THE VATICAN MYTHOGRAPHERS

The Vatican Mythographers

RONALD E. PEPIN

Fordham University Press | New York | 2008

Library of Congress Cataloging-in-Publication Data

Mythographi Vaticani. English
The Vatican mythographers : an English translation / Ronald E. Pepin.
    p. cm.
Includes bibliographical references and index.
ISBN 978-0-8232-2892-8 (cloth : alk. paper)
1. Mythology, Roman—Early works to 1800.   2. Mythology, Classical—Early works to
1800.   I. Pepin, Ronald E.   II. Title.
PA6139.M9M9713   2008
292.1'3—dc22   2008003832

Printed in the United States of America
10 09 08   5 4 3 2 1
First edition

CONTENTS

PREFACE

In 1831, Angelo Mai, Prefect of the Vatican Library, published three separate Latin compilations of classical myths composed during the Middle Ages. Mai had discovered these in Vatican manuscripts, one of which had once belonged to Christina, the expatriate Queen of Sweden. Only three years later, Georg H. Bode decided to issue a new edition of these three Latin writers, based on Mai's texts, at Celle. Since then, the so-called Vatican Mythographers have been widely studied and cited. Many of their sources have been discovered and their influence traced.

Two of the writers remain anonymous, despite numerous attempts to identify them. Based on a dozen manuscript attributions, the Third Vatican Mythographer is generally accepted to be Alberic of London, of whom nothing is definitively known apart from his name and *locus*. New editions of the first two have appeared in the last twenty years, and there is now a French translation of the First Vatican Mythographer. However, no English translation of these works has been published to date. In the following pages, I offer an accurate, literal translation of these three important witnesses to the enduring vitality of classical myths, the legacy of medieval schools, and beyond those to a wide range of medieval and Renaissance literary and intellectual culture.

ACKNOWLEDGMENTS

I am glad to acknowledge my debts of gratitude to colleagues and friends, to scholars and strangers who have encouraged this project in ways large and small.

First, I am deeply grateful to the anonymous readers of Fordham University Press for their insightful suggestions and candid assessments of my work. My translation and introduction are better for their input, and they are, of course, absolved of responsibility for any mistakes or infelicities that might remain.

For many years of generous assistance, encouragement and scholarly collaboration, I thank Hugh Feiss, o.s.b.; Johanna Glazewski; Peter Wursthorn; and my reliable computer consultant, Matthew P. Pepin.

I am also pleased to acknowledge the competent direction and gracious assistance rendered to me by Helen Tartar, Editorial Director of Fordham University Press, and Professor Gyula Klima, Editor of the Fordham Series in Medieval Studies. Indeed, the entire staff of the Press was most helpful and welcoming to me throughout the production phases of this book, and I am grateful to them all.

My thanks for four decades of patient partnership go to Beth.

Introduction

Since their first appearance together over one hundred and seventy years ago, the Three Vatican Mythographers have been viewed as a single entity. They have been treated collectively in histories and studies of medieval literature, although their individual substance and style have invited closer scrutiny in recent years. Before characterizing each Mythographer separately, it might be well to discuss their common purposes, audience and influence.

PURPOSE AND INFLUENCE

Mythology is universal and everlasting. Throughout human history, myths, in both oral and written form, have been preserved, transmitted, analyzed, assimilated, and interpreted. They have survived, even in hostile cultures, for a host of reasons, including their ability to entertain, inspire, instruct, and sometimes horrify us. Their transmission has often met with resistance from established faiths and philosophical schools opposed to fiction and fable on religious and intellectual grounds. This has surely been true for classical mythology and, indeed, all "pagan" literature. Yet the surpassing charms and insights associated with these ancient stories compelled their defenders to justify them and their perpetuators. Scholars have amply defined and documented the clever use of biblical topoi such as *Spoliatio Aegyptiorum* (despoiling the Egyptians) and *Captiva Gentilis* (gentile captive) by Church Fathers for this purpose.[1] They have traced the euhemeristic tradition and its place in the comprehension of myths in the ancient world and the Middle Ages.[2] Another integral part of the rationalization for the study of pagan works was the allegorical method used to develop spiritual, physical, and moral interpretations. The medieval reliance on allegory has been widely researched and insightfully described by modern specialists in various disciplines. C. S.

Lewis, Jean Pepin, Adolph Katzenellenbogen, Winthrop Wetherbee, and many others have illuminated our understanding of a technique that was ubiquitous in schools of grammar, philosophy, and theology. Indeed, by the twelfth century "allegory became the universal vehicle of all pious expression; mythological exegesis . . . grew to astonishing proportions."[3]

I have introduced the preceding generalizations as a basis for analyzing the purposes of the Vatican Mythographers who also employ these rationales. In fact, all three of these medieval grammarians were engaged in transmission of classical myths and in teaching the truths embedded in them. Euhemerism and allegorization are abundantly evident in their works, especially that of the Third Mythographer. Thus, their approaches were traditional. The question is, why did they compose their works, and for whom?

Literary historians of recent decades have discussed the audiences and purposes of Classical, Medieval, and Renaissance mythography at length. Though the field remains open to research into texts and sources, important new studies have clarified our perception of particular eras and authors. For example, Alan Cameron's book on mythographers in early imperial Rome traces the role of mythology, "the cultural currency of even the remotest corners of the Roman world," in popular culture.[4] Cameron proves that the influence of mythographers extended far beyond the poets and their accepted audience, infusing such areas as oratory, tourism, drama, dance, and other entertainments. Even gladiators' names were commonly drawn from myth.

The audiences and purposes of mythographers in the Middle Ages were certainly more confined. Of course, we are dealing with a vast period characterized by widespread illiteracy and a religious culture still hostile in many ways to all things "pagan." It is sometimes suggested that pagan mythology was powerfully subversive to medieval Christian culture, and thus controlling and confining it offered an opportunity for Christian thinkers to present the greater authority of their own worldview. Jane Chance takes this position to its fullest and most complex expression:

Within and during these different periods when interest in classical texts resulted in reinterpretations of the antique, the common purpose of medieval mythography involved the repressed transmission of human sexuality, essentialized as female and textualized, embodied as text. Because of this scholastic context and because of its allegorical methodology, mythography served the purposes of patriarchy within the Church.[5]

This view leads Chance to suggest a more fully subversive reading of such materials in our own time:

> Yet even in these terms mythography, if not allegory, as *translatio studii* would have occupied a role as institutionally subversive, empowering authority regarded as marginal, whether pagan or feminine, and therefore in the context of postmodern discourse to be designated as female in its difference, its 'otherness.'[6]

It is clear that pagan myth presented a potential threat to Judeo-Christian authority and worldview, but the vast range of literary, historical, and ethical resources pagan myth comprised could never be entirely overlooked and were indeed increasingly pondered. Common strategies for framing and exploiting them—as well as containing and denouncing them—were (false but suggestive) etymologies, moral allegory, and that species of euhemerism offered by the book of Wisdom 14:11–20 (Douay-Rheims):

> Therefore there shall be no respect had even to the idols of the Gentiles: because the creatures of God are turned to an abomination, and a temptation to the souls of men, and a snare to the feet of the unwise. . . . For by the vanity of men they came into the world: and therefore they shall be found to come shortly to an end. For a father, being afflicted with bitter grief, made to himself the image of his son who was quickly taken away: and him who then had died as a man, he began now to worship as a god, and appointed him rites and sacrifices among his servants. Then in process of time, wicked custom prevailing, this error was kept as a law, and statues were worshipped by the commandment of tyrants. . . . And the multitude of men, carried away by the beauty of the work, took him now for a god that a little before was but honored as a man.

Thus a simple response to our earlier question why and for whom the Three Vatican Mythographers composed their works: to provide handbooks of mythological stories that might facilitate reading and reappropriating in various ways the classical poets who formed the basis of the grammar course in schools. The handbooks were intended to elucidate in terms consonant with Christian purposes the fabulous figures, themes, and places that appear in the works of Ovid, Vergil, Horace, Lucan, Statius, and other curriculum authors. This is surely true of the rather straightforward narratives of the First and Second Vatican Mythographers. The Third Vatican Mythographer often explicitly links a particular discussion to its usefulness in reading "the poets." For example, his elucidation of soothsaying opens with these words: "The subject now seems to demand that we touch on the superstitious absurdities of soothsayers here, not elsewhere, since poets are sometimes concerned with these." He frequently underscores his point with direct supporting quotations from poetic texts.

In addition, the extensive allegorization that we observe in the Second and Third Mythographers (pervasive in the latter) illustrates the moral purpose of their teaching, constituting a "philosophia moralis," to use the words of Hildebert of Lavardin.[7] Thus all of the gods, goddesses, and heroes were identified with virtues and vices. Perseus slays the Gorgon with Minerva's help: virtue conquers fear through wisdom. Bacchus is a naked youth who rides a tiger: drunkenness is never mature, denudes us of possessions, and begets ferocity. Ulysses, husband of Penelope, passes by the monstrous Scylla unharmed: a wise man bound to chastity overcomes lust.

Students, poets, artists, philosophers, astronomers—indeed, all literate people—were beneficiaries of these works. For example, we know that the First and Second Vatican Mythographers supplied Jean de Meung with his knowledge of myths for *Roman de la Rose*.[8] The Third Mythographer, whose book has been called "a precious auxiliary in reading the poets," was used by Petrarch for his epic *Africa* and Bersuire in his *Ovidius moralizatus*.[9] The Third Mythographer also profoundly influenced artists and became "not merely a precursor, but one of the principal agents of the Renaissance."[10] He did this not only by providing inspirational themes, but also by offering a detailed iconography of mythological characters. In fact, his primary formula for introduction of a divinity is *depingitur*, literally "he/she is depicted as." This term occurs again and again in the text as a guide to visual and verbal representation of the figures in question.

Certainly, there are numerous similarities among the Three Vatican Mythographers, especially the First and Second. These two followed some of the same sources and sometimes used the same expressions to relate the same stories. Possibly the two depended on a common primary text. The Third Vatican Mythographer has been hailed as the more interesting, the most popular, and the most insightful of the three, with a superior style as well. But since all three exhibit unique features, and all wrote in different eras, I will now characterize each briefly.

FIRST VATICAN MYTHOGRAPHER

The First Vatican Mythographer's work, preserved in a single surviving manuscript of the twelfth century (Vatican Reg. lat. 1401), has now been edited four times (Mai: 1831; Bode: 1834; Kulcsar: 1987; Zorzetti: 1995). The text is divided into three uneven books, with a total of 234 individual myths recounted (229 in Kulcsar). The stories are presented with no evident order or stated purpose, save a few groupings of related materials, e.g. the labors of Hercules or Trojan War tales. All are relatively brief retellings of classical myths, the longer ones averaging thirty or forty lines, the shortest a single sentence. The third book opens with a genealogy of gods and heroes that extends to eighty-two lines. The author refrains from comment on the myths he relates, and there is no intrusion of personality, no first-person remarks that might offer a clue to his identity.

Several scholars have suggested that the First Vatican Mythographer was an Irish writer of the eighth or ninth century.[11]Another finds "Adanan the Scot" to be "perhaps the most sensible attribution."[12] The most complete study of the work to date concludes that the author must remain anonymous.[13]

The First Vatican Mythographer's Latin prose is uninspired, his style entirely lacking verve and charm. He does cite numerous writers of classical antiquity as sources, though he offers only infrequent and brief quotes from Vergil, Horace, Ovid, and Statius. The careful researches of scholars have detected a heavy reliance by this mythographer on other unnamed sources. These include Servius, the Scholiasts on Statius, and the highly influential works of later authorities in the field, notably Hyginus (indirectly) and Fulgentius. A recent, comprehensive study includes the *Narrationes*, a summary of transformation tales from Ovid's *Metamorphoses* dated between 150 and 250 CE, among the "substantial mythographic sources drawn on by the first and second Vatican mythographers."[14] This mythographic compilation was sometimes credited in the Middle Ages to "Lactantius Placidus," an ascription not to be taken seriously.[15] In fact, our Third Vatican Mythographer occasionally cites "Lactantius" as a source. The most recent traceable source employed by the First Vatican Mythographer was Remigius of Auxerre (841–908). In light of this fact, the suggestion made by K. Elliott and J.P. Elder that he probably lived in the seventh or eighth century must be rejected in favor of a later date. Zorzetti's conclusion that he lived between 875 and 1075 is more likely.[16]

SECOND VATICAN MYTHOGRAPHER

The text of the Second Vatican Mythographer is considerably longer than that of the First. The recent edition by Kulcsar employs eleven manuscripts and includes 275 individual chapters of varying lengths, while the older editions of Mai and Bode, based on Vatican Reg. lat. 1401 only, contains 230 chapters. The presentation resembles that of the First Mythographer, except that the myths seem to be grouped more systematically and purposefully. This compiler also seems to have consulted more sources, and this probably accounts for the greater frequency of explanations (*explanationes*) and interpretations (*interpretationes*) appended to the various stories. These are often introduced by a formula: *veritas autem est* (but the truth is) and in one instance (ch. 129) a traditional bias is revealed in the statement, "Just as in Latin discourse nothing is more pleasing than truth, so in Greek discourse nothing is more honored than falsehood." Moreover, this mythographer has won greater, albeit faint, praise for style: "Better . . . though it would hardly win any prize for composition today."[17]

The Second Vatican Mythographer remains anonymous, though there have been attempts to identify him with "Lactantius Placidus" or Remigius of Auxerre, and his dates are uncertain. Some commentators opt for the Carolingian period.[18] One modern assessment places him "not much later than the first Vatican Mythography" and then concludes "perhaps I would suggest on the gendered basis of some of the unusual interpretations, by an anonymous woman ecclesiastic familiar with Remigius's mythographic commentaries."[19] But this tentative conclusion remains unsupported. We cannot at this point be more definitive, but we are sure that the Second Vatican Mythographer lived and worked later than the First.[20]

THIRD VATICAN MYTHOGRAPHER

The text of the Third Vatican Mythographer contains fifteen lengthy chapters in Bode's edition (1834; reprinted, Hildesheim, 1968). A new edition of all three mythographers was promised in 1947 by Elliott and Elder, but never appeared.

By universal agreement, it seems, the Third Vatican Mythographer is the "most interesting."[21] The reasons typically advanced for this assessment include the author's "excellent" Latin style and the extensive allegorical interpretations that he offers for the myths he has assembled. Indeed, his treatise often contains several variant and frequently conflicting opinions on the meanings of individual myths based on different sources. Also, an impressive array of sources has been established, and their influences on the Third Vatican Mythographer have been carefully analyzed. These ancient authorities include the *Narrationes* (attributed to "Lactantius Placidus"), Fulgentius' *Mitologiae*, the *Commentary on the Aeneid* of Servius, Macrobius' *Saturnalia* and *Commentary on the Dream of Scipio*, Martianus Capella's *Marriage of Mercury and Philology*, and the commentary on the latter by Remigius of Auxerre. Our mythographer regularly cites his sources by name in the text, especially Fulgentius and Remigius, whose views are often contrasted in detail. Moreover, many times he illustrates a point with a quotation or series of them from the ancient poets, in particular Vergil, Horace, Lucan, Ovid, and Statius. Even Lucretius, a rare author in the Middle Ages, is named several times.

In addition, a host of fascinating, often bizarre etymologies, many drawn from Isidore of Seville's *Etymologiae*, lend added interest to the narration and explanation of the myths. The Third Vatican Mythographer is given to digression also, mostly when a vexing question of interpretation arises, but sometimes because of the complexity of subject or theme. Longest among these, as one might expect, is the excursus on the nature of the soul in chapter 6 (on Pluto). Here the writer acknowledges the difficulty of the material "for the inexperienced," but proposes to set forth a few "easy theories" and thereby avoid "inappropriate silence" on a vital subject. There are also fascinating passages on ancient death and burial practices, religious rites and sacrificial animals, and soothsayers and signs of the Zodiac.

Moreover, a personality emerges from the Third Vatican Mythographer's narration, unlike the other two texts, which remain devoid of notable marks of authorial individuality. This uniqueness reveals itself in several first-person intrusions through which the writer comments on a point, expresses impatience or frustration, renders an opinion, and so on. Sometimes there is a candid admission of uncertainty ("Judging that to be obscure, as far as I am concerned, I leave it to be studied by astronomers"). Sometimes he admits confusion due to the unreliability of sources ("Since I have not found these names in any authentic accounts, I consider them commonplaces or hastily-invented or false or apocryphal"). Occasionally our author records his moral viewpoint ("Among the ancients, some tyrants exhibited this [immoral] way of life; among us, the whole world does!" or "Glaucus is rightly called one-eyed, because one who devotes himself to lust is blind and foolish and rotten"). In one instance, adopting a sentiment from Fulgentius, the Third Vatican Mythographer reveals his disdain for merchants ("He is said to be the god of theft and himself a thief, because merchants, while cheating others through their lies and deceptions, are not far removed from thieves"). Also, his expressed outlook is Christian, sometimes supported by Scriptural citations, and even monastic in some cases, as when he seems to embrace *contemptus mundi* ("Just as the peacock adorns its front parts but shamefully bares its backside, so indeed do riches and worldly glory adorn for the moment, but later leave bare those whom they have adorned"). Once he assures his readers that "I am not setting forth Catholic truth in these matters, but the opinions and fictions of the pagans." Passing remarks of this kind by the author are too few to offer more than scant insight into his personality, but they do provide at least a welcome glimpse, and a contrast to the almost-total darkness in which the First and Second Vatican Mythographers reside.

Despite these traces of personality in the text, the Third Vatican Mythographer's identity remains elusive. Among the more than forty surviving manuscripts of this work ranging from the twelfth to the fifteenth centuries, a dozen attribute it to "Alberic." The epithet "Londinensis" appears in four of them. This Alberic of London has been identified with a Master Alberic, Canon of Saint Paul's, whose name occurs in Cathedral charters around 1160.[22] In some manuscripts Alberic's name is stricken in favor of "Nequam." Alexander Neckam lived from 1157 to 1217. This well-known English author, Abbot of Cirencester, was a polymath whose most notable work is the encyclopedic *De naturis rerum*, essentially a moralization of scientific facts. His biographer has referred to him as a grammarian, versifier, scientist, preacher, commentator, and theologian, but he has also excluded "Mythographus tertius" from his corpus of authentic writings.[23]

The problem of identification is further compounded by the fact that in one important manuscript used by Mai (Vatican Reg. lat. 1290) there are actually two texts: our Third Vatican Mythographer under the title *Liber Ymaginum deorum*, and a shorter, illustrated work entitled *De deorum imaginibus libellus*. The latter was long considered an abridgement of the former, a view disproved by Seznec, who showed that the *Libellus* indeed derived from the *Liber Ymaginum*, but was composed two centuries later.[24] Added complication results from new titles that emerged in later manuscripts to identify the longer work of the Third Vatican Mythographer, or copies of it. By the fourteenth century the book was called *Scintillarium poetarum*, or simply *Poetarius*. Indeed, Petrarch owned a manuscript of it and referred to it as "Poetarius Albrici."[25]

One scholar's solution to the identity problem was to conflate three attributions by suggesting that Alberic was a pseudonym of Neckam. "Mythographus tertius, Albricus and Neckam would thus be one and the same person."[26] In summary, modern scholarly opinion is divided on the authorship question. Some favor Alberic of London; others allow for the possibility that Neckam is the Third Vatican Mythographer. Given Neckam's range of interests as evidenced by his lengthy list of known writings, his dates, and the attribution of the work to him in several manuscripts, chiefly ones of English provenance, I would incline toward the view that he is *Mythographus tertius,* but only tentatively. A definitive identification relies upon further research.

The text of the Third Vatican Mythographer commences with a preface in which the author relates the legend of Syrophanes, a rich Egyptian of ancient times whose beloved son died. Overwhelmed by grief, the father set up a statue of the son in his house, and before this "image of sorrow" the entire household used to place garlands and burn incense. Soon, accused persons took refuge there, and out of fear people venerated that statue. Thus, "fear first made gods in the world," and the worship of pagan idols began to be diffused. Later, the philosophers of old taught that there is but one god, the creator of all things. However, this god was known by various names because of his many diverse manifestations and the manifold ways in which the world is governed. This same god has feminine names as well as masculine according to his dispositions and actions. This summary account of the origin of the gods concludes with the author's statement of purpose:

> Now let us refute in turn some unexplained errors of antiquity, and if we cannot pour light into them, at least let us drive away in some measure the mists of ignorance with the scourge of mightier authorities.

There follow fourteen detailed chapters on these gods, goddesses, and heroes of classical mythology: Saturn, Cybele, Jupiter, Juno, Neptune, Pluto, Proserpina, Apollo, Mercury, Pallas, Venus, Bacchus, Hercules, Perseus. The chapters are uneven in length for the obvious reason that more stories are associated with some gods than with others, but also because some accounts prompt more expansive digressions. For example, the story of Pluto contains a lengthy treatment of the classical Underworld and includes an extensive discourse on the nature of the soul as well. This discussion is amplified by the Third Vatican Mythographer's summarization of many philosophical schools of thought on the subject, including comparisons and contrasts among them. The book closes with a chapter on the twelve signs of the zodiac, recounting mainly how each was created and placed in the heavens. In fact, this final section ends quite abruptly, leaving the impression that the book was hastily concluded, or is incomplete as it stands. One symptom of its hurried conclusion is the unusual repetition of the phrase *immensae magnitudinis* (of immense size) in the concise passages describing the animals that became the constellations Cancer, Leo, Scorpio (2), and Pisces. Overall, acclaim for the content and quality of the Third Vatican Mythographer's book seems entirely justified.

SUMMARY

The Three Vatican Mythographers are not equal in esteem or influence. The First has a bland style and survived in a single manuscript, which is at least one indicator of sparse influence. The Second displays better style, is longer, and survived in eleven manuscripts. This testifies to a wider, though certainly not vast, influence. The Third reveals a mature Latin style. This author is intrinsically more interesting because of the clever allegorizations and curious etymologies blended into the marvelous myths he recounts. This work has survived in over forty manuscripts, which attests to its significant influence.

THE TRANSLATION

This translation is based on the edition of Peter Kulcsar for the First and Second Vatican Mythographers; the basis for the Third Vatican Mythographer is Bode's edition. Unfortunately, in the latter case the editor founded his text on the sometimes inaccurate and often euphemized previous edition of Mai, though he did offer emendations.[27] A new edition for the Third Mythographer, like those provided by Kulcsar for the First and Second, is still sorely needed, although even Kulcsar's text has not gone without criticism.[28]

For the convenience of readers who might want to cross-reference my translation with the Latin text of the Third Vatican Mythographer, I have retained Bode's numeration of segments under each separate chapter.

Works of inferior style tend to be more difficult to translate and often cause added frustrations for the translator because of their infelicities, repetitions, and other weaknesses. The First and Second Vatican Mythographers produced Latin prose that is dry and uninspired despite the enduring charm of their material; the Third Vatican Mythographer's prose is more pleasing to translate, and, as we have noted, he has been credited with "an excellent Latin style" (Krill, 176). Even so, this author relies heavily on repeated formulas such as "they say" or "it is said," probably to underscore his reliance on sources and to declare his lack of credence in the fabulous stories he recounts. Thus, to avoid needless repetition and to promote English fluency, I have sometimes taken these liberties in translating the Latin:

> Omitted such connectives as *autem* (moreover) and *etiam* (also). The Vatican mythographers relied heavily on these to secure the flow of sentences, but in English they tend to impede the flow.
> Broken up lengthy sentences and changed some subordinate clauses into independent ones.
> Changed Latin passives into active voice, and rendered the pluperfect "had been" into a simple past tense.
> Omitted *dicitur* (it is said), especially when it is used repeatedly in a single story. This favored formula of the mythographers was surely employed to confirm that they were relating fables, not creating them, but it also distanced them from pagan stories which lacked literal truth.

In every other way, I have tried to provide a clear, accurate translation. I trust that it will be of use to those without Latin who wish to study works that form a part of the legacy of medieval schools.

FIRST MYTHOGRAPHER

BOOK ONE

1. Prometheus.

After Prometheus created men, he is said to have ascended into the sky with the help of Minerva. With a little torch applied to the Sun's chariot wheel, he stole fire, which he made known to mankind. Angered by this, the gods sent two evils upon the earth: fevers, that is emaciation, and diseases. Also, with the help of Mercury, they bound Prometheus to a rock on Mount Caucasus, where an eagle was summoned to devour his heart. There is a rational explanation for these stories: Prometheus was a most intelligent man, and he was the first to teach astrology to the Assyrians. He studied this with the greatest care while living on Mount Caucasus. An eagle devours his heart: this refers to his very great solicitude, by which he observed and understood all the motions of the stars. And since he did this with intelligence, with Mercury, the god of intelligence and reason, as his guide, he is said to have been bound to a rock. Beyond this, he comprehended the nature of thunderbolts and revealed it to mankind; thus he is said to have stolen fire from heaven. For through a certain art taught by him, fire was once brought forth from above; this benefited men while they used it well. But afterward, through the wicked use of mankind, it was turned to destruction, just as we read in Livy concerning Tullus Hostilius, who was consumed by this fire with all his possessions. For this reason, when fire was stolen, the angry gods sent disease upon mankind.

2. The Story of Neptune and Minerva.

When Neptune and Minerva were fighting over a name for Athens, it pleased the gods that the city be called by the name of the one who would bestow the better gift on mankind. Then Neptune struck the shore and brought forth the horse, an animal suited to war. Minerva hurled her spear and created the olive tree, which was confirmed to be the better gift and an emblem of peace. On this account the city was called Athens from the name of Minerva, who is called Attis [*sic*] in Greek.

3. The Story of Scylla.

There were two Scyllas: one was the daughter of Phorcys and Crateis. Since the sea god Glaucus loved her, while he himself was loved by Circe, and he despised her, the angry Circe poisoned a spring where Scylla used to wash herself. When the girl lowered herself into it, the middle part of her body was changed into wild beasts. The other Scylla, in fact, was the daughter of Nisus, king of the Megarians. While Minos was fighting against them (after the Athenians had already been conquered) on account of the death of his son Androgeus, whom the Athenians and Megarians had killed by deception, Scylla, Nisus' daughter, loved him. To please the enemy, she cut off her father's purple lock of hair and presented it to Minos. Nisus considered the lock sacred, since he would possess his kingdom so long as he kept it intact. Afterward, despised by Minos, Scylla was transformed because of her sorrow into a bird, and Nisus, killed through the mercy of the gods, was also changed into a bird. Today these birds are violently stirred against each other by great discord.

4. The Story of Tereus and Procne.

Tereus was king of the Thracians. He married Procne, the daughter of Pandion, king of Athens. After a short time she asked him to fetch Philomela, her sister, for a visit. He proceeded to Athens, and while he was bringing the girl back, he violated her on the way and cut out her tongue so that she would not tell of his wicked deed. Yet the girl sent the true story to her sister depicted in her own blood on a tapestry. When this accusation became clear, Procne killed her son, Itys, and set him before his father to be eaten. Afterward, all were changed into birds: Tereus into a hoopoe, Itys into a pheasant, Procne into a swallow, Philomela into a nightingale.

5. The Story of the Cyclops and Acis.

The Cyclops is said to have loved the nymph, Galatea. Since she loved a certain shepherd, Acis, and spurned Polyphemus, in his anger the Cyclops killed Acis. He was afterward changed through the mercy of Galatea into a spring which even today is called Acilius (from Acis).

6. The Story of Silvanus and Cyparissus.

Silvanus is the god of forests. He loved a boy named Cyparissus, who had a very tame deer. When Silvanus unknowingly killed this deer, the boy died of sorrow. The god, his lover, turned him into a cypress, the tree that bears his name. He is said to have this as a consolation.

7. The Story of Ceres and Proserpina.

After Ceres had long searched for her daughter Proserpina (who had been snatched away by Pluto), at last she found her in the Underworld, since she had been seized by Pluto, or Orcus, the brother of Jove. When Ceres begged Jove's help in the matter, he responded that the girl could return if she had eaten nothing in the Underworld. However, she had eaten pomegranate seeds in Elysium. Alscalaphus, the son of Styx, gave her this food. Thus Proserpina could not go back to those living on the earth. To be sure, Ceres is said to have obtained this favor afterward: that Proserpina would spend six months with her mother, six with her husband. The story is fashioned this way because Proserpina is both herself and the moon, which waxes for six months in the whole year and wanes for six, that is, fifteen days in each of the months, so that she seems to be increasing in the Upper World and decreasing in the Underworld.

8. The Story of Celeus and Triptolemus.

Eleusis is a city in the region of Attica, not far from Athens. When Celeus reigned there, he very generously received Ceres with hospitality while she sought her daughter. As remuneration she taught him every kind of agriculture; she even warmed his newborn son, Triptolemus, with fire through the night and nourished him with divine milk by day. After she put Celeus in charge of her winged dragons, she sent him through the whole world to teach men the use of grains.

9. The Story of Ceyx and Alcyone.

Ceyx, the son of Lucifer, had a wife, Alcyone. After she prohibited him from consulting Apollo about the state of his kingdom, he perished in a shipwreck. When his body floated back to his wife Alcyone, she threw herself into the sea. Afterward, through the mercy of Thetis and Lucifer, both were changed into seabirds called halcyons. These birds make their nests on the sea in midwinter; during this time there is so great a calm that nothing at all moves on the sea. For this reason those days are called "halcyon days."

10. The Story of Ceres and Lyncus.

When Ceres was searching for her daughter Proserpina, she approached a certain spring to relieve her thirst. Then Lyncus' peasants stirred up the water with their feet and prevented her from drinking. Also, Lyncus farted in her presence. The goddess, angry at those who had wanted to kill Triptolemus in Scythia, changed Lyncus into a wild lynx.

11. The Story of the Titans and the Giants.

Earth, that is Ceres, was angered by Saturn's scorn for herself and Tantalus. She brought forth Titans and Giants against Saturn, and later against Jove, but also for the purpose of driving out all the gods in her revenge. By collecting and piling mountains upon mountains, these brothers tried to climb to the sky and cast down the gods from there. To oppose them, Jupiter assembled all the gods, and among the rest came Father Liber, Vulcan, Satyrs, and Sileni riding on asses. Frightened by the loud, disorderly braying of the terrified asses, a sound unknown to the Giants, they fled from their enemies. Even the gods themselves, terrified at the sight of Typhoeus the Giant, had fled, transformed into diverse monsters and animals. Moreover, with the help of an eagle that served him by carrying his thunderbolts, Jupiter defeated them and shut them up in Aetna, except for one Titan only, that is, the Sun.

12. Pelops.

The Giant, Tantalus, the father of Pelops, wishing to test the gods' divinity, served his own son Pelops to them to eat. For this savagery he was condemned to stand in the river Eridanus, dying of thirst and suffering from hunger, for he saw but could not reach the fruits on the bank of the aforementioned river. Later, when the gods wanted to recall his son from the Underworld at Tantalus' request, Ceres, who alone had eaten the arm of Pelops while the other gods had abstained, restored to him an arm of ivory. The story is fashioned this way because Ceres is the earth, which consumes all bodies, yet saves the bones.

13. *The Story of Tityus.*

Tityus was one of the Giants. Wishing to lie with Latona, he was killed by the arrows of Apollo and Diana. He was condemned to the Underworld. There two vultures take turns devouring his liver, which then grows again for renewed punishment.

14. *The Story of Ixion.*

Ixion was a Giant who wanted to lie with Juno; a cloud (nubes) enveloped him and in this way he had his affair. When he boasted that he had done the same as if sleeping with Juno, he was condemned to this punishment: in the Underworld he forever rolls a wheel encircled by snakes up a mountain.

15. *The Story of Circe and Ulysses.*

Dwelling on Meonia, Circe, the daughter of the Sun, changed men who came to her island into wild beasts. Ulysses came there by chance and sent Eurylochus with twenty-two companions to visit her. She deprived the others of their human form, but Eurylochus escaped and reported to Ulysses. Alone, he went to her. On his way, Mercury gave him an antidote and showed him how he might trick Circe. After Ulysses came to her and had accepted a drink from her, he mixed in Mercury's antidote and drew his sword; he warned her to restore his companions to him. Then Circe perceived that this was done with the consent of the gods. She gave him assurances and restored his companions to him. Indeed, Ulysses slept with her. By her he begot Telegonus, at whose hand he was later struck down and died.

16. *The Story of Tiresias.*

While Tiresias was strolling through the forest he saw two snakes copulating. When he struck them with a stick, he was changed into a woman. After eight years, when he saw them having intercourse in like manner and struck them again, he was restored to his former nature. And when there was contention between Jove and Juno about which sex enjoyed the greater pleasure in sexual passion, Tiresias was summoned as a judge who had experienced each sex. When asked, he declared that a woman's pleasure was three times greater than a man's. For this, an angered Juno deprived him of his sight, as if he were obliging toward Jove and injurious toward herself. Since he was blinded on account of this insult, Jupiter granted him foreknowledge of things to come.

17. The Story of Lycaon.

Impatient over human wickedness, Jupiter came disguised as a man to Lycaon, the king of Arcadia. Lycaon planned death for him as if for a mortal man and served him human limbs to eat. When Jupiter recognized these, he did not utterly destroy Lycaon, but wanted him to perceive his punishment. Jupiter changed him into the shape of a wolf who still has Lycaon's habits in his fury and his name in the appellation "lycaon." This same Lycaon had a daughter, Callisto. After Jupiter violated her, Juno changed her into a bear. Taking pity on her, Jupiter later transformed her into a constellation in the sky.

18. Io and Argus.

Since Io, the daughter of King Inachus (a river), surpassed girls of the same age in beauty, she was loved by Jove. After he had made entreaties, he fulfilled his desire; so that the girl might not provoke the wrath of Juno, her seducer transformed her into a cow. When Juno discovered his trick, she asked that Jove give the cow to her as a gift because it would be more beautiful than the rest of the cattle that are seen in the Peloponnesus. So that he would not betray the girl by refusing, he handed her over. So that Io might not be Jove's mistress any longer, Juno appointed Argus, who had a hundred eyes, as a guard over her; at the command of Jove, Mercury killed Argus. Because he died keeping watch for her, Juno transformed Argus into a peacock and, after he was taken under her protection, she placed his lost eyes among the peacock's wondrous tailfeathers. Since Io was harried by the Furies, she wandered over the earth; at last she was brought to Egypt. There, after Juno was placated by Jove, Io received her former shape again and was named Isis.

19. The Story of Icarius and Erigone.[1]

Icarius, the father of Erigone, revealed to mortal men the gift of wine, which he had received from his father, Liber. He was killed by peasants after they had drunk too much, and in their drunkenness believed that they had been given poison. Icarius' dog returned to his daughter, Erigone; she followed his tracks and, when she found her father's corpse, she ended her life with a noose. Through the mercy of the gods she was restored to life again among the constellations; men call her Virgo. That dog also was placed among the stars. But after some time such a sickness was sent upon the Athenians that their maidens were driven by a certain madness to hang themselves. The oracle responded that this pestilence could be stopped if the corpses of Erigone and Icarius were sought again. These were found nowhere after being sought for a long time. Then, to show their devotedness, and to appear to seek them in another element, the Athenians hung rope from trees. Holding on to this rope, the men were tossed here and there so that they seemed to seek their corpses in the air. But since most were falling from the trees, they decided to make shapes in the likeness of their own faces and hang these in place of themselves. Hence, little masks are called *oscilla* because in them faces oscillate, that is, move.

20. *The Story of Iphigenia and Orestes and Pylades.*[2]

When the Greeks were proceeding against Troy and had come to the island called Aulis, King Agamemnon, wishing to practice archery, spied a doe belonging to Diana; not knowing it was hers, he killed the doe. When the Greeks were detained there for a long time by contrary winds, the answer from Apollo's oracle was that the winds had to be appeased by the blood of Agamemnon. Then Ulysses, as he was very shrewd, returned to his homeland and, feigning marriage, brought back with him Agamemnon's daughter, Iphigenia. But when the girl was about to be sacrificed, merciful Minerva sent a cloud before the eyes of those surrounding her and put a doe in place of the girl. Then she was transported to the Taurian territory and given in marriage to Thoas, king of the Scythians, and she became a priestess of Diana Dictynna. While she was appeasing the deity with human blood, especially the blood of foreigners, according to established custom, she recognized her brother, Orestes. He had received an oracle and come to the Colchians with his most faithful friend, Pylades, to free himself from madness. After Thoas was killed, Iphigenia carried off with them a statue of Diana concealed in a bundle of sticks and brought it to Aricia. It is called Fascelis from this, not so much from *face*, the torch that accompanies the statue.

21. *The Story of Hippodame.*

Hippodame was the daughter of Oenomaus, king of Elis and Pisa. He had very swift horses because they had been created from the blowing of the winds. He killed many of his daughter's suitors who were challenged to a chariot race under the stipulation that either he would hand over his daughter, or he would kill the defeated suitors. When Hippodame fell in love with Pelops, she bribed Myrtilus, her father's charioteer, with a promise of first intercourse. Myrtilus made axles of wax for Oenomaus' chariot and Pelops was the victor. When Myrtilus demanded the reward promised by the girl, her husband hurled him into the sea. To this he gave his name, for it is called the Myrtoan Sea after him.

22. The Story of Myrtilus, Atreus, and Thyestes.

Vexed that his son Myrtilus had been hurled into the sea and robbed of life, Mercury found a vengeance to console his childlessness. Indeed, he caused so much discord for Pelops' sons, Atreus and Thyestes, that they broke the laws of brotherhood. They were ruling a kingdom by turns, and Thyestes knew that it was fated to remain in the possession of the one who had a ram with golden fleece. At that time Atreus was ruling the kingdom and possessed the fleece. Thyestes hoped that it could be transferred to himself when he seduced Europa, his brother's wife. After Atreus learned this, he drove Thyestes out, along with his two sons. Later, he sent greetings to him and feigned forgiveness. After he had summoned Thyestes' sons to him and murdered them, he served Thyestes' own dead sons to him to eat. After the meal, he showed the heads of his sons to Thyestes as a sign of the deadly banquet. When Thyestes sought advice from the oracles concerning revenge in this matter, they responded that certain vengeance would come through one who was born of himself and his daughter, Pelopia. He swiftly embraced and penetrated his daughter, by whom a boy was born. Aware of her incest, she threw the child into the woods. This boy, nourished by the teats of a she-goat, took the name Aegisthus from this. Indeed, when he grew up, he killed Atreus to avenge his father. Afterward Aegisthus was killed by Agamemnon's son Orestes, along with the woman with whom he had committed adultery. This same Aegisthus also had killed Agamemnon after he committed adultery with Agamemnon's wife, Clytemnestra.

23. The Story of Phrixus and Helle.

Phrixus and Helle were brother and sister, the children of King Athamas and Neobola. They were stricken with madness by Liber when they were wandering in the forest. Their mother, Neobola, is said to have come and shown them a ram distinguished by a golden fleece. She ordered the forenamed brother and sister to climb upon the ram and to go to King Aeetes[3] in Colchis, and there to sacrifice the ram. Or in another version: When Neobola (who was also called Nubes), incited by the frenzy of Father Liber, went to the forest and did not return to her husband's hearth, Athamas brought in a stepmother named Ino for his children, Phrixus and Helle. Plotting death for the children because of a stepmother's hatred, she asked women to destroy the grain that was to be sown. After this was done, a famine arose. When the citizens consulted Apollo, Ino bribed the messenger to report that the oracle had declared that the children of Nubes must be sacrificed; she even said that they had burned the grain. Fearing the ill will of the people, their father handed over his own children to their stepmother's judgment, but secretly he gave them a remedy. For he dispatched Phrixus, who was unmindful of his own death, to deliver the ram with the golden fleece. Urged on by the command of Juno to flee with his sister, Phrixus immediately escaped from death with her. Then, when they floated above the sea while clinging to the ram, the girl, Helle, fell into the sea and gave her name to it, for it is called the Hellespont after her. Carried to Colchis, Phrixus sacrificed the ram, and in the temple of Mars he dedicated the golden fleece. A hideous dragon guarded it. King Aeetes received Phrixus with pleasure, and gave him his daughter for a wife. When Phrixus had children by her, Aeetes feared that he would drive him out of his kingdom, for prophetic signs had been given to him advising him to guard against death from a stranger, a descendant of Aeolus. So he killed Phrixus, but his sons climbed into a boat to go to their grandfather, Athamas. Aeson received them after they were shipwrecked. Afterward, Jason went to Colchis to take the golden fleece; he killed the dragon and carried off the fleece.

24. The Story of Pelias and Jason.

Pelias, or Peleus, was the king of Peloponnesus. His brother was Aeson, and this Aeson had a son named Jason. The forenamed Pelias was afraid of his brother's son on account of his strength and uprightness, lest he might expel him from his kingdom. So he sent him to Colchis to bring back the golden fleece[4] on which Jove had ascended into the sky. Indeed, he thought this task would cause Jason's death. However, a certain Argos made a ship that was called Argo from his name; Jason and his companions were called Argonauts after this ship. In fact, its steersman was Tiphys. While sailing to Colchis, they came to Troy, but Laomedon, the king of Troy, did not allow them to enter the harbor. Then they went back and told the things that Laomedon, the king of Troy, did to them. For this reason Pelias and Hercules came to Troy and conquered it. Laomedon was killed.

25. The Story of Jason.

In accordance with Apollo's oracle, Jason went to Colchis to seize the golden fleece, which Phrixus had consecrated to Mars. It was under this condition: that he first yoke bulls that could not be tamed by the Colchians. Medea, the greatest of sorceresses, marveled at Jason's beauty. Through her sorcery she caused him to subdue the bulls and to kill the watchful dragon. After it was killed and the bulls breathing Vulcan's fire were yoked, Jason sowed its teeth. The armed men born from these teeth killed each other with reciprocal wounds. Indeed, King Aeetes had proposed these conditions to Jason. Apollo had told Aeetes that he would reign as long as that fleece was in the temple. After he had taken possession of the golden fleece, Jason later married Medea. But when Jason brought home a mistress named Glauce, the daughter of Creon, Medea gave his mistress a tunic tinged with poisons and garlic [sic]. When Glauce put this on, she began to be consumed by fire. When Medea could not endure the wrath of Jason, who was raging against her, she fled on a winged serpent.

26. The Story of Orithyia.

A very beautiful maiden, Orithyia, daughter of the Athenian king Erechtheus and Penthesilea, was loved by Aquilo, the north wind. After she was married, she had two sons by him, Zetes and Calais, winged youths who were among the Argonauts with Jason. They drove the Harpies away from Phineus.

27. The Story of Phineus.

Phineus was the king of Arcadia. He placed a stepmother over his children, and at her instigation he blinded them. Angered at this, the gods blinded him and summoned the Harpies. After they had been snatching food from him for a long time, he welcomed Jason with hospitality. Jason had come to Colchis with the Argonauts on account of the golden fleece, and Phineus gave him a guide. Thus, influenced by this favor, the Argonauts dispatched the winged youths, Zetes and Calais, the sons of Boreas and Orithyia, to drive the Harpies away. When they pursued the Harpies with drawn swords as they were being driven from Arcadia, the youths came to islands called Plotae. And when they wanted to go farther on, they were warned by Iris to stay away from the hounds of Jove. They turned their course around, and this turning, that is strophe, gave its name to the islands.* Also, this is the reason that the hounds of Jove were named Furies. Thus also greedy men are thought to submit to the Furies, since they hold back from using their possessions. Indeed, in the world below they are called "Furies" and "hounds," and among those in the world above "Dirae" and "birds." In the middle region they are called "Harpies." Thus a double form is found in them.

28. The Story of Leander and Hero.

Sestos and Abydos were neighboring cities divided by a narrow stretch of sea flowing between them. One of these cities was famous for Leander, a very handsome youth; the other for Hero, a very beautiful woman. When they were apart from each other, love glowed in the depths of their hearts. Unable to bear love's flame, the young man sought in every way an opportunity to have the maiden. But when he found no approach to Hero by land, he entrusted himself to the sea, impelled by ardent passion and daring. Thus by swimming he came to the girl every night when the light of a tower shone from the opposite shore thanks to the girl's effort; by this he could guide his nightly journey to her. Indeed, on a certain night when the wind, blowing more violently than usual, extinguished the little torch, Leander strayed and lost his way. He perished as he swam. When Hero saw his body cast up by the waves onto the shore the next day, driven by grief, she fell from the top of the tower. Thus with this man, the one with whom she shared worldly pleasure, she also suffered the bitterness of death.

29. The Story of Cleobis and Bito.

It was the custom for a Greek priestess to go with yoked oxen to the shrines of Juno. On the appointed day oxen were not found, for a pestilence that swept across Attica had killed everything. The two sons of the

*The islands came to be called Strophades.

priestess, Cleobis and Bito, submitted to the yoke and carried their mother to the shrines. Then, approving of their conscientiousness, Juno granted that their mother might ask what she wished for her sons. Giving a faithful answer, the mother said that the goddess herself should bestow what she knew to be beneficial to mortal men. And so on the next day the sons of the priestess were found dead. From this it is shown that nothing is more preeminent than death.

30. The History of Amulius and Numitor.

Amulius and Numitor were brothers. Amulius expelled his brother from his realm and killed his son; in fact, he made his daughter, Ilia, a priestess of Vesta to remove her hope of offspring, by whom he thought he would be punished. Many say that Mars lay with her and thus were born Remus and Romus, whom Amulius ordered to be thrown with their mother into the Tiber. Then, as certain ones say, the Anio made Ilia his wife, and as others say, she was the wife of Tiber. Indeed, her boys were left exposed on the nearby riverbank. Faustus the shepherd found them; his wife, Acca Larentia, had recently been a prostitute. She nursed the boys, who had been rescued by them. Later, when Amulius had been killed, the boys recalled their uncle, Numitor, to the kingdom. Since the realm of Alba seemed small for them and their uncle, they departed, and, after auguries had been observed, they founded a city. But Remus had first seen six vultures; then Romus saw twelve. This fact caused a war in which Remus was killed, and the Romans were named after Romus. Moreover, it happened by a kind of flattery that he was called Romulus instead of Romus, since he was pleased with the diminutive name. That they are said to have been nourished by a *lupa*, a she-wolf, is a fabulous invention to conceal the baseness of the founders of the Roman nation. Nor was this story invented unsuitably, for we call prostitutes *lupas*, "she-wolves." From this also comes *lupanaria*, "brothels." It is well known that this animal is under the protection of Mars.

31. The Story of Lyncus.

Lyncus was the king of Scythia. He planned to kill Triptolemus, after receiving him with hospitality. Triptolemus had been sent by Ceres to teach all men about grain, and Lyncus wanted such great glory to come to himself. On account of this, an angry Ceres changed him into a wild lynx of the mottled kind, as he had been conspicuous for his mottled mind.

32. The Story of Oenopion.

King Oenopion had no children. He asked Jove, Mercury, and Neptune to grant him offspring. They were urging him to request something from them, since he had received them with hospitality. The gods ordered that the urine[5] of an ox sacrificed to them be placed in a skin and covered with earth, to be removed from the ground after the months of pregnancy were completed. When this was done, a boy was found, to whom a name was given from urine, so that he was called Orion. Later, he became a hunter. When he wanted to lie with Diana, as Horace tells us,[6] he was killed by her arrows. Lucan says he died when a serpent was sent against him, and through the pity of the gods he was carried off and placed among the constellations.[7]

33. The Story of Orion.

Orion, the forenamed son of Neptune, was a very fierce hunter. Visiting Minos, king of the Cretans, he was received with hospitality, but he violently attempted to ravish his daughters. Minos sacrificed to his father, Liber, whose son he seems to have been. Then, his father Liber sent satyrs who tied up the drunken Orion and handed him over in fetters to Minos so that he might punish him. Minos put out his eyes. Later, in fact, Orion learned from an oracle that he would recover his sight if he went to the East. He heard the sound of the Cyclopes fashioning thunderbolts, seized one of them, and asked that he carry him on his shoulders to the East. Transported thus to the East, he recovered his sight.

34. The Story of Amaracus.

Amaracus was a royal perfumer. By accident he fell while carrying perfumes and created a better fragrance from their mingling together. For this reason the best perfumes are called "amaracina." Later he was turned into the marjoram plant, which men now also call "amaracum."

35. The History of Palamedes.

When Palamedes was recruiting throughout Greece, he lead away an unwilling Ulysses, who had been feigning madness. Ulysses had yoked animals of a different nature from each other and was sowing salt when

Palamedes placed his son in his way. When he saw his son, Ulysses stopped. Led off to war, he had a just cause for animosity. Later, when Ulysses was sent to fetch grain and brought nothing back to Troy,[8] he was rebuked vehemently by Palamedes. Ulysses said that the cause was not negligence, for if Palamedes himself were to go, he could not bring back anything. Palamedes went and brought back endless amounts of grain. With his enmity increased by envy of this feat, Ulysses gave to a captive a false letter to Palamedes in Priam's name. In this letter Priam gave thanks for Palamedes' betrayal [of the Greeks] and reminded him that a secret mass of gold had been sent to him. Then Ulysses caused the captive to be killed on his journey. The letter was found, and, in the military custom, brought to the king and read to the assembled captains. Then when Ulysses had dissembled himself to Palamedes, he said [to the Greeks]: "If you believe that it is true, search for the gold in his tent." When this was done and the gold found, which Ulysses had bribed servants to hide there in the night, Palamedes was stoned to death. However, it is well known that he was a wise man, for he invented a board game to repress the insurrections of an idle army. According to certain ones, he discovered letters, which is perhaps a doubtful thing. Yet it is certain that X (chi) with an aspiration was invented by this man.

36. The Story of Achilles.

Bathed in the Stygian swamp by his mother, Achilles was invulnerable in his whole body, except the part by which she held him. When he decided to have intercourse with his beloved Polyxena in a temple, Paris hid in ambush behind a statue and killed him. It is thought that Paris aimed the darts, while Apollo held them.

37. The Story of Latona and Asterie.

After Latona had been violated, Jupiter also wanted to violate her sister, Asterie. She asked the gods to be changed into a bird, and she was turned into a quail. When she wanted to cross over the sea called Coturnicus, Jove blew upon her and changed her into a stone. Thus she lay concealed for a long time under the waves. Later, after Latona implored Jove, Asterie was lifted up and began to float upon the waters. She was consecrated to Neptune first, and then to Doris. Later, Juno sent the Python against the pregnant Latona and pursued her. She was expelled from all the lands. Finally, Latona was received at last by her sister Asterie, who directed her to shore, and there she gave birth to Diana first and Apollo after. He avenged the injury to his mother immediately when he killed the Python. Indeed, after Diana was born, she performed the duty of midwife to her mother as she gave birth to Apollo. For this reason, although Diana is a virgin, she is invoked by women giving birth. This is also true of Juno, Diana, and Proserpina. After the two deities were born, they did not allow Latona to wander the land of her birth, but they bound her to the two islands. In fact, the truth was far otherwise. Indeed, since this island (Delos) is troubled by earthquakes, which happen because of winds concealed under the earth, it has no oracle of Apollo. In fact, he ordered that a dead man not be buried there, and he commanded certain sacrifices to be performed. Later, people came from the nearby islands of Mykonos and Gyaros to occupy this island. Also, there is a reason that we say Diana was born first, for it is clear that night was first, whose ornament is the moon, that is, Diana. Day comes after, which the sun makes, who is Apollo. Moreover, the fact that Delos was first called Ortygia happened because of the quail, called *ortux* in Greek. Delos is so called because it lay hidden for a long time and appeared later. For the Greeks express "clear" by the word *delon*, or, what is truer, clear oracles are given there, even though the responses of Apollo are obscure everywhere else. Furthermore, Delos is called both a city-state and an island. For this reason it sometimes receives a postpositioning.

38. The Story of the Hesperides.

According to the fable, the Hesperides, the daughters of Atlas, were nymphs. They had a garden in which there were golden apples consecrated to Venus. Sent there by Eurystheus, Hercules carried off these apples after he killed an ever-watchful serpent. But in fact the Hesperides were noble girls whose flocks Hercules drove off when their guard had been killed. For this reason it is supposed that he had carried off apples (mala), that is, sheep, for a flock of sheep is called *mala*, and a shepherd is called *melonomos*.

39. The Story of Atalanta and Hippomenes.

Schoeneus is a city-state. Atalanta was a maiden from there, one so powerful at running that she killed suitors who had been challenged to race and were defeated. Later, Hippomenes asked Venus to help him. When he received from her three golden apples from the garden of the Hesperides, he challenged the girl and began to throw down the apples one at a time. Then, held back by her desire to gather up the apples, Atalanta was defeated in the race. But after he gained the victory, Hippomenes, because of impatience for love, had intercourse with the vanquished Atalanta in a grove of the Mother of the gods.[9] For this reason the angry goddess changed them into lions and yoked them to her chariot; she also ordered that lions never copulate with each other. For, as Pliny says in his *Natural History*, the lion has intercourse with a female panther, and the panther with a lioness. Thus the Mother of the gods is said to ride in a chariot, since she is the earth, which hangs in the air. So, she is borne on wheels, since the world turns like a wheel, and it is able to revolve. Therefore lions are yoked to it to show that maternal piety can overcome everything. Her attendants, the Corybantes, are thought to carry drawn swords to signify that all men ought to fight for their own land. The fact that she wears a tiered crown shows that city-states have been set up on earth. These, it is well known, are distinguished by towers.

40. The Story of Helenus.

Helenus was captured by the Greeks at Arisba and forced to reveal the fate of Troy, including that concerning the Palladium. He is said to have obtained realms from Pyrrhus, for he had shown Pyrrhus that he should return home by land, telling him that all the Greeks would perish by shipwreck (and this happened). Then Diomedes and Ulysses entered the citadel by underground passages, as some say, or by sewers, as others say, and they carried off the statue, after the guards had been killed. Since they were worshippers of Minerva, this most important task was given to them. Later, when Diomedes had this statue, he believed that it was not meant for him on account of its dangers. He tried to give it to Aeneas as he was passing through, but when Aeneas turned away while offering sacrifice with his head covered, a certain Nautes took the statue. For this reason the Julian clan does not preserve the sacred rites of Minerva, but the clan of the Nautii does. Although some say that the Trojans hid this statue within a raised wall, they later understood that Troy would fall. Afterward, in the war with Mithridates, a certain Roman, Fimbria, is said to have revealed the discovered statue that, it is well known, was brought to Rome. It had been prophesied that supreme power would reside there, where also the statue was. So Mamurius the craftsman was summoned, and he made many similar statues. Nevertheless, the Palladium was recognized by only one priestess through the movement of its spear and eyes. Indeed, some say that only one statue had fallen from the sky near Athens. Others propose two: this one of which we have spoken, and that Athenian one.

41. The Story of Andromache and Molossus.

It was a custom of kings that, not having a lawful wife, they might nevertheless have someone, even a captive, in place of a lawful wife. This was so that children born of her might succeed them. And so Pyrrhus took the captive Andromache as if she were a lawful wife, and from her he received a son, Molossus. Later, when Pyrrhus wanted to marry Hermione, the daughter of Menelaus and Helen, who had been betrothed already to Orestes, he was killed in an ambush set by Orestes in the temple of Apollo at Delphi. Even so the dying Pyrrhus ordered that Andromache, who held the place of a wife in his house, be given to Helenus on account of his good deed; Helenus had prevented him from sailing home.[10] Then it happened that Helenus held also the kingdom of his stepson, who had succeeded his father. Part of Epirus is named Molossia after him. Helenus later named this country Chaonia, after his brother Chaon. He did this as a consolation for the death of his brother, whom he is said to have killed unknowingly in a hunt.

42. The Story of the Sirens.

According to the story, the three Sirens were part maidens, part birds, the daughters of the river Achelous and Calliope the Muse. They used to make music, one of them with her voice, another with pipes, the other with a lyre. First they lived near Pelorus, and later on Capri; they led those enticed by their singing to shipwreck. In truth, they were harlots who led those passing by to poverty; on account of this, they were thought to cause shipwreck. By scorning them, Ulysses killed them.

43. The Story of Venus and Pasiphae.

After the adultery of Mars and Venus was revealed by the Sun, Vulcan encircled their bed with very fine chains. The unknowing Mars and

Venus were enveloped by these and shown in their great shame, with all the gods witnessing. Exceedingly pained by what had been done, Venus began to afflict every offspring of the Sun with unspeakable passions. Therefore, Pasiphae, the Sun's daughter, the wife of king Minos of Crete, was inflamed by love of a bull. Through the skill of Daedalus, she was enclosed in a wooden cow covered with the hide of a very beautiful heifer and had intercourse with the bull. From this was born the Minotaur, which was shut up in a labyrinth and used to eat human flesh. But Minos had more children by Pasiphae: Androgeus, Ariadne, and Phaedra. Since Androgeus was the strongest athlete and defeated all the Athenians in contests of sport, he was killed after the Athenians and the neighboring Megarians formed a conspiracy. Grieving over this, Minos gathered his ships, provoked a war, and established this penalty for the conquered Athenians: that each and every year they would send seven of their sons and seven of their daughters to be devoured by the Minotaur. But in the third year, Aegeus' son Theseus was sent, a man as mighty in strength as in appearance. He was loved by the king's daughter, Ariadne. With the advice of Daedalus he guided his way by a thread, slew the Minotaur and fled as the victor with the ravished Ariadne. When Minos discovered that all these things had been accomplished through the work of Daedalus, he imprisoned him and his son Icarus, in the labyrinth. But when the guards were bribed, Daedalus received wax and feathers under the pretext of making a gift to appease the king. Then putting wings on himself as well as his son, he flew away. As Icarus flew higher and higher, his wings dissolved from the heat of the sun, and he gave his name to the sea into which he fell. Daedalus was carried first to Sardinia, then to Cumae, and in a shrine built for Apollo, he depicted the fall of his son. However, this is the truth: certainly, Taurus was Minos' clerk, whom Pasiphae loved; she slept with him in the house of Daedalus. And since she bore two sons, one by Minos and the other by Taurus, she is said to have brought forth the Minotaur. The queen freed the imprisoned Daedalus when his guards were bribed. After his son was lost at sea, he was brought to Cumae in a ship. Vergil touches upon this when he says "the oarage of wings."[11] For wings are both of birds and of ships, as in "we unfurl the wings of the sails."[12]

44. The Story of Procris.

Procris, the daughter of Iphilis, was the wife of Cephalus. When he was taken with a zeal for hunting and exhausted by the effort, he used to go to a certain place and there to summon the breeze (*aura*) to refresh him. Since he did this often, he stirred the love of Aurora toward himself. She gave him a very swift hound named Lelepa and two unavoidable spears. While they were embracing, she asked Cephalus to love her and to spurn his wife. He said that he had sworn an oath of mutual chastity with his spouse. When she heard this, Aurora responded: "To prove your spouse's chastity, transform yourself into a merchant." When this was done, he went to Procris. After gifts were offered and intercourse was procured, he revealed himself as her husband. Grieving over this, Procris went to the forest and hid among the bushes to catch her husband, since she had heard from a rustic that he loved Aurora and summoned her to him. When he called the dawn (Aurora) in his usual way, Procris tried to come forth, and she moved the bushes. Expecting it to be a wild animal, Cephalus hurled the unavoidable spear and killed his wife.

45. The Story of Amymone and Palamedes.

While Amymone, the daughter of Danaus, was zealously practicing with a javelin on an island, she struck a satyr without knowing it, and when the satyr wanted to violate her, she implored Neptune for help. When Neptune saw this, he had intercourse with her himself, after the satyr was chased away. From this intercourse, Nauplius was born, the father of Palamedes. Thus Vergil writes: "The name of Palamedes, descendant of Belus."[13] In fact, Neptune is said to have struck the place with his trident where he had intercourse with Amymone. When water flowed from here, the spring was called Lerna, and the stream Amymone.

46. Theseus and Hippolytus.

After the death of Hippolyte, Theseus made Phaedra, the daughter of Minos and Pasiphae, stepmother to Hippolytus. When she tried to seduce him, Hippolytus despised her for her lewdness. Phaedra falsely accused him to Theseus because she wished to harm him. Theseus then asked his father Aegeus to avenge him. While Hippolytus was driving his chariot along the shore, Aegeus sent a sea beast to frighten the horses, and they tore him to pieces. Then Diana, moved by his chastity, recalled him to life through the help of Aesculapius, the son of Apollo and Coronis. Aesculapius was born when his mother's womb was cut open. This had happened because Apollo was angry at Coronis when he heard from the raven, his spy, that she committed adultery. When her time for giving birth arrived, he pierced her with his arrows. Indeed, he also changed the raven from white to black. From Coronis' cut-open womb, Apollo brought forth Aesculapius, who became skilled in medicine. Jupiter later killed him because he called Hippolytus back to life. Then an angry Apollo shot the Cyclopes, the fashioners of thunderbolts, with his arrows. For this he was ordered by Jove to pasture the herds of King Admetus for nine years, with his divinity set aside for that time. But Diana commended Hippolytus, who had been called back from the Underworld, to the nymph Egeria, and she ordered that he be called Virbius, as if to say *vir bis* (twice a man).

47. The Story of Minos and the Bull and Hercules.

When Minos, the son of Jove and Europa, approached the altars to sacrifice to his father, he begged the divine power that he might offer a victim worthy of his altars. And so, a bull bathed in wondrous brightness suddenly appeared. Minos marveled at the bull and, forgetful of his religious duty, he preferred to make it the leader of his herd. Pasiphae is even said to have burned with love for this bull. Therefore, scorned by his son, an indignant Jupiter brought a raging fury upon the bull, and it not only devastated the fields of Crete, but even all the cities. Sent by Eurystheus, Hercules overcame the bull, and he led the subdued animal to Argos. There it was dedicated to Juno by Eurystheus. But Juno hated the gift because it lead to the glory of Hercules; she drove the bull into the territory of Attica, where it was also called "Marathonian." Later Aegeus' son, Theseus, killed this bull.

48. The Story of Theseus and Pirithous and Hercules.

When Theseus, the son of Aegeus and Aethra, had been raised by his mother and reached the age of youth, he traveled to the territory of Attica to learn of his father. So that he would come to him with honor, he freed Greece of robbers. Moreover, after Medea was cast aside by Jason and wedded to Aegeus, she persuaded him to send the bull that was devastating the territory of Attica against the approaching youth. She said that he would deprive Aegeus of his realm. Indeed, after the bull was killed, Theseus increased the king's fear. Then Aegeus wanted to destroy him when he was invited to a banquet. Finally, when Aegeus recognized a sword that he had formerly left with Aethra, he gladly acknowledged his son and compelled Medea, who was responsible for the ambush, to flee. After his father's death, Theseus obtained the kingdom of Athens. His strength gave him confidence, and he conspired with Pirithous, Ixion's son, to ravish Proserpina. After they descended into the infernal regions, Pirithous was bound to a rock with coils of serpents; he endures these punishments forever. In fact, while Hercules was descending to the Underworld to capture Cerberus, he found Theseus, a youth very dear to himself, clinging to the rock. Hercules entreated Dis, as certain sources say, and asked pardon for Theseus; as others say, he tore him so forcefully from the rock that part of his buttocks clung to it.

49. The Story of Hercules and Hylas.

When Hercules became the comrade of the Argonauts, he took Hylas with him, the son of Theodamas, a youth of admirable beauty. Because of his strength, Hylas broke his oar in the sea while he rowed. Proceeding to Mysia to repair it, he entered a forest there. In fact, when Hylas had gone to fetch water, he was seen and seized by nymphs. While searching for him, Hercules was left behind in Mysia by the Argonauts.

50. The Story of Hercules and Alcmena.

This was the origin of Hercules: Jupiter lay with Alcmena in the shape of her own husband, Amphitryon; Hercules was born of her. So that his birth would be concealed from Juno, who hated the sons of Jove's mistresses, the night was doubled. But when this did not deceive Juno, she sent two serpents to devour Hercules lying in his cradle. There were two boys: Ephytus by Amphitryon, Hercules by Jove. Frightened at the arrival of the serpents, Ephytus fell from his cradle and woke his sleeping parents with his crying. Rising, they saw Hercules strangling the snakes and choking their throats.

51. The Story of Hercules and the Nemean Lion.

Sent by Eurystheus, king of Thebes, Hercules killed the Nemean lion, whose hide with its claws he took for spoils.

52. The Story of Molorchus.

Molorchus was a certain shepherd who received Hercules with kindness and hospitality as he came to kill the Nemean lion.

53. The Story of Eryx and Hercules.

Eryx was the son of Venus and Butes. Killed by Hercules, he gave his name to a mountain because of his burial there. On this mountain he had made a shrine for his mother. The poet credits this to Aeneas: "then a temple near the stars on the peak of Eryx."[14]

54. The Story of Hercules and Lake Ciminus.

Once Hercules came to a people who were called Cimini, either from the mountain or from the lake. When he was challenged by certain individuals to demonstrate his strength, he is said to have fixed an iron pole in the ground where he exercised. Since the pole was fixed in the earth and could be withdrawn by no one, Hercules, when asked, pulled it up. Then an immense quantity of water followed it, which made Lake Ciminus.

55. The Story of Antaeus and Hercules.

Antaeus, the son of Earth, was king of Libya. When Hercules came to visit him, Antaeus wrestled with him but could not overpower him. Indeed, Antaeus thought that he was falling, and he took strength from his mother, Earth, and rose up even stronger. Seeing this, Hercules strangled him by choking him as he was suspended in air.

56. The Story of Hercules and Alcinous and the Harpies.

Alcinous, king of Phaecia, was plagued by the Harpies. When Hercules came to visit him and recognized this, he waited for their approach as they came in their accustomed way to the table; after they were wounded, he drove them from the kingdom. Ovid calls them "Stymphalian birds."[15]

57. The Story of Hercules and Tricerberus.

While descending to the infernal regions to rescue Theseus, Hercules feared that Tricerberus might attack him and tear him to pieces. So, leaping upon Cerberus first, he dragged him up from the infernal regions. When Cerberus saw the unaccustomed light of the upper world, he foamed at the mouth; from this foam a poisonous plant called aconite is said to have originated. For Cerberus is the earth, "she who consumes." Hence Cerberus is said to be named from *creoboros*, that is "devouring flesh."

58. The Story of Hercules, Deianira, Oeneus, and the Centaur.

Oeneus, son of Parthaon and king of Aetolia, had the seat of his realm in Calydon. He had a daughter, Deianira, whom Hercules and Alpheus, who is also Achelous, sought in marriage. The father proposed this condition to them: that wrestling one another, the victor in the struggle would take Deianira as his wife. When they entered the contest, Achelous, capable of magical arts, changed himself into various shapes of wild beasts, and at last he changed into the form of a bull. When Hercules conquered him and tore off his right horn, he was thrown into confusion. The nymphs took the horn and offered it to Fortuna as a gift. Fortuna filled it with all good things and handed it over to Copia, her attendant, so that for those whom Fortuna wishes to favor, abundance (copia) flows copiously from it. Thus Horace says: "Here in the country, abundance, rich in goods, will flow copiously from a fruitful horn."[16] Alpheus, or Achelous, disfigured by the strength of Alceus' grandson,[17] was changed into a river and slipped away from the hands of his enemy. Fearing always lest his enemy should ever appear, he flows with his streams through the hollows of the land in Sicily.

Later, taking Deianira under his care, Hercules came to a river of very great depth. When he could not cross it, he put her down and carried across his club and the rest of his arms with him so that after he was freed from the burden, he might carry her unimpeded. Meanwhile, he entrusted her to the Centaur, Nessus. Then when he wanted to return to carry her across, he saw Nessus the Centaur having intercourse with her. Seething with anger, Hercules wounded him with a poisoned arrow shot from his bow; the blood of Nessus was turned into poison. As he was dying, Nessus said to Deianira: "Gather up this blood and it will be given as a gift from me to you. For if ever the love of Hercules turns away from you, give a garment tinged with this blood to your husband and you will recall his love." And so, when Hercules loved a certain harlot, Deianira, filled with hatred, sent him a garment tinged with that poison. She sent word through Lichas, his servant, that he should put it on at the hour of sacrifice. After Hercules was clothed in it, the garment clung to his skin, and the poison began to pour through his limbs and to set them on fire. Then Hercules cast Lichas, who had brought the garment to him, into the Euboean Sea. He hurled himself into the fire of Mount Aetna, and thus he was conveyed to a place among the gods.

59. The Story of Philoctetes and Hercules.

Philoctetes, the son of Poeas, was Hercules' companion. When Hercules laid aside his human body on Mount Oeta, he asked Philoctetes not to reveal the remains of his body to anyone. He made him swear an oath concerning this matter, and as a gift he gave him arrows tinged with the hydra's gall. Later, during the Trojan War, an oracle answered that Hercules' arrows were needed for the storming of Troy, just as they were needed against the hydra. And so Philoctetes was found. He was asked about Hercules, and he first denied that he knew where Hercules was. Finally, he acknowledged that Hercules was dead. Also, when he was violently forced to reveal Hercules' grave, he struck the place with his foot, since he was unwilling to tell. Later, he went to war. While training, he was wounded by a falling arrow on the foot with which he had struck Hercules' tomb. Later, when the Greeks could not bear the stench of his incurable wound, at last they left him on Lemnos, although they kept him with them for a long time because of the oracle. The arrows were taken from him. He did not care to return to his homeland afterward because of the horror of his wound, but he founded little Petalia for himself in the region of Calabria.

60. The Story of the Grandsons of Hercules.

After Hercules departed from the earth, his grandsons feared the plots of those whom their grandfather had afflicted in various ways. First, they established a sanctuary for themselves at Athens; this is the temple of Minerva, from which no one could be led away. Statius even says this: "It is a tradition that the grandsons of Hercules founded it."[18] For this reason, therefore, Vergil says: "Brave Romulus brought back this sanctuary";[19] that is, he made a temple in imitation of the Athenian sanctuary. Romulus did this so that he might have many foreigners with whom he could settle Rome. Thus Juvenal says: "And yet, although you might long repeat and long read over the name, the race you take from an infamous sanctuary."[20]

61. The Story of Pholus and Hercules.

Pholoe, a forest in Thessaly, was named after the Centaur, Pholus, who dwelt in it. At the time Hercules was sent by King Eurystheus into Thrace to tame the horses of Diomedes (which ate human flesh), this Pholus received him with hospitality. Others, who say that Hercules killed Pholus after he had been received with hospitality by him, are mistaken. But Velius Asper Longus relates that Pholus was led against the Centaurs by Hercules when he had received Hercules with hospitality. Asper even relates that while Pholus marveled at Hercules' arrows, which had killed so many Centaurs, one of them fell on his foot. He could not be cured of this wound. Thus some believe that he was killed by Hercules.

62. The Story of the Hydra and Hercules.

The Hydra was a serpent in Lerna, a marsh of Argos. Having fifty heads, or, as certain writers say, seven heads, it devoured the whole region. When Hercules had heard this, he went there and fought it, and when one head was cut off, three grew. Hence also in Latin it was called Excetra; later Hercules conquered this Hydra. Yet it is established that Hydra was a place spewing forth waters that ravaged a nearby city; when one channel was closed, many others burst forth. Seeing this, Hercules set these places on fire and thus closed the channel of water. The Hydra is named from water. Moreover, the place where it is written, "the blemish is burned away, and the useless moisture oozes out,"[21] indicates that these things could happen.

63. The Story of the Hardships of Hercules.

Certain other stories are sketched out about Hercules besides the ones contained here. Indeed, it is said that he also killed a certain Erymanthean boar, and stole away the golden horns from a certain stag; he stripped the Amazon of her girdle, and snatched victory from the horses of Diomedes. Also, as Lucan attests, he cast down Mount Ossa, which had been placed upon Olympus by the Giants. In a single breath, he traversed 125 paces on the run. However, these aforementioned stories are not fully described here, since they are rarely found.[22]

64. The Story of Eurystheus and Hercules.

Eurystheus, a descendant of Perseus, was a king in Greece. At the instigation of Juno, he ordered Hercules to overcome various monsters by which he could be killed. For this reason the poet called him "pitiless,"[23] one capable of fulfilling a stepmother's hatred.

65. The Story of Busiris and Hercules.

Busiris was a king of Egypt. He sacrificed guests who visited him. Busiris was slain by Hercules when he also wanted to kill him.

66. The Story of Cacus and Hercules.

Cacus was the son of Vulcan. Spewing fire from his mouth, he ravaged all the nearby places. Hercules killed him. In truth, he was a very wicked slave of Evander, and a thief, and so he is called Cacus, which in Greek means "wicked." He is said to spew fire from his mouth because he used to devastate the fields with fire.

When Aeacus,[24] Jove's son, saw ants, that is *myrmicas*, on a fig tree, he wished for just so many companions. Immediately the ants were turned into men. But this is a fable, for the Myrmidons were named after King Myrmidon, as Sosthenes tells us.

67. The Story of Geryon and Hercules.

Geryon was a king of the island of Erythia, or Spain. He is called "three-born" or "three-bodied" since he had three heads; or according to others, fifty-three heads; or since he ruled three islands; or since there were three most-amicable brothers. At the instigation of Juno, King Eurystheus sent Hercules to kill Geryon, hoping that he would perish at the same time. While proceeding there with a bronze jar and a two-headed dog, Hercules came to the ocean. "Bronze jar" because of his bronzed ships; "two-headed dog" since he was exceedingly strong in a naval battle as well as a land battle. When Hercules found no ship, he climbed on board a piece of alder-wood and went to the island of Erythia, where first he killed Geryon's dog, Orthrum, and then his daughter Ithimia. Then Hercules killed Erython the herdsman, the son of Mars. Last of all, he killed Geryon himself. Thus, as a victor, he led away Geryon's herds into Greece.

68. The Story of Evander and Hercules.

At first, Hercules was not welcomed by Evander. After Hercules declared that he was Jove's son and proved his strength by killing Cacus, he was accepted and esteemed as a god. Then Evander set up a mighty altar to him. When Hercules decided to sacrifice certain of Geryon's cattle to his father, two old men, Pinarius and Potitius, were called upon. To them Hercules showed the rites by which he wanted to be honored, namely, that he be sacrificed to in the morning and in the evening. And so after the morning sacrifice was completed, when Potitius arrived first for the evening sacrifice, an angry Hercules ordered that the house of Pinarius should serve the house of Potitius at its feasts.

69. The Story of Evander.

Evander was a descendant of Pallas, the king of Arcadia. He killed his own father. With his mother Nicostrata (who was later called Carmentis) urging him on, Evander drove out the old inhabitants and acquired the place where Rome was later built. He then founded a little town on Mount Pallanteum, which had its name from Pallas, his ancestor.

70. The Story of Bellerophon, Who Is Also Perseus.

When Bellerophon (who is also Perseus), the son of Glaucus, had unknowingly come to Proetus seeking hospitality, Proetus' wife Sthenoboea (or Anteia) loved him. She could not gain from him her desire that he sleep with her, so she lied to her husband that Bellerophon had forced her on account of his lewdness. Proetus sent Bellerophon to his father-in-law, Iobates, and he gave him a written account of the matter to be brought to his father-in-law. When Iobates read this, he wanted to kill such a man. But Bellerophon freed himself from the impending danger by his prudence and the help of his chastity. Yet, so that a monstrous danger might prove his virtue, he was sent to slay the Chimaera, which he destroyed with the help of Pegasus. Finally, Iobates sent him to conquer the Calydonians. When Bellerophon had conquered them, Iobates at last recognized the reason for his own great misfortunes. He wiped away the charges against Bellerophon and wondrously praised his virtue. He gave to Bellerophon his own daughter Alcimene as his wife. But Sthenoboea (who is also Anteia) perished by her own hand when this fact was made known.

71. The Story of the Chimaera and Bellerophon.

The Chimaera, a monster, was the daughter of Typhon and Achemenida. She is said to have had a threefold shape, for she looked frightful, with the appearance of a lion above, then a goat in the middle, and her tail stuck out as a serpent. When she devastated the lands in Lycia near Mount Gargarum, she was killed by Bellerophon. Some sources say that the Chimaera was not an animal, but a mountain in Lycia that nurtured lions and goats in certain places, was burning in certain places, and was full of serpents in certain other places. Bellerophon made this mountain habitable, and thus he is said to have killed the Chimaera.

72. Perseus.

While Perseus was making his way through Ethiopia, he saw Andromeda bound to a rock and exposed to a sea beast on account of the pride of her mother, who preferred her own beauty to that of the nymphs. Captivated by Andromeda's appearance, Perseus was inflamed with love. The maiden's parents, Cepheus and Cassiopeia, promised that they would join her to him in marriage if he would kill the beast. Perseus accomplished this, and Cepheus kept his plighted word. The foremost men were present at the wedding banquet. Phineus (to whom Andromeda had been betrothed before) thought that a grievous insult had been inflicted upon himself because he, a kinsman, was esteemed less than a stranger. He stirred the passions of those who were eating at the banquet, and they started a fight. When the deplorable affair of men fighting was going on in the palace, and many men on each side took up the arms that chance offered them, at last Perseus, fearing the multitude of adversaries, brought forth the Gorgon's head. When they saw this, Phineus and his helpers became as rigid as stone.

73. The Story of Tarquin and Lucretia.

Tarquin the Proud had profligate sons, among whom was Arruns. He was in the camp when his father was besieging Ardea, and a conversation arose between him and Collatinus, the husband of Lucretia, about their wives. The dispute proceeded to such a point that they seized their horses and immediately set out together to their homes to test the morals of their wives. And so, they entered the town of Collatia, where the home of Lucretia was. They found her attending to her weaving, and sad on account of her husband's absence. Then they proceeded to Arruns' house. When they found his wife indulging in songs and dances, they returned to camp. Arruns grieved over this. He thought about Lucretia's chastity, that it could be assailed. He composed a letter in her husband's name and sent it to Lucretia. This was contained in the letter: that Arruns should be received with hospitality. When this was done, he entered her bed-chamber at night with a drawn sword and accompanied by an Ethiopian. He used this stratagem to force her to have intercourse with him, saying: "Unless you lie with me, I shall kill the Ethiopian along with you as if you were caught together in adultery." Lucretia feared that because of this lust she might lose her reputation for chastity. She thought there would surely be no expiation for this, so she unwillingly obeyed his shameful orders. On the next day, her relatives were called together, along with her husband Collatinus, her father Tricipitinus, and her uncle Brutus, who was tribune of the patrician knights. She told of the incident and asked that her violated modesty not perish unavenged. Then with a sword thrust, she killed herself. Taking the sword drawn from her body, Brutus came before the populace and, after he had complained much about the pride of Tarquin and the baseness of his sons, he saw to it that they were not admitted into the city. This was done on his authority, for he was exceedingly powerful. As we said above, Brutus was tribune of the knights. But when he was not admitted to the city, Tarquin went to Porsenna, the king of Etruria, who violently besieged Rome for Tarquin with mighty forces after the Janiculum was captured and camps were set up there. When he tried to cross over a pile bridge, that is a wooden one, Cocles alone held back the enemy attack, while behind him his comrades dismantled the bridge. When it was dismantled, he threw himself with his weapons into the Tiber. Though injured in the hip, he survived the flowing waters. Thus, when the defect of his hip was thrown up at him in the assembly, he said: "By every step I am reminded of my triumph." Further, under the great compulsion of the siege, the populace also gave hostages. When she found an opportunity, one of these, Cloelia, swam across the river and then returned to Rome with a peace proposal; she went back again when Porsenna asked for her. He admired the girl's courage and gave her the option to go back with whom she wished. She chose maidens. Porsenna marveled at this also; he granted her wish, and in a letter asked the Roman people to decree some manly reward for her. To her was dedicated the equestrian statue that we see today on the Via Sacra.

74. The Story of Hymeneus.

Hymeneus, a most handsome boy, was of Athenian origin. When he surpassed the years of boyhood and still could not achieve manhood, it is said that he had been endowed with this beauty so that he might imitate being a woman. When one of his fellow citizens, a noble maiden, loved him, he despaired of marriage, since he was born of common parents.

Yet he did what he could: loving her at a distance with his heart alone, he made himself a girl in appearance. When the noble women and maidens were celebrating the sacred rites of Eleusinian Ceres, pirates arrived suddenly and captured them. Among the women was also Hymeneus, who had followed his beloved; he was carried off along with the girl. Then, when the pirates had carried their booty over the distant seas, finally they reached a certain region where, overcome by sleep, they were slain by those pursuing them. With the maidens left there, Hymeneus returned to Athens and was promised marriage to his beloved by the citizens if he would restore their own daughters to them. When he restored them according to his vow, he received his desired wife. Since this union was happy, it pleased the Athenians to join the name of Hymeneus to marriage.

75. The Story of Orpheus and Eurydice.

Certain writers think that Orpheus, the son of Oeagrus and Calliope the Muse, had Eurydice, the daughter of Apollo, as his wife. When the lustful shepherd Aristeus, the son of Cirene, pursued Eurydice and wanted to ravish her, she fled from this union. As she was fleeing, she could not avoid a serpent, and this was the cause of her death. Compelled by a longing for his wife, Orpheus tried to assuage Dis and Proserpina. He wanted to see if he could recall Eurydice to the world of the living through the sweetness of the music of his cithara. Descending to the land of the dead, he moved them to pity by his music. He obtained Eurydice under this accepted condition: that he should not look back before he reached the world of the living. But perseverance in lovers is difficult. Fearing that there was no trust in spoken promises, Orpheus looked back and made his effort worthless. Then he returned to the world of the living. He had experienced too little of happy marriage, and, hateful of the whole race of women, gave himself over to solitude.

76. The Story of Castor and Pollux.

Castor and Pollux were the sons of Jove and Leda. They loved Phoebe and Dianisa, the wives of Lynceus and Idas (the son of Aphoreus), and wanted to ravish them. Lynceus had the power of seeing all things and roused his brother Idas to vengeance. Idas owned a spear that had the likeness of a divine weapon, so that no one could escape it. When he hurled it, he killed Castor, and then when he wanted to slay Pollux, he was stricken by Jove's thunderbolt. Seeing his brother dead, Pollux descended to the Underworld. He regained his brother and ascended from there to the world above. Then he begged Jove to give him celestial glory. The brothers were placed among the constellations and had their celestial glory.

77. *The Story of the Swan and Leda.*

Striving after the love of the maiden Leda, Jupiter changed himself into a swan and pretended that he was fleeing from an eagle. He had transformed Mercury into the eagle. Thus, received into the lap of Leda, he had intercourse with her; she produced an egg from which three offspring were born: Castor, Pollux, and Helen.

78. *The Story of Apis.*

Solinus relates that among all the things that Egypt holds worthy of mention, the people especially marvel at a bull called Apis. This bull is notable for a spot, a white mark engendered by nature on its right flank, which bears the appearance of the horned Moon. Egypt worships this bull like a god because it gives certain clear signs about the future. The bull is seen also in Memphis. There its length of life is decided, for it is drowned in the depth of a sacred spring. It is killed so that it might not live longer than allowed. Soon, without public mourning, another bull is sought. A hundred priests accompany this bull to Memphis, and suddenly, as if panic-stricken, they utter predictions. The bull reveals everything clearly about future events, especially if it takes food from the hand of the one consulting it. The Jews made an image of its head for themselves in the wilderness.

79. *The Story of Tydeus and Polynices.*

Tydeus, the son of Oeneius and Passiope, was the father of Diomedes. He killed his own son Maniplus and came as an exile to Argos. There he was joined in friendship to King Adrastus. At that time, Polynices was expelled from his kingdom by his brother Eteocles, who ruled Thebes, and he also came as an exile to Adrastus. When Adrastus considered an oracle of Apollo, which stated that he would give his daughters to a boar and a lion, he decided to give them to Polynices and Tydeus in marriage, for they were clothed in the hides of these wild beasts. The king decided that he ought to give his daughters to them in marriage. Then, when they were received as fellow citizens, Adrastus obtained the help of Polynices against Eteocles. There Tydeus was killed, and Polynices fell, along with his brother, from the wounds they inflicted on each other.

80. The Story of Sinicrus[25] and Branchus.

When a certain king named Cius ate on the seashore while traveling and then set out again, he forgot his son, whose name was Sinicrus. The boy came to the grove of a certain Patronus, who took him in, and he began to pasture she-goats with his sons. Once, they caught a swan and covered Sinicrus with its feathers. While the sons were fighting about offering Sinicrus as a gift to Patronus, they became weary of the struggle. After they cast aside the feather covering, they came upon a woman. When they fled, she called them back and advised that Patronus would love the boy Sinicrus in a special way. The sons told Patronus what they had heard. Then Patronus loved Sinicrus as his own son with very great affection and arranged for his own daughter to be his wife. When she became pregnant by him, she saw in a dream that the Sun entered her through her throat and came out through her belly. Thus the infant that came forth was called Branchus, since his mother had seen him enter her womb through her throat. When Branchus kissed Apollo in the forest, he was embraced by him. After he received a crown and a staff, he began to prophecy, and suddenly he entirely disappeared. A temple called Branchiadon was built for him. Likewise temples were consecrated to Apollo. These are called Philesia, either from the kiss of Branchus or from the struggle of the boys.

81. The Story of Salmoneus.

Salmoneus was a king of Elis. Uplifted by excessive good fortune, he ordered his citizens who were priests to transfer the worship of Jove to himself, and to devote Jove's ceremonies and sacred rites to himself. Carried through the air in a chariot, he imitated the thunder and carried firebrands in the manner of lightning. Jove, hurling a real thunderbolt, plunged him headlong into Tartarus.

82. The Story of Aloeus, Othus, and Ephialtes.

Aloeus had a wife, Iphimidia, who had intercourse with Neptune and bore two sons, Othus and Ephialtes. During each month, they grew nine inches. Indeed, relying on their height, they tried to overthrow Heaven, but they were pierced by the arrows of Diana and Apollo.

83. The Story of Ceculus.

A certain infant was placed by a certain servant next to a hearth in which shepherds used to light a fire. Drawn by the warmth, the infant threw himself into the glowing ashes. The shepherds discovered him there and thought he was the son of Vulcan. They raised him. He was called Ceculus[26] since he had very narrow eyes because of the fire. When he reached young manhood, he founded a city in the mountains called Preneste. Observing that people frequented the place, he constructed a wooden theater so that the neighboring peoples might come to that city. Ceculus built the town, Preneste, at that time. When no one believed that he was Vulcan's son, he handed torches to his friends. At a given signal he attacked the spectators with fire after they were surrounded. When they begged for mercy and accepted him as the son of Vulcan, he put out the flames.

84. The Story of the Three Proetides.

The Proetides were daughters born of Proetus, king of the Argives, and his wife Sanabilia, or Stenoboea. Their names are Cresipe, Iphinoe, and Ephianasa. Boasting insolently, they preferred their own beauty to Juno's. Learning of this, Juno drove them to insanity; they thought they were cows. They looked for horns on their heads and did not find them, and they put forth confused bellowing until they were cured by a certain Melampos.

85. The Story of the Pierides.

King Pierus of Macedonia and his wife Euipe had nine daughters. When these girls boasted insolently and challenged the Muses to a contest of song, one of them began to sing about the giants who had contended against the gods. Typheus, one of the giants, used his earth-born hideous-ness to terrify the gods, who were driven into Egypt. There, out of fear, Jupiter was turned into a ram, Apollo into a raven, Liber into a goat, Diana into a cat, Juno into a cow, Venus into a fish. However, when the Muses had sung in turn the praises of Ceres and about how Typheus had been put under Mount Etna on Sicily, the defeated Pierides were transformed into magpies.

86. The Story of Orista.

When the shepherd Orista, son of King Oinos, saw a goat frequently leaving the herd, he followed it and found the goat feeding on grapes on the bank of the river Achelous. He immediately pressed a bunch of grapes and mixed this with the water of the river Achelous next to which it had been found. He brought this to the king who called it after his own name, Oinos, in Greek, that is, wine (vinum).

87. The Story of Liber, Silenus, King Midas and the River Pactolus.

When Liber departed from Thrace and made his way to Mount Tmolus, his foster father, Silenus, was captured by the Phrygians and brought to King Midas. After the king recognized Silenus, he was welcomed and restored to Liber upon his arrival. On account of this good deed, the god gave the king the right to ask him for anything he wished. Midas asked that whatever he touched might become gold. This was a harmful re-quest, for he began to be tormented by the effect of this wish, since what-ever he touched immediately became gold. When the king asked to be restored to his former condition, Liber did this. He ordered that Midas go to the river Pactolus and immerse himself entirely, and thus he would return to his original state. After he did this, the river Pactolus flowed with sands of gold.

88. On the Birth of Pan.

After the death of Ulysses, Mercury slept with his wife, Penelope. Near the town of Tegeum she bore him a son named Pan, and for this reason he is called Tegeus.

89. The Story of Pan.

While Pan was visiting Mount Tmolus in Lydia, he amused himself with a reed pipe. He challenged Apollo to a contest, with Tmolus as judge, since it was his mountain. When the victory was awarded to Apollo, it displeased King Midas, who was sitting on his throne, because the angry god had given him the ears of an ass. Midas showed this mark of reproach only to his barber, telling him that he would make him the sharer of his realm if he kept his defect secret. The barber dug in the earth, told his lord's secret to the hole in the earth and covered it over. In that very place a reed grew, from which a shepherd made a pipe for himself. When this was played, it used to sound out "King Midas has the ears of an ass," nothing less than what it had absorbed from the earth. Certain authors teach that not Pan, but Marsyas, vied with Apollo.

90. The Story of Arachne and Minerva.

Arachne the Lydian, daughter of Edmon and Ippopis, sought fame for her skill in woolworking. Through diligence derived from her mother, she surpassed all others in performing this work. During the festal days, she boasted more insolently than befits a mortal woman, for she challenged Minerva to a contest. Transformed at this time into an old woman, Minerva came to Arachne to restrain her boldness. When she observed Arachne persisting in the contest, she reverted to her own shape. Minerva proposed a task and entered into the contest. After Arachne was defeated and reproachfully driven away by Minerva, she hanged herself. On account of the skill she had received from Minerva, she was turned into a spider, so that she could have no satisfaction from her useless efforts.

91. The Story of Alcestis.

Admetus, the king of Greece, sought Alcestis in marriage. Her father had published a proclamation saying that if anyone yoked two dissimilar wild beasts to his chariot, that man could take her in marriage. Admetus besought the help of Apollo and Hercules. They yoked a lion and a boar to his chariot, and so he received Alcestis in marriage. After King Admetus fell sick and learned that he was dying, he prayed to Apollo. In truth, Apollo said that he could not do anything for him unless one of his own relatives voluntarily offered herself to death in his place. This his wife did. And so, when he went down to drag back the three-headed dog, Hercules raised her up from the infernal regions also. In people's opinion, Admetus stands for "mind," Alcestis for "boldness."

92. *The Story of Neptune and Amycus.*

Neptune fell in love with Merope the nymph. By her he had a son, Amycus, the king of the Bebrycians. Amycus broke the rule of hospitality when he used to receive visitors who came to him. He forced them to wear boxing gloves and to fight with him. After he emerged as the victor, he put them to death. When many had endured this ferocity of his, he was finally defeated in the same kind of contest and punished with death by Pollux, who sought the golden fleece with the Argonauts at Colchis.

93. *The Story of Neptune and Eryx.*

When Neptune observed Venus strolling on the shore of the Sicilian Sea, he had intercourse with her. Made pregnant by him, she bore a son whom she named Eryx. He ruled in Sicily. Trusting in his own strength, he made a law for those coming to visit him that they put on boxing gloves and do battle with him. While driving the herds of Geryon from Spain, Hercules visited him. He fought with Eryx, defeated him, and killed him. From his name a mountain of Sicily is called Eryx.

94. *The Story of Arion and the Dolphins.*

Arion of Lesbos was the best cithara player.[27] When he was traveling from Tarentum to Corinth with many riches, he saw that ambushes were laid for him by the sailors at sea. He asked to play for a little while on his cithara. When dolphins gathered around at this sound, he leaped upon one and thus escaped imminent danger.

95. *[Untitled]*

There is said to have been a grove on Cyprus where doves gave oracular responses. The story is fashioned this way because in the language of Thessaly, both doves and prophetesses are called *peliades*.

96. *The Story of Antiope, Zethus, and Amphion.*

Epaphus deceived Antiope, the daughter of Nycteus, and ravished her. On account of this, she was forcibly cast out by her husband, Lycus. After she was driven out, he took Dirce as his wife. He ordered his servants to bind Antiope and hide her in the darkness. When her time for giving birth drew near, she escaped her chains by the will of Jove. On Mount Citheron (or Aracynthus), she brought forth her offspring and gave birth to Zethus and Amphion. A certain shepherd raised them as his own. Afterward, when their mother recognized them, they killed Lycus and avenged his wrongdoing; in fact, they bound Dirce to a fierce bull and killed her in that manner. From her blood the pool called Dirce in Thebes is said to have been formed. One of the sons, Amphion, had a zeal for playing the cithara. He played in such a way, so men say, that he summoned mountains and forests and rocks to himself. His brother Zethus[28] brought these rocks and stones to Thebes, and with them he built the walls of Thebes. In fact, Amphion was called Dirceus from Dirce, the spring, since the gods had changed his mother into a spring. This was formed from her blood in Thebes "on Attic Aracynthus."[29]

97. The Story of Nyctimene.

After Nyctimene slept with her father and then recognized her crime, she hid herself in the woods and shunned the light. There, through the pity of the gods, she was changed into a bird that is a wonder to the other birds on account of so great a crime.

98. The Story of Glaucus.

Glaucus was a fisherman from the city of Anthedon. When he placed the fishes that he caught upon the grass on the shore, he sensed a certain power in those grasses, for life was restored to the fishes and they sought the sea again. After he ate this grass, Glaucus was changed into a sea deity.

99. The Story of Glaucus and Venus.

Pothnia was the country from which Glaucus came. When he spurned the sacred rites of Venus, in anger she sent a frenzy into the mares he used for his chariot. They tore him to pieces. The story of Venus sending madness into them is fashioned in this way because Glaucus was actually torn to pieces by unbridled mares which were overeager after he kept them from intercourse so that they would be faster.

100. The Story of Chelone and Mercury.

A certain maiden named Chelone had an unrestrained tongue. In fact, when Jupiter married Juno, he ordered Mercury to summon all the gods and men and animals to the wedding. Of these, only Chelone, mocking and disparaging the marriage, disdained to come. When Mercury noted that she did not come, he descended to earth once again and hurled her house, which was set above a stream, into the sea. He changed Chelone herself into an animal of her own name,[30] which we call "tortoise." For a punishment he made the girl bend forward and carry her roof on her back. Thus this name is given to arched buildings.

BOOK TWO

101. The Story of Saturn and His Sons.

Saturn, the son of Pollus, was the husband of Ops. An old god with his head covered, carrying a scythe, he is said to have reigned thus and to have subjugated many realms to himself. For this reason, and since he had great power, he was considered the supreme god. He had three sons by Rhea: Jove, Neptune and Pluto. One of them, Jupiter, cut off his father's testicles and cast them into the sea. From their foam was born Venus, the goddess of sensual desire. Afterward, these brothers divided the whole world by lot among themselves: Jupiter took possession of the sky, Neptune the sea, Pluto the underworld. There is an indication that the individual brothers have power in the realm: Jupiter has a three-forked thunderbolt, Neptune a trident, Pluto a three-headed hound.

102. The Story of Saturn and Philyra and Chiron.

When Saturn was having intercourse with his beloved Philyra, his wife Ops arrived. Fearing her presence, he changed himself into a horse of such kind as a deity could imitate. From this union, Chiron was born, a man in half his body, a horse in half. This Chiron was the first inventor of medicine. Later he taught this to Aesculapius.

103. The Story of Jove's Birth.

Saturn learned through a prophecy from Themis that he could be driven from his kingdom by his own son. Thus he used to devour his children by his wife, Rhea. Delighted with her son Jove because of his beauty, Rhea entrusted him to nymphs on Mount Dictaeus in Crete, where bees nourished him. Curetes and Corybantes were summoned to create an uproar and prevent the child's squalling from being heard. Hence they are the attendants of the Mother of the gods.[31] When Jupiter was born and his mother hid her child, she sent to Saturn a precious stone concealed in the likeness of a child. Men call this *abidir*; its nature is always changing. Accepting this, the father crushed it with his teeth and ate it.

104. The Story of Jove and Saturn and Venus.

When Saturn went forth on a certain day to exercise his body, the young Jupiter cut off his testicles with a knife he had brought. These he cast into the sea, and from their foam Venus was born. Soon Jupiter drove his father from his kingdom. Saturn fled to Latium in Italy and hid there. Under the sway of Jove, the age ceased to be golden; until his time it had been called golden on account of Man's simple way of life. Jupiter took his own sister Juno as his wife. Symbolically, men consider Jove to be first as fire; thus he is called Zeus in Greek, which means "life" or "heat." They consider Juno to be second as air.

105. The Story of Juno and the Garden of the Hesperides.

It is recorded that when Jupiter took Juno as his wife, he met Earth carrying golden apples with their branches. Then Juno, marveling at them, asked Earth to plant these apples in her gardens, which extended as far as Mount Atlas. When Atlas' daughters often plucked the apples from the trees, Juno stationed an ever-watchful dragon there as a guard. Hercules later killed it.

106. The Story of Neptune.

Neptune means "thundering from a cloud," as it were; the Greeks call him Poseidon. Third in power after Jove and Juno, he presides over the element of water. He is depicted as bearing a trident because he exercises the threefold virtue of water, that is, flowing, fertile, and potable. Men name Amphitrite as the wife of Neptune, since water is in all three elements, and "all around" in Greek is expressed as *amphi*. Neptune had a son by Venus: Eryx, king of Sicily. By the nymph Merope he had Amycus, king of the Bebryces.

107. The Story of Pluto.

Pluto, the brother of Jove and Neptune, is said to preside over the lands, because riches in Greek are called "Plutos." Others call him Orcus, receiver of the dead, since they say that the One Renounced rules over the darkness below. At his feet they place the three-headed dog, because the ill will of mortal strife is produced by a triple condition, that is, by nature, by a cause, and by accident.

108. On the Three Furies, or Eumenides.

Men say that the three Eumenides, called Furies, serve Pluto. The first of these, Allecto, means "incessant" in Greek; Tisiphone is "their voice"; Megaera is "mighty strife." The Furies have snakes for hair.

109. On the Three Fates.

Indeed, the three Fates destine men for Pluto. They are also called Parcae, ironically, because they spare (parcant) no one. Clotho carries the distaff, Lachesis draws the thread, Atropos cuts it. Clotho in Greek is expressed as "summoning" in Latin, Lachesis means "lot," and Atropos means "without order."

110. On the Three Harpies, or Stymphalides.

Vergil assigns three Harpies to the Underworld: Aello desires, Occipito seizes, Celaeno conceals. Aello means "taking away the property of another"; Occipito means "carrying off quickly"; Celaeno means "black."

111. On Proserpina, or Diana.

They say that Proserpina, the daughter of Ceres, is Pluto's bride. Indeed, Ceres means "joy," and she is the goddess of grain. In fact, Proserpina is so named because from her the fruits come forth (proserpere). She is also named Vesta because she is clothed in green crops or various plants. The same goddess is named Diana, (duana, as it were), since the moon (luna) appears both in the day and at night. They also say that the same goddess is Lucina, because she shines (lucrat). The same goddess is Trivia, because she is observed in three forms. Of her Vergil says, "the three faces of maiden Diana,"[32] since the same goddess is called Luna, Diana, and Proserpina. This maiden is also named Latonia, from her mother Latona, and as a wife she is named Plutonia. In Greek, she is named Hecate.

112. The Story of Apollo, or the Sun.

They say that Apollo, son of Jove and brother of Diana, is the Sun. They consider him the god of divination because the Sun shows all obscure things clearly in the light. Moreover, they name him Sol, as if to say the sole Titan, the one who did not oppose Jove. They name him Phoebus, as if to say *ephebus*, that is, "youth." Thus the Sun is depicted as a boy because daily he rises and springs forth with new light. Also they call this same Apollo by the name Pithius, from the Python, a serpent of enormous size that Apollo destroyed with his arrows. He even carried back the spoils of the Python, so he is called Pithius. To him men also ascribe a four-horse team, since he traverses the space of a day by a four-part path, or because there are four seasons of the year. The names of the Sun's four horses are: Acteon, Lampus, Eritreus, and Philogeus. Eritreus in Greek means "reddish" because the Sun rises red in the morning light. Acteon means "shining"; Lampus means "burning." Philogeus means "earth-loving" because the Sun inclines directly toward the earth at his setting in the evening.

113. On the Nine Muses.

Men assign the nine Muses to Apollo and add him to their number as the tenth, because there are ten melodious measures of the human voice. These are the names and explanations of the Muses:

> Clio means "the idea of seeking knowledge." She discovered
>   history;
> Euterpe means "well-pleasing." She invented the flute;
> Melpomene means "practicing meditation." She produced
>   tragedies;
> Thalia means "capacity." She produced comedies;
> Polyhymnia means "making much memory." She invented
>   rhetoric;
> Erato means "finding likeness." She discovered geometry;
> Terpsichore means "delighting in instruction." She furnished the
>   psaltery;
> Urania means "heavenly." She invented astronomy;
> Calliope means "of best voice." She taught literature.

114. The Story of Apollo, the Raven, and Coronis,
the Daughter of Phlegyas.

Men place the raven under the protection of Apollo, either because it alone brings forth oviparous young in the midst of the summer heat contrary to the nature of things, or because in the books that cast nativities it alone among all birds has sixty-four meanings in its calls. This is the story: the raven enjoyed Apollo's protection. When the god was offering a sacrifice, he sent the raven to a spring to fetch pure water; there it saw very many young fig trees. The raven perched in a certain one of these trees while waiting for the figs to ripen. After several days, the figs ripened and the raven ate many of them. As Apollo was waiting for the raven, he saw it making haste to fly with a full water pail. For this offense, because it had long delayed Apollo and he had been forced by the raven's lingering to use other water, he inflicted this shame upon it: as long as the figs were ripening, the raven could not drink, so that it had a useless throat for those days. Moreover, Ister and many others have said that Coronis was the daughter of Phlegyas, and that by Apollo she bore Aesculapius, but afterward she had intercourse with Ischys, the son of Elatus. The raven observed and reported this to Apollo. Although it had been white before, for this disagreeable report Apollo made the raven black, and he shot Ischys with his arrows.

115. The Story of Apollo and Daphne, or the Laurel.

Men assign the laurel to the protection of Apollo, for we know that he loved Daphne, daughter of the river Ladon in Arcadia. She was changed into a laurel through the mercy of Earth. And where could laurel spring forth from except river water? The poets say that if you place laurel at the head of those who sleep, they will see dreams that are true. Boreas, they say, loved Hyacinth as much as Apollo did, but Hyacinth rejoiced more in Apollo's love. While he was exercising with a discus, he was killed with the same discus by an angry Boreas and changed into the flower that bears his name.

116. The Story of Apollo and Eridanus.

Apollo, who is also the Sun, sired Phaethon, or Eridanus, by having intercourse with the nymph Clymene. Through the prayers of his father and Diana, Eridanus restored Hippolytus to life when he was killed. He could not drive the chariot obtained from his father. When he strayed off course and the world was burning, he was blasted by Jove's lightning and fell into a river of Italy. He was called Phaethon from the light of the flames as he burned, and he gave his former name to the river. Thus we find these two names shared between the son of the Sun and the river. Later, his sisters, Fetusa and Lampetusa, were changed into poplar trees as they wept. Moved by anger, Apollo killed the Sicilian smiths who made Jove's thunderbolts. For this Jupiter stripped him of his divinity and cast him from the sky. Banished, Apollo pastured the cattle of King Admetus for four years above the river Euphrates, where he had very many sons.

117. The Story of Mercury and His Mother, Maia.

Jupiter lay with Maia on Mount Cilleno and had a son, Mercury, whom Juno loved so much that she gave him milk from her own breast and introduced him to the art of healing. His father gave him a herald's staff. If he touched anyone with it on the thicker part of the head, the person would die; one whom he touched on the thin part would live. The name Mercury is said to come from *medius currens*, "running in the middle," because speech runs between all men, as it were. Thus Mercury is represented as both swift and wandering. The wings on his head and feet signify that speech flies swiftly through the air. He is called a messenger, since all thoughts are made known through speech. Men call him the master of theft, since speech deceives the minds of listeners. He has a staff with which he separates serpents, that is to say, poisons, for people who wage war and those who disagree are appeased by the speech of negotiators. This is why legates of peace are called heralds (caduceatores), according to Livy. For just as wars are declared through the *fetiales*, so peace comes about through the *caduceatores*.* Moreover, in Greek he is called Hermes, from *apo tes ermeo*, i.e., "interpreter" in Latin. On account of his power and knowledge of many arts, he was named Trismegistus, that is, "three-times greatest" (ter maximus). This reason is given for why men imagine him with a dog's head: among all animals, the dog is considered the more acute and perceptive species.

118. The Story of Semele and Her Son, Father Liber.

Jupiter had intercourse with Semele, by whom Father Liber was born. When Jupiter appeared to her with his thunderbolt, she was consumed by a crackling flame. Then his father took the boy and put him in his own thigh, and later gave him to Maro to be reared. Liber vanquished

*Caduceatores: heralds who bore a flag of truce.

India and was counted among the gods. Including Semele, there were four sisters: Ino, Autonoe, Semele, and Agave; this same Agave violently cut off the head of her own son. These four sisters were called Bacchae, and symbolically four kinds of drunkenness are signified through them: intoxication from wine, forgetfulness, lust, and madness. Juno suspected this same Semele, the daughter of Cadmus and Hermione, because she had had intercourse with Jove. The goddess changed herself into an old woman so that by this deception she might gain revenge without incurring anyone's ill will. She encouraged Semele to ask Jove for a pledge of his love so that there would be verification of this remarkable intercourse. Semele succeeded in gaining her request, and the god entered her home adorned by his thunder and lightning. Semele was deceived by her desires, for flame consumed her house and the girl herself. From the fire Jove snatched Liber, who had been conceived in the womb of the pregnant girl, and he sewed him into his own thigh. After the months of gestation were completed, he secretly handed him over to be reared by nymphs who frequented Mount Nisa in India. Indeed, there were seven sisters. These same nymphs were called Dodonidae. Driven away by Lycurgus, they fled to Thetis, according to Pherecydes and Asclepiades. For this reason, Jove granted them the favor of placing them among the constellations. Seven in number, they are called Hyades. Father Liber, or Dionysus, is said to ride upon tigers because every intoxication from wine always persists in wildness. He is called Lyaeus, as if to say "manifesting mildness" (lenitas). He is also depicted as a youth, since drunkenness is never mature.

119. The Story of Liber and Jove Ammon.

When Liber, or Dionysus, assailed the Indians and led his army through Xerolibia, he was tormented by thirst and begged the aid of his father Jove. After he observed a ram, immediately a spring appeared. Thus he made a statue with a ram's head for Jove, thereafter called Ammon, "from the sands" (arenis). This story is fashioned so because his oracles are quite obscure.

120. The Story of Liber and the Tyrrhenians.

When Tyrrhenian sailors found Father Liber sleeping on the shore, they stealthily carried him onto their ship. When he awoke on the ship, he asked where he was being taken. They answered that they would take him wherever he wished. Liber said, to Naxos, an island consecrated to him. But they began to turn their sails elsewhere. On account of this, the angry deity made tigers devoted to himself appear before their eyes. Utterly terrified through dread of these, the sailors hurled themselves headlong into the waves.

121. The Story of Father Liber and King Lygurgus [sic].

Lygurgus was a king of Thrace. As the story has it, he was hacking down vines out of disdain for Liber and cut through his own legs, but the truth is that he was abstemious, that is, refraining from wine. It is well known that such men are of a more acute nature, which also was said about Demosthenes.

122. The Story of Minerva.

Minerva, the goddess of wisdom, was the discoverer of many clever talents. She is called Athena in Greek, but Minerva among the Romans, as if to say *munus artium variarum*, "gift of various skills." Moreover, on that account it is said she had been born from the head of Jove, since the understanding of the wise one who discovered all things is in the head. She is also called Tritonia, since she appeared at a maidenly age around Lake Triton. The same goddess is called Pallas, either from the island of Pallene where she was raised, or from *apo tou pallein*, that is, "from the attack of a spear," or because she killed Pallas the giant. This same Minerva invented pipes from bones. She made music with these at the banquet of the gods, and all the gods laughed at her puffed up cheeks. She went to the Tritonian pool and looked at her own face in the water. When she conceded that the puffing out of her cheeks was ugly, she threw away the pipes. Marsyas found them and became skilled at playing music. He challenged Apollo to a contest. Both chose King Midas to be the judge. Through his judgment Marsyas was defeated and paid the penalty: he was hanged, stripped and scourged to death. So much of his blood poured out that from it a spring arose. Juvenal recalled him when he said: "just as defeated Marsyas."[33] Others say that nymphs, satyrs, and other country-dwellers followed Marsyas the satyr with so much weeping that from their tears a stream arose. It is called Marsyas. They did this because they would be without his music. Certain ones say that Midas the king had not judged rightly, and for this Apollo gave him ass' ears. But this tale at another time.

123. The Story of Priapus and Lotus the Nymph.

There was a certain nymph named Lotus. When Priapus loved her and pursued her, she was changed through the pity of the gods into a tree that is commonly called Syrian bean. Priapus himself was driven out of the city of Lampsacus. Later, on account of the huge size of his male part, he was received into the ranks of the gods and entitled to be the deity of gardens. Concerning him Statius[34] says: "My right hand restrains thieves, and there is a red stake stretched out from my indecent groin, but a wreath fixed on my head frightens bold birds." Priapus is said to preside over gardens because of their fertility, for although other ground might produce something once, gardens are never without fruits.

124. The Figurative Story of Pan.

Pan is a rustic god formed in the likeness of nature; thus he also is called Pan, "all." Indeed, he has horns like the rays of the Sun and the horns of the Moon; his face is ruddy like the sky. On his breast he has a fawn-skin covered with starry markings like the stars. His lower part is shaggy because of the trees, bushes and wild beasts; he has goats' feet to show the firmness of the earth. He has pipes of seven reeds on account of the harmony of the heavens, in which there are seven sounds. Thus Vergil says "seven distinctions of tone."[35] He has a curved staff, a shepherd's crook, since the year curves back upon itself. Since Pan is the god of all nature, the poets imagine that he wrestled with Amor, the god of Love, and was conquered by him, for "love conquers all."[36] He loved the nymph Syrinx. When he pursued her, she begged Earth for aid and was turned into a reed. To assuage his love, Pan carved into it and made a reed pipe for himself.

125. The Story of Vulcan.

Since Vulcan was misshapen, he was rejected by his parents, Jove and Juno, and cast down onto the island of Lemnos. He was raised there by the Sintians. Although Vulcan fashioned thunderbolts here for Jove, he was not admitted to the banquets of the gods. Afterward, he asked his father Jove if by chance he might marry Minerva. This was granted if he could gain the consent of Minerva herself. However, since she scorned his love and greatly resisted it, he spilled his lustful seed upon the earth. From this was born a boy with a serpent's tail. He was called Erichthonius, as if to say "begotten from earth and strife," for *eris* is "strife" and *chthon* is "earth." To conceal his disgusting feet, he yoked horses and rode in a chariot to hide the ugliness of his body.

126. The Story of Phorcys.

Phorcys was the son of Thoose the nymph and Neptune. Varro says that he was the king of Corsica and Sardinia. When he and a great part of his army were overwhelmed by King Atlas in a naval battle, his comrades supposed that he had been transformed into a sea god.

127. The Story of the Three Gorgons and Perseus.

Phorcys had three daughters: Sthenno, Euryale, and Medusa. They saw with a single eye, and those who looked upon them were turned into stone. For this reason they were called Gorgons, from fear, for fear is called gorgon. Perseus attacked them with a shield made of crystal and a falchion, a kind of curved sword. With Minerva's help, he killed them. In fact, the three sisters were of singular beauty (unius pulchritudinis); this is why their story says that they saw with a single eye. Furthermore, they were very rich in lands. Thus they were called Gorgons, as if from *ge oreges*, that is, "cultivators of earth," for *ge* in Greek means earth in Latin, and *orgia* means cultivation. When her father died, Medusa, the elder daughter, received his kingdom by succession. Perseus, the king of Asia, killed her and took her kingdom. However, the truth is this: Gorgon is interpreted to mean "fear"; Sthenno means "weakness"; Euryale means "vast depth"; Medusa means "madness" or "forgetfulness." All of these produce fear in all people. Perseus is regarded as a form of virtue; he killed the Gorgon with Minerva's help because virtue overcomes all fears with the help of wisdom. In addition, Pegasus was born from the Gorgon's blood. Pegasus is interpreted to mean "fame." With his hoof he brought forth the spring of Castalia, or Pegaseum, since virtue, overcoming all things, acquires fair fame for itself. Poets are thought to drink from that spring, since fame is especially aided by the fictions of poets. Indeed, it should be noted that Pegasus was Neptune's horse.

128. The Story of Medusa the Gorgon.

Although Medusa the Gorgon was pursued by many because of her beauty, she could not escape sexual union with Neptune. She had intercourse with him in the temple of Minerva. Since Medusa defiled the holiness of the place, Minerva changed her hair into snakes. She had initially been sought by suitors, but now turned to flight those she met when her deformity was exposed.

129. The Story of the Three Graces.

We read that Jupiter had three daughters with Juno. They are servants of Venus whose names are Basithea, Eugiale, and Euphrosyne, and since they are charming and gentle, they are called the Graces.

130. The Story of the Lemnian Women and Hypsipyle.

Although the Lemnian women paid a tenth part of their produce to all the gods each year, they decided that Venus alone must be passed over. In anger, the goddess let loose a goatish stench upon them. Their husbands cursed their wives and left Lemnos out of loathing for them. The husbands went to the men of Thrace and took their daughters for themselves in marriage. When this became known to the women of Lemnos, they swore an oath against the whole race of men. Venus urged them on, and they killed all the men when they returned from Thrace. Among these women only Hypsipyle aided her father Thoas. She not only spared him, but even followed him as he fled to the seashore. Then Liber appeared to Thoas and guided him by a prosperous sea voyage to the island of Chion. Later, the Argonauts came to Lemnos, and the Lemnian women received them with hospitality and had intercourse with them. Hypsipyle had two sons by Jason: Euneus and Thoas. Although the Argonauts were detained for many days, they departed after Hercules chided them. Moreover, after the Lemnian women learned that Hypsipyle had saved her father, they tried to kill her. As she fled, she was captured by robbers and carried off to Nemea. She was sold into servitude to Lycurgus, the king of that territory.

131. The Story of Danaus and Aegyptus.[37]

Danaus, the son of Belus, had fifty daughters by his many wives, and his brother Aegyptus had just so many sons. Aegyptus asked his brother

Danaus to join his daughters to his sons in matrimony. After an oracle from the gods informed Danaus that he would die at the hands of his own son-in-law, he went to Argos. He is said to have made the first ship there. From the place-name the ship was called Argo. Aegyptus sent his sons to pursue his brother. He ordered them either to slay Danaus or not to return home, as Agenor had once commanded his son Cadmus. After they reached Argos, the sons of Aegyptus began to besiege their uncle. Danaus saw that he could not resist them and betrothed his daughters to them. At the bidding of their father, all of them murdered their husbands in the night, except Clytemnestra and Hypermestra. The latter alone spared her husband, Lynceus. Because of their crime, the daughters of Danaus were sentenced to this punishment in the Underworld: they put water into jars that have holes.

132. The History of Dardanus and the Origin of the Trojans.

Dardanus and Iasius were brothers, the sons of Atlas' daughter Electra. However, Dardanus was sired by Jove and Iasius by Corinthus. From him the mountain and town took their name. Later, Dardanus killed Iasius. This same Dardanus left his place of abode in the Tuscan district of Italy due to an oracle. He traveled through Thrace to Samos, which he named Samothrace. From here he came to Phrygia, which he called Dardania after his own name. He sired Ericthonius, who ruled in those places. Ericthonius sired Tros, who was praiseworthy for his justice and loyalty. Tros called Erichthona by the name Troy, in order to perpetuate the memory of his own name. Tros had two sons: Ilus and Assaracus. Since Ilus was older and ruled Troy, he named it Ilium from his own name. Assaracus yielded the place of primacy. Ilus had a son, Laomedon, and Priam was the firstborn of Laomedon. Assaracus sired Capys, by whom Anchises was begotten, and Anchises sired Aeneas.

133. The Story of Laomedon and Hercules and Hesione.

Laomedon was king of the Trojans, the father of Priam. He asked Neptune and Apollo to build the city of Troy and promised to pay them. After they had constructed it, he cheated them of their rewards. Angered by this, Apollo sent a pestilence upon the Trojans, and Neptune sent a massive sea monster. When Apollo was consulted about these, he responded with oracles hostile to the Trojans. He said that all Laomedon's daughters should be offered to the sea monster that was devastating the entire city. Then Hercules arrived there while on his way to Colchis. He asked to marry Hesione, Laomedon's daughter. Laomedon promised her to Hercules if he could free her from the sea monster. Hercules killed the sea monster and asked for the bride he had been promised, but Laomedon deceived him. Angered by this, Hercules tore down the walls of Troy and gave Hesione to a certain comrade of his named Telamon. She gave birth to Teucer, but it is known that Ajax* was born of another woman. Then Hercules established Priam, who had been rescued by his companions, in his father's kingdom.

134. The Story of Acesta and Hippotes.

The forenamed King Laomedon cheated Neptune and Apollo of the pay that had been promised after they constructed the city of Troy for him. An angry Neptune sent a huge sea monster against the city. Consulted about this, Apollo answered that noble maidens must be offered to the beast. While this was happening, a certain nobleman named Hippotes feared for his daughter Acesta, since the daughter of King Laomedon was already bound to a rock in the sea. When a storm arose, Hippotes placed Acesta on a ship and sent it where chance would take it. She was carried to Sicily. There the River Crimisus had intercourse with her after he was changed into a dog or a bear. She gave birth to a son, Acestes, who founded a city for the Trojans. Today this is called Acesta, after his mother's name.

135. The Story of Teucer.

After Troy was sacked, Teucer returned home without his brother, who had killed himself in a rage because he lost the arms of Achilles. Teucer was driven away from Salamis and went to Sidon. From him, Dido learned everything. Certain sources say that Teucer did not give aid to his own brother who was killed at Troy. He also did not carry back his bones to his homeland nor bring his brother's small son with him. Thus it was believed that he had killed him so that he would not be his co-heir. Driven into exile by his father, Teucer went to Belus, the king of the Carthaginians, who had overcome the island of Cyprus by arms. There, after a long war, Teucer founded a city that he called Salamina, from the

*Also Telamon's son.

name of his homeland. This Teucer was with the host[38] of the Greeks. There is another Teucer, and the Trojans are called Teucri after him. This Teucer built up and enlarged the walls of Troy after the death of Dardanus. Moreover, Ajax and Achilles were his cousins, since Thelamon and Peleus were brothers, the sons of Aeacus.

136. The Story of Tithonus and Aurora.

Tithonus was the brother of Laomedon, king of the Trojans. When he had become the beloved of Dawn (Aurora), he asked her for length of life. Because of this he lived a very long time, until he was changed, on account of his excessive old age, into a cricket. He sent his son Memnon, born of Aurora, to the aid of Troy. Memnon was called "Black Ethiopian," since the light is faint where dawn first rises. In their yearly flight, birds dutifully gather in assembly at the tomb of Memnon, who died and was buried at Troy.

137. The Story of Pyrrhus and Helenus.

As we read in the story, Achilles was shot with an arrow by Paris. As he was dying in the temple of Apollo Thymbraeus, he asked that Polyxena be sacrificed at his tomb when Troy was conquered. His son Pyrrhus, whom he had by Deidamia, fulfilled this wish. Later, in his homeland, as an insult to Apollo he set up altars to his father in the god's Delphic temple and began to offer sacrifices to him there. Pyrrhus was killed by Orestes when he tried to seize his betrothed, Hermione. As he was expiring, Pyrrhus ordered that his wife Andromache be given to Helenus. He had taken Helenus captive at Troy, but on many occasions he had been faithfully forewarned by this same Helenus and made cautious. For this reason also he rendered this good deed to him.

138. The Story of Diomedes.

Diomedes, also called Tytides, learned that his wife was living shamefully at Argos because of the wrath of Venus. He had wounded the goddess in battle when she rescued her son Aeneas from his hands by interposing a cloud between them. Diomedes refused to return to Argos, but took possession of parts of Apulia. After he subdued the inhabitants on the whole of Mount Garganus, he founded many cities in that same region. Indeed, he founded Beneventum and Equus Tuticus and Arpos, which is also called Agrippa. Venulus the Greek was sent from the territory of

Tibur to this place, not to Arpinum, which is known to be in Campania. From this comes the line: "He bore plunder seized from the army of the Tiburtines."[39]

139. On Diomedes and the Palladium.

Since Diomedes was afflicted by many misfortunes, an oracle ordered him to return the Palladium, which he kept with him, to the Trojans. When he attempted to do this, he found Aeneas in the act of offering sacrifice. So that Diomedes would not interrupt the sacrificial process, Nautes accepted the Palladium. For this reason, the family of the Nautii preserves the holy rites of Minerva.

140. The Story of Diomedes' Companions.

It is known that Diomedes' companions were changed into birds after the death of their leader, for whom they grieved uncontrollably when he was killed. Even today these birds are called *diomedeae* in Latin; the Greeks named them *herodii*. They inhabit the island of Electride, or Febra, not far from Calabria, in sight of the city of Tarentina. Indeed, these birds are said to rush happily to meet Greek sailors, but, mindful of their origin, they eagerly flee from Roman[40] sailors.

141. On the Island of Euboea, and Nauplius, the Father of Palamedes.

Euboea is an island, and Mount Caphareus is there. Near this mountain the Greeks perished in a shipwreck because Nauplius, the father of Palamedes, was grieving that his son's death was caused by their conspiracy. When he saw the Greeks struggling in a storm, he climbed Mount Caphareus. With a raised torch, he gave the signal that a harbor was nearby. This deceived the Greeks, and they suffered shipwreck among the rugged crags.

142. On Another Euboea and the City of Cumae.

Euboea is also an island from which the Chalchidians proceeded to seek new dwelling places. Not far from Baiae, they found an empty shore. This place took its name from Baius, Ulysses' companion who was buried there. After they observed a pregnant woman, they founded a city there. This showed that their republic would be fertile. They called it Cumae, either from the woman with child or from the waves there.

143. The Story of Meleager and Oeneus.

Oeneus, the father of Tydeus and Meleager, was the son of Parthaon and king of Aetolia, whose most noble city is Calydon. He threw the supreme power of his own kingdom into disorder by his negligence of the sacred rites. In fact, while celebrating the annual prayers for the success of his empire, he neglected the divine majesty of Diana. For her sake the indignant gods oppressed him to such an extent that it seems as if he would have pleased all the gods if he had worshipped her alone. Diana sent a boar of immense size to the region. It was called the Destroyer of the Calydonian Land, from the city of that nation. Overwhelmed by the ferocity of this boar, Oeneus published an edict that the man who would kill the monster would have half his kingdom. Meleager, with his courage, did not fear the danger; in fact, Oeneus' son summoned youth gathered from everywhere to this expedition of a new sort. Among these came Atalanta, daughter of Iasius, the greatest huntress. Leading all the hunters in the woodlands, she struck the aforementioned boar with an arrow. Later, Meleager intercepted the wild beast as it came toward him and killed it. He was grateful to the girl who had shone among men through her success. He gave the hide of the monster to her as proof of her glory, along with its head. But envy betrayed the reward earned by her bravery, for Plexippus and Agenor, the uncles of Meleager, were indignant that a maiden was preferred to them. They robbed her of the gift. Because of this strife, they hastened their deaths. Angry over their actions, Meleager spurned the blood relationship with his mother's brothers. He killed Plexippus and destroyed his mother's affection for himself. Indeed, Althea vented her rage and avenged her brothers. There was a firebrand that she had kept hidden since Meleager's birth. It had suddenly appeared in the palace as a sign of his destiny and foretold that the youth would live so long as it was preserved. His mother thrust this into the fire and extinguished it along with her son's life. After she recognized the wicked deed she had committed, she hanged herself.

144. On Clytemnestra and Her son, Orestes.

Clytemnestra was the wife of Agamemnon. After he returned from the Trojan War, he was killed by the adulterer, Aegisthus, for when he entered his own house, his wife brought him a garment without an opening for the head. As he tried to put it on and could not find the opening,

Aegisthus the adulterer murdered him. Later, Orestes killed Aegisthus, together with his own mother, and because of this he was driven to madness. Indeed, this Orestes, the son of Agamemnon and Clytemnestra, was famous on the stage, since he was the best tragic actor [*sic*]. He was insane when he killed his mother and Aegisthus. At the suggestion of Pylades, his comrade, he entered the temple of Apollo to escape the Furies. When he wished to depart, the Furies attacked him. From this story comes: "On the threshold sit the avenging Furies."[41]

145. The Story of Europa and Jove.

Europa was the daughter of Agenor, king of the Greeks. While she was gathering flowers in the meadows according to the custom of girls, Jupiter changed into the shape of a handsome bull and violated her in the following manner. When Mercury had crossed over to Phoenicia at his father's bidding to drive the herds of that region to the shore, Jupiter changed into a bull. He intermingled with King Agenor's young bullocks and compelled the maidens to love him as he strutted about on the sand. He sported with individual ones little by little, and at last with Agenor's daughter. He was driven by love for her to change his shape. Jupiter carried Europa off to the island of Crete as she sat on his back, and there he enjoyed sex with her.

146. The Story of Agenor and His Son, Cadmus.

After his daughter Europa had been ravished, Agenor sent his sons Cadmus, Cilex, and Phoenix to find their sister; he ordered them not to return to him unless they found her. Cilex traveled to different regions, and at last he founded Cilicia; also, Phoenix named Phoenicia from his own name. After he lost hope of seeing his father again, Cadmus went to the oracle of Apollo seeking to know where in the world he might settle. He received the response that he should drive a cow that had been separated from the herd, one with the image of the moon on her flank. Where she would lie down from fatigue, there he should establish his city. Obeying this command, Cadmus came to the land that later was called Boetia, from *bos*, "cow." When he sent his companions to the fountain of Mars to fetch water and went there himself after them, he found that a dragon had devoured them. When he saw this, he killed the serpent and sowed its torn-out teeth. From these sprang forth a host of armed men.

While they were fighting among themselves in their own war, it happened that from this host only five men were left. By the will of Minerva these men were joined to Cadmus as companions in founding the city of Thebes. These are the names of those men: Echion, Ideus, Ciominus, Pelorus, Hypereon.

147. The Story of Cadmus and Harmonia.[42]

After Agenor's son Cadmus witnessed his own misfortunes at the death of his grandsons, he detested the city of Thebes. With his wife Harmonia, the daughter of Venus and Mars, he fled to the Illyrian gulf. There he sought mercy from the gods. He asked to be changed into the shape of a dragon, which in the beginning was the cause of his trouble. His wishes were fulfilled, and both he and his wife were turned into serpents.

148. On the Necklace of Harmonia.

Harmonia was born of the adultery of Mars and Venus. She was united in marriage to the forenamed Cadmus. Harmonia received a golden necklace as a gift of Vulcan. It was tinged with poisons of such a kind that one wearing this gold would be crushed by a heap of troubles. Statius describes very clearly the potent poisons with which this necklace was tinged, according to the stories. This same Harmonia and her husband Cadmus were changed into serpents. Then Agave received the necklace; she became insane and cruelly killed her own son Pentheus. Then Semele had it. Mislead by Juno, she was stricken by Jove's lightning. Then Laius' wife, Jocasta, had the necklace. She slept with her own son Oedipus and from this union produced sons and daughters. Later Argia, the daughter of King Adrastus and wife of Polynices, owned it. She caused the Theban war through her instigation. Finally Eriphyle, the wife of Amphiaraus the seer, received it. She revealed that her husband did not want to go to war, and thus she forced the utterly-unwilling man to go.

149. The Story of Eteocles and Polynices and Amphiaraus.

The Theban brothers, Eteocles and Polynices, divided their kingdom. They agreed upon this covenant: one would have the kingdom for a year, and the other would leave the country until the year was completed; then he would have the kingdom. In the first year, the younger brother, Polynices, gave up the kingdom. He sought it again after a year, but it was denied him by his brother. Then the exile went to Adrastus, king of the Argives, and served bravely as a soldier under him. He received the king's daughter as his wife. Later, when he returned and his brother denied the kingdom to him again, he started a war. Fate decreed that if Amphiaraus the priest took part in the war, Polynices would be the victor after the earth swallowed up Amphiaraus. Knowing of this predicted death, Amphiaraus hid in his house. His own wife Eriphiyle betrayed him after Argia, Polynices' wife, gave her the necklace that Vulcan had fashioned for his stepdaughter Harmonia. Then Polynices led Amphiaraus off to war. He was transported alive to the infernal regions, along with his chariot, when the earth swallowed him up. Alcmaeon, his son, wanted to avenge his father, so he killed his mother, as Orestes had done.

150. The Story of Apollo and Sibyl.

Apollo loved Sibyl with a devoted love, and he gave her the power to demand what she wanted. She took up sand in her hands and demanded so long a life. Apollo replied that this could happen if she would leave the island of Erythrea, where she dwelt, and never see it again. Thus she traveled to Cumae and stayed there; weakened in bodily strength, she retained life in her voice alone. When the citizens of Erythrea learned this, they were moved either by envy or by mercy; it is uncertain which. They sent her a letter marked according to ancient custom with chalk; when she saw this earth, since it was from her island, she died. Some say that she is the one who composed the Roman prophecies because, when Apollo's temple was burned, the books were brought to Rome from there, where she was.

151. The Story of Caenis (neither a Man nor a Woman) and Neptune.

Caenis was a maiden who obtained a change of sex from Neptune as recompense for her defilement. Indeed, the young man was invulnerable. While fighting for the Lapiths against the Centaurs, he was fixed in the ground gradually by the repeated blows of their clubs. After his death, however, he returned to the former sex. This story illustrates that pronouncement of Plato or Aristotle that souls commonly change their sex through metempsychosis, that is, permutation.

152. The Story of Tarpeia.

The Tarpeian citadel was named after the maiden, Tarpeia. When Romulus waged war against the Sabines, he handed over the Capitolium to a certain Tarpeius to be defended. This man's daughter Tarpeia fell among the enemy when she went to fetch water. They incited her to betrayal. She asked for a reward: the adornments on their left hands, that is, their bracelets. And so, after she betrayed the citadel to them, the enemy kept their promises and paid her with an ingenious death. They killed her by laying their shields, that is, the adornments on their left hands, upon her. Buried there, she gave her name to the Tarpeian rock.

153. The Story of Niobe and Her Children.

Niobe, the daughter of Tantalus and wife of Amphion, came from Sipylus in Lydia. By Amphion she had seven sons and seven daughters, that is, fourteen children, whose names are these: Archemorus, Antagorus, Tantulus, Phadimus, Sipylus, Xenarchus, and Epinitus; likewise, the daughters are Asticratia, Pelopia, Cheloris, Chleodoxe, Ogime, Phegia, and Neera. Niobe boasted over their great number and said, "if Latona is so revered because she thrives with her twin children as her assurance, how much more worthy am I of veneration. I produced fourteen children!" Then she and her husband and all her children were slain by the arrows of Apollo and Diana, who is also called Trivia. For this reason Juvenal wrote: " 'Spare them, I pray, O Paean, and you, Goddess,[43] put down your arrows. The children have done nothing! Strike the mother!', Amphion cries out, but Paean draws his bow."

154. The Story of Acrisius and Danae.

Acrisius, king of the Argives, had a daughter of wondrous elegance named Danae. He learned from an oracle that he could be destroyed by her offspring. Acrisius made a bronze tower and shut his daughter within it. He gave orders to guard her with a continuous watch. Then Jupiter transformed himself into a shower of gold and had intercourse with her when he flowed down through the roof into the maiden's lap. Perseus was born of this union. Thus Terence wrote: "The god had come secretly through an opening in the roof; the deception of the woman was accomplished."[44] It is said that Jupiter transformed into a shower of gold because he bribed the guards with gold and thus had intercourse with her.

After her father realized that she was pregnant, he put her in a ship to go where chance would take her. Through the mercy of the gods she was carried to a safe place, namely, Italy. Perseus the fisherman found her. Danae gave birth there and named her son Perseus. Also, she was brought to the king of that territory, who made her his wife. He founded Ardea with her. Men say that Turnus derived his origin from them. Jupiter entrusted Perseus to a certain king to be raised. Pained by this, Juno was filled with unspeakable hatred. She decided to persecute Perseus and urged the king to destroy him somehow. The king sent Perseus to slay various monsters, such as the Chimaera, the Gorgon, and Medusa.

155. The Story of Laodamia.

Laodamia was the wife of Protesilaus. When she learned that her husband died in the Trojan War, she wished that she might visit his spirit. When this was granted, she was unwilling to forsake the spirit and perished in its embrace.

156. The Story of Phyllis and Demophoon.

Phyllis was the queen of the Thracians. As Demophoon, son of Theseus and king of the Athenians, was returning from the Trojan War, she fell in love with him and proposed marriage to him. He said that first he would set his affairs in order and then return for his wedding. He departed, and when he tarried, Phyllis hanged herself. She did this because of the impatience of love more than the influence of sorrow, since she believed that she had been spurned. She was transformed into an almond tree without leaves. Later, when Demophoon returned and learned the truth, he embraced the tree trunk. As if it sensed the bridegroom's arrival, the tree put forth leaves. For this reason they are called *phyllera*, from Phyllis; formerly they used to be called *petala*.

157. The Story of Alcon.

Alcon was the best archer of Crete. When a dragon attacked his son, he shot an arrow with such great skill that it flew and fixed itself in the wound of the serpent, and did not pass through into his son. For this reason, he deserved praise.

158. The Story of Codrus.

Codrus was King of the Athenians. After war had started between the Spartans and the Athenians, an oracle responded that those whose leader perished would be victorious. Codrus set out in humble garb to the nearby tents of the enemy. There, by railing at them, he incited them to his own murder, and, recognized by no one, he fulfilled the prophecy.

159. The Story of Pirithous and Mars.

Pirithous, King of the Lapiths, took a wife. He invited the neighboring peoples, the Centaurs, to the feast, along with his relatives and all the gods, except Mars. The angered god sent a madness upon them, so that the Centaurs and the Lapiths entered into a war. Thus Vergil writes: "Mars wanted to destroy the mighty race of Lapiths."[45] The Centaurs were sons of Ixion and a cloud (Nubes). Juno sent this cloud to him in the shape of herself.

160. The Story of the Thessalians and the Centaurs.

Pelethronium is a town of Thessaly where the practice of taming horses was first discovered. Now a certain Thessalian king ordered his attendants to recover his oxen after a gadfly drove them off. The servants were unable to do it by running, so they mounted horses. Thanks to the swiftness of the horses, they pursued the oxen and brought them back to their stables. But the men were seen, either when they were riding swiftly or when their horses were drinking at the river Peneon with their heads bent forward. They furnished the occasion for the fable that Centaurs exist.

161. The Story of the Phoenician Priestess.

Dryope, a Phoenician priestess of Father Liber, secretly became pregnant. While she led a sacrificial bull by the horns to the altar, she forgot her burden. Because of her excessive weariness, the infant fell from her womb.

162. The Story of Sisyphus and Aegina.

Sisyphus was punished for his actions according to a penalty such as this: Since Jupiter loved Aegina, the daughter of Asopus, he secretly stole her from the guardian appointed by her father. He confessed the deed to

Sisyphus. Out of human fickleness, Sisyphus made this known to her lamenting father. Hence he is said to roll a rock endlessly up a mountain. Sisyphus is the one who rolled a mighty stone in the Underworld because he killed many men with a huge rock.

163. The Story of Arethusa and Alpheus.

We read that Arethusa the nymph washed herself in the river Alpheus after hunting. Alpheus desired her. She fled from him as he sought his pleasure and was turned into a spring by the mercy of the gods. The spring flowed through hidden passages to Sicily. It is said that Alpheus pursued her all the way to Sicily.

164. The Story of Sciron.

Sciron lived on a high crag. He is said to have forced those passing by to wash his feet. While they were doing this, he suddenly threw them off the precipice.

165. On Crotopus and Chorebus.

Crotopus was a king of the Argives whose daughter Apollo violated. Outraged over this, the father killed his daughter because she was a priestess of Vesta and ought to have remained a virgin forever. To avenge her, Apollo sent a horrible monster, which a certain very brave youth, Corebus, killed. Statius also wrote about this story in a very seemly manner. Indeed, the monster was called Lamia, for lamiae are ditches filled to overflowing in the fields, or whirlpools in streams. Hence this most ferocious beast was named Lamia.

166. The Story of the Sphinx.

The Sphinx was a certain monster that sat upon a rock and proposed a riddle to passersby. She tore those unable to solve it to pieces with her claws and fangs. Coming to this monster, Oedipus explained her allegory and killed her.

167. On Athracias the Magician.

Athracias was King of Thessaly and the father of Hippocatia, whom Pirithous took as his wife. Athracias first established the art of magic among the Thracians.

168. The Story of the River Licornus.

Licornus is a certain river, also called Hebenus. Next to this river, Hercules killed Nessus while he was copulating with Deianira, the wife of Hercules. She put a certain shirt smeared with the blood of Nessus the Centaur on Hercules; because of this he suffered unbearable burning throughout his body.

169. On Minos.

The renown of his lineage alone sufficed for the glory and fame of Minos of Crete. However, because of the gentleness of his soul, he deserved to have men marvel at him more for his morals than for the power of his family. In fact, the King of Crete was so gentle in his way of life that those whom he ruled rejoiced that he was their lord. When he died, he was not deprived of honor by death. His gentleness was so revered that he is said to judge the final outcome for mortal men among the spirits of the dead. Indeed, the ancient Greeks said that just as wicked and cruel men suffer punishments in the Underworld, so does each good man receive after death the rewards of a good life. The fact that Minos did not conduct himself as a king or tyrant, but as one of the common people, is an example of his goodness. This is his highest praise.

170. On the Centaurica.

The Centaurica, which Orestes brought over from Scythia, used to be appeased by human blood. Her statue was taken into Laconia. So that guilt should not arise from the neglect of a solemn sacrifice, and so that the people of Greece should not obey through cruelty, they devised a plan: young boys vied among themselves in enduring scourges and challenged themselves in this penance. Then, placed upon the altar of Diana, they were scourged with whips until blood would flow from the human body. This would be equivalent to a sacrifice.

171. The Story of Atalanta and Meleager.

While fleeing from copulation with a certain man, Atalanta, the daughter of King Iasius, became Diana's companion in hunting. Forced to have intercourse by Meleager, she bore a son. Since she concealed his conception for a long time under the guise of her virginity, she called him Parthenopius (virgin-born).

172. *Why the Dove Is Consecrated to Venus.*

We read that the gods, Cupid and Venus, came down into certain bright meadows for enjoyment and vied in a playful contest to see which of them might gather more flowers. Of the two, Cupid gathered more, since he was carried by the swiftness of his wings. But a certain nymph named Peristera ran up suddenly and made Venus the winner over Cupid by helping her and gathering flowers for her. Angered that the palm of glory was snatched from him, Cupid changed the nymph into a dove, which is still called *peristera* in Greek. Accordingly, the dove is said to be under Venus' protection.

173. *The Story of Jove and Juno and Vulcan.*

Jupiter and Juno wanted to make known their divinity, and they produced offspring without sexual union. Jupiter brought forth Minerva from his beard, and Juno brought forth Vulcan from her thigh. Vulcan was deformed and thus was hurled from the sky. Through the mercy of Pluto he was placed in charge of the Cyclopes, who make thunderbolts for Jove. Yet he remained lame. When Vulcan grew up, with Pluto's counsel he made a golden chair so that he could recognize his mother. Sitting on it, Juno laughed. From this, Vulcan knew that she was his mother.

174. *On the Temple of Juno.*

There was a temple of Juno in which Hercules had a table and Diana had a bed. Boys were brought there to eat from the table and receive strength from it, and to sleep on Diana's bed, so that they might become loveable to all, and their generation might increase.

175. *The Story of Styx and Victory.*

Styx is a certain swamp in the Underworld. We read this about it: "by which the gods swear and fear to deceive the deity."[46] This is so, according to the stories, because Victory, the daughter of Styx, favored Jove in the war of the Giants. As a reward, Jupiter granted that when the gods swore oaths by her mother, they would not dare to deceive. The reason is this: Styx means sorrow, and Styx is also named from *tristitia* (sadness). The gods are forever happy and immortal; thus they do not feel sorrow. They swear by something contrary to their nature. Thetis dipped Achilles in the Styx, fearing his death because he had been born of a mortal father. Thus she made him entirely invulnerable, except his feet.

176. The Story of Antigone.

With her lovely hair, Antigone, the daughter of Laomedon, preferred her own beauty to Juno's. Angered at this, Juno changed Antigone's hair into snakes. While bathing, she was turned into a stork through the mercy of the gods. For this reason she grieves, as she is said to be hostile to Jove.[47]

177. The Story of Apollo and Cassandra.

Apollo loved Priam's daughter Cassandra. She had intercourse with him on this condition: that he would grant her a knowledge of prophecy. When she promised him what he wanted, he granted her the knowledge of prophecy. Later, upset because he had given her the faculty of foreseeing in expectation of a promised sexual union, Apollo took away credence from her even though she spoke the truth.

178. The Story of Minerva, Who Was Enraged at the Greeks.

This story says that Minerva was angry at the Greeks because of the defilement of Cassandra. Oileus' son Ajax, one of the Greek leaders, violated her in Minerva's temple. Or Minerva was angry because the victors, through pride, refused to sacrifice to her. Thus, while they were returning home, she scattered them in different directions, harried as they were by a very violent storm. Horace wrote: "when Pallas turned her wrath from burned Ilion."[48] In fact it is well known that the Greeks struggled in the storm during the vernal equinox when the lightning strokes of Minerva, that is, thunderbolts, stir up the most violent storms. For we know that Gemini belongs to Apollo and Hercules, so Aries belongs to Minerva.

179. The Story of Picus and Pomona.

Pomona, the goddess of fruit, loved Picus and secured a marriage with him, since he was willing. Later, Circe, because she loved him and was rejected, in her anger transformed him into a bird, the woodpecker sacred to Mars (picus Martius), for the magpie (pica) is another kind of bird. Moreover, this is thought to be so because Picus was an augur, and he kept a woodpecker in his house, through which he knew the future; the pontifical books reveal this. Furthermore, the poet correctly gave to him a wand, which is the possession of augurs.

180. The Story of Astraeus and Aurora.

According to the Greeks, the Zephyri are western winds born of Astraeus and Aurora; from them the Titans, with Atlas as their leader, take their origin. Because of Epaphus, the son born of Io, Juno incited them to take up arms against Jove. As a result, the conquered winds paid penalties, along with the gods who helped them, and Jove imposed on Atlas the burden of the vault of heaven. Hence Vergil writes: "Did so great a confidence in your race hold you?"[49] Moreover, they are called by different names by the Greeks and by us: they say Zephyrus (west wind); we say Auster (south wind); we call the north wind Aquilo; they call the north wind Boreas; they say Eurus (east wind); we say Africus (south-west wind); Vergil writes: "The warmth slipped away and life vanished into the winds."[50]

181. The Story of Jove and Ganymede.

Ganymede, the son of Troilus (Priam's son), was preferred to the rest of the Trojans for his eminent beauty. He used to hunt constantly in the forest of Ida. Ganymede was snatched up into the sky by Jove's armorbearer, namely, the eagle that formerly brought him his thunderbolts. He was made cupbearer to the gods. Hebe, the daughter of Minos, Jove's son, had first held this office. Or, in another version: So that Jupiter might not subject himself to the disgrace of sexual union with a youth, that is, a male, he changed into an eagle. He snatched Ganymede from Mount Ida and made him the cup-bearer in heaven.

182. The Story of Lyriope and Narcissus.

Lyriope the nymph gave birth to Narcissus; his father was the River Cephisus. Tiresias promised Narcissus every good fortune if he would have no knowledge of his own beauty. When Echo loved Narcissus and found no way to possess him, she pined away with love for the young man. She pursued him with her last cries as he fled. The remains of her body were turned into stone. Juno's wrath fell upon her because Echo often delayed her with her chattering. Thus Juno could not catch Jupiter when he pursued nymphs in the mountains. Echo is said to be Juno's daughter, and she was concealed in the mountains because of her deformity. Nothing of her could be perceived except her voice, which is still heard after her death. Nemesis, that is, Fortune, the avenger of those who are disdainful, drove the above-named Narcissus to love of himself because of his excessive cruelty toward Echo. He burned with no less a flame than she. When he was worn out by constant hunting, he stretched out in the shade next to a spring. While drinking the water, he caught sight of his own likeness and tarried very long in the same place. Finally, he so pined away that he died. From his remains a flower appeared. The water nymphs, weeping over their brother's death, called it by his name, Narcissus.

183. The Story of the Sirens and Proserpina.

The Sirens were daughters of the River Achelous and the Muse Melpomene. When they were searching for Proserpina, who had been carried off, they could not find her. They finally begged the gods to turn them into birds so that they might be able to follow after the one they were seeking not only on land, but even on the sea. Finally, they came to the rock of Mars, which is close to the sea and hangs over it. And so it was their fate to remain safe as long as mortals heard their voices. By chance Ulysses sailed past. Circe, daughter of the Sun, warned him about the Sirens. Then the Sirens threw themselves down from the rock.

184. The Story of Latona and the Lycian Peasants.

Latona was the daughter of Coeius the giant. She could not bring forth Apollo and Diana, who had been conceived of Jove, because of Juno's anger over his adultery. As she wandered about and no region would welcome her, at last she came to Lycia. When she wished to quench her thirst in the summer heat, those who were gathering rushes along the shore prevented her from approaching. Her wrath was inflamed on account of this, and she asked the gods that the Lycians might always live in that pond. Her prayers were heard: Jupiter turned the peasants into frogs.

185. The Story of Medea and Jason; Aeson and the Nurses of Father Liber.

Jason promised to marry Medea and took her to Greece, where he had intercourse with her. Since he had witnessed her skills in many instances, he asked her to restore his father Aeson to his youth. Since the love she bore Jason had not yet been put aside, she refused him nothing. She set up a bronze cauldron and cooked different kinds of herbs she knew and had gathered from diverse regions. Medea immersed Aeson, who had been killed, in the warm herbs and brought him back to his former vigor. When Father Liber observed that Aeson's old age had been banished by Medea's medicines, he asked her to bring help to his nurses and to restore them to the vigor of youth. Moved by his authority and aid, she granted this everlasting favor to Liber by using the same medicines with which she had restored Aeson to his early youth.

186. The Story of Deucalion and Pyrrha.

Because of the audacity of mortals, of Lycaon and others who tested even the power of the gods by their wickedness, Jupiter inundated the world with a deluge of profuse rains. Indeed, the first deluge occurred under Ogyges, King of the Thebans, not under Saturn; the second, that of Deucalion, occurred under Jove. Since two mortals surpassed the rest in piety, Deucalion, the son of Prometheus, and Pyrrha, his sister and wife, they escaped the inundation of rains on Mount Parnasus. Instructed by the oracle of Themis, the priestess of Earth at that time, they prayed to the gods and received the favor of producing offspring. When Apollo was consulted in his temple on the same hill, the oracle answered that on that mountain they should cast upon the ground the bones of their mother. They were greatly puzzled about what the bones of their mother might be. At length, they recalled that Earth was their mother, and rocks were the bones of Earth. Then they immediately cast stones behind them. The ones that Deucalion threw became men, and those that Pyrrha threw became women. Afterward, Prometheus came and put life into those human beings when he brought his heavenly torch to them.

187. The Story of the Divine Palici.

Symaethus is a river in Sicily not far from the town of Catina. In the region around this river dwell the Palici, gods whose story is as follows: when Jupiter violated Aetna the nymph and made her pregnant, he entrusted the girl to Earth out of fear of Juno. According to certain writers, Aetna brought forth her children there; according to others, Jupiter later entrusted her offspring to Earth. When the two boys burst forth from

Earth, they were called Palici, as if to say, "coming a second time." At first they were placated by human victims; later they were appeased by certain holy rites, and their sacrifices were altered. Moreover, their altar is "placable" because their divinities were appeased.

188. The Story of Consus and the Games of the Circus.

Consus is the god of counsels. He has his shrine under the earth to show that counsel ought to be concealed. So also, sacrifice is offered to Faith by a hand covered with a cloth, since faith ought to be concealed. This Consus is also called Neptune the horseman; therefore the Circus games were celebrated in his honor. Moreover, the Circus games (circenses) are either named after the circular course (circuitu), or because swords were once set up where the turning posts are now. In fact, the circus games are named after the swords around which they used to race.[51]

189. The Story of Hercules; on the Games of the Olympiad.

Hercules and his soldiers fought on horses for the first time near Mount Olympus. Seeing them on their horses from a distance, their enemies believed them to be Centaurs. Stunned, they turned in flight. Thus Hercules instituted the games there. Revered among the Greeks for his strength, Hercules used to run in various foot races for a third of a mile with a single breath, that is, one hundred and twenty-five paces. Also, near Mount Olympus he set up (statuit) the finish line. Thus it is called a "stadium" from "setting up"; namely, at the goal when the course was finished. A "stadium" is an eighth part of a mile. Later, games were instituted in imitation of Hercules and they were called Olympiad. The time span of four years is called an olympiad. In fact, after three years are completed and the fourth year is approaching, a festival is celebrated in honor of Olympic Jove. He is the deity who is called Olympic from the Olympian mountain where he dwelt. The poets situate him there in place of heaven, for it is of wondrous height. Moreover, at that festival men engaged in all kinds of games and contests. There was running of diverse kinds, with foot races and horses, and also with chariots. They established a finish line, ran to it, and immediately turned back to the other side.

190. The Story of Tiber.

Tiber was a king of the Tuscans. He died near this river and gave the name Tiber to it. Some would have it that this same king committed robberies along the banks of this river and brought much harm to those crossing over it. Thus Tiber is understood as hubris,[52] that is, "from harm." Others would have it that those who came from Sicily called it Tiber for its resemblance to a trench at Syracuse which the Africans had made without just cause, and likewise the Athenians had made around the wall of their city. Livy says that the Tiber is named after an Alban king, Tiberinus, but that is not true, since the Tiber is known to have been named before that Alban king.

191. On the Grynean Grove.

Gryneum is a grove consecrated to Apollo in the Ionian territory. There Calchas and Mopsus once held a contest over their skill in prophesy. When they contended over the number of fruits on a certain tree, the glory rested with Mopsus; in grief over this matter, Calchas died. Euphorion preserved this story in song, and Gallus translated it into the Latin language. From this comes that line at the end of Vergil where Gallus says: "I shall go, and the songs composed by me in Chalcidian verse."[53] Euphorion came from Chalchis, a town in Euboea.

192. On King Idomeneus and His Son.

When Idomeneus, King of the Cretans, was returning home after the fall of Troy, he vowed during a storm that he would sacrifice from his property that which first presented itself to him. And so it happened that his son presented himself first. Some say that Idomeneus immolated him. Others say he wished to immolate him. Driven from his realm by the citizens, Idomeneus occupied the Salentine promontory in Calabria. Near there he founded a city, as it is written, "And he besieged the Salentine fields with his army."[54] There are five Greek languages: Aeolic, Ionic, Doric, Attic, and demotic. The names of the seven hills of Rome are Palatine, Quirinal, Caelian, Viminal, Esquiline, Janiculum, and Aventine.

193. The History of Croesus, King of Lydia.

Croesus, King of the Lydians, was captured once by Cyrus, King of the Persians, who placed him upon a pyre. Suddenly, so great a rain shower arose that the fire was extinguished, and he found an opportunity to escape. Croesus bragged that this matter had turned out favorably for him, and he even boasted excessively about the vastness of his wealth.

Solon, one of the Seven Sages, told him that no one ought to brag about riches and prosperity, since we do not know what the coming day might bring. That same night Croesus saw in his dreams that Jupiter drenched him with water and the Sun dried him. When he reported this to his daughter Phania, she wisely revealed how the matter stood, saying that he would be fastened upon a cross, drenched by rain and dried by the sun. Later this happened so, for he was again captured and crucified.

194. The Story of Thamyras and the Muses.

Thamyras was a certain poet. The Muses blinded him when he competed for a long time against them and Apollo with his poetry.

195. The Story of Meleager's Sisters.

Pleuron is a city that belonged to Meleager. There the gods in their mercy turned his sisters, the Meleagrids, into birds because of their intolerable weeping after his brother Tydeus killed him.[55] Those birds are guinea hens.

196. The Story of the Sons of Jason and Hypsipyle, and Phaeton.

The Jasonids were the sons of Jason and Hypsipyle. One of them had a maternal name, Thoas, because his mother was the daughter of Thoas; the other son was called Euneus, after his father the sailor, since "good" in Greek is *eu* and "ship" is *neus*. Euneus means "sailing well," as it were. Also, Phaeton, or Thion, was the son of Liber. He ruled on the island of Chios and was the father of King Thoas. Hypsipyle, the daughter of Thoas, was the only one to save her father when a conspiracy was formed against all the men. Her great-grandfather Liber protected her.

197. The Story of Myrrha and Adonis.

Myrrha loved her own father and had intercourse with him when he was drunk. After her father learned that she was pregnant and her crime was known, he pursued her with his drawn sword. She was turned into a myrrh tree. When her father struck this tree with his sword, Adonis was born from it. They say that Venus loved this Adonis. Thus it is thought that the myrrh, namely, the tree, produced Adonis, which means "sweetness" in Greek, since the gum of the myrrh is sweet in its scent. So also Venus loves it, since this kind of juice is very hot.

198. The Story of Aeneas and the River Lethe.

While Aeneas was wandering through the Underworld, he spied a certain stream in a distant region. A countless throng of souls was making its way toward it. He asked his father what stream it was and why the souls were proceeding to it. His father said: "It is Lethe. The souls proceed there to drink and experience forgetfulness, so that they might want to return again." Astonished, Aeneas asked: "Father, tell me. Are even souls that have endured many punishments on account of their past life able to have the longing to return to their bodies? It is not likely that souls released from the prison of the body would return to its bonds." After he heard this speech, Anchises said these words: "First, it is necessary that they return; next, they are able; then they wish." Since these matters are obscure, they are made known in other subdivisions: Why "it is necessary?": All living beings take their origin from God. Since we discern that they are born, undoubtedly they return to the place from which all are created. Then "they are able" is proved as follows: since souls are immortal, they are also able to return again. The third point is whether they wish to return. Anchises says that this happens through the River Lethe. And this is what he is about to speak of, but the interrupting questions create obscurity. Certainly, concerning this stream wiser men ask whether it is one of those nine that encircle the infernal regions, or besides the nine, and we are to understand that it is separate from those nine. Indeed, they say this stream is the representation of old age, for our minds thrive and are lively and full of memory from childhood up to old age. Later, in extreme old age, all memory is lost. When this has been lost, death occurs, and souls return to another body. Thus the poets imagine that souls, in drinking from Lethe, return again to the body. Lethe is oblivion, always the neighbor to death. If the soul is eternal and part of the highest spirit, why does it not see all while in the body? Is it not of such great wisdom and such great vivacity that it could know all things? In fact, since it begins to descend into the body, it drinks in foolishness and forgetfulness. Thus it cannot exercise the power of its divinity after forgetting its own nature.

199. Likewise, on the Escape of Aeneas.

During the destruction of Troy, Aeneas, son of Venus and Anchises, rescued two Penates from the flames, along with his father and his son Ascanius. He went with them to Mount Ida. Advised by the oracles of the gods, Aeneas built twenty ships there and sailed to Thrace. There he founded a city. He called it Aenea, after his own name. Then, warned by signs from the gods, he sailed to the island of Delos where Anius was king and also priest of Apollo. Proceeding from here through the Cyclades, Aeneas came to the island of Crete, where he founded the city of Pergamum. Encouraged by the gods, he proceeded toward Italy. Passing by the Strophades and many islands of Greece also, he visited Helenus in Achaia. Guided by the soothsaying of Helenus, Aeneas reached the coast of Italy, which he saw not far off. Sailing by these shores, which the Greeks say lie between Italy and Sicily, he came after great hardship to the Cyclopes. After he arrived at the harbor of Trephanum and lost his aged father there, he came along Africa again to Sicily. There he founded the city of Acheste. Then, sailing toward Italy, he came to the Euboean coast not far from Campania and there consulted the Cumaean Sibyl. With her, Aeneas descended to the Underworld to understand everything. And then, sailing past Circe's island, at last he came to Italy. There, entering the mouth of the Tiber, he occupied himself in the search for peace. He was joined in friendship with Evander and was supported by the aid of the Tuscans. But Turnus, the son of Glaucus and Venilia, Queen of the Rutuli, started a war. Turnus was killed, and Aeneas took as his wife Lavinia, the daughter of King Latinus. He founded the town of Lavinium, named after her, and ruled there for three years. It is said that then, while walking near the River Numicus, he was conveyed to heaven, since he was nowhere visible. Likewise, in another version, this same Aeneas, as Cato says, took King Latinus' daughter Lavinia as his wife while Turnus, her suitor, was living. This same Turnus in his anger started wars against Latinus, as well as against Aeneas, with help from Mezentius. In the first of these wars, Latinus perished, and in like manner Aeneas died in the second. Afterward, Ascanius killed Mezentius and took Laurolavinium. Fearing ambushes, Lavinia, heavy with child, fled into the forest and hid in the cottage of Tyrrhus the shepherd. "Father Tyrrhus"[56] refers to this. He welcomed her and supported her, and there she brought forth Silvius. But although Ascanius burned with envy, he summoned his stepmother and ceded Laurolavinium to her. Indeed, he founded Alba for himself. Since he died without children, he left his realm to Silvius, who was also called Ascanius.

200. [Untitled]

Rhesus was a king of Thrace. He came to the aid of Troy and pitched his tents on the shore, for the gates were closed. He was killed by Diomedes and Ulysses, who had both come to spy; Dolon, who had been sent as a scout, betrayed him. The horses of Rhesus, on which the fate of Troy depended, were led away.

The Second Book, Having 100 Stories, just as the First Book, ends here. The Third Book begins.

BOOK THREE

201. On the Geneology of the Gods and Heroes.

Ophion or, according to the philosophers, Ocean, who is also Nereus, begot Caelus by the elder Thetis [sic].[57] Caelus begot Saturn, Phorcys, and Rhea. Phorcys begot Stheno, Euryale, and Medusa, who was the Gorgon. By Rhea, Saturn begot Jove, Juno, Neptune, and Pluto. By Pleione, Atlas begot Sterope, Maia, Electra, and their four other sisters. By Electra, Jupiter begot Dardanus and Teucer; Dardanus begot Ilus and Asaracus; Ilus begot Laomedon and Ganymede. Laomedon begot Anchises, Tithonus, Antenor, Antigone, (who was turned into a stork), Hesione, and Priam. By Hecuba, daughter of King Dymas of Thebes, Priam begot Troilus and Helenus, Polydamas, Deiphobus, Cassandra, Paris, and Hector, who begot Astyanax by Andromache. By Venus, Anchises begot Aeneas. By Creusa, Aeneas begot Iulus, who is also Ascanius. After Anchises died, Aeneas, coming then to Italy, begot Silvius Aeneas by Latinus' daughter Lavinia, who had been betrothed to Turnus. Silvius begot Latinus; Latinus begot Epytus, Capys, and Capetus. Capetus begot Romulus and Acrota; Acrota begot Aventinus; Aventinus begot Palatinus; Palatinus begot Amulius and Numitor. Amulius begot Ilia. She was the priestess with whom Mars had intercourse and begot Romulus and Remus. The wife of Romulus was Hersilia; Julius was from her family. Likewise, Jupiter had intercourse with one of Atlas' four daughters, whose names are not found, and by her he begot Tantalus. By Stirope, Tantalus begot Niobe and Pelops. Pelops begot Atreus and Thyestes by Hippodamia, the daughter of Oenomaeus, whom he defeated in a chariot race with the help of Myrtilus. Atreus begot Agamemnon and Menelaus.

By Helen, Menelaus begot Hermione; by Clytemnestra, Agamemnon begot Orestes and Iphigenia. The elder Thetis, the wife of Ocean, bore Thetis, the mother of Achilles, and Clymene. Clymene was the wife of the Sun, and she bore Phaethon. Also, she bore Oetra, and Oetra bore Theseus. Neptune begot Aegeus; Aegeus begot Theseus. By Hippolyta, Queen of the Amazons, whom he had captured, Theseus begot Hippolytus. The same hero begot Demophon. Likewise, [Jupiter][58] had intercourse with Alcmena, the wife of Amphitryon, and he begot Hercules; by Deidamia, Hercules begot Hyllus. Likewise, Agenor begot Cadmus, Europa, Cilix, and Phoenix. Cadmus took for himself Hermione, the daughter of Venus (Vulcan's wife) and Mars; by her he begot Agave, Semele, Autonoe, and Ino. Agave bore Pentheus, and Semele bore Bacchus; Autonoe bore Actaeon. Ino was the wife of Athamas after Nephele, who had borne Phrixus and Helle; she bore Learcus and Melicertes. Lycus succeeded Cadmus. His wife was Antiope, the daughter of Nycteus. (Jupiter) had intercourse with her in prison in the form of a satyr. She bore Zethus and Amphion, who succeeded Lycus and took Niobe to himself. By her, he begot seven sons and just as many daughters. Likewise, Laius begot Oedipus by Jocasta; Oedipus begot Eteocles and Polynices, Ismene and Antigone, all by Jocasta. Likewise, Adrastus begot Argia and Deipyle. Also, Mars begot Parthaon; Parthaon begot Oeneus. Cestius begot Althaea, Toxeus, and Plexippus. By Althaea, Oeneus begot Meleager and Tydeus, Gorge and Deianira. Meleager begot Parthenopaeus; Tydeus begot Tytides, who was a leader in the Trojan War. Likewise, Jupiter begot Apollo and Diana by Latona, daughter of Coeus. According to certain writers, Coeus was the son of Titan who had intercourse with Earth. He begot twelve sons who rose up against the gods. Indeed, since Apollo and Diana did not take part in their iniquity, they deserved to ascend in a heavenly chariot. Likewise, Jupiter had intercourse with Maia and begot Mercury. Vulcan came from [Jupiter's] seed or from the thigh of Juno; Pallas, who is also Minerva, came from the head of Jove. By Jove, Juno bore Hebe; according to certain writers, she came from lettuce. Likewise, Venus came from the foam of Saturn's testicles after he had been driven out of his kingdom by Jove. Likewise, Jupiter had intercourse with Danae, the daughter of Acrisius, and by her he begot Perseus. Likewise, in the form of a swan, he had intercourse with Leda, the wife of Tyndarus. Thus two eggs were produced. Castor and Pollux came from one of these eggs;

from the other was born Clytemnestra and Helen. Also, Lycurgus begot Phyllis and Archemorus. Likewise, by Hypsea, Aeetes begot Chalciope, Medea, and Absyrtus; hence the verse: "not her mother Hypsea and Chalciope her sister."[59] By Alcestis, Admetus begot Nisa and Sthenoboea. Apollo served him seven years for Nisa; Pretus [sic] took Sthenoboea as his wife. Likewise, by Coronis, Apollo begot Aesculapius. Likewise, according to certain writers, Apollo had intercourse with Aethea and begot Circe. Also he begot Pasiphae. Likewise, Jupiter had intercourse with Europa, the daughter of Agenor, and by her he begot Minos. Pasiphae bore the Minotaur, sired by a bull; Minos begot Phaedra, Ariadne, and Androgeus by Pasiphae. Bacchus took Ariadne after Theseus abandoned her on an island, and by her he begot Thoas. Thoas begot Hypsipyle, who dwelt on the island of Lemnos. Likewise, Laertes begot Ulysses; by Penelope, Ulysses begot Telemachus. Likewise, Nauplius begot Palamedes. Also, Teucontus begot Telephus. Antenor begot Artilochus and Acamas. Phoebus begot Miletus. By Cyanae, the daughter of Meander, Miletus begot Caunus and Bibylis. Erectheus, King of Athens, succeeded Pandion, the father of Philomela and Procne. She was the wife of Tereus and mother of Itys. Erectheus begot Procris and Orythia. Cephalus, who was from the stock of Aeolus, had Procris as his wife. Boreas carried off Orythia and by her begot Zetes and Calais.

202. The Story of the Double Name and the Downfall of Phlegyas.

According to Euphorion, the Phlegyans, an island people, were very irreverent and sacrilegious toward the gods. Thus an angry Neptune struck the part of the island that the Phlegyans inhabited with his trident and destroyed them. Phlegyas, Ixion's father, had a daughter named Coronis. Apollo violated her and she bore Aesculapius. Grieving over this, her father set fire to Apollo's temple and was driven into the Underworld by his arrows. Thus Statius writes: "He oppresses Phlegyas as he lies on his everlasting couch beneath the hollow rocks."[60] To those now placed in torments Vergil wrote: "Learn justice!"[61]

203. The History of the Sons of the Laconians[62] Born of Uncertain Fathers.

The Laconians were worn down by the Athenians in a long war and feared a scarcity of men. They ordered their maidens to have intercourse with any men at all. This was done. After their victory, the young men born of uncertain fathers were ashamed of their origin, for they were called "maidens' children." With Phalanthus as their leader, the eighth one after Hercules, they sailed to a town of Calabria founded by Taras, Neptune's son, and they dwelt in this enlarged city.

204. The Story of Jove and Thetis and Achilles.

Although Jupiter wished to marry Thetis, the Fates prevented it because the offspring that would be born would drive him from his realm, just as he had expelled Saturn. Thetis, a goddess, married Peleus, a mortal man. By him, she bore Achilles. Fearing the death of Achilles, she was consoled in vain by Neptune.

205. On the Wedding of Peleus and Thetis.

Peleus, the son of Aeacus (or Aceus) married Thetis, daughter of Nereus and the nymph Doris. All the gods were invited to the wedding except Discord. In anger over this, Discord threw a golden apple into the banquet hall. On it was inscribed: "a gift for the most beautiful goddess." When the apple was picked up, a contention over it arose among Juno and Minerva and Venus; they asked Jove to be the judge. Unwilling to offend his wife or daughters, he sent them to Paris (Alexandros), the son of Priam and Hecuba, who was pasturing his flock on Mount Ida in Phrygia. Paris was known never to regard persons in a judgment. When Juno promised him the kingdom of Asia, and Minerva promised knowledge of all arts, Venus promised whatever woman he wanted. Paris judged Venus most worthy of that apple. When this was done, Juno and Minerva became enraged at the Trojans over the insult to their scorned beauty.

206. The Story of Achilles and Agamemnon and the Death of Hector.

Achilles, the son of Thetis and Peleus, came with fifty ships from the city of Larissa to aid Agamemnon and Menelaus, the sons of Atreus, against the Trojans. Agamemnon besieged Troy with his army and many weapons, while Achilles attacked the nearby cities with his Myrmidons. Among those he joined to himself were Thebes and Lyrnesus, and two very beautiful women: Briseis and Chryseis. Meanwhile, a pestilence fell upon the Greek army. Convinced by the warnings of Calchas, Agamemnon restored Chryseis to her father Chryses, the priest of Apollo. He said that Achilles ought to do this. On account of this discord between them, each army was inflamed to mutual slaughter, such that Minerva scarcely calmed their strife. After this, Achilles for some time did not oppose the Trojans, who were fighting successfully. Finally, when the Greeks were being overcome, Hector even set their ships on fire and fought in their very camps. Patroclus, the armor-bearer of Achilles, went into battle wearing Achilles' arms. Hector killed him and carried off the arms. Moved by grief over this, Achilles received the arms of Vulcan from his mother Thetis when he wished to fight again and did not have arms. He took these up and returned to the battle. After he killed many Trojans, he fought with Hector himself in single combat. Achilles killed Hector and stripped him of his arms. He tied his body to a chariot and dragged it. Priam came unarmed and redeemed the body for burial after he payed for it with gold.

207. On the Death of Troilus.

Troilus, the son of Priam and Hecuba, used to exercise his horses outside the city walls. He was wounded by Achilles in an ambush and brought lifeless into the city, bound to his horses. There was a prophecy that said that if Troilus reached twenty years of age, Troy could not be destroyed.

208. On the Victory of Hector and the Flight of Palamedes.

Achilles refused to fight against Troy because he had been bribed by King Priam, who promised to give him his daughter Polyxena in marriage. One day Diomedes, the son of Tydeus, came and asked Achilles to return to the battle line, but he refused. Then Palamedes asked Achilles to give him his chariot and horses and clothing; Achilles gave them. Later, Hector commanded the battle line, and he carried off the clothing, chariot and horses. Thus the poet writes: "having put on the spoils (of Achilles)."[63]

209. The History of Priam's Son, Killed by His Own Father.

By Arisbe, Priam had a son who was a seer. This son declared that on a certain night a boy was born by whom Troy could be destroyed. It so happened that the wife of Thymoetes and Hecuba, Priam's lawful wife, had both given birth. Priam ordered the death of the son of Thymoetes, and the wife also.

210. Varying Opinion on the Death of Priam.

One reads various opinions on the death of Priam. For example, some say that Pyrrhus captured him in his own house, dragged him to Achilles' tomb, and killed him near the Sigean promontory, for Achilles was buried there. Then Priam's head was carried about, fixed on a pike. Others say that he was killed near the altar of Hercean Jove. Thus Lucan writes: "Do you not see, the guide says, the Hercean altars."[65] Vergil follows this latter opinion completely, although he also mentions the one written before.

211. The Story of Dido and the History of Saturn.

Dido was the daughter of Meton, whom Vergil calls Belus. After her husband Acerbus was killed (Vergil names him Sychaeus), she escaped from her brother, King Pygmalion. She took a great weight of gold and boarded ships; she came to the shores of Africa. Once there she bought from Iarbas, King of the Moors, as much land as could be measured or encompassed by the hide of an ox. Dido claimed her city by deception, for she stretched out a hide cut into the thinnest strips and encompassed twenty-two stadia. For this reason, she called it Byrsa (later, Carthage). After he had lost possession of the sky, Saturn wandered in exile over the whole earth accompanied by Juno. So that she might not become fatigued by the tedium of the journey, he entrusted her to nymphs in Africa to be raised. Because of this, Juno always kept Carthage mighty.

212. Likewise on Dido and the Founding of Carthage.

When Dido was passing through a certain island of Juno's, she received an oracular response and carried off the priest of Juno with her, since she had little trust in him when he prophesied the site of Carthage. When they arrived there, the priest chose the place for constructing the city. After it was excavated, the head of an ox was found. This displeased Juno, since an ox is always brought under the yoke. A different place was excavated, and there the head of a horse was found. This pleased Dido, since this animal, although it is subjugated, is still warlike and conquers and usually is friendly. Therefore they built temples to Juno there. Thus Carthage is both warlike, through the omen of the horse, and fertile, through the omen of the ox.

213. On Anchises and Venus.

It should be known that Anchises was a shepherd, and Venus had intercourse with him as her lover. Thus Aeneas was born near the river Simois in Troy. Indeed, goddesses or nymphs bring forth their children near rivers or groves. When Anchises boasted of this, he was scorched by lightning and deprived of an eye, for he was one-eyed.

214. The History of Dionysius the Tyrant.

A certain tyrant, Dionysius, used fraud and deception to invade all of Sicily. He utterly plundered it, so that he even laid waste the statues and temples of the gods. In fact, he carried off the beard of bearded Jove and plundered his statue, which was clothed in the most precious garments. He clothed himself with them, saying that a divinity should not be cold in such stiff garments. One day, a certain friend of his questioned him, asking if he were happy. Dionysius said, "why not?" Then he ordered the man to sit upon his throne clothed in royal garments and holding his scepter. He commanded that a very sharp sword held by a very slender thread be suspended over the man's head, and he asked him if he seemed blessed. The man responded that in no way was a person blessed who thought that he was about to die swiftly at the falling of a sword. Dionysius said to him: "Now you know what kind of fear I endure constantly."

215. The History of Regulus, Roman Consul.

Regulus was a Roman consul who captured many men in the war with Africa and put them in chains. Once, while waging war against them, he was captured and bound in chains. Not esteeming him lightly, the Romans gave hostages and freed him from chains. When he came to the senate and his wife, along with his sons, wished to kiss him, he responded that a captive ought not be kissed by a noble person. Then when they wanted to redeem him for a price, he forbade it vehemently, saying that he could in no way serve worthily again as a soldier. And so, as Orosius says, Regulus was returned to the enemy by his own wish and cast into chains. Sleepless after his eyelids were cut away, he died.

216. The History of Torquatus' Victory and His Parricide.

Lucius Mallius Torquatus overcame a certain Gaul in single combat and put a neck chain (torquis) on him; he took his name from this. Proceeding to the City, he ordered his son merely to guard his camp. When an occasion arose, the son went to battle and attained a victory. When the father returned later, he praised the good fortune of the Roman people, but the son, as Livy says, he clubbed to death on account of his disobedience. Therefore "cruel with his axe" means cruel in his justice of killing; it does not mean with a kind of steel, for he did not punish his son with an axe.

217. The History of Camillus' Victory.

After the Roman legions had been annihilated near the river Allia, Brennus led the Gauls, and they destroyed the city of Rome, except for the Capitol. For this they accepted a vast amount of money. Then Camillus was made Dictator. He had been away, since he was in exile near Ardea because he had not shared booty from Veia equally. He pursued the departing Gauls and after they were killed, he took their gold and their standards. Since he weighed this gold there, he gave a name to the city. It is called Pisaurum, because gold (aurum) was weighed (pensatum) there. After this was done, he went again into exile but was called back and returned to Rome.

218. On the Seven Civil Wars of the Romans.

From the time of Caesar, the Roman people made a habit of civil wars, for they were waged seven times. There were three from Caesar's time: first, against Pompey in Thessaly; second, against his son Magnus in Spain; also, against Juba and Cato in Africa. After the death of Caesar, from the time of Augustus Octavian, there were four: against Cassius and Brutus at Philippi in the region of Thessaly, and also against Lucius Antonius at Perusia in the district of Etruria. The sixth was against Sextus Pompeius in Sicily; the seventh against Mark Antony and Cleopatra in Epirus.

219. The History of Atilius' Good Fortune.

Atilius was a certain senator who was summoned while cultivating his fields. He merited the office of Dictator because of his virtue. He was called Serranus, from "sowing" (serendo). He was also named Quintius Cincinnatus. Finally, the same man became a conqueror when he cut down the enemy. He was the first to drive his defeated enemies before him.

220. On the Three Hundred Fabii Killed and the One Survivor.

There were three hundred and six men from the one family of Fabii who swore an oath together and fought along with their slaves and retainers against the Veientians. Near the river Cremera, they were slain in an ambush. Only one, Fabius Maximus, survived. He had remained in the city because of his still-tender youth. Later, when he could not resist the attack of Hannibal, he avoided him by delay. He drew Hannibal toward Campania, where his strength was weakened by pleasures. Fabius is the one of whom Ennius says: "You who alone restored our state to us by delaying."[66] Vergil knew and cited this verse as an example.

221. On the Victory of Marcellus.

Marcellus overcame the Gauls and the Carthaginians in a cavalry battle. He even killed Viridomarus, the leader of the Gauls, with his own hand and brought back the *spolia opima*, "spoils of honor," that he had taken away from that general. Cossus did the same thing to Lars Tolurnnius.

222. On the Praises and Death of Another Marcellus.

According to the poems of Vergil, various qualities are observed in the young: beauty, youth, and strength. Moreover, Vergil singles out Marcellus, whom Augustus adopted. He was the son of Octavia, sister of Augustus. In his sixteenth year, while he held the office of Aedile, he fell into ill health and died in his seventeenth year in the region of Baiae. The City grieved exceedingly over his death, for he was affable, as well as Augustus' son. To glorify his funeral procession, Augustus ordered five hundred biers to enter the City. In fact, among our ancestors this was glorious and was granted in accordance with one's prosperity, for Sulla had six thousand. So, Marcellus was carried in a mighty procession and buried in the Campus Martius. In adulation of Augustus, Vergil delivers Marcellus' eulogy, as it were.

223. On the God Fatuus and the Goddess Fatua.

There is a certain god, Fatuus; his wife is Fatua. The same god is Faunus, and the same goddess is Fauna. They are called Faunus and Fauna from "talking wildly"; thus we also call those who speak rashly "fatuous."

Indeed, physiology holds this view: that the eyes are signified by the "gate of horn." Eyes are of the color of horn and harder than other bodily members, for they do not sense cold. The mouth is designated by the "gate of ivory," from the teeth. Thus Aeneas is sent forth through the gate of ivory. This gate of ivory is even said to be more ornate, as it were; in fact, these are things that are beyond Fortune.

224. The Story of Endymion and the Moon (Luna).

The shepherd Endymion loved the Moon, or Diana. She scorned him, but he drove his shining-white flocks to pasture and thus drew her to his embrace. Men propose a certain mystical explanation for this event. Indeed, Endymion is said to have loved the Moon in a twofold way: (1) because he was the first among men to discover the course of the moon; he is also reported to have slept for thirty years, since he strove for nothing else in his life except this discovery; (2) because the dampness of nightly dew benefits the successes of shepherds. The vapors of stars and the moon itself drench this with life-giving juices of plants.[67]

225. The Story of Berecyntia and Attis.

Berecyntia, the Mother of the gods, loved Attis, a most-handsome boy. Burning with jealousy, she made him half male by castrating him. Men call her Berecyntia, as if to say "Mistress of mountains." Thus they name her Mother of the gods, since mountains are called gods because of their loftiness. They also give her the name "Mother of the gods" as a measure of her power. So she is called Cybele, as if to say *cidos bebeon*, that is, "the firmness of glory." Thus the glory of power is always inflamed by love and tormented by envy. It swiftly cuts away what it loves, while it might also cut off what it hates.

226. The Story of Psyche and Cupid.

In his *Metamorphoses*, Apuleius writes that in a certain country a king and queen had three daughters. The two elder ones were of moderate beauty, but the younger one, named Psyche, was of such wondrous elegance that she was thought to be an earthly Venus. Finally, after husbands took the elder two in marriage, no one dared to love Psyche, as if she were a goddess, but every man endeavored to supplicate her and to win her for himself with sacrifices. Therefore, burning with envy, Venus asked Cupid to punish her insolent beauty. Coming to avenge his mother, Cupid loved the girl when he saw her, and he pierced himself with his own arrow. Thus Apollo sent a message ordering the girl to be sent alone to a mountain peak where she would be the bride of a winged serpent. And so, when the wedding dance was completed, that is, the virginal procession, the girl glided down over the mountain slopes on the gentle wafting of the blowing west wind. She was carried into a certain precious, golden house. There, with only voices to serve her, Psyche was intimate with an unknown husband, for he came to her at night. Just as he arrived unseen in the evening, so also he departed unknown in the twilight, after the struggles of Venus had been carried out in the dark. But Psyche's sisters came to weep at her death. After they climbed the mountain peak, they called upon their sister with mournful cries. Although the light-shunning husband forbade the sight of her sisters and threatened her, the unconquerable ardor of sisterly love overcame Psyche. She guided her sisters' thoughts to herself on the breeze of the blowing west wind. Because of their poisonous counsels that she seek out her husband's looks, she consented to curiosity, the stepmother of her own welfare. Finally, Psyche believed her sisters, who said that she was united like a beast to a serpent-husband, and she was about to slay him. She concealed a dagger under her couch and covered the lamp with a basket. When her husband was in a deep sleep, Psyche armed herself with the sword and brought out the lamp. She recognized Cupid and was inflamed by an unrestrained desire for love, but she burned her husband when the glowing lamp oil bubbled over. He fled, exclaiming many reproaches over the girl's curiosity, and abandoned her. Psyche was banished from the house and exiled. Later, Jove procured their marriage. At last Cupid married the girl, who had been persecuted with many torments by Venus.

227. The Story of Perdicca.

Perdicca was a hunter of wild beasts. Seized by a love for his own mother, he was weakened and brought to a final wasting-away, while his unrestrained lust seethed and his shame resisted the force of this new outrage.

According to Vergil, he was the first to invent the saw. The truth is this: Although Perdicca was a hunter, the bloody destruction involved in the slaughter of wild animals and the wandering chase in the wilderness displeased him. He was even more displeased when he considered his fellow youths, Actaeon, Adonis, and Hippolytus, who had died a wretched death. Cursing the hunt, he pursued agriculture. Because of this he is said to have loved his mother, that is, Earth, the mother of all. Because of his toil, he became emaciated.

228. The Story of the Dog Transported to the Constellations.

This is the story of the dog placed among the constellations. Jove made this dog a protector of Europa. The dog came to Crete because Europa was fond of hunting and because no wild beast could outrun it. After her death, the dog went to Cephalus, whose wife was Procris. Cephalus took the dog with him to Thebes where, it was said, there was a fox that could elude all dogs. And so, when the dog and the fox had reached the same spot, Jupiter did not know what to do, as Histrius says, and he changed both into stone. Some have said that this dog was Orion's. Since Orion was fond of hunting, the dog was placed with him among the constellations. But others have said that he was Icarus' dog.

229. On the Seven Pleiades.

We know of seven stars named Pleiades, or Hyades. They are called Pleiades because they were seven daughters born of Pleione, who is also Aethra, the daughter of Oceanus, and Atlas. They are said to be seven in number, but no one can see more than six. This is the reason given: Six of the seven had intercourse with immortal gods; three with Jove, two with Neptune, one with Mars. But the remaining one was the wife of Sisyphus. The Pleiades begot the following: Dardanus by Electra and Jove; Mercury by Maia; Lacedaemon by Taygete. Hyrieus was born of Alcyone and Neptune; Lycus and Nicteus were born of Celaeno. Mars begot Oenomaus by Sterope. Merope, the wife of Sisyphus, bore Glaucus, whom many have said is the father of Bellerophon. Thus Merope was placed among the constellations near the rest of her sisters, but since she wed a mortal man, her star is obscured. Other writers say that Electra is not visible as she weeps for captured Troy and for her offspring expelled from Troy. There is another tradition concerning the Pleiades.

When these seven sisters were taking a journey with their girls, Orion tried to violate one of them, and she fled with her sisters. Orion pursued her for twelve years and could not find her. Jove pitied the girls, and established both among the stars. And so Orion is still seen following them as they flee toward their setting.

SECOND MYTHOGRAPHER

1. Where Fable Got Its Name.

Poets gave a name to fables from *fando*, "speaking," since they are not deeds that have been done, but only invented in speech. Thus, they were introduced so that a certain representation of the life of human beings might be recognized in the conversations of imaginary dumb animals among themselves. Tradition has it that Alcmaeon of Croton first invented fables, and they are only called Aesopic because he practiced this art among the Phrygians. Moreover, fables are either Aesopic or Lybistic.[1] They are Aesopic when the dumb animals are imagined to have conversed among themselves, or things converse that do not have a soul, such as cities, trees, mountains, rocks, and streams. They are Lybistic when it is imagined that there is verbal communication of men with beasts or of beasts with men.

Poets invented certain fables for the sake of amusing; they expounded certain ones that pertain to the nature of things and some pertaining to the morals of human beings. Those invented for the sake of amusing are the kind that men commonly tell, or such as Plautus and Terence composed. Men invented fables pertaining to the nature of things. The lame Vulcan story is an example, since by nature fire is never perfectly straight. Men invented fables such as that three-shaped beast the Chimaera: a lion above, a serpent below, a she-goat in the middle.[2] Through this they wanted to distinguish the ages of men, whose early youth is wild and rough, like a lion; whose half-way point in life is most perspicuous, like a she-goat, because it sees most sharply; then old age, subject to constant misfortunes, like a serpent. So also they invented the fable of the Hippocentaur, that is, a man mingled with a horse, to represent the swiftness of human life, since it is well known that a horse is very swift. Men invented fables pertaining to morals, such as in Horace when a mouse speaks to a mouse and a weasel speaks to a little fox, so that after the story has been made up according to what is done, the true meaning is given. So too are such fables of Aesop concluded with a moral, as also in the Book of Judges. There the woods sought a king for themselves and spoke to the olive and the fig and the vine and the bramble. Certainly, this entire story is invented according to morals, so that after the story has been made up, it arrives at the point intended in its true meaning. Demosthenes the orator also used a fable against Philip, who demanded that the Athenians hand over ten orators to him and he would leave their country. Demosthenes made up this fable to dissuade them: once upon a time, a wolf wanted to beguile the attentiveness of the shepherds. He urged them to join him in friendship, but on this condition, that the dogs, the cause of their strife, would be handed over under the law to the wolves. In hope of security, the shepherds agreed and gave the dogs, whom they had as the most watchful guardians of their sheep. Then, with all fear removed, the wolves tore to pieces everything that was in the shepherds' flocks, not only for their satiety, but really for their pleasure. The leaders of the people asked Philip how much more easily he also could overpower a city deprived of its guardians.

2. On the Different Names of the Gods.

Those whom the pagans revere and call gods are said to have been men once, and they began to worship them after death because of their way of life or the merits of each one. Examples include Isis in Egypt, Jupiter on Crete, Juba among the Moors, Faunus in Latium, Quirinus among the Romans, Minerva among the Athenians, Juno on Samos, Venus on Paphos, Vulcan on Lemnos, Liber on Naxos, Apollo in Delphi. Indeed, poets took up their praises and transported them to the heavens in the poems they composed. Moreover, the gods were named after their deeds, such as Mercury, since he presides over merchandise, and Liber, who presides over liberty. Also, statues were set up to certain brave men or founders of cities. When they died, those who loved them did this so that they might have some solace from contemplation of their likeness. But little by little this error crept in among their descendants through the persuasion of demons: those whom they honored solely for the memory of their name, their successors later thought to be gods and worshipped them. Stoics say that there is only one god and one goddess, and they are the same in might; they are called by various names according to the nature of their offices and acts. They call the same god Sun and Liber and

Apollo. Likewise, they say that the same goddess is Luna and Diana and Ceres and Juno and Proserpina. Moreover, the deities seem to be of each sex; thus, because they are incorporeal, they assume whatever body they wish.

3. On Saturn.

Saturn, the son of Coelus and Pollus, was the husband of the goddess Ops. He is depicted as old, with his head covered, and carrying a scythe. Fearing the might of Jove, Saturn took flight from Olympus. He went to Italy and first ruled that realm. By giving it laws, he united a race that was untaught and scattered in the mountains, and he called it Latium, since there he had hidden (latuisset) in safety. Thus, he is depicted with his head covered, as if hiding (latens). Certain authors want to call him Saturn, from *saturando*, "saturating," since he drew people to himself through the distribution of grain. Others say that Saturn is, as it were, "saturated with years" (annis saturetur). He is imagined to be old, either on account of his slowness of motion, or because he is at a farther distance from the Sun, or because he is called the god of rain, for we know that old people are always cold, like the rains. He holds a scythe, either because he is the god of the seasons, which hasten back upon themselves like a scythe, or on account of the wisdom that is sharp within him. Others say that Saturn does no harm in going forward, but he is dangerous in going backward. So he is imagined to be armed with a scythe, since a scythe stretched forth causes less harm, but indeed a scythe brought back cuts down whatever it hits. This is the reason that he is said to have eaten his own children: Saturn is the god of the seasons, and time consumes whatever it brings forth; on the other hand, the ages disperse the years born of themselves. Men say that Saturn had four children: Jove, Juno, Neptune, and Pluto. While assigning possession of the elements to these deities, the poets ascribed to Saturn, as god of the seasons, four children, that is, four elements. They allotted the upper regions to Jove, with his wife Juno as his companion, and the lower regions to Neptune and Pluto. Thus the three brothers are said to have divided dominion of the world among themselves, and by lot Jupiter received the sky, Neptune the sea and Pluto the earth. Indeed, Neptune is called the ruler of the second share, since water is nearer to the sky than the land is. Also, these three deities, although they have different dominions, yet seem to have power over the entire realm mutually. So also the elements which they hold in check are joined together by a certain natural plan, and the scepters of these deities signify this, for Jupiter has his three-forked thunderbolt, Neptune his trident, and Pluto his Cerberus.

4. On Jove.

Therefore the poets ascribe to Jove, as fire, the first place next to Saturn. They call him Jove from *juvando*, "assisting," for nothing so warms everything as the heat of fire.

5. On the Eagle of Jove.

The eagle is placed in the care of Jove and said to be his armor-bearer, since the eagle is of such great warmth that it might even cook the eggs upon which it sits unless it applies to them a huge, freezing-cold stone, as Lucan testifies: "Stones when warmed under a breeding eagle."[3] The eagle is even thought to have supplied arms to Jove in the war of the giants. In fact, Jupiter and Saturn were kings, but when Jupiter had a dispute with his father Saturn over their domains, a war began. Going forth to war, Jupiter looked to the eagle for an omen. When he was victorious because of this augury, it was supposed that the eagle had supplied weapons to him as he fought. Thus, from this auspicious omen it came about that eagles accompany the soldiers' standards.

6. On Juno.

Jupiter is said to have bound a bride to himself with golden chains. She is Juno, the air. The poets called her queen of the gods. She is even called Curetis, since she used a chariot (curru) and spear. Juno is named from *iuvando*, "assisting," and she is said to rule realms because this way of life strives after riches. Men say that she is the goddess of birth and presides over marriages because riches are always pregnant and never miscarry.

7. On Her Peacock.

Men place the peacock under Juno's care because every life that strives after power always seeks adornment. According to the stories, this peacock was the son of Aristo, and before he was changed into a kind of bird, he had eyes in all his limbs. Juno set him as a guard over Jove's beloved

Io, the daughter of Inachus, King of the Argives, so that Jupiter could not approach her. When Jupiter employed Mercury to kill him, Juno changed him into a peacock and took him into her care.

8. On Iris, Her Rainbow.

To this goddess men join Iris, the rainbow, because just as the rainbow has various adornments, so also fortune, although adorned for a short time, is quickly fleeting. Also, according to the poets, Iris, the attendant of Juno, was called Thaumantias, that is, daughter of Thaumas. She received this name out of an admiration[4] that proceeds from her colors. Iris is said to be just like *eris*, that is, strife, for she is never sent for conciliation, as Mercury is, but always for destruction. Moreover, she is said to be an attendant only of goddesses, but this is false, since she is also dispatched very often by Jove. We read, for example, "For Jupiter sent Iris from heaven through the air."[5] Also, the rainbow does not appear except from the region of the Sun, to which it lends various colors when irradiated, since a little water, clear air and dark clouds create various colors.

9. On the Reason Why Juno Is Called Jove's Sister and Wife.

The reason why Juno is called sister and wife of Jove is that these elements [fire and air] are equal in their fineness. They are called sisters, but since they are in harmony when mixed, and air wedded to fire grows hot, they are said to be joined in marriage. Since Juno, air, is subject to Jove, fire, the name of husband is given to the element rightly placed above. Furthermore, Jupiter is said to have bound her with chains because air nearer to heavenly fire is mixed with the two elements from below, water and earth, which are heavier than the two above.

10. Who First Made Temples for Her.

Phoroneus, the son of Inachus, King of the Argives, was the first to dedicate temples to Juno and to institute the practice of sacrifices. He also first ruled over mortals. Jupiter is said to have first lain with a mortal, Phoroneus' daughter Niobe (since there is another Niobe, daughter of Tantalus).

11. On Neptune.

Men assign the sea to Neptune. They call him ruler of the second lot, since water is closer to the sky than earth is; because everything that contains is above that which is contained. Moreover, they assign Amphiena to Neptune as his wife, for in Greek we say *amphiena* for "around," since water is surrounded by three elements. Thus men say that he holds a trident because the nature of water has a triple quality: flowing, fertile, and potable.

12. On Pluto.

Men say that Pluto presides over the earth, for riches are called *plutos* in Greek; they believe that riches are allotted to earth alone. They also call this god Orcus, that is to say, "swearing," so that no one might depart from him unpunished.

13. On His Three-Headed Hound.

At Pluto's feet they place a three-headed hound because the ill will of quarrels is inflamed by a triple circumstance, that is, natural, causal, and accidental. The natural one is hatred, as of dogs and hares, wolves and sheep, men and serpents. The causal one is like the jealousy of love. The accidental one is either what arises by chance, as relates to men, or because of grazing together, as relates to the herds. Or, since Cerberus is the earth, the devourer of all bodies, he is called Cerberus, as if to say *creoborus*, "devouring flesh."

14. On His Furies.

The three Furies serve Pluto. These daughters of Night and Acheron have serpents for hair. They are also called Eumenides by antiphrasis, since they are not good. The first of these is Allecto, "incessant"; the second is Tisiphone, as if to say *tuton phone*, "the voice of these women"; the third is Megaera, as if to say *megala eris*, "great discord." Therefore, to rave without ceasing is first, to burst forth with the voice is second, and to bring strife is third.

15. On the Causes of the Plague.

At a certain time, the Nile rose above the plain and remained long in the fields. From the water of that river and the heat of that province, many diverse animals were formed in the mud. Some were whole and some half complete. When the Nile receded into its channels, these animals rotted. Then a pestilence arose because of the putrid air. Blowing from

Egypt, the south wind drove it first to the province of Attica, then to the region of Venetia and Illyria, and it even ravaged the whole world. Lucretius writes extensively about this pestilence.[6]

16. On the Spartans.

The Spartans were worn down by a long war with the Athenians and feared a shortage of men. They ordered virgins to lie with any men at all. After this was done and a victory won, the young men blushed over their uncertain fathers, for they were being called "sons of maidens." They sailed away in a ship with Phalantus as their leader, the eighth after Hercules. They came to the town in Calabria founded by Taras, the son of Neptune. This place, exalted by an ancient name, they called Tarentum.

17. A History.

Italy is part of Europe. Italus, King of the Sicilians, left Sicily and came to the lands next to the Tiber, and from his own name he called the place Italy.

18. A History.

Lavinum was named after Lavinus, the brother of Latinus. Afterward, it was called Laurentum, from the laurel found by Latinus when he came to the city and took command after his brother's death. Later, it was named Lavinium, after Lavinia, Aeneas' wife.

19. A History.

It is known that Ascanius founded Alba, but which Ascanius is uncertain: the son of Creusa or Lavinia. Even Livy is uncertain about the matter. When Tullus Hostilius conquered this town, he brought all the noble families to Rome. The same Ascanius had other names besides Iulus and Ilus. He was also called Dardanus and Leontodamas as a consolation for his dead brothers.

20. A History.

There were two Decii. One of these sacrificed himself for the republic in the Italic War, the other in the Gallic War.

21. On the Harpies of Jove.

The Harpies, also called Furies, are three in number according to Vergil: Aello, Occipite, and Celaeno. According to Apollonius, whom even Vergil follows in Book Twelve, there are only two. They are also said to be the hounds of Jove and called Harpies from the word "snatching" (rapiendo). Moreover, Aello is from *aedomallon*, "taking another's"; Occipite, "carrying off quickly"; *celenum* in Greek is rendered as "black" in Latin. Indeed, the first thing is to want another's goods, the second is to seize what is wanted, the third is to conceal what is seized. The Harpies are the daughters of Sea and Earth. Thus they dwell on islands, being part land and part sea. Others call the Harpies daughters of Thaumas and Electra. This is the reason that they are called hounds of Jove, since these same ones are said to be Furies: because they also snatch food, which is characteristic of the Furies, as in the line "And she prevents them from touching the tables with their hands."[7] Thus also greedy men are thought to suffer the Furies, since they hold back from what has been prepared. Likewise, Vergil asserts that they are Furies, saying in Book Three: "I, eldest of the Furies, reveal to you."[8] Lucan also asserts that the Furies are called hounds, as in the line "in the light above I left behind the Stygian hounds,"[9] and as Vergil says in Book Six: "The hounds seemed to howl through the shadows at the arrival of the goddess."[10] Truly, they are called Furies and hounds among those below the earth, Dirae and birds among those above, as Vergil shows in Book Twelve. In between, they are called Harpies. Thus they have a double shape. Vergil names these three Aello, Occipite, and Celaeno; Apollonius, whom Vergil follows in Book Twelve, says there are two.

22. On the Parcae of Pluto.

The three Fates are assigned to Pluto. By the poets they are called Parcae, through antiphrasis.[11] According to the pagans, they determine human life. Therefore one of them has a distaff; she presides over birth. Another draws the thread; she determines the life. The third severs it; she brings death. Thus it is said: "Clotho carries the distaff, Lachesis draws the thread, Atropos cuts it." The first is called Clotho, that is, "calling forth." The second is Lachesis, that is, "lot." The third is Atropos, that is, "without order." Thus the first is the calling forth in birth, the second is the lot of life, how one is able to live, and the third is the manner of death, which comes without order.

23. On His Wife.

They say that Pluto's bride is Proserpina, the daughter of Ceres. Men said that Proserpina was joined to Pluto as if she were a crop, that is, creeping forward in roots through the ground.[12] She is also called Hecate, that is, bringing forth fruit a hundredfold, or having a hundred powers, for the Greeks call one hundred a hecaton. Thus we call a spacious house a "hecatomb." This goddess is Luna in the sky, Diana on the earth, and Proserpina in the Underworld. In fact, joy is called Ceres in Greek. And so, Ceres is said to be the goddess of grain because joy abounds when there is abundance of produce.

24. On the Elysian Fields.

Sallust says that the blessed islands mentioned in Homer's poems are called Elysium.[13] According to theologians, they are around the lunar circle, where the air is purer. Thus Vergil says: "in the fields of air."[14] Likewise Lucan says: "The place between earth and the paths of the moon . . . they do not come there placed in gold, nor buried with incense."[15]

25. On the Nine Circles.

There are said to be nine circles in the Underworld. The first holds the souls of infants; the second of those who cannot help themselves on account of their simplicity; the third of those who kill themselves to avoid hardships; the fourth of those who are insane; the fifth of brave warriors; the sixth of criminals punished by a judicial sentence. In the seventh circle, souls are purged; in the eighth, souls are purged so that they might return to bodies; and in the ninth, so that they might no longer return to the Elysian Fields.

26. On the Life of Jove.

Saturn learned from a prophecy of Themis, the high priestess of Earth, that he could be driven out of his realm by his own son. According to certain writers, he learned this from a prophecy of Proteus. Thus he ordered his wife Ops, also called Rhea or Cybele, to give him right away whatever offspring she should bring forth. She was pregnant and brought forth Jove. Charmed by Jove's beauty, Ops entrusted him to the nymphs on Mount Dicte in Crete to be nourished. When Saturn asked where her offspring was, she showed him a stone wrapped in a garment. Saturn devoured it. But Jupiter was raised by the nymphs to whom his mother had entrusted him. He was suckled by a she-goat named Amalthea and is even said to have used her hide afterward in the war against the Titans. Then the Curetes and Corybantes were summoned to prevent the boy's wailing from being heard by the clanging of bronze. The Corybantes are spirits, attendants of the Mother of the gods, spirits who know all, as it were. Also, bees then followed the sound of the bronze. They nourished Jove with honey. For this Jupiter later allowed them to have young without any sexual union. Moreover, the adult Jupiter drove his father from his realm and became the worst of ravishers. He caused the age under his sway to be called silver, while it had been called golden when Saturn reigned. Because of his crimes of sexual impurity, Astraea, sister of the Titans, is said to have retired into the heavens with her sister, called Modesty. Astraea is called Justice because of her equity.

27. On Latona and Her Sister.

Jupiter violated Latona, daughter of Coeus the Titan. Later, when he wanted to violate her sister Asterie also, she begged the gods to change her into a bird. She was changed into a quail, which we call *coturnix*. When she wished to cross the sea, which is "Coturnicus," Jove blew upon her and changed her into a stone. She was hidden beneath the waves for a long time. Afterward, when Latona implored Jove, Asterie was raised up and, now called Ortygia, began to float on the waters. She was first consecrated to Neptune and Doris. Later, the Python was sent against Latona. Earth had shown the Python in an unknown form to mortals after a flood. Latona had been made pregnant by Jove, and while Juno was pursuing her, no region accepted her in her wandering. She came at last to Lycia. When she wanted to slake her thirst caused by the summer heat, she was prevented from coming nearer by those who were gathering rushes along the shore of a pond. Angered by this, Latona prayed to the gods. She asked that the people who lived there might never be away from their water. Her prayers were heard, and Jupiter transformed those peasants into frogs. Moreover, Latona could not give birth to Apollo and Diana, the children she had conceived, while Juno was pursuing her. She was driven out of every land. At last she was welcomed by her sister when Ortygia brought her to her shores. There she bore Diana first, then Apollo, who immediately killed the Python and avenged the injury to his mother. After Diana was born, she performed the duty of midwife to her mother as she gave birth to Apollo. Thus, although Diana is a virgin, she is still invoked by women giving birth. Truly, she is Diana, Luna, and Proserpina. After the two deities were born, they did not suffer the land of their birth to wander, but they bound Ortygia to two islands, Mykonos and Gyaros. Certainly the truth is far otherwise. This island is troubled by earthquakes, which happen because of winds concealed beneath the land. Thus Lucan wrote: "He believed the wind was seeking to burst forth."[16] The island lacked an oracle of Apollo because of earthquakes, for he had commanded that a dead man not be buried there, and he ordered certain sacrifices to be performed. Later, people came from Mykonos and Gyaros, the nearby islands, to take possession of these lands. Also, this is the reason we say that Diana was born first: It is well known that night was first, whose ornament is the moon, Diana. Then came the day, which the sun, Apollo, produces. It happened that Delos was first named Ortygia from the quail, called *ortux* in Greek. Furthermore, it is called Delos because it lay hidden for a long time and appeared later, for "clear" is expressed as *delon* in Greek; or what is truer: because the oracles given there are clear, although everywhere else the responses of Apollo are obscure.

28. On the Triple Power of Apollo.

It is well known that Apollo has a triple power: he is the Sun among the gods, Father Liber on earth, and Apollo in the Underworld. Thus, we even see three signs around his statue: the lyre, which shows us the image of celestial harmony; the chariot, which indicates that he is an earthly deity; arrows, by which he is seen to be a god of the lower regions, and injurious. Thus he is called Apollo in Greek, Destroyer in Latin.

29. On His Various Names.

Apollo is called by various names by different peoples: Titan among the Achaemenians, Osiris among the Egyptians, and Mithras among the Persians, where he is worshipped in a cave. This is because of an eclipse which he undergoes through an interposition of the moon. Indeed, there the Sun has the face of a lion; he wears a tiara and Persian dress, sits on an ox and holds its horns in both his hands. This latter is understood to pertain to the moon. Moreover, he is called Apollo, which means "destroyer" in Latin, either because he is the god of pestilence or because he destroys all the moisture in plants with his heat. Men say that he is also the god of auspices, by which cities are ruled. He is the god of divination because the sun makes all dark things clear, or because in his rising and setting he shows the various outcomes of signs. Furthermore, Apollo is called a Titan, as if he were one of the Titans who took up arms against the gods, although he held back in the war against the gods. He is thought to have merited heaven for this good deed. Also, he is called Sol, as if he alone (solus) of the Titans did not bear arms against the gods. He is called Phoebus, as if he were a youth, that is, a young man. Thus he is also depicted as a boy, since he is born at the new dawn each day with a boyish face, as it were. He is called Pythius from the Python, a serpent of immense size, which he killed. So also the Pythian games, whose winners are crowned with laurel, are celebrated in honor of him. Moreover, credulity is called python in Greek because false credulity is suppressed when the light makes things clear.

30. On His Tripod, Bow, and Arrows.

Men speak of Apollo's tripod because he knew the past, perceives the present, and will see the future. They ascribe to him a bow and arrows, either because his rays shoot forth from a circle like arrows, or because he breaks through the mists of doubt by his manifestation. They say that he drives a four-horse chariot because he completes the cycle of the year in the four-part variations of the seasons. It is also said that he gave responses at Lycia for six months and at Delos for six months. So do we read about other gods, that they prophecy at times on the kalends, at times on the ides, sometimes at the first or middle or last part of the day. Thus the day is rightly divided, that is, the whole day is not sacred (religiosus) to the gods.

31. On His Four Horses.

Thus they have given fitting names to his horses: Eritreus, Acteon, Lampus, and Philogeus. Eritreus is called "reddish" in Greek because the sun rises red in the morning light. Acteon is called "shining" because the sun shines more brightly at the third hour. Lampus means "burning" because the sun is burning more brightly when it climbs to the highest circle of the day. Philogeus is called "earth-loving" in Greek because at the ninth hour the sun inclines toward its setting.

32. On His Raven.

This story shows why men place the raven under Apollo's protection. Coronis was the daughter of Phlegyas. Apollo made her pregnant and made the raven her guardian, so that no ravisher might approach her in secret. When Lycus lay with her secretly and Jupiter destroyed him with a thunderbolt, her adultery became known. Apollo killed Coronis with his arrows. After the dead girl's womb was cut open, Apollo brought forth Aesculapius, who became skilled in medicine. He changed the raven, which was by nature covered with white feathers, from white to black and took it under his protection. But the truth is that the raven is under Apollo's protection either because it alone brings forth the eggs of its young in the midst of summer's heat, contrary to the nature of things, or because it has many meanings in its calls.

33. On His Laurel.

This is a story concerning the laurel, which is consecrated to Apollo. Daphne, the daughter of the River Peneus, was the most beautiful of all maidens. Once he saw her beauty, Apollo burned with desire to force himself upon her. After Daphne appealed to her father to protect her virginity, she was changed through the mercy of Earth into a laurel tree before any copulation. Apollo welcomed her into his care. This is the truth: she is said to be the daughter of the River Peneus because laurel, which abounds on the banks of the same River Peneus, springs forth from river-water. She is called the friend of Apollo because those who have written about the interpretation of dreams promise that if laurel is placed near the head of those who sleep, they will see true dreams.

34. On His Nine Muses.

Men assign nine Muses to Apollo, and they add him to the Muses as the tenth, because there are ten modulations of the human voice. But in fact, we say that the Muses are the nine modes of learning and knowledge. The first is Clio, the initial thought of learning, as it were. She discovers history, since no one seeks knowledge except where he advances the dignity of his own fame, and fame is called *clyos* in Greek. The second Muse is Euterpe, "well-pleasing." She holds a pair of brass pipes because the first thing is to seek knowledge, the second to be pleased by it. Third is Melpomene, "saying sweet things" or "meditating." She has tragedies in her keeping, as the first thing is to want, the second is to desire what you want, the third is to meditate upon what you desire. Fourth is Thalia, "giving capability." She discovers comedies; because after desire, there is need of capability. Fifth is Polyhymnia, "recalling many things" or "much memory." She discovers rhetoric, since after capability, memory is necessary. Sixth is Erato, "finding resemblance." She discovers geometry, since after knowledge and memory, one tries to find something resembling itself on its own. Seventh is Terpsichore, "shaping instruction." She discovers the psaltery. Thus after finding it is also necessary to divide and judge what you find. Eighth is Urania, "heavenly melodiousness" or "good voice." She discovers astrology because after deciding you choose what you say or what you reject, since it is a heavenly quality to choose what is useful and to despise what is fleeting. Ninth is Calliope, either "of the best voice" or "assigning the best things." She discovers literature. Thus the order is as follows: first, to want knowledge; second, to be pleased by what you want; third, to pursue that by which you have been pleased; fourth, to grasp that which you pursue or which is desired; fifth, to remember what you grasp; sixth, to find something similar on your own to what you remember; seventh, to judge what you find; eighth, to choose from what you judge; ninth, to make known what you have chosen.

35. On Diana, the Sister of Apollo.

They say that Diana, namely Luna, is the sister of Apollo and the guardian of ways. They also say that she is a virgin, because a way (via) brings forth nothing. Thus men think that both of these gods have arrows because these two stars send forth their rays from the sky to the earth. Moreover, they say that Diana is called Duana, as it were, since the moon (Luna) appears both in the day and at night. Men also declare that she is Lucina because she shines (luceat), and the same goddess is called Trivia because she is thought of in three forms. Thus Vergil writes "the three faces of virgin Diana"[17] because the same goddess is called Luna, Diana, and Proserpina. But when she is thought of as Luna, "She shines in a glimmering garment; when she reclines armed with arrows, she is the virgin Latonia; when she sits resting on her throne, she is Pluto's wife."[18] Men say that this same Luna is Proserpina among the dead, either because she shines at night or because she runs nearer the earth and presides over it. Not only does the earth sense the waxing and waning of the moon, but also stones and brains of living things or even seeds do, because while the moon increases, seeds degenerate and produce little worms. Finally, while the moon increases, wood grows weak, split by holes bored by moths. Also, Diana is said to live in groves because all hunted game feeds more at night and rests by day.

36. Why She Is Called Dictynna.

The reason she is called Dictynna is this: Minos, King of the Cretans, wanted to ravish Bryte, the daughter of Mars, who was consecrated to Diana the Cretan. Bryte cast herself into the sea and was caught in the nets of fishermen, who drew her body out of the sea. The nets are called *dictia* in Greek. Also, Crete began to be afflicted by pestilence. An oracle stated that the people could not escape this plague unless they set up a temple to Diana and called her Dictynna, "from the nets."

37. On the Temple at Carya.

At Carya in Laconia there is a temple sacred to Diana. It is even called Cariatium for this reason: while maidens were at play, the entire group of them thought that the building was falling down. They fled to a nut tree and hung down in its branches. The Greeks call this nut a *carya*, and so from this tree both the temple and the goddess take their name.

38. On Endymion.

Endymion the shepherd loved the Moon. She scorned him, but he drove his shining-white flocks to pasture and thus drew her to his embrace. This is said to be so because Endymion was first among men to discover the course of the moon. Thus he is also said to have slept for thirty years, since he strove for nothing else in his life except this discovery; or it is so because the moisture of nocturnal dew benefits the success of shepherds.

39. On Mars.

Mars is the god of war, and he is called Mars because war is fought between males (mares). Mars is named for *mas*, "male," as it were. Likewise, he is called "maker of deaths," for death (mors) is named after Mars. Men say that he is an adulterer because the outcome is uncertain for those who wage war. In fact, he stands with a naked chest, so that in war each man might expose himself without fear in his heart. Venus slept with Mars, and the Sun discovered this. He made it known to Vulcan, for virtue corrupted by lust becomes clear with the Sun as its witness, and it is held shamefully chained by the bonds of passion.

40. On the Birth of Venus.

Saturn was angry at his father Caelus and cut off his manly parts with a sickle. They fell into the sea. Venus was born from their blood and the foam of the sea. Thus she is named Aphrodite, for in Greek *aphros* means "foam." Venus first married Vulcan. Later, she committed adultery with Mars, and the Sun revealed this crime. Vulcan enclosed their bed in chains as they were lying together. Saturn is called Chronos, "time," in Greek. Thus, when the virile forces of time, that is, its fruits, have been cut away by the sickle and cast into the sea, as it were, they produce desire in the fluids of the testicles, for abundance of satiety[19] nurtures desire. Venus is thought to have been born through this loss because all virile forces are weakened by venereal use, which does not take place without loss in the body. This is the reason for "from the sea": because physicians say that sweat, which sexual union always produces, is salty. Men imagine Venus swimming in the sea because all desire suffers shipwreck. Vulcan is thought to be the husband of Venus because the venereal function does not occur without heat. Thus Vergil says in the Third Book of the Georgics: "Old, he is cool toward Love."[20] Since Venus was born from the sea, myrtle, which delights in the seashore, is consecrated to her, as in "The shores delighting most in myrtle-groves."[21] Or as the medical books say, this tree is suited to many needs of women. Venus slept with Mars. The Sun discovered this and revealed it to Vulcan, for virtue corrupted by lust becomes clear with the Sun as its witness, and it is held shamefully chained by the bonds of passion.[22]

41. The Story of Why the Myrtle Is Consecrated to Venus.

Myrina[23] was a very beautiful maiden betrothed to a certain man. Robbers seized her and hid her in a cave until they had completed their robberies. But she escaped and went home. Since she was freed by the gods, she was consecrated as a priestess of Venus. Afterward, when her betrothed took her, she killed him. In fact, she was changed into a tree. Because of the dignity of her priesthood, Venus granted a pleasant aroma to the tree and placed it under her own protection.

42. On the Roses of Venus.

Men also place roses under the protection of Venus, for roses are red and they prick. Lust is red because of the reproach of shame, and it pricks with the sting of sin.

43. On the Seashell of Venus.

Venus is depicted as carrying a seashell because an animal of this kind is joined in sexual intercourse with its entire body exposed at once.

44. On the Doves of Venus.

Men also place doves under her protection because birds of this kind are fervid in sexual union. This is the story of why doves are under the protection of Venus. Once when Venus and Cupid descended into certain flourishing fields for pleasure, they began to vie with each other in playful strife to see who might gather more budding flowers. Aided by the swiftness of his wings, Cupid conquered nature with the flight of his body, and he was winning. Suddenly, Peristeia rushed up and with her wings made Venus the winner. Cupid was indignant. He changed the girl into a dove, called *peristeia* by the Greeks. But glory lessened her punishment. To mitigate the transfiguration of the innocent girl, Venus placed the dove under her own protection.

45. On Adonis.

This is the story of Adonis, who was subject to Venus. Myrrha loved her own father, and slept with him when he was drunk. When Myrrha's father learned that she was pregnant and her crime was known, he began to chase her with his drawn sword. She was changed into a myrrh tree. After Myrrha's father struck this tree with his sword, Adonis was born from it. Venus took Adonis to herself and loved him. But let us say what this story means. The myrrh is a kind of tree of great hardness. Yet in the heat of the sun it exudes a sap called myrrh. Since this tree has a sweet fragrance, it is said to have given birth to Adonis, for "sweetness" in Latin is called *adon* in Greek. Furthermore, it is said that Venus loved him because this kind of juice is very hot.

46. On Venus' Cupid.

They join Cupid to Venus because venereal pleasure cannot be enjoyed without love. Simonides says that Cupid, the god of love, was born of Venus only, although others say of her and Mars, others say of her and Vulcan. Indeed still others want to make him the son of Chaos and the prime nature of things. He is depicted as a winged boy, naked, with a quiver and a torch. He is wearing a quiver because love wounds the soul just as arrows wound the body. He is naked because the shamefulness of love is apparent always and never hidden. Cupid is depicted with a torch because shameful love is inflamed by heat and a certain fervor. He is winged because love passes quickly; nothing is found to be more fickle or changeable than lovers. Also, he is thought of as a boy because just as eloquence is wanting to boys through their inexperience, so also it is wanting through pleasure to those who love excessively. There are two Venuses: one is devoted to pleasure; she is the mother of desires who gave birth to Hermaphroditus. The other is the chaste one who presides over chaste, licit loves. Likewise, there are two loves: chaste and unchaste. The latter we always speak of in the plural in contradistinction to that chaste love.

47. On the Three Graces.

There are three Graces: Pasithea, Eugiale, and Euphrosine. They are depicted nude and together, with one turned away, but two looking back at us. Also, they are consecrated to Venus because through their impulse all animals are prone to sexual union. They bathe in the fountain of Acidalia in Orchomenus, a city of Boetia. Venus is called Acidalia for this reason, or because from there she inflicts the cares of love. The Graces are deservedly called daughters of Venus and Liber, for they are entirely won over through the gifts of these deities. So are they naked because favors ought to be without rouge, that is, without pretense. So are they together because it is fitting that graces be indissoluble. This is the reason that one is depicted as turned away and two look back at us: because a favor that has proceeded from us is accustomed to return double.

48. On Erichthonius.

When Jupiter and Juno had produced many children through their union, at last it pleased them to beget children without sexual union, to prove their divinity. Then from his beard Jupiter sired Pallas, also called Diana. She was of noble shape. Since she sprang from his head, and the five senses are distributed in the head, she is called the goddess of wisdom. After Juno touched her own genital parts, she brought forth Vulcan. Since genital parts are unclean and unsightly, he appeared in an unsightly form: dark and lame. Since Vulcan was unsightly and Juno was not pleased with him, Jove hurled him onto the island of Lemnos. He was raised there by a Sintian. Vulcan did not merit divine honors, to which one comes through the company of the deities or through sexual union with goddesses. Thus Vergil says: "On whom his parents have not smiled, nor has a god honored him at his table, nor has a goddess deemed him worthy of her bed."[24] After Vulcan fashioned thunderbolts for him, Jove finally procured his marriage to Minerva. She spurned him and struggled against him, so he spilled his lustful seed onto the ground. Moved by shame, Minerva put dust over it with her foot. From this was born a boy with a serpent's tail. He was called Erichthonius, as if he had been produced from earth and strife, for strife is *eris* and earth is *chthon*. Minerva hid him in a basket. After a serpent was positioned as a guardian for him, she handed him over to be watched by two sisters, Aglauro and Pandora, the daughters of Erethia. She forbade them to open the basket. But, all the more desirous of what was forbidden, these maidens opened the basket and saw the snake. After Minerva drove them insane, they threw themselves from the citadel of Athens. As a snake, Erichthonius fled to the shield of Minerva[25] and was brought up by her. To conceal the hideousness of his tail, he yoked horses and rode in a chariot. By this he concealed the deformity of his body. Thus Vergil says in the Third Book of the Georgics: "Erichthonius first dared to yoke a chariot and four horses and to stand as a conqueror upon swift wheels."[26]

49. On Priapus.

Priapus was from Lampsacus, a city on the Hellespont. He was driven out of the city and later, because of the hugeness of his male member, was received into the ranks of the gods, where he was entitled to be the deity of gardens. Priapus is said to preside over gardens on account of their fertility, for although other ground might produce something once in a year, gardens are never without fruit, and although other ground might have produce once in a year, a garden truly has many crops. Also, he is the attendant of Father Liber, the god of lust and sexual union. Hence he attends his sacred rites, for "Without Ceres and Liber, Venus is cold."[27] Some people say that Priapus is Adonis, the son of Venus, who is worshipped by women. According to others, this Adonis was Venus' lover. A boar killed him, and thus Venus wept exceedingly. The story is fashioned this way because Adonis is the Sun and the boar is winter. Indeed, the boar killed Adonis because when winter comes, the sun runs out of heat and dies. Venus, the earth, weeps, because the earth produces nothing when winter obscures the sun.

50. On Minerva.

Minerva is the goddess of wisdom, war, and weaving. She is depicted bearing arms, clothed in a triple garment and wearing the Gorgon's head on her breast. She was born from the head of Jove for this reason: because intellect is situated in the brain. She bears arms for this reason: because wisdom is fortified. Men attach the Gorgon to her on her breast because a wise man will have fear in his heart against adversaries. They place on her head a helmet and crest, so that the understanding of wisdom might be armed and adorned. Men also imagine her clothed with a triple garment because wisdom is hidden, rarely recognized from without. They say that she is the foundress of Athens, for Minerva is named Athena in Greek, as if to call her *athanate parthene*, "immortal maiden," because wisdom cannot die nor be corrupted. Men place the owl under her protection because wisdom retains its own splendor even in darkness. This is the story of how she took the owl under her protection: Nycteus, King of Ethiopia, would have been happy if he had never been a father. He had a daughter named Nyctimene, who loved her father with an impious love. She confessed her love to her nurse and sought her shameful assistance. In fact, this nurse lied to her own master, Nycteus, and told him that a certain maiden, a foreigner, loved him. She brought it about that he embraced his own daughter without knowing it. He decided to punish the crime too late once it became known, and he wanted to kill the daughter he recognized in his embraces. Nyctimene implored the help of Minerva; under Minerva's protection she was snatched from danger. She was turned into a bird that flees the sight of day out of consciousness of the crime committed, and it was entrusted to Minerva's protection. Others say that she was the daughter of Pretus[28] and that she fled, fearing her father's violence. Minerva changed her into a night owl.

51. On Vulcan.

Now Vulcan is fire, and he is called Vulcan as if to say *volicanus* because he flies (volet) through the sky. Vulcan was cast aside by Juno because of his deformity. It is well known that she is the Sky, where thunderbolts are produced. Vulcan is thought to have been born from Juno's thigh, since thunderbolts proceed from the lowest part of the sky. Thus Homer says that he was hurled from the sky to earth because every thunderbolt falls from the sky. Since the thunderbolt appears often on the island of Lemnos, so Vulcan is said to have fallen onto this island. He is lame because by its nature fire is never straight. Men say that he is married to Minerva because sometimes fierce passion even creeps stealthily into wise people. Indeed, she defended her virginity with arms because all wisdom protects the integrity of its ways against violent passion by virtue of the mind. In fact, from this struggle Erichthonius was born, for strife is called *eris* in Greek. For what else can passion stealing upon wisdom produce except the strife of envy? Wisdom, Minerva, conceals this strife in a basket, that is, hides it in the heart, for every wise man hides his own passion in his heart. Thus Minerva stationed a serpent there, that is, destruction. This she entrusted to two maidens, Aglauro and Pandora. Pandora means "universal gift," but Aglauro is as if to say *acoloron*, "forgetfulness of sorrow." In fact, a wise man entrusts his grief to kindness, which is the gift of all, or to forgetfulness.

52. [Untitled]

It should be known that there were three Atlases: one was Moorish; he is the greatest. Another was Italian, the father of Electra, who gave birth to Dardanus. A third was Arcadian, the father of Maia, who gave birth to Mercury. But from the similarity of names there came about an error, and Maia and Electra are said to have been the daughters of the greatest

Atlas for this reason: he had daughters of these names, that is, Electra and Maia.

53. On the Mercuries.

Corvilius says that there are four Mercuries: one is the son of Jove and Maia, Atlas' daughter; another is the son of Coelus and Dies; a third, who summons souls, is the son of Liber and Proserpina; the fourth, Mercury, who killed Argus, is the son of Jove and Cyllene. But since truth is ignored in reference to the gods, we must follow up on these stories. Jupiter had intercourse with Maia, the daughter of Arcadian Atlas. Thus Mercury was born on Mount Cyllenus in Arcadia. He taught us letters, established the months, discovered the constellations and invented the lyre. He even provided this with seven strings because of the number of Atlas' female descendants, since his mother was one of them. Also, he presides over business affairs and is the god of theft and plunder. Mercury is depicted carrying a staff, wearing winged sandals on his feet, and with a dog's head. He is reddish and sunburned.

54. Why He Is Called Mercury.

He is called Mercury as if to say *mercium curius*, "merchandise courier," or *medius currens*, "running in the middle," since speech is between men, or since he is the messenger of the gods. He is said to be running, as it were, between gods and men. Mercury is thought to be the god of plunder and theft because tradesmen are always surrounded by plunder and perjury. He holds a staff. With this he separated serpents, that is, poisons, because those who wage war and those who disagree are appeased by the eloquence of negotiators. He wears winged sandals on his feet because he returns to his origin more quickly than the other planets. Thus he is said to be swift and straying. Moreover, he is represented as reddish and sunburned because he is known to be nearer to the Sun than the other stars. He is depicted with a dog's head, and therefore also called Anubis, because nothing is known to be more sagacious than a dog. He invented the lyre, and for this he received his staff as a gift from Apollo. This is the story:

55. On the Lyre.

While the Nile was returning to its own channels, it left behind various living things upon the land. Even the tortoise was left. After it had putrefied and its sinews remained stretched out within the shell, it yielded a sound when Mercury struck it. Through imitation of this, he invented the lyre. Later, when Mercury drove away the cattle of King Admetus that Apollo was pasturing, Apollo caught him. He demanded that Mercury allow him to say that he had invented the lyre. Mercury agreed, and received from Apollo a certain staff called a herald's staff (caduceum). Holding this staff in his hand, Mercury proceeded to Arcadia. When he saw two entwined serpents fighting among themselves, he threw down the staff between them, and soon they were separated and went away. When this happened, he knew that this little staff had been provided for the sake of peace. Here is the story of this staff: Mercury is the god of eloquence and the messenger of the gods. His staff separated the serpents, that is, poison, for those who wage war are pacified by the eloquence of messengers. Thus legates of peace are called *caduceatores*, "heralds." For just as wars were proclaimed by the fetial priests, so peace came about through the heralds. Moreover, a messenger (interpres) in Latin is called *hermes* in Greek.

56. On Orpheus.

After Apollo received the lyre, he taught Orpheus, the son of the River Oeager and Calliope the Muse, and he ceded the lyre to Orpheus after he himself invented the cithara. Orpheus was a theologian (theologus), and he first instituted orgies. Since he calmed the wildness of men by the establishment of morals, he is said to have enticed the trees and rocks by moving them to listen to him. His wife was one of the Dryads, named Eurydice. By a certain misfortune, she stepped on a snake hidden in the meadow grass while she was fleeing from the ambush of Austeus, son of Apollo and Cyrene the nymph, daughter of the River Peneus in Thessalia. She died from its venom. Thus, distraught over his inability to endure the grief, Orpheus took his lyre and approached the entrance to the Underworld. He soothed the ferocity of Dis by the sweetness of his singing. He gained his wish that Eurydice be restored to him, on this condition: he should precede her as she followed and not turn back his gaze for her sake. But due to the impatience of his love, he forgot the condition placed on him. He looked back at the wife now under his power. When the law of the Fates drew her back, he suddenly lost her as she slipped from his view.

57. On Jove and Etna the Nymph.

Jupiter had intercourse with Etna the nymph and made her pregnant. When Juno persecuted her, Etna implored Earth for help and was received into her bosom. She gave birth to twins prematurely. Or, as some say, fearing Juno, Jupiter entrusted Etna to Earth, and according to others, he entrusted her offspring. Earth nourished them in her bosom as long as the law of the womb demanded, and then she brought them forth. Thus they are called Palici, "twice-born." According to the story, they were savage and used to be appeased by human blood. Later they were pacified by certain sacred rites, and their sacrifices were changed.

58. On Cybele.

Cybele is the Mother of the gods; she rides in a chariot with lions yoked to it. She is imagined to have Corybantes armed with drawn swords as her attendants, and to wear a turreted crown. The Mother of the gods is said to ride in a chariot because she is the earth, which is suspended in air. She is borne up on wheels because the world turns in a circle and revolves. Lions are yoked to her chariot to show that maternal tenderness can overcome everything. The Corybantes with drawn swords are imagined to be her attendants to signify that all men ought to fight for their own land. The fact that she wears a turreted crown shows that cities are placed upon the earth, and they are marked by towers. The next story demonstrates why the lions are yoked to her chariot.

59. On Atalanta.

There was a certain maiden named Atalanta from the city called Schoeneus. She was the daughter of Scineus. Atalanta was so superior in running that she killed suitors whom she challenged to race and defeated. Later, Hippomenes asked Venus to help him. She gave him three golden apples from the garden of the Hesperides. He challenged the girl and began to throw down the apples one at a time. Then, held back by her desire to gather up the apples, Atalanta was defeated and Hippomenes gained the victory. Because of his impatience for love, he had intercourse with the vanquished Atalanta in a grove of the Mother of the gods. For this reason the angry goddess changed them into lions and yoked them to her chariot, commanding that lions never copulate with each other. In fact, Pliny says in his *Natural History* that the lion has intercourse with a female panther, and the panther with a lioness.

60. On Pan.

Pan is a rustic god formed in the likeness of nature; and so, he is called Pan, "all." Indeed, he has horns like the rays of the Sun and the horns of the Moon. His face is ruddy in imitation of the sky. On his breast he wears a fawnskin covered with stars in the likeness of the stars. His lower part is shaggy because of trees, bushes, and wild beasts. Pan has goats' feet to show the firmness of the earth. He has a pipe of seven reeds because of the harmony of the heavens, in which there are seven planets, as Vergil says: "seven distinctions of tone."[29] And so he has a crooked staff called a *kaluropa*, that is, a shepherd's crook, because of the year, which curves back upon itself. Since he is the god of all nature, the poets imagine that he wrestled with Love and lost because "Love conquers all," as we have read.[30] According to the stories, Pan loved the nymph Syrinx. When he pursued her, she implored Earth for help. She was turned into a reed that Pan carved into and made a reed pipe (fistula) for himself to assuage his love. Thus the reed pipe is called *syringa* in Greek.

61. The Story of Aeneas.

As soon as Aeneas came to Italy and took a wife, as Cato says,[31] Turnus started wars against both Latinus and Aeneas because of this, and he obtained help from Mezentius. In the first war Latinus perished, in the second Turnus, and Aeneas died as well. Afterward Ascanius killed Mezentius and took Laurolavinium. Fearing ambushes by Ascanius, the pregnant Lavinia fled into the forest and hid in the cottage of Tyrrhus the shepherd. There she gave birth to a son whom she called Silvius. Fearing that the people's envy might be inflamed against him, Ascanius summoned his stepmother and ceded Laurolavinium to her. He founded Alba for himself and died without children. He left his realm to Silvius, who was also called Ascanius. Thus in Livy there is an error that says: "Ascanius established Alba."[32] Afterward, all the Alban kings were called "Silvius" from his name, just as today the Roman emperors are called "Augustus," Egyptian kings are called "Ptolomey," the Persians "Arsacidus," and the Latins "Muranus."

62. A History.

According to Vergil, the cause of fire on Mount Etna is this: there are lands exuding sulfur through hidden courses, such as Mount Vesuvius in Campania and Mount Taurus, and the smell of hot water indicates this. Likewise, we know that wind is created from the motion of water, and also that there are hollow lands. We know that Etna is in the part of the world where the East or Southwest wind blows; it has caves full of sulfur, and they lead down right to the sea. These caves receive streams into themselves and create wind. After the wind has been stirred up, it produces fire from the sulfur. Thus there is the fire that we see. Moreover, the correctness of this explanation is proven because when the other winds blow, Etna emits nothing from itself. Also, according to the manner in which the East wind or Southwest wind blows, Etna sometimes emits smoke, sometimes ashes, sometimes fire.

63. On Faunus.

Faunus is said to be a lower god, and rightly so, for nothing is lower than the earth on which he dwells and from which he gives oracles. He is also called Fatuus. His wife is Fatua. He is the same as Faunus and she is Fauna. They are called Faunus and Fauna from *fando,* "talking wildly." Thus we call those who speak rashly "fatuous." Fauns are commonly called demons or shaggy creatures; they proclaimed oracles by speaking with their voices when the country folk consulted them.

64. On Nymphs.

The nymphs of mountains are called Oreads. Those who dwell in forests and delight in trees are Dryads. Those who are born and die in trees are Hamadryads, for very often, when a tree has been cut, a voice bursts forth and blood flows out. The nymphs of wooded vales are Napaeae, those of springs are Naiads, those of rivers are Potamides, and those of the sea are Nereids. There are certain goddesses of place, that is, local deities who do not go to other places, such as Marica, a goddess who dwells near the River Liris on the shores of Minturnae. Poets call them Muses because there are nymphs who are also Muses, according to Varro. But we should know that this same Varro says that there are only three:

one born from the motion of water, another whom the sound of air produces when it has been struck, and a third who consists only of pure voice.

65. On Astraeus.

Astraeus was one of the Titans who took up arms against the gods. He lay with Aurora and thus the winds were born, according to Hesiod. But, in truth, clouds are created from air, water comes from clouds, and winds from the motion of water. Aeolus is said to be king of the winds and to curb their fury by his command. The truth is as follows:

66. On Aeolus.

Aeolus, the son of Hippotas, was the king of eight islands that are below the Strait of Sicily. These islands are called Aeolic after him, although they also have their own names.

Aeolus foretold the blasts of winds to come by the mists on these islands and the smoke on the isle of Vulcan. Thus to inexperienced people he also seemed to hold back the winds by his power. The poets imagined that he was king of the winds. He is said to have restrained the winds in a cave because hollow places are filled with winds.

67. On the Titans.

The fables tell us that Earth was angry at the gods who refused to dwell upon her. For revenge, she created the Titans, also called Giants. They were armed with the tails of serpents. Trusting in their strength, they set about to destroy the heavens by heaping up piles of rock on the mountains and driving the gods down to earth. They were overthrown by Jove's thunderbolts and by the Gorgon's head when Minerva held it before them. After the burden of the sky was placed upon their leader, Atlas, they were buried under heaps of earth. One of them, Enceladus, also called Briareus or Egeon, was placed under fiery Etna. Thus he is still said to burn. As he changes sides, he causes the whole of Sicily to tremble, and he fills it with steamy smoke. In fact, we have accepted these stories as fables, except what we read about the Giants. Reason does not favor this part, for since the Giants are said to have fought in Phlegia, a place in Thessaly, how is Enceladus in Sicily? How is Otus in Crete, according to Sallust, when he says "the fields of Otus"?[33] How is Typhoeus in Campania, as in the line "Inarime placed over Typhoeus by Jove's commands"?[34] Varro says that some men fled to the mountains with their tools during a flood. Later, they were provoked into war by men who came from other mountains, and they easily prevailed from the higher places. Thus it happened that the higher ones were called gods and the lower ones were called earth-born, and since they crept from the depths to the heights, they were said to have tails in place of feet.

68. On the Decree of Jove.

In this war of the Giants against the gods, Victory, the daughter of Styx, favored Jove. For this she merited a reward: the gods would not dare to deceive when they swore oaths by her mother. Styx is a swamp in the Underworld. Indeed, Jove decreed that if any god swore falsely by this deity, he should be prohibited from having ambrosia and nectar for a whole year and nine days. The reason is this: Styx means sorrow; the name comes from *tristitia*, "sadness." The gods are happy forever, and thus also immortal. Thus, since they do not feel sorrow, they swear oaths by something contrary to their nature, that is, sadness, which is contrary to eternity.

69. [Untitled].

Phlegethon, a river of the infernal regions, means fire, for *phlox* in Greek is *calor*, "heat," in Latin. From this all things are created and, in truth, nothing is born without heat. Acheron arises as if from the depths of Tartarus. The estuaries of this river create Styx, and Cocytus arises from the Styx. This is the etymology, for philosophy holds this view: one who lacks joy is sad. Sadness is near to mourning, which is produced by death. Thus these streams are said to be among the dead.

70. A Story About Gallus.

Helicon is a mountain in Boeotia, also called Aonius. As he was strolling near this mountain, Gallus was led by one Muse to the rest, and there the one who said "mouldering fungus grows"[35] was made a poet. Pliny says that when air begins to be humid, the glowing ash that is accustomed to ascend with smoke is held back by the density of the air. It remains in lamps and imitates certain shapes, as of fungi.[36]

71. [Untitled][37]

A union of things has been effected that maintains itself in turn through eternity. It is varied in its order and law, so that even variety itself has eternity.

72. The Story of Peleus.

Peleus was loved by Hippolyta, the wife of Acastus. When he scorned her, she complained to her husband that she had been accosted about illicit sex. Angered, Acastus took Peleus hunting on Mount Pelius and left him there, unarmed, to be killed by Centaurs. He was saved by Chiron. After Peleus gathered an army, he destroyed the kingdom of Acastus and afflicted Hippolyta with a fitting punishment.

73. On Otus and Ophialtes.

Otus and Ophialtes were giants, the sons of Aloeus. They were so bold that they piled up mountains and endeavored to attack the heavens. In fact, they grew nine inches each month. However, they were struck by a thunderbolt and plunged into Tartarus.

74. On Salmoneus.

Salmoneus was the son of Aeolus (not the king of the winds, but a certain Aeolus who ruled in Elis). After he constructed a bronze bridge, Salmoneus drove his chariot over it to imitate thunder, and he ordered a man against whom he had hurled a firebrand to be killed. Later, he was struck by Jove's lightning and experienced a true thunderbolt.

75. On Phaethon.

Phaethon, son of Clymene and the Sun, grieved over a taunt made to him by King Epaphus of Egypt that he was not sired by the Sun, but by adultery. With his mother leading the way, Phaethon went to the Sun and demanded that, if he were truly his son, he should grant his request. When the Sun swore by the River Styx that he would do this, Phaethon asked that he be allowed to drive his chariot. The Sun could not refuse after he had sworn an oath. Phaethon took the chariot. When he veered out of the Sun's orbit and began to burn up the world, he was struck by Jove's lightning. He plunged into the River Eridanus in Italy, which is also called the Po. His sisters, Phaetusa and Lampedusa, wept over his death. Through the mercy of the gods they were changed into trees; some say into alders, others say poplars. This same man was first called Eridanus, but later he was called Phaethon from the light of the fire he caused.

76. On Lycaon.

Born from the blood of the Giants, Lycaon was a tyrant of Arcadia. When Jupiter saw his daughter Callisto in the retinue of Diana, he fell in love with her. Changed into Diana, Jupiter lay with her when she was separated from the rest of the nymphs, and he made her pregnant. When her swollen uterus betrayed the crime, an angry Diana removed her from her retinue. After ten months had passed, Callisto brought forth a little boy who was named Arctos. Angry that Jove's mistress was also a mother by him, Juno turned Callisto into a bear. After her son Arctos reached adulthood, believing she was a bear, he unknowingly attacked his mother. He tried to kill her with the javelin he threw. Jupiter did not allow the unknowing man to commit matricide. He immediately placed them among the stars. He is called Arcturus, and by another name, Arctophylax; she is called Arctos Mizon, and in Latin, Septentrio Major. This constellation does not move from its place, nor does it sink, for the reason which we are about to reveal.

77. On Thetis.

Thetis, daughter of Nereus and wife of Ocean, was Juno's nurse. When Juno was angry that Jove's mistress had been carried up into the heavens, she asked Thetis, out of love for the one she nursed, to prevent Callisto from sinking into the ocean.

78. On Lycaon.

Lycaon used to kill guests whom he had welcomed with hospitality. Provoked by grief over his ravished daughter, he wanted to discover whether he was the true Jupiter when he welcomed Jove with hospitality. Lycaon placed human flesh before him to eat so that after he violated the law of hospitality, he might kill him quickly if he were proven to be a mortal man. Jupiter was stirred to anger and burned his house. He changed Lycaon into a wolf and taught that the laws of hospitality must not be violated.

79. On Icarus (Icarius).[38]

A certain Icarus was the companion of Athenian Liber, who instructed him to pass on the use of wine to mortal men. When Icarus planted the vine and made it flourish, a he-goat went into the vineyard and ate the leaves, which seemed very tender. After the goat did this, Icarus killed it. He made a bag from its skin, tied it in the wind and made his companions dance around it. Thus a goat is still sacrificed to Bacchus because it injures vines. Indeed, victims are sacrificed to deities either through similarity or contrariety: through similarity, as a black sheep to Pluto; through contra-riety, as a sow, which is injurious to crops, to Ceres or a goat, which is injurious to vines, to Liber. Also, a she-goat is sacrificed to Aesculapius, the god of health, since a she-goat is never without a fever. Moreover, when the peasants drank to excess the wine Icarus gave them and became inebriated, they thought that they had received poison from him. They killed him on a mountain in the region of Marathon. His dog, whose name was Mera, returned to his daughter Erigone. When she followed the dog's tracks as he drew her along by her clothes, she came to her father's corpse and ended her life by hanging. The dog made amends for her death by his own. By the will of the gods Erigone was placed with the dog in the heavens. She is called Virgo and the dog is Syrius. Like-wise, Icarus was welcomed in the sky with his wagon. The wagon is called Septentrio or Arctos, and he is called Bootes or Artophilax. But after some time, such a sickness was let loose among the Athenians that their maidens were driven by a certain madness to hang themselves. Thus an oracle was consulted. It responded that this pestilence could be stopped if the corpses of Erigone and Icarus were sought again. These were sought for a long time and found nowhere. Then to show their devotedness, and to appear to seek them in another element, the Athenians hung ropes from trees. Holding on to these ropes, men were tossed here and there so that they seemed to seek the corpses in the air. Since most were falling, they decided to make shapes in the likeness of their own faces and hang these in place of themselves. Thus little masks are called *oscilla* from the fact that in them faces oscillate, that is, move, for *cillere* is "to move." So also they are called "little forks," by which grains are stirred.

80. On Saturn and Philyra.

When Saturn was having intercourse with his beloved Philyra, his wife Ops arrived. Fearing her presence, he changed himself into a horse. From this union Chiron was born, a man in half his body, a horse in half. Then Chiron dwelt on Pelion, a mountain in Thessaly; Achilles and Aesculapius are said to have been raised by him. Later he was placed among the stars by Saturn and became Sagittarius, "The Archer."

81. On Prometheus.

When Prometheus made man by command of the gods, he added parts from all the animals according to their nature. Thus he added the strength of the lion to man's stomach. He added fear from the hare, shrewdness from the fox, intelligence from the snake, simplicity from the dove. Moreover, he made man lifeless and senseless. Minerva marveled at his work. She promised him that if he wanted anything from the heavens, he might seek it for his work. Prometheus said that he did not know what goods were kept in the heavens, but if it could happen, he would raise himself up even to the gods above and from there, if he saw something suited to his work, he would carry it off better when he was present to judge. She brought him to the sky, transported within the borders of her sevenfold shield. When he saw that heavenly things were animated, enlivened by the force of fire, he stole fire by applying a torch to the wheels of Phoebus' chariot. He rendered man animate by applying fire to his breast. We say that he was named Prometheus, as if from the word *promanteci*, which in Latin we call "the foresight of god," because man was created from the foresight of god, and Minerva from heavenly wisdom, as it were.

82. On the Sacrifice of Prometheus.

The ancients used to consume whole victims in the holy flames. Prometheus, who used the excellence of his mind to fashion men, obtained a favor from Jove, namely, that men should throw part of the victim into the fire and consume part among their victuals. While this custom continued, Prometheus himself sacrificed two bulls. When he had first placed their livers on the altar, he covered the flesh of each bull, which had been put in one place, with the hide of an ox. The bones, which were next to it and covered with the rest of the skin, he put in their midst and gave Jove the opportunity to take the part he wanted. Thinking that each was a bull, Jupiter chose the bones for his portion. When he realized what he had done, Jupiter took fire away from mortals so that flesh would not be useful when it could not be cooked. But, thinking about restoring fire to mortals with Minerva's help, Prometheus ascended to heaven and, with a little torch applied to the Sun's rays, he stole fire. He made this known to mankind. The gods were angry because of this and sent two evils upon earth: emaciation and diseases. Moreover, with Mercury's help, Jupiter bound Prometheus with iron chains to a rock on Mount Caucasus in Scythia for thirty thousand years. He sent against him an eagle to devour his heart. Hercules visited Prometheus on Mount Caucasus. Eurystheus had sent him to fetch the apples of the Hesperides, but he did not know his way. Prometheus showed him the way. After his victory, as an act of gratitude, Hercules killed the eagle that was devouring Prometheus' heart. Concerning the release of Prometheus, this following reason was handed down to memory.

83. On Jove and Thetis.

When Jupiter was seduced by the beauty of Thetis, he wanted to take her for his wife. The Parcae foretold in their songs that Jupiter would be driven from his kingdom by a man who was born of him and Thetis. When Jupiter learned this from Prometheus, who had heard these sayings, he abandoned his wish to marry Thetis. For his good deed, Jupiter freed Prometheus from his chains and ordered his finger to be bound with stone and iron as a remembrance. Because of this custom, men still use rings comprised of stone and silver as a remembrance of friendship, and they began to keep them as a token of friendship. Now all these stories were devised for a reason. Indeed, Prometheus was a very intelligent man. Thus he is called Prometheus, "from intelligence." He was the first to teach astrology to the Assyrians; he studied it with very great care while living on Mount Caucasus. This mountain is positioned in the territory of the Assyrians, near almost to the stars. Thus he pointed out even the greater constellations and diligently indicated their risings and settings. An eagle is said to have devoured his heart because his solicitude was in the sky. Inspired by this study, he understood all the motions of the stars. Because Prometheus did this through intelligence, with Mercury, the god of intelligence and reason, as his guide, he is said to have been bound to a rock. Beyond this, he comprehended the nature of thunderbolts and revealed it to men. Through a certain art taught by him, fire from above was elicited. This benefited mortal men while they used it well. But afterward, through the evil use of mankind, it was turned to their destruction, as we read in Livy about Tullius Hostilius, who was consumed by fire with all his possessions. In fact, Numa Pompilius used fire with impunity only in sacrifices to the gods. Thus, when fire was stolen, disease is said to have been sent upon mankind by the angry gods.

84. On Cleobis and Bito.

It was the custom for a Greek priestess to proceed with yoked oxen to the shrines of Juno. On the solemn day oxen could not be found, for a pestilence had killed everything. The two sons of the priestess, Cleobis and Bito, submitted to the yoke for their mother and brought her to the shrines. Approving of their conscientiousness, Juno granted that their mother might ask what she wished for her sons. Giving a faithful answer, the mother said that the goddess herself should bestow what she knew to be beneficial to mortal men. And so, on the next day the sons of the priestess were found dead. From this it is shown that nothing is more preeminent than death.

85. On Chelone.

A certain maiden, Chelone, had an unrestrained tongue. In fact, when Jupiter married Juno, he ordered Mercury to summon all the gods and men and animals to the wedding. After this was done, only Chelone, mocking and refusing to go to the wedding, disdained to come. When Mercury noticed that she had not come, at Jove's command he descended to earth and hurled the dwelling of Chelone, which was situated above the water, into the sea. He changed Chelone herself into an animal of her own name.[39] In Latin we call this *testudo*, "tortoise." For a punishment, he made Chelone carry her roof on her back. Thus this name was given to arched buildings.

86. On King Proetus.

Proetus, the son of Abas, was King of the Argives. His wife's fertility proved inimical to his own happiness. Indeed, he raised three daughters and even brought them up to the time of marriage, but the intemperate tongues of those maidens produced the reasons for his unhappiness. For they are reported to have solemnly entered the temple of Juno and preferred themselves to the goddess. For this reason, the offended Juno turned the girls into heifers. She inspired in them the desire to seek out the woods to such an extent that they frequently bellowed and feared yokes on their necks. They thought that they had the shape of cows. They endured this condition until Proetus proposed to give part of his kingdom and one of these daughters as a wife to anyone who restored them to their former state of mind. Melampus, who was very skilled in the use of herbs, released the daughters of Proetus from their insanity, and he married one of the maidens. He became a partner in the kingdom and a son-in-law.

87. On Antigone.

Antigone was the daughter of Laomedon, King of the Trojans. Because of her arrogance over her own beauty, she preferred herself to Juno, who changed her into a stork.

88. On Arachne.

Arachne, also known as Lydia, was a certain girl who was a priestess of Minerva. She was very skilled in wool working. When she impudently preferred her own work to Minerva's and challenged her in weaving, Minerva changed her into a small creature of her own name, that is, a spider (arachne). She ended her life with a noose. Thus she hangs forever on high in the task in which she rejoiced, forever[40] spinning webs.

89. On Niobe.

Niobe, daughter of Tantalus, or Pelops, was the wife of Amphion. Because of her insolence regarding her offspring, she proved the power of Apollo and Diana. In fact, Niobe used to rejoice as she was accompanied by seven sons and just as many virgin daughters, to whom she had given birth by Amphion. Once, Tiresias' daughter, Manto, warned the Thebans in an oracle to pray to Latona and her children, Apollo and Diana. Niobe refused to be present at the holy rites, proclaiming that she was more potent than the power of Latona and her children. When Latona complained of this to her children, Apollo and Diana came to Thebes hidden in clouds. They slew Niobe, along with her sons and daughters. Niobe is said to have taken the children killed at Thebes to her homeland, that is, to

Mount Sipylus. There she grew hard. Indeed, she was changed into stone. These are Niobe's sons: Archemorus, Antogonus, Tantalus, Phedimus, Sipylus, Xenarchus, and Apinitos. Her daughters are Asticratia, Pelopia, Cheloris, Cleodoxe, Ogime, Etia, and Neera.

90. On Glaucus.

Glaucus was a certain man from the city of Pothnia. When he spurned the sacred rites of Venus, she became angry. She sent a frenzy into the mares that he used for his chariot, and they immediately tore him to pieces.

91. On Deucalion and Pyrrha.

To punish the vices of the human race, Jupiter covered the land with a deluge of rain and destroyed the race of men in the flood. But, through the mercy of the gods, Deucalion, the son of Prometheus, and Pyrrha, his sister, were carried in a little boat and escaped the downpour of rains on Mount Parnasus. At Delphi they learned through an oracle of Themis, a priestess of Earth, that the human race could return if they cast behind them the bones of their mother. They understood that "mother" meant the earth, for she is the mother of all things, and "bones" meant the stones of the earth. Therefore the oracle was fulfilled: the stones that Deucalion cast behind his back were turned into men and the stones that Pyrrha cast were turned into women. According to others, when they had fled to Parnasus, they made a fire to use at night, but, thinking that Jove could be displeased by this, Deucalion extinguished the fire. Because of this, Jupiter had mercy on them. He told them through Mercury to cast stones behind them.

92. On Lycus and Antiope.

Antiope, daughter of King Nycteus, was the wife of Lycus. After she was ravished through the deceit of Epaphus, the son of Io and Jove, she was cast out by her husband Lycus. When she had been driven away, Jupiter changed into a satyr, or, as some say, a bull, and had intercourse with her. He made her pregnant. An angry Lycus took Dirce as his wife. When she suspected that her husband Lycus had slept with Antiope, whom he first loved, she ordered her servants to bind his mistress and shut her up in the darkness. When the birth of her offspring approached, Antiope escaped from her chains through the will of Jove and left her sons, Zethus and Amphion, on Mount Cithaeron. Zethus was a rustic, but Amphion was skilled in music. Mercury gave him a lyre. To avenge the injuries to their mother, these sons killed Lycus. In fact, they tied Dirce to a fierce bull and killed her. From her blood originated the spring called Dirceus, named after her. This same Amphion came as a helper to Cadmus, Agenor's son, as he was founding Thebes. Amphion moved stones by the sweetness of his music, and by his singing he caused them to place themselves in the walls of their own accord.

93. On Epaphus.

Jupiter ordered Epaphus, the son of Jove and Io, to build a town in Egypt and to reign there. He established the town of Memphis and many others. By his wife Cassiope he had a daughter, Libya, who later possessed a realm in Africa. From her name the land is called Libya. She also left the inheritance of her realm to her son, Agenor.

94. On Lycurgus.

Lycurgus was the King of Thrace. He scorned Liber, and while he was cutting down vines, he cut his own legs and died.

95. Whence Wrestling Was Invented.

The sport of wrestling was first discovered by the Athenians. Also, the Trojans are said to take their origin from the Athenians, before Dardanus and Teucer. Thus they also worship Minerva.

96. On Jove and Europa.

When Mercury crossed over to Phoenicia at his father's bidding to drive the herds of that region to the shore, Jupiter changed into a bull. He intermingled with the cattle of King Agenor of Libya and compelled the maidens walking about on the sand to fall in love with him. Sporting with individual ones little by little, at last he violated Agenor's daughter Europa as she picked flowers in the fields, as is the custom of girls. Then he carried her to the island of Crete as she rode on his back, and by her he sired three sons: Minos, Rhadamanthus, and Aeacus. He named the third part of the world after Europa.

97. A Repetition.

Agenor had a daughter named Europa. Jupiter changed himself into a bull, a form that pleased him, and intermingled with Agenor's cattle. He violated Europa as she picked flowers in the fields, as is the custom of girls. Then he carried her to the island of Crete as she rode on his back. By her he sired three sons: Minos, Rhadamanthus, and Aeacus. They were made judges among the dead, and he named the third part of the world after Europa.

98. On Agenor and His Sons.

After his daughter Europa had been ravished, Agenor sent her brothers, Cilex, Cadmus, and Phoenix, to find their sister under this condition: not to return to him unless they found her. Cilex traveled to different regions and at last he founded Cilicia. Also, Phoenix founded Phoenicia. Since he could not find his sister, Cadmus learned from the oracle of Apollo where he should settle. He received the response that he should drive a cow separated from the herd, one with the sign of the moon on her flank. Where the cow would lie down from fatigue, there he should establish his city. Cadmus obeyed this command and came to the land that was later called Boetia, from *bos* (cow). When he sent his companions to the fountain of Mars to fetch water and went there himself after them, he saw that a dragon devoted to Mars had devoured them. He killed the serpent and sowed its teeth. From these sprang forth a host of earth-born men who killed each other by mutual wounds. But there were five survivors whose names are these: Echion, Ideus, Ciominus, Pelorus, and Hypereon. By the will of Minerva, these men joined Cadmus and Agenor, who made them helpers in founding Thebes. This was because of the sweetness of their singing, such that stones placed themselves in the walls of their own accord. They became leaders of the city.

99. On Cadmus.

Cadmus married Harmonia,[41] who was born of the adultery of Mars and Venus, but under a bad omen. After Venus instilled love in the daughters of the Sun and they died in the throes of this fatal disease, Vulcan, on the advice of Minerva, used his craft to make a necklace. The Gorgon's eyes, which were inserted as gems in this necklace, made Minerva an accomplice. Thus, Vulcan made a very beautiful necklace of unfortunate omen in such a way that the one wearing it would necessarily be overwhelmed by a heap of troubles. He gave it to Harmonia, the daughter of Mars and Venus. When she married Agenor's son Cadmus, she suffered many adversities due to this evil omen. Finally, when Cadmus fled the insolence of the Thebans and went to Illyrica, Harmonia was changed into a serpent along with him. Then Semele wore this necklace; she was killed by Jove's thunderbolt. Then Ino had the same necklace. When her husband Athamas killed her sons, Learchos and Palemon, she hurled herself into the sea to escape the madness of the husband pursuing her. Later, Agave had the necklace. She also killed her son due to her madness. These forenamed women were daughters of Cadmus and Harmonia. Jocasta also owned the necklace. By mistake she married her son Oedipus. Also Argia, daughter of King Adrastus, possessed this necklace; she was presented with it by her husband Polynices, who had received it through inheritance. She gave this same necklace to Eriphyle, the wife of Amphiaraus, to betray her husband. Later, her son Alcmaeon killed her to avenge his father. Seized by madness after his mother had been killed, Orestes consecrated this same necklace to Apollo; thrown into a spring, it is said to be visible there today. If anyone touches it, they say that the Sun is offended and that storms arise. The four sisters—Ino, Autonoe, Semele, and Agave—are said to be daughters of Cadmus because there are four kinds of drunkenness: from wine, forgetfulness, lust, and insanity. Thus these four received the name Bacchae. First is Ino. *Oinos* in Greek means wine. Second is Autonoe, as if to say *autonynone*, "not knowing herself." Third is Semele, as if to say *samalion*. In Latin we call this "unfettered body." Thus she gave birth to Father Liber, that is, drunkenness born of lust. The fourth is Agave, who is compared to insanity because, inebriated from wine, she cut off her son's head.

100. On Juno and Semele.

When Juno saw that Jove loved Cadmus' daughter Semele, also called Thione, she transformed herself into an old woman. Approaching Semele's door, she spoke to her thus: "If Jupiter loves you truly, as they say, demand that he come to you in the same way as he appears to Juno." When Semele requested this favor of Jove, he said that a mortal could in no way endure such a visit. But, as she was insistent, he finally promised that he would come to her in the same way as he comes to Juno. When he arrived with his thunderbolt, Semele could not bear it and died. After her womb was swiftly opened, Jupiter himself and Mercury concealed Father Liber in Jupiter's thigh so that he might be properly born after nine months. After the months of pregnancy were completed, Jupiter secretly handed him over to be raised by nymphs, who were then assembled on Mount Nisa. Later, Ino, the wife of Athamas, son of Aeolus, raised him. She was his aunt, the sister of Semele. Because of this, an angry Juno instilled madness in Ino's husband Athamas so that he wanted to kill his own sons. She hoped that if Athamas could find Father Liber, he might destroy him by the same fate as his sons. Athamas soon killed one son, Learchos, with the arrows of Hercules. After he killed the son and placed him on his own shoulders, he pursued his wife Ino, as Statius reports. Indeed, he says: "With his right hand turned toward his back, the descendant of Aeolus, bearing the corpse on his burdened shoulder."[42] Ino caught sight of her husband as he raved and pursued her. She snatched up her other son, Melicerta, and leapt with him into the sea. Then they were changed into sea gods: Melicerta into Portunus, called Palaemon in Greek, and Ino into the sea goddess called Leucothea in Greek.

101. Palaemon.

The body of Palaemon was driven toward Corinth, which is also called Ephyra. When people observed from his appearance that he was a king's son, they buried him. It is said that lustral games were instituted to honor him when he was buried.

102. On Liber.

After Liber reached adulthood, he made India subject to himself. Then on his return home he was in distress, plagued by thirst in the desert in the farthest part of Libya. He asked Jove to prove that he was his father by showing him water. Soon, from the sand a ram appeared; with its raised hoof it showed the place where Liber could dig and find water. Then, after the earth was opened, an abundance of water came forth. Or as others say, a ram appeared to him. With it as his guide, Liber found water. After the water was found, Liber asked Jove to place the ram among the stars. In the place where the water flowed, he set up a temple to Jove Ammon. He also made a statue with ram's horns. It was fashioned with ram's horns because the oracles given there are rendered amidst howling noises, and they are shrouded in obscurity. Also, he is called Jupiter Ammon because he was found in the sand, for the Greeks call sand *ammonia*. Moreover, Liber, also called Lyaeus, was received among the gods. He is said to sit on tigers, and he is depicted as a naked youth. Father Lyaeus is called Liber because the effect of wine makes minds free (liberas). He subdued the Indians, since this race is given to wine. Thus he is also called Lyaeus, as if to say "providing mildness." He is depicted as a youth because drunkenness is always hot, and as naked because a drunken man lays bare the secrets of his mind.

103. On Autonoe.

Autonoe, the third daughter of Cadmus, married Aristaeus, son of Apollo and the nymph Cyrene. By him she conceived her son Actaeon. When Actaeon was hunting in the woods, he suddenly came upon the naked Diana. She was bathing at a spring, worn out from the summer heat and continual hunting in the valley of Gargaphia. The angry goddess changed Actaeon into a stag, so that he could not speak. He was torn to pieces by his own hounds and died. Anaximenes explains this story so: "Actaeon loved hunting, but when he reached a mature age, he was afraid after he considered the dangers of hunting. He saw the rationale for this skill exposed. While he fled the danger of hunting, he did not set aside his love of hounds. By sustaining them for no purpose, he lost almost all his own substance. For this reason Actaeon is said to have been devoured by his own hounds."

104. On Aristaeus.

After his son was torn to pieces by hounds, Aristaeus left Thebes at the instigation of his mother and took possession of the island of Ceos. At this time Ceos was still empty of men. Later, he abandoned this island and made the crossing to Sardinia.

105. On Agave.

Agave, the fourth daughter of Cadmus, was the wife of Echion. She held Father Liber in such contempt that she even climbed a tree and ambushed him with an arrow. Likewise, her son Pentheus, King of the Thebans, despised Liber's sacred rites and denied that he was born of Semele.

Moreover, he scorned the words of Tiresias the seer, who warned that at the arrival of this same Liber, the Thebans would go forth wreathed with ivy and receive his sacred rites. Pentheus prevented his people from complying with these prophecies. He immediately ordered his servants to bring Liber before him in chains when he came to Thebes. To mock him in his madness, Liber changed into his companion Acetes. He was led away in chains and placed in custody. Thus madness was inflicted on mother and son. Agave, armed with fury, decapitated her son as he came to meet her; she thought that he was a bullock. Liber escaped unharmed. But, soon after the slaughter, Agave recovered her senses and realized that she had decapitated her own son.

106. On Tiresias.

Tiresias was a Theban, the son of Perieros. When he struck two serpents joined in intercourse on Mount Cyllene with his walking stick, he was changed into a woman. After a span of time, he saw the serpents a second time in the same place and, when he struck them again with his staff, he returned to his former shape. At this time there was a facetious debate between Jove and Juno as to whether a male or a female felt the greater pleasure in sexual intercourse. Tiresias, who had experienced each nature, was led before them as judge. He affirmed that a woman's passion is triple that of a man's. Angered by this, Juno cut off his hands and blinded him. Because of this Jupiter granted that he might live seven lifetimes and be regarded as the most veracious seer. Men say that Tiresias, of whom we are speaking, is understood to be time. This is said to be masculine in the spring because then there is firmness and planting of seeds. Therefore, while the springtime sees living things coming together with desire, it strikes them with its staff, that is, the heat of passion. Time is converted into the female sex when it is changed into the heat of summer. Indeed, men think of summer as a woman because then all things emerge, exposed, from their pods. Summer's bearing is prevented when autumn comes, and time changes to its prior state of receiving and binding. Finally, when Tiresias is brought to the two gods, that is, to the two elements, fire and air, for the sake of judging, he pronounces a just judgment. In fact, a triple means of fructifying seeds is present in air before fire, for air is wedded to the soil, abides in leaves, and is pregnant in pods. The sun, however, only knows how to promote ripeness in grains. Tiresias was blinded by Juno because the season of winter is enveloped in a cloudy atmosphere. Jupiter gave him foreknowledge in the dark mists, that is, conception of the future sprouts.

107. On Branchus.

Branchus, beloved of Apollo, was knowledgeable about future events. This is his story. When a certain man from Chios ate on the seashore and then set out again, he forgot his son, whose name was Smicrus. The boy came to the grove of a certain Patron,[43] who took him in. He began to pasture the she-goats with Patron's sons. Once they even caught a swan and covered the boy with its feathers. While fighting over which of them would offer Smicrus as a gift to their father, they grew weary of the struggle. After they cast aside the feathers, they found a woman. When they fled in fear, they were called back by her and advised that Patron would love Smicrus in a special way as his own son. The boys told Patron what they had heard. Then Patron loved Smicrus as his own son and gave him his own daughter as a wife. After she became pregnant by him, she saw in a dream that the Sun entered through her mouth and came out through her belly. Thus when the infant was born, he was called Branchus, since his mother had seen the Sun enter her uterus. When Branchus kissed Apollo in the forest, the god embraced him. After he received a crown and a staff, Branchus began to prophesy, and suddenly he entirely disappeared. A temple was built for him called Branchiadon, and temples were also consecrated to Apollo. These are known as Philesia, from the kiss of Branchus.

108. On Mopsus.

Mopsus, the son of Apollo and Ymas, was Jason's faithful friend. He was so skilled in prophecy that temples were dedicated to him after his death. From these sanctuaries people often receive oracular responses.

109. On the Sibyl.

Apollo loved Sibyl with a devoted love and allowed her to demand whatever she wanted from him. She took up sand in her hands and demanded so long a life. Apollo replied that this could happen if she would leave the island of Erythea,[44] where she dwelt, and never see it again. So she traveled to Cumae and stayed there. Weakened in bodily strength, she retained life in her voice alone. When the citizens of Cumae realized this, they were moved either by envy or mercy. They sent her a letter marked with chalk, according to ancient custom. When she saw this, she died. Some writers say that she is the one who composed the Roman prophecies because, after Apollo's temple was burned, the books were brought to Rome from where she was. The Sibyl was called Femonoe, for the name is an adjective. Indeed, every girl whose breast received the deity is called "sibyl." As others say, *sios* means "gods"; *bule* is "opinion." Therefore they say *sibyllas*, as if to say *siobulas*.

110. On Her Books.

It is known that during the reign of Tarquinius, a certain woman brought him nine books of the Cumaean Sibyl, according to Vergil. According to Varro, they were books of the Erythrean Sibyl. In these books were the oracles and remedies of the Romans. For them she demanded three hundred Philippics, which at that time were valuable. When she was scorned, she burned three books. She returned on another day and again demanded as much. Likewise, she returned on the third day with three books after another three had been burned, and she received as much as she demanded. These books were very diligently preserved in the temple of Apollo. In the time of the civil war, their verses were published among the people, and the evils of the Roman fate were made known to all.

111. On Io.

Io was the daughter of Inachus, King of the Argives. Jove loved her and was lingering with her, when Juno came upon them. Fearing that Io might be discovered, he changed her into a cow. He gave her to Juno, who asked for her, so that he would not have to reveal his mistress. Juno set Argus, the son of Aristos, over her as a guard; he had eyes in all his limbs. When Jupiter had Mercury kill him, Juno changed Argus into a peacock. In fact, she set a gadfly on Io. Tormented by this gadfly throughout the whole world, Io at last came to Egypt. There, according to the will of Jove, she was changed into Isis. Moreover, Isis is thought to have crossed the sea in the likeness of a cow because she crossed in a ship that had a picture of a cow on it. So that you might understand this more clearly, Egypt worships the boat of Isis.

112. On Isis.

Isis is a tutelary deity of Egypt. Through the motion of a rattle that she carries in her right hand, Isis signifies the accession and recession of the

Nile. Through a bucket that she holds in her left hand, she signifies the flowing of all waters. Furthermore, in the language of the Egyptians Isis is the earth, which they call Isim.

113. On Osiris.

Osiris was a giant, the husband of Isis. He was torn to pieces by his own brother, Typhon. Isis, Queen of Egypt, wept long for Osiris and searched for him. Finally, when he was found, she preserved him. Thus the people who keep his feasts pretend that they are seeking Osiris. Finding him at last, they greet him in Greek with these words: "We worship you."

114. On the Winnowing Fan of Father Liber.

Isis is said to have placed the discovered limbs of Osiris in a sieve. The same is true of Father Liber, among whose mysteries there is a winnowing fan because the rites of Father Liber pertain to purging of the soul. Men were cleansed by his mysteries just as a winnowing fan purges grains. Thus he is called Liber from this, since he liberates. Orpheus says that he was torn to pieces by the Giants.

115. On Venus.

Venus was angry because Proserpina, the daughter of Jove and Ceres, spurned marriage. She stirred up desire in Pluto to snatch Proserpina, daughter of Jove and Ceres, as she was picking flowers near the peak of Aetna. He had emerged from the Underworld out of fear of Typhoeus, who was spewing forth Aetna. Pluto seized Proserpina and was hurrying to flee, but he was impeded by Cyane the nymph who hindered him. The river Anapus loved her. Incensed with anger at the delay, Pluto struck her with his scepter to remove her as she hindered him. As a result, Cyane plunged headlong into the Underworld and was changed into water. This lake is near Arethusa.

116. On Proserpina.

Ceres searched the world with lighted torches for Proserpina, that is, Persephone. She had been snatched away by Father Dis. Ceres raised a cry along the highways and at the crossroads. Thus it remained part of her sacred rites that on certain days matrons howl all along the highways.

117. On Ceres.

Ceres did not cease her search for her daughter. When she approached a certain spring to quench her thirst, the Lycian peasants[45] saw her and prevented her from drinking. They stirred up the water with their feet and made a sound with their noses in front of her. Angered by this, Ceres changed them into frogs, which still croak in imitation of that sound. When the Pantagias, a river of Sicily, flows fully, it fills almost all of Sicily with its sound. Thus it is called Pantagias. Later, when this river was roaring as Ceres was seeking her daughter, it was ordered to be silent by the will of the deity.

118. On Her Search.

Ceres did not cease to seek Proserpina, who had been snatched away. She came to Celeus, King of the Athenians, in the city of Eleusis. When he welcomed her courteously and told her who had snatched Proserpina away, she was pleased by his kindness. Ceres promised that she herself would be the nurse for his son, Triptolemus, whom his wife Hiona had borne. The queen gladly accepted this nurse for her son and handed him over to her to be nourished.

119. On the Immortality of Her Nursling.

When Ceres wished to render her nursling immortal, she used to nourish him with divine milk by day, and at night she secretly buried him in a fire. Thus he grew beyond what mortal men were accustomed to. When his father marveled at this, he watched at night and, when Ceres buried the boy in the fire, he cried out. Angered, Ceres destroyed Eleusis. She also bestowed an eternal blessing on her nursling, Triptolemus, for she gave him fruits to propagate and a chariot hitched to serpents. Riding in this, he sowed the earth with fruits.

120. On Triptolemus.

When Triptolemus was scattering fruits among all peoples through the blessing of Ceres, he came to King Lyncus[46] and was almost ensnared there. For Lyncus, wanting to show that what his guest had brought was his own, tried to slay Triptolemus in an ambush. When he recognized the danger, Triptolemus began to pursue Lyncus with his sword. Changed into a wild beast of his own name, Lyncus was marked with the color of his ways.[47]

121. On King Cepheus.[48]

After Triptolemus returned home, King Cepheus was envious of him and tried to kill him. When the plan was discovered, he handed over his kingdom to Triptolemus at the command of Ceres. There Triptolemus established a town that he named after his father. He first instituted the sacred rites for Ceres. These are called Thesmophoria in Greek.

122. On the Finding of Proserpina.

When Ceres had long sought Proserpina, whom Pluto had snatched away, at last she found her in the Underworld. When she implored Jove's assistance in this matter, he responded that Proserpina could return if she had tasted nothing in the Underworld. But, she had already tasted the seeds of a pomegranate in Elysium. Ascalaphus, the son of Styx, had given these to her. Thus Proserpina could not return to the Upper World. In her anger, Ceres changed Ascalaphus into an owl. But Ceres later obtained this favor from Jove: Proserpina would be with her mother for six months and with her husband for six months. The story is fashioned this way because Proserpina is herself and also the moon. In the whole year the moon waxes for six months and wanes for six, that is, for fifteen days each month she seems to be waxing in the Upper World and waning in the Underworld.

123. On the Sirens.

The Sirens were daughters of Melpomene the Muse and the River Achelous. When they searched for Proserpina, whom Pluto had snatched away, and did not find her, they finally begged the gods to turn them into birds, so that they could pursue the one they were seeking not only on land but also on the sea. After this was granted, they searched for a long time. Finally, they came to the rock of Mars, which hung down close to the sea, and they began to dwell there. This was also granted to them: that they would remain safe as long as their voices were heard. The Sirens were part birds, part maidens, and they had the feet of cocks. They used to make music, one of them with her voice, another with pipes and the third with a lyre. They lived first near Pelorus, then on the island of

Capri. When sailors were enticed by their songs and approached the rocks where the Sirens sat as they sang, they were led to ruin. Their ships were dashed upon the cliffs, and the Sirens devoured them. Ulysses killed them by spurning them, for when he was sailing past the Sirens, he blocked the ears of all his companions with wax so that they did not hear them. He ordered that he himself be bound to the mast of his ship. Thus he heard the sweetness of their song and escaped danger. But the Sirens grieved so much over their defeat that they hurled themselves into the waves, and thus they tasted death. In truth, the Sirens were harlots. Since they led those passing by into poverty, they were thought to bring ruin upon them. Therefore Sirens in Greek are called in Latin *trahitoriae*, "those who draw to ruin," for enticement is brought about in three ways: either by song or by sight or by custom. The Sirens are said to be winged because they swiftly penetrate the minds of lovers. They are imagined with the feet of cocks because all habits are scattered by the state of lust. They were killed by Ulysses, who is called *olon xenos*, "stranger to all things," as it were, since wisdom is a stranger to all enticements of the world.

124. On Tantalus.

Tantalus, King of the Corinthians, was a friend of the gods. When he entertained them on a certain occasion and food was lacking, he wished to test their divinity. He killed his own son Pelops and set him as food before the invited deities. Then, although all the rest abstained, Ceres ate Pelops' shoulder. When the gods wanted Mercury to summon him to the heavens, an ivory shoulder was restored to him. Ceres alone is said to have eaten because she is the earth, which dissolves the body, preserving only the bones. Pelops is thought to have been recalled by Mercury for this reason: Mercury is the god of intelligence. Tantalus was condemned to the Underworld on this condition, that while standing in the river Eridanus in the Underworld and weak with hunger, he might not drink of the waters at hand or enjoy the nearby fruits. Thus avarice is shown through him, as Horace says: "Why do you laugh? With the name changed, the story is about you."[49] Canopus is a city near Alexandria, which Alexander founded in the likeness of his cloak.

125. On Danaus and Aegyptus.[50]

Danaus and Aegyptus were brothers. In fact, they were the sons of Belus and the brothers of Agenor, the father of Cadmus. By his many wives

Danaus had fifty daughters, and his brother Aegyptus had just as many sons. Aegyptus asked his brother Danaus to give his daughters to his sons in marriage. Danaus learned from an oracle that he would be killed at the hands of his own son-in-law. He went to Argos and is said to have been the first man to make a ship; from the name of the place, the ship was called Argo. Learning of this, Aegyptus sent his sons to pursue his brother and ordered them either to kill Danaus or not to return to him. After they reached Argos, they began to besiege their uncle. After Danaus saw that he could not resist, he joined his daughters in marriage to the sons of his brother. At the command of their father, the brides all killed their own husbands. Only Hypermnestra, the youngest, spared her husband, Lynceus. Later, Danaus was killed by him, so that the truth of the oracle was fulfilled. Because of this crime, the daughters are punished in the Underworld by this penalty: pouring water into perforated jars, they never see an end to their toil.

126. On Tityus.[51]

Tityus was the son of Earth. He was of such gigantic size that he filled up nine acres with the bulk of his body. He loved Latona. Because of this he was pierced by the arrows of Apollo and punished in the Underworld by this penalty: a vulture forever devours his liver, which is ever renewed.

127. On Sisyphus.

Through cruel villainy, Sisyphus seized a mountain positioned between two seas, the Sisyphean and Lechaean. He used to kill men who were passing that way by hurling a huge rock on them. In payment for this crime, he is said to roll a stone toward the peak of a mountain in the Underworld. Since the stone always slides back, he never rests from his labor of rolling it. Moreover, Jove admitted to him that he had seized Aegina, the daughter of the River Asopus. In his faithless inconstancy, the same Sisyphus revealed this to her father, who was looking for her, and for this he was condemned to that penalty in the Underworld. Of course Lucretius explains[52] everything wonderfully, confirming that all these things that are imagined among the dead are in our life. Indeed, he says that Tityus is love, that is, desire. According to physicians and doctors, this is in the liver, just as laughter is in the spleen and anger in the bile. Thus also the liver devoured by the vulture is said to be reborn as a punishment, for something done once does not suffice for desire, but it always breaks out again. Lucretius also says that the superstitious are meant by those over whom hangs the rock that is ready to fall. They always fear in vain and have a bad opinion of the gods and of heaven, for people who fear through reverence are religious. Through those who roll the stone he wishes to signify soliciting and rejection, since seekers, once rejected, do not cease to solicit. Also, through the wheel he intends to show tradesmen.

128. On Ixion.

Ixion, the son of Phlegyas, was ruler of the Lapiths, a race of Thessaly. Beloved of Jove, he was transported by his mercy to heaven; there he dared to seduce Juno to debauchery. She complained to Jove about his audacity, and, with his encouragement, she presented a cloud to Ixion in place of herself. Ixion had intercourse with it, and from this the Centaurs were born. But after he returned to mortal men, Ixion boasted that he had lain with Juno. For this reason Jupiter struck him with a thunderbolt and bound him to a wheel surrounded by snakes, to be whirled around in the Underworld.

129. An Explanation of This Same Story.

Just as in Latin discourse nothing is more pleasing than truth, so in Greek discourse nothing is more honored than falsehood. Men assert that Ixion is as if to say *axion*, that is, "worthiness," and Juno is the goddess of realms. Therefore worthiness striving after a realm deserves a cloud, that is, the likeness of a realm. And so Democritus writes that in Greece Ixion was the first man to seek the glory of a realm. He first gathered to himself one hundred horsemen. They were called Centaurs, one hundred armed men, as it were. In fact, they ought to be called *centippi*, from the fact that they are depicted as combined with horses. But in a short time Ixion secured a realm, and then was driven out and lost it. Thus he is said to be punished on a wheel because a whirling wheel is always turning in an unstable way. From this it is clear that all who strive after a realm through arms and violence suffer sudden seizures of their possessions and sudden forced removals. Furthermore, here is what we think Centaurs are and the setting of their story: a certain Thessalian king sent his servants to Peletronium to recover oxen that were tormented by a gadfly.

This is a town in Thessaly where the practice of taming horses was first discovered. The men were unable to overtake the oxen by running. After they invented the practice of taming horses, they were the first to mount them. Using the speed of the horses, they drove the oxen back to their stables with goads. While these men were riding the horses, they gave rise to the myth that they were Centaurs either by riding swiftly or by watering the horses with their heads bent down at the River Peneos. Other writers say that the story of the Centaurs was invented to express the swiftness of human life, since it is well known that a horse is very swift.

130. On Perithous.

Perithous, King of the Lapiths, a race of Thessaly, took Hippotamia as his wife. He invited the Centaurs, a neighboring people, to a wedding banquet, even Rhetus, Phobus, Hileus, along with very many others, and all the gods except Mars. Incited by wrath, the angry deity roused the banqueters to arms. Now the Centaurs had grown warm with wine, and they wanted to burst into the bedchamber of the girl who was being married. Full of wine, they also tried to seize the wives of other Lapiths, but they failed, overcome by the Lapiths and their king, Perithous. In this same fight Ceneus was killed. He was first a maiden, but later obtained a change of sex from Neptune as a recompense for being violated. He was invulnerable, but while fighting with the Lapiths against the Centaurs, he perished, fixed in the earth by repeated blows of their clubs. After death, he returned to his former sex.

131. The Story of Amulius and Numitor.

Amulius and Numitor were brothers. Amulius drove Numitor from his realm and killed his son. In fact, he made Numitor's daughter Ilia a priestess of Vesta to remove her hope of offspring, by whom he thought he could be punished. Mars lay with her, as they say. Thus Remus and Romulus were born. Amulius ordered them to be thrown into the Tiber along with their mother. Then, as certain writers say, the Arno made Ilia his wife, and as others say, Horace among them, she was the wife of the Tiber. Thus "uxorious river."[53] Suffering with Ilia as she lamented the murder of Caesar, the Tiber is said to have overflowed all the way to Rome, as if to avenge him. Faustulus the shepherd found these boys. His wife had recently been a prostitute named Acca Laurentia; she nursed the boys, who had been rescued by them. Later, after Amulius was killed, they recalled their uncle, Numitor, to his kingdom. Since the realm of Alba seemed small for them and their uncle too, Romulus and Remus departed. After they observed auguries, they founded a city. Indeed, Remus first saw six vultures; then Romulus saw twelve. This fact caused a war in which Remus was killed, and the Romans were named after Romulus. It happened by a kind of flattery that he was called Romulus, since he was pleased with a diminutive name. They are said to have been nursed by a she-wolf (lupa) to conceal the baseness of the founders of the Roman nation, and not unsuitably so, for we call prostitutes she-wolves (lupae). From this also comes the word for brothels (lupanaria), since it is well known that this animal is under the protection of Mars. Ilia was the mother of Remus and Romulus; she conceived them by Mars. After her death, she was buried on the banks of the River Anio, which flows into the Tiber, and since the Anio is an abounding stream, it took Ilia's ashes into the Tiber. Thus Ilia is said to have married Tiber. We know that Carthage was founded seventy years before Rome. In fact, between the fall of Troy and the origin of the city of Rome, there were three hundred and sixty years.

132. On the People of Phlegyae.

The Phlegyae were a certain island people who were irreverent and sacrilegious toward the gods. Thus an angry Neptune struck the part of the island that the Phlegyans inhabited with his trident and destroyed all of them.

133. On Acrisius.

Acrisius, a king of the Argives, received an oracular response that a man born of his daughter would be the cause of his death. Troubled by this, Acrisius made a bronze tower and put his daughter Danae into it. He placed girls as guards within; outside he stationed attendants and watchdogs. But Jupiter turned himself into a golden shower and lowered himself into her lap through chinks in the roof tiles. He made her pregnant. When this was discovered, her father shut her up in a chest and hurled her into the sea. Danae was carried to Italy, where a fisherman found her along with Perseus, whom she had brought forth there. She was taken to the king, who married her, and with her he founded Ardea. Turnus took his origin from here.

134. On Perseus.

Later, Perseus was sent by King Polydectes to slay the Gorgon. While he was on his way back, he carried her decapitated head in his hand as he flew. When the Gorgon's head was exposed, he changed his grandfather Acrisius into a rock.

135. On the Gorgons.

The three Gorgons were Sthenno,[54] Euryale, and Medusa, the daughters of Phorcys and the nymph Cretis. They used a single eye by turns. If anyone looked upon them, he was immediately turned to stone in amazement. Serenus says that they were three girls of singular beauty. When young men looked upon their beauty, they became stupefied in amazement. Thus it is thought that if anyone looked upon them, he was turned to stone. Moreover, they were very rich. Thus they are called Gorgons, as if to say "cultivators of earth," for the earth is called *ge* and cultivation is *orgia*. Now when their father died, Medusa succeeded to his realm. When she was sought by many in marriage because of her beauty, she could not flee from Neptune. Because she had intercourse with him in the temple of Minerva, and because she boasted over her looks, preferring herself to the goddess, Minerva transformed her hair into snakes. Thus she who had been sought at first by many suitors later feared these same suitors because of the ugliness of her countenance. Perseus, the son of Jove and Danae, killed her. He was sent by King Polydectes after he received from Minerva a shield of crystal, so that the Gorgon could not see him. Also, he first snatched away the eye of Phorcys' daughters, which they used for watching. Perseus took her decapitated head to Pallas to wear on her breast. From its blood was born a species of snakes. From her womb came forth a horse with wings, Pegasus, which flew to Mount Aonium in Boeotia. The horse struck the earth with its hoof and brought forth the Castalian spring, called either Pegasus or Helicon; it is sacred to Apollo and the Muses. From this philosophers and poets are thought to drink, for poets are priests of the Muses, as it were. Also, Medusa is said to have had snakes for hair because she was more cunning than her sisters. Perseus is said to have carried off her head because he killed her and carried off her fortune. He is said to have come there by flying because he came in ships.

136. The Interpretation of This Same Story.

The truth, honestly, is this: Gorgon is fear. First, it is the fear that weakens the mind; second, the fear that spreads profound terror over the mind; third, the fear that brings darkness not only over the mind, but even over our sight. Thus they receive their names. Sthenno is "weakness," Euryale is "vast depth," and Medusa is "forgetfulness." These names produce fear in people. Perseus destroyed all of these, for virtue is called *perseus* in Greek. He killed Medusa with the help of Minerva because virtue overcomes all fears with wisdom as its helper. Moreover, Minerva is imagined to have Medusa's head on her breast because all prudence is in that place, and prudence confounds others and shows them to be "stony" and ignorant. Pegasus was born from the Gorgon's seed, for fame is called *pegasus*, since virtue, overcoming all things, seeks fame for itself. From this [stream] poets drink because when they see this victress, they leap up in praise of virtue.

137. On Atlas.

Atlas was the son of Iapetus and Clymene. He received an oracular response from Themis, who was a priestess of the gods from the beginning. It said that he should not receive with hospitality anyone from the progeny of Jove if he wished to retain custody of the garden where golden apples grew. For this reason he kept Perseus, the son of Jove and Danae, out of the territory of Libya. Perseus had been sent by King Polydectes, the son of Magnes, to slay Medusa the Gorgon. After Perseus killed Medusa with Minerva's help, he returned and changed Atlas into a mountain by showing him the Gorgon's head.

138. On Minerva.

Once, while Minerva was making music on the pipes at a banquet of the gods, the deities observed her cheeks puffed up in so unsightly a manner, and they began to laugh. Not knowing why they were laughing, she went to Lake Triton and there, when she saw the puffing of her lips, she threw away the pipes. Marsyas found these and became skilled in playing them to such an extent that he likened himself to Apollo. When Apollo contended with him for a long time and could not surpass him, he turned his cithara upside down and began to make music. When the pipes were turned upside down, Marsyas was unable to equal Apollo. The god bound him to a tree and began to punish him by beating him to death with rods. From his blood arose a spring named after him. In memory of his infamy, Marsyas is depicted with a swine's tail.

139. On the Song of Apollo and Marsyas.

Midas, King of Lydia, was summoned to judge this contest. When he had heard their songs, he preferred Marsyas. An angry Apollo punished his foolishness by giving him the ears of an ass. Midas kept these from the sight of all by always wearing a crown on his head. While his freedman was cutting his hair, Midas feared that he would be defamed by him. He placed a crown on the freedman, promising that if he concealed his shame, Midas would make him a sharer in his kingdom. When the man could not keep what he saw to himself, he dug a pit and entrusted the secret to it by reporting to the earth that King Midas had the ears of an ass. Indeed, in this pit a reed grew. When shepherds made a reed pipe for themselves from this and wanted to play anything, the reed pipe made known what the king's barber had entrusted to the earth.

140. The Story of Midas.

Midas the king asked this of Apollo: that everything he touched should become gold. After this was granted, he was tormented by the effect of this wish, since he could not touch food without it being changed immediately into gold. He turned back to prayer and received the response from Apollo that if he submerged his head three times in the River Pactolus, he would soon be released from his suffering. After Midas did this and escaped his suffering, the river is said to have had golden sands from then on.

141. The Explanation of This Same Story.

But the truth is this: every greedy man dies of hunger because he puts a price on all things. Midas was a king who gathered all his money together, as Socrates says, and diverted the River Pactolus through countless turnings to water his own territory. The river customarily ran down to the sea. Because of avarice, he made the river productive at his own expense. In fact, Midas in Greek is *meden idon,* "knowing nothing," for a greedy man is so foolish that he does not even know how to benefit himself.

142. On the Contest of Neptune and Minerva.

Neptune and Minerva were contending over the name of Athens on the pinnacle of the acropolis at Thebes. It pleased the gods to name the city after the one who bestowed the better gift on mortal men. Neptune struck the shore with his trident and brought forth the horse, an animal suited to war. Minerva hurled her spear and created the olive. This was acknowledged as the better thing and was considered a sign of peace. Then the city was called Athens, as if from a *thanate,* "immortal." So, since the gift of Minerva was preferred over the gift of Neptune, someone who is offered an olive branch is said to be better than the one offering it. Thus there is that saying: "I give grass," that is, "I concede victory," for when someone in a struggle gives grass like a palm to one with whom he does not attempt to fight, he asserts that he is a better man. The olive branch is bound with fillets to show the sluggishness and weakness of the one offering it, for sheep always need help from others. Some say that the horse produced by Neptune was named Scitium, others say Siros, and others say Airos, which was the horse Adrastus had in the Theban War. Neptune is said to have created the horse because he is a swift deity, and mobile like a horse. Also, Castor and Pollux are said to keep horses under their protection because their stars are very swift.

143. On Minos.

When Minos, the son of Jove and Europa, approached the altars of his father to offer sacrifice, he begged the divine power that he might offer a victim worthy of his altars. And so, a bull bathed in wondrous brightness suddenly appeared. Minos marveled at it, and, forgetful of his religious duty, he preferred to make it the leader of his herd. Pasiphae, the daughter of the Sun and wife of Minos, is even said to have burned with passion for this bull. Therefore, scorned by his son, Jupiter brought a raging fury upon the bull, so that it devastated not only the fields of Crete, but all the cities too. King Eurystheus sent Hercules, and he overcame the bull by his power. He led it, bound, all the way to Argos. Although Eurystheus wanted to consecrate the bull to Juno, she hated the gift because it brought glory to Hercules. She drove the bull away into the territory of Attica, where it was called Marathonius, from Mount Marathon. Later, Theseus, the son of Aegeus, killed it. But let us speak more fully about Pasiphae and this same bull.

144. On Venus.

And so, after the adultery of Mars and Venus was revealed by the Sun, Vulcan encompassed their bed with very fine chains of steel. The unsuspecting Mars and Venus were enveloped by these and displayed in their mighty shame. All the gods witnessed it. Exceedingly pained by what had been done, Venus began to afflict every offspring of the Sun with unspeakable passions. Therefore Venus inflamed Pasiphae, the daughter of the Sun and wife of King Minos of Crete, to burn with love for a bull. Daedalus used his skill to enclose her in a wooden cow covered with the hide of a very beautiful heifer. She had intercourse with the bull. From this union was born the Minotaur, which was shut up in a labyrinth and used to eat human flesh. But Minos had more children by Pasiphae: Androgeus, Ariadne, and Phaedra.

145. On Androgeus.

Androgeus was a very strong athlete who defeated all opponents in the games at Athens. After a conspiracy was formed against him by the Athenians and the neighboring Megarians, whose king was Nisus, they killed him in an ambush. Grieving over this, Minos gathered his ships and started a war. After the Athenians were defeated, he established this penalty: each and every year they would send seven of their sons and seven of their daughters to be devoured by the Minotaur.

146. On Scylla.

When Minos was waging war against the Megarians, after the Athenians had been defeated, Scylla, the daughter of Nisus, the Megarians' king, loved him because he was handsome. To please the enemy, she brought to him a purple lock of hair cut from her father's head. Nisus considered the lock sacred, since he would possess his kingdom so long as he kept it intact. After he received the hair, Minos conquered the city and killed

Nisus. Later, after Minos rejected Scylla, she was changed into a bird because of her sorrow, and the dead Nisus was changed into a bird through the mercy of the gods. Today these birds are hostile to each other, for out of hatred for the old theft, that is, of the hair, the sparrow-hawk (nisus) pursues the ciris (scylla) to kill it.

147. On Theseus.

The Athenians sent their children to the Minotaur each year. In the third year, they sent Theseus, son of Aegeus, King of the Athenians. He was as mighty in strength as he was in beauty. Ariadne, the king's daughter, loved him. She feared that even if the Minotaur were slain, Theseus would not be able to free himself from the winding, intricate path of the labyrinth. She pleaded with Daedalus, the creator of the labyrinth, to help him by some stratagem. Daedalus ordered Theseus to unwind a ball of thread when he entered the labyrinth, so that as he came out he could master the twists and turns by rewinding it. This was done, and after the Minotaur was slain, Theseus the victor came forth. He fled and carried off Ariadne with him. But, wearied of love, he rejected her and abandoned her as she slept on Naxos, an island consecrated to Liber. When Liber took her as his wife, Vulcan gave him a crown adorned with seven stars. Liber placed it among the constellations in honor of his wife.

148. On Aegeus.

Now Aegeus gave this order to his son: if he returned as a victor, he would change his sails, that is, he would put white sails on his ships. Otherwise, he would come back with black sails. Theseus forgot this and did not do it. When Aegeus looked out over the sea from the shore, he thought that his son, who was returning without his sails changed, had been defeated. He hurled himself into the sea, to which he gave his name. In fact, because of his hatred of that place, Theseus sailed away. He came to Italy and founded Brundisium. When Minos learned that all these things had been done through the work of Daedalus, he thrust him into the labyrinth to be kept there, along with Icarus. But after the guards were bribed with gifts, Daedalus obtained wax and clay, under the appearance of making something with which to please the king. Then, after he put wings on himself and his son, he flew away. While Icarus was striving for higher places, the heat of the sun loosened the feathers on his wings.

He fell into the sea, to which he gave his name. The truth is that he escaped on the wings of his sail, that is, by sailing; or he spread his cloak on a ship to secure the help of the winds. In fact, Daedalus was first transported to Sardinia, then to Cumae. There he built a temple to Apollo and depicted all these things on its doors.

149. On Taurus.

But this is the truth: Taurus was a clerk of King Minos. Pasiphae loved him, and she had intercourse with him in the house of Daedalus. Since she gave birth to twins, one child by Minos and one by Taurus, she is said to have brought forth the Minotaur. After the guards were bribed, the queen freed Daedalus, who had been confined on account of this crime. After his son was cast into the sea, he was carried by ship to Cumae.

150. On Sciron.

Sciron lived on a cliff. He used to force his guests or passersby to wash his feet, and then he unexpectedly hurled them down the cliff. Theseus killed him.

151. On Theseus.

After the death of Hippolyta, Theseus, son of Aegeus and Aetra, made Phaedra, the daughter of Minos and Pasiphae, stepmother to Hippolytus. She tried to seduce him to debauchery. When Hippolytus scorned her, Phaedra falsely accused him to his father; she said that he tried to violate her. Theseus asked his father Aegeus, who was then a sea god, to avenge him. While Hippolytus was driving his chariot on the seashore, Aegeus sent a sea beast against him. Frightened by it, his horses tore him to pieces after he had been hurled from the chariot. After Hippolytus was killed, Phaedra hanged herself because she could not bear her passion. Moved by the chastity of Hippolytus, Diana recalled him to life with the help of Aesculapius, son of Apollo and Coronis, the daughter of Phlegyas. He was born when his mother's womb was cut open. Apollo had heard from the raven, which he used as a guardian for Coronis, that she committed adultery with Lycus. The angry god pierced her with his arrows when her offspring was ready to be born. In fact, he made the raven, which was covered with white feathers, black instead of white and took it under his protection. When the womb of Coronis was cut open, Apollo brought forth Aesculapius, who became skilled in medicine. Grieving because his daughter had been violated by Apollo, Phlegyas, the father of Coronis, burned his temple at Delphi. Thus he was sent to the Underworld by the arrows of Apollo. Later, Jupiter killed Aesculapius because he had recalled Hippolytus to life. Thus an angry Apollo shot the Cyclopes, the fashioners of Jupiter's thunderbolts, with arrows. On account of this deed, Apollo set aside his divinity and took on the shape of a mortal man. He was sent by Jove to pasture the herds of King Admetus for a period of nine years near the River Amphrysus in Thessaly. But Diana commended Hippolytus, who had been recalled from the Underworld, to the nymph Egeria in Aricia. She ordered him to be called Virbius, as if to say *vir bis*, "twice a man." But these stories are fables, for this man, although he is introduced everywhere as chaste, and he always lived alone, is said to have had a son. In truth, however, Virbius is a deity joined to Diana, as Attis is joined to the Mother of the gods, Erichthonius to Minerva and Adonis to Venus. Indeed, individual deities have lesser powers as their attendants. Also, poets vary the fables, for Vergil says that Hippolytus was recalled from the Underworld, but Horace, on the contrary, says "Diana does not free the chaste Hippolytus."[55] Although the mangled Hippolytus returned to life according to the fables, he could not escape the demands of death.

152. On Oenopion.[56]

Oenopion, also called Pelargus, was a king who had no children. When he was encouraged by Jove, Mercury, and Neptune, whom he had received hospitably, to request something from them, he asked them to grant him children, without a wife. They ordered that the urine of an ox sacrificed to them be put in a skin and covered with earth, to be removed from the ground when the months of pregnancy were completed.[57] After this was done, a boy was found, to whom a name was given from the urine, so that he was called Orion. In the Doric dialect this was changed: the diphthong *ou* was changed into *o*, because the first syllable is generally found to be short, although it might be naturally long, for in Greek the letter *u* is withdrawn, and the *o* remains short. Later, Orion became a hunter. When he wanted to lie with Diana, as Horace tells us, he was killed by her arrows. According to Lucan, he perished when a scorpion was sent against him with the help of Earth. Jupiter bore him up to heaven and made his constellation famous for storms. Diana also carried her avenger up to heaven, but actually Orion is said to have been killed by the scorpion because when it rises, he sets. In fact, because of his great size, Orion rises for many days. Therefore, those who are inexperienced [in astronomy] are doubtful about the time of a storm. At a certain time this same Orion was caught by a king when he wanted to ravish his daughter. In his anger, the king put out his eyes. When the blind Orion consulted an oracle about how to recover his sight, the response came to him that his sight could be restored if he would proceed over the sea to the east so that he might look forever at the Sun's rays, which he could therefore do. For when he heard the roar of the Cyclopes fashioning thunderbolts for Jove, he was led by the sound to them. He placed one of them on his shoulders and, with him as a guide, he carried out the oracle's directions.

153. On Perdicca.

Perdicca, the son of Polycaste, was a hunter. Seized by love for the Mother of the gods, he seethed with immodest desire and pined away with shame for this new outrage; he was brought to a state of extreme thinness. Perdicca is also said to have invented the saw. But as Fenestella Martialis writes, he was first a hunter. When the bloody devastation of the slaughter of wild animals and the wandering chase displeased him, and when he saw his young fellow hunters, Actaeon, Adonis, and Hippolytus, suffer a wretched death, he repudiated his former skill and pursued agriculture. For this reason he is said to have loved the Mother of the gods, as if to say the earth, the "mother" of all. Also, worn out by this toil, he became emaciated. And since he drew all hunters away from the disgrace of their former skill, he is said to have invented the saw, that is, evil speaking. His mother was Polycaste, as if to say *polycarpe*, which in Latin we call *multifructum*, "abounding in fruit," that is, Earth.

154. On Bellerophon.[58]

When Bellerophon, the son of Glaucus, came unknowingly to King Proetus, the son of Abas, Proetus' wife Sthenoboea, or Anteia, burned with love for him. She could in no way gain her desire that he sleep with her, so she lied to her husband that Bellerophon had solicited her for sexual intercourse. Proetus sent Bellerophon to his father-in-law, Adiuvates, also called Gabates, and he gave him a written account of the matter to be brought to his father-in-law. After he read this, Adiuvates wanted to kill such a man. Bellerophon freed himself from the impending danger by his prudence and the help of his chastity. Yet, so a monstrous danger might prove his virtue, he was sent to slay the Chimaera, which was then devastating the lands of Lycia. Mounted on Pegasus, the horse born of the Gorgon's blood, which he had received through the mercy of the gods, he destroyed the Chimaera. While he was returning from there, riding Pegasus, the horse he had taken, and delighting in his victory in so great an adventure, he penetrated the heights of heaven. Because of the disturbance of his mind as he looked down at the earth, he was stupefied and fell. In fact, Pegasus was received among the constellations. The Chimaera was said to be a beast with the face of a lion, its lowest parts a serpent and its middle part a she-goat. But the truth is that there is a mountain in Cilicia whose peak burns even today. It was so called [Chimaera] because there are lions there. Furthermore, the middle parts are pastures and the lowest parts of the mountain are indeed full of snakes. Bellerophon made this place habitable. Thus he is said to have killed the Chimaera. Also, after Bellerophon slew the Chimaera, he was sent to conquer the Calydonians. After they were defeated, Adiuvates wiped away the charges made against Bellerophon. He praised his virtue and gave him another daughter of his, Alcimene, as his wife. After this fact was made known, Sthenoboea killed herself.

155. On Jove and Leda.

Jupiter changed into a swan and had intercourse with Leda, daughter of Thestius[59] and wife of Tyndareus. She gave birth to Pollux and Helen by Jove, and by Tyndareus she gave birth to Castor. But, feeling pity for his brother's mortality, Pollux rescued him from death by going alternately in place of his brother to the Underworld. As a reward for their unanimity, Jupiter brought them to heaven and made their stars beneficial to sailors, although their sister's star is a sign of ruin to sailors. It is thought that they go to the infernal regions by turns, one for the other, because their stars are so disposed that one rises while the other sets. Moreover, time indicates that Helen was immortal, since she endured for so long. It is known that her brothers were with the Argonauts, that the sons of the Argonauts fought with the Thebans, and that the sons of those fighting there were present at the fall of Troy. Thus if Helen were not immortal, without a doubt she could not have endured for so many ages. We read that before she wed Menelaos, she was carried off by Theseus and entrusted to the care of Proteus in Egypt. Her star, called Urania, is said to hollow out an apple tree, and to bore through the bottom of a ship by blazing with so great a burning fire that the bronze is melted by the heat. When sailors observe this star fixed over a ship, they do not doubt that they will perish.

156. On Theseus and Perithous.

Theseus and Perithous, one of the Lapiths, formed a conspiracy to take as wives the daughters of Jove. For Theseus, they seized Helen, daughter of Jove and Leda, while she was still a small girl, and they entrusted her to the care of Proteus in Egypt. When they did not find anyone who might be joined to Perithous, they conspired to go to the Underworld to seize Proserpina. When this was done, they were caught there and condemned to harsh punishment. Yet Hercules freed Theseus in such a way that part of his body was detained there and part was torn off by Hercules and taken away. But Vergil says the contrary: "Wretched Theseus sits [there] and will sit forever."[60] Thus are stories generally varied by poets.

157. On King Athamas.

King Athamas, son of Aeolus and brother of Creteius, had a wife called Nubes, or Nephile. By her he had Phrixus and Helle. When Nubes was aroused by the frenzy of Father Liber, she sought out the forest and did not want to return to her husband's hearth. Athamas put a stepmother named Ino over his children. With a stepmother's hatred, Ino plotted the death of the children. She asked women to destroy the grain that was to be sown. After this was done, a famine arose. When the city sent a messenger to consult Apollo, Ino bribed him to report that the oracle had declared that the children of Nubes should be sacrificed; indeed, Ino said that they had set fire to the grain. Fearing the ill will of the people, their father handed over his children to their stepmother's judgment. When the hostile stepmother was pursuing them as they were wandering in the forest, their own mother came and pointed out to them a ram distinguished by its golden fleece. Under the inspiration of Juno, their mother ordered the children to climb onto it and to cross over to the island of Colchis, to King Oeta, son of the Sun, and there to sacrifice the ram. They obeyed their mother's command and the ram carried them over the sea. Helle, the girl, one of the weaker sex, fell and gave her name to the Hellespont. Phrixus reached Colchis. There he obeyed his mother's order and sacrificed the ram. In the temple of Mars he dedicated the golden fleece and set a sleepless dragon as a guardian over it.

158. On Pelias.

Pelias, the son of Neptune, possessed the summit of Hiulcus [sic]. Prophecies said that he would be deprived of his citadel by a man who would arrive there with one foot bare on a day when he was sacrificing to Neptune. Thus, when Pelias was carrying out the annual sacrifice to his father Neptune, Jason, the son of Aeson, came to him wearing a shoe on one foot only. The shoe on the other foot had been lost in the mud of the River Anaurus. Pelias observed him and remembered the oracles. He sent Jason under the pretext of glory to seek the golden fleece from King Oeta at Colchis, yet with this intention: that the dragon would kill him. But an oracle had informed Oeta that he could abide in his kingdom as long as that golden fleece remained in the temple of Mars. Jason was eager to acquire the golden fleece, and he gathered together certain brave men of Greece. He took with him Hercules and Castor, along with his brother [Pollux]. After a ship was built called Argo (hence they were called Argonauts), and Tiphys was made helmsman of the ship, Jason ventured to sail upon a sea untried before.

159. On Jason.

When the ship Argo was built on Mount Pelius in Thessaly, Earth grieved that the sea, untouched before, had now become a passageway, so she put rocks into the sea. When those who were building the ship saw this, they sent her unfinished onto the sea. Thus Lucan writes: "Carried off with smaller stern, the Argo was led down the mountain slopes."[61] Indeed, the whole ship is not formed [as a constellation] in the sky, but only from the helm to the mast. When they reached Colchis, Jason was welcomed by King Oeta. He loved the king's daughter Medea and had sons by her. But after Oeta received responses from oracles saying that he should beware of death from a stranger, the offspring of Aeolus, he killed Phrixus, whose sons boarded a ship to cross over to Athamas, their uncle. After they were shipwrecked, they were welcomed by Aeson. Although Jason was eager to get the golden fleece, he feared the watchful dragon that he saw. King Oeta granted him the right to take away the fleece under this condition: if he would yoke bulls breathing fire from their nostrils and then sow the dragon's teeth. The Colchians had not tamed these bulls. Although this seemed difficult to him, Medea, daughter of King Oeta, was an enchantress. Delighted by Jason's strength, she loved him. Medea enchanted the serpent and put it to sleep. Jason immediately killed it and took its teeth. After he had yoked the fire-breathing bulls with the help of Medea's skills, he went into the field and sowed the teeth. On the third day an armed host arose from the field and attacked Jason. Then, thanks to Medea's craft, this army was incited against itself and destroyed by mutual wounds. Having obtained the victory, Jason took the fleece and carried it back to his country. When Medea left Colchis and followed Jason, she reached Italy. There she taught remedies against snakes to certain people around the vast Lake Fucinum. These people called her Anguitia because snakes were distressed (angere) by her charms.

160. On Medea.

After Jason promised marriage and took Medea to Greece, he was united to her. Since he had witnessed her skills in many ways before, he asked her at length to transform his father Aeson into a youth. She had not yet set aside the love that she had for him. In a cauldron, she boiled herbs whose power she knew; they had been acquired from diverse regions. After Aeson had been killed and cooked in the warm herbs, she restored him to his former vigor.

161. On the Nurses of Liber.

When Father Liber observed that Aeson's old age had been banished by Medea's medicines, he asked her to restore his nurses to the vigor of youth also. She consented to his request and restored his nurses to youthful vigor by the same medicines as she used to make Aeson young again. Then Medea confirmed an eternal pledge of good will with him. But when Jason spurned her and took as his concubine Glauce, Creon's daughter, Medea gave his mistress a tunic imbued with poisons and garlic [*sic*]. When she put this on, Glauce began to burn with fire. Jason raged against Medea, but she did not endure his wrath. She fled on a winged serpent, after her own and Jason's sons were slain.

162. On Pontia.

Pontia, the daughter of Petronius, was a harlot. For the sake of money, this woman killed her own sons, so that she might give the money to a lover. Afterward, she betrayed herself; she held a great banquet, where she died when her veins were cut open.

163. On Amycus the King.

Amycus, King of the Bebrycians, was the son of Neptune and Merope.[62] He always used to set a trap in the woods of Bebrycia, so that if any stranger happened to come there, he was killed in a contest when Amycus provoked him into a boxing match. After Amycus did this for a long time, finally he met with Pollux, who had come to Bebrycia with the Argonauts. Provoking him into a boxing match, Amycus was defeated and killed by Pollux in the same contest.

164. On Venus.

After the Sun detected the adultery of Venus and Mars, Vulcan bound both of them in bed with very fine chains on the island of Lemnos where he lived. Although the women there paid a tenth part of their produce to all the gods each year, they said that Venus alone should be passed over. In honor of Vulcan they condemned her for her adultery. In anger, Venus let loose a goatish stench upon them. Their husbands cursed them and abandoned Lemnos out of loathing for their wives. They went to the Thracians and took their daughters for themselves in marriage. When this became known to the women of Lemnos, they all swore an oath against the whole race of men. Venus urged them on, and they killed all the men when they returned from Thrace. Among them only Hypsipyle had mercy on Thoas, her father. Not only did she spare him, but even followed him as he fled to the seashore. Then Liber, who was actually his father, appeared to Thoas and guided him to the island of Chion by a prosperous voyage. When the Argonauts came to Lemnos, the Lemnian women received them with hospitality and had intercourse with them. Hypsipyle had two sons by Jason: Euneus and Thoas. Although the

Argonauts were detained there for many days, they departed after Hercules chided them. After the Lemnian women learned that Hypsipyle had saved her father, they tried to kill her. As she was fleeing, she was captured by robbers and carried off to Nemea. There she was sold into servitude to Lycurgus, the king of that region. In his service, she nursed his son Opheltes, later called Archemorus. The boy was killed by a serpent. Angered by this loss of his child, King Lycurgus wanted to exercise the right of ownership over Hypsipyle and to sacrifice her in honor of his son. He was prevented by the Greeks to whom she showed a spring when they were thirsty, while in the meantime the boy perished. Also, the Greeks had received an oracular response that they would not reach Thebes unless the shades of Archemorus were placated. For this reason they established funeral games. Jason's two sons by Hypsipyle were present at these games. She had left them on Lemnos when she fled, and they were now seeking their mother. They prevailed in running races, and when the herald announced their names as sons of Jason and Hypsipyle, their mother knew them. After they recognized her and persuaded the king, they soon took her back to Lemnos.

165. On Phineus.

Phineus, the King of Arcadia, placed a stepmother over his children, and at her instigation he blinded them. Angered over this, the gods took away his sight and sent the Harpies against him. For a long time they snatched his food away from him. He welcomed Jason with hospitality when he came to Colchis with the Argonauts because of the golden fleece. Phineus even gave him a guide. Prompted by this act of kindness, the Argonauts sent him winged youths to drive away the Harpies. They sent, I say, Zetes and Calais, the sons of Boreas and Orythia, the daughter of Erectheus. When the young men pursued them with drawn swords, the Harpies were driven from Arcadia. Then the youths came to the islands called Plotae. When they wanted to go farther, they were warned by Iris to stay away from the hounds of Jove, so they changed the direction of their flight. Their turning, that is strophe, gave its name to the islands [Strophades]. Phineus is put forth as a model of avarice; he is called Phineus from *faenerando*, "lending at interest." Therefore he is blind because all avarice is blind; it does not see its own goods. So the Harpies plunder his food, since their plundering does not permit him to consume anything of his own. Also, Zetes and Calais drive them from his sight [sic], for in Greek "seeking after good" is called *zetrocalon*, since all plundering is put to flight with the coming of goodness.

166. On Oedipus and the Monster That Was Called Sphinx.

The Sphinx was a monster with wings and claws like the Harpies. Sitting on a rock overlooking the highway, she proposed riddles to those passing by. When they could not solve them, she suddenly swept down with her wings and dragged them to herself on the cliff with her claws. Oedipus, King of Thebes, solved the obscurities of her speech by his cleverness and defeated her. Thus he killed her.

167. On Oeneus.

Oeneus was the son of Parthaeon and king of Aetolia, whose chief city was Calydon. By his negligence of sacred rites, he threw the state of his kingdom into disorder. Indeed, while celebrating the annual prayers for the success of his empire, he neglected the divine majesty of Diana. She sent a boar of immense size to his territory. After the boar devastated the Calydonian lands, it was called Calydonius, from the city of that nation. Overwhelmed by its ferocity, Oeneus published an edict declaring that the man who should kill the monster would have half his kingdom. His son Meleager summoned youths who were gathered from everywhere to this expedition of a new sort. Among these also came Atalanta, daughter of Iasius, the greatest huntress, actually a companion of Diana. She was the first among all those in the woodlands to strike the aforementioned boar with an arrow. Meleager later intercepted the wild beast as it came toward him and killed it. To show his thanks to the girl who shone among men by her success, he gave the hide of that monster to her, along with its head, as proof of her glory. Also, among the retinue of Diana, she is the one who had intercourse with this same Meleager; she bore a son named Parthenopaeus, who later perished in the war at Thebes. But when Atalanta was honored with such a gift, Plexippus and Agenor, the maternal uncles of Meleager, were indignant that a maiden was preferred to them. They deprived her of the spoils she had received. When an angry Meleager killed his uncle Plexippus because of this, he hastened his own death, for he lost his mother's affection. His mother Althea secretly kept a firebrand that had suddenly appeared in the palace when Meleager was born. Clearly it was of this sort: that the young man would enjoy life so long as it was preserved. In anger his mother immersed it in flames and extinguished it; the death of her son followed. Later, when she realized the crime she had committed, she hanged herself. Another calamity followed this sorrow, for Meleager's sisters wept for their brother so much that, through the mercy of the gods, they were turned into birds, which today are called *meleagrides*.

168. On Harpalyce.

After a multitude had surrounded her aged father, Harpalyce freed him more quickly than can be believed of a woman. Hence she is said to surpass even a river in swiftness.

169. On Oenomaus.

Oenomaus was the King of Elis and Pisa. He had very swift horses, seeing as they had been sired by the blowing of the winds. He killed many of his daughter Hippodamia's suitors. They were challenged to a chariot race under the stipulation that he would hand over his daughter if he were defeated, or he would slay them if he were victorious. Hippodamia loved Pelops, son of Tantalus, who had received horses from Neptune that were suited to chariot racing. By their speed they surpassed everyone. Thus Hippodamia bribed her father's charioteer, Myrtilus, with a promise of first intercourse. He made axles of wax for Oenomaus' chariot and Pelops won the race. Then Myrtilus demanded the reward that the girl had promised. Her husband hurled him into the sea. To this he gave his name, for it is called the Myrtoan Sea after him.

170. On Mercury.

Vexed that his son Myrtilus had been hurled into the sea and robbed of life by Pelops, the son of Tantalus, Mercury found a vengeance to console a father's childlessness. He caused so much discord for Pelops' sons, Atreus and Thyestes, that they violated the laws of brotherhood. Thyestes knew that the kingdom was fated to remain in possession of the one who had a ram with golden fleece. At that time Atreus was ruling the kingdom and possessed the fleece. Thyestes hoped that by seducing Europa, his brother Atreus' wife, it could be transferred to himself. After Atreus learned this, he expelled his brother, along with his two sons.

Later, he feigned forgiveness and summoned Thyestes. Then he set before him his own murdered sons to eat. At this outrage committed toward a brother, the Sun is said to have turned himself away from their territory. Moved by grief, Thyestes sought advice from the oracles. They responded that certain vengeance would come to him through one who was born of himself and his own daughter Pelopia. He swiftly embraced his daughter and penetrated her. By her a boy was born whom she threw into the woods because of her conscience. This boy was nourished by the teats of a she-goat. From this he took his name, Aegisthus. When he grew up, he killed Atreus to avenge his father. This same Aegisthus killed Agamemnon after he committed adultery with his wife, Clytemnestra. Later he himself was overthrown and killed by Orestes, the son of Agamemnon, who also killed Clytemnestra, his mother. She had killed her husband for the sake of Aegisthus, her lover. Indeed, when Agamemnon had entered his house, she brought him a garment without an opening for the head. When he wanted to put it on and could not find the opening, he was killed by Aegisthus, the adulterer. Thus she was later killed with Aegisthus by her son Orestes.

171. On Jove and Alcmena.

When Jupiter loved Alcmena, the wife of Amphitryon, he changed his appearance into that of Amphitryon. Then he came to the city of Tyrinthia to seduce her. So that the pleasure of sleeping together with her would not be lessened by the arrival of day, Jupiter commanded that night to last three times as long. So on that night the Moon completed her journey three times. Hercules was conceived from this intercourse with Alcmena.

172. On Hercules.

Hercules was born with Iphicles, the son of Amphitryon. But since Juno hated all the children of Jove except Mercury, she sent two serpents against Hercules. Iphicles fell back with fear in his cradle. By his wailing he roused his parents. When they got up, they saw Hercules holding in his hands the snakes sent against him by his stepmother's hatred.

173. Why He Is Called Hercules.

Certain authors want Hercules to be called Alcides, from *apo tes alkes,* that is, "from strength." It is not because in his youth he had this name from Alceus, Amphitryon's father. Also, we know that surnames are given from accidentals. Wiser men imagined Hercules to be strong more in mind than in body, so that his twelve labors could be referred to something, for although he did many things, only twelve are attributed to him on account of twelve known signs. The reason Hercules is said to have dragged Cerberus out of the Underworld is because he scorned and subdued all passionate desires and all worldly vices. For Cerberus is earth, that is, she who consumes all bodies. He is called Cerberus as if to say *creoborus*, "devouring flesh." Aconite is said to have sprung forth from the foam of this Cerberus, which he spewed when he was dragged, and it is called *a cote* because it springs forth from stones. Thus we read in Vergil: "Reclining on bones,"[63] for the earth quickly consumes bones. When Hercules went to the Underworld to drag Cerberus out and also to seize Proserpina, he was exhausted by his labor. He covered his head with a poplar crown. Thus the inner part of the leaves clinging to his temples cleansed the sweat from his head, but the outer part remained black because of the heat of the Underworld. Since Charon the boatman took him on board, he spent a whole year in chains. Hercules is said to have shuddered in horror when Juno offered Megara to him.

174. On Diomedes.

Diomedes, King of the Thracians, had horses that used to eat human flesh. In fact, when many guests had died in his lodgings, he welcomed Hercules with hospitality. So that he might not be deceived by him and perish, Hercules made Diomedes become food for his own horses. After the cruel tyrant had been killed, Hercules led away the horses. He tamed their ferocity and brought them back to their accustomed food, that is, to pasture, and gave them to his son Cromis to keep.

175. On Geryon.

Geryon, who had three sets of limbs, was the King of Spain. Hercules sailed there in a bronze jar and killed a two-headed dog that Geryon had. Geryon is imagined to have had triple limbs because he ruled over three islands that lie near Spain: Balearica Minorca, Balearica Majorca, and Ebusa.[64] He is thought to have had a two-headed dog for this reason: because he was very powerful in both land and naval battles. Hercules conquered him and led away his cattle. Hercules is thought to have sailed to his land in a bronze jar because he had a strong ship fortified with bronze. When Hercules returned from Spain through Campania, he held a triumphal procession in a certain town. From this, the town is called Pompeii. Later, near Baiae, he made a pen for the cattle and enclosed it. This place was formerly named Boaulia, but today is called Boale. Coming then to Italy, he was welcomed hospitably by Evander.

176. On Evander.

Evander the Arcadian was a grandson of Pallas, prince of Arcadia. He killed his own father, with the encouragement of his mother Nicostrata, who was also called Carmentis because she prophesied through songs (carminibus). Because of this murder, Evander abandoned his own land and came to Italy. He drove out the native peoples, took the lands where Rome is now, and founded a small town on the Palatine hill. His hill was called Palatine after Pallas, his grandfather, or after his own daughter Pallas. She was ravished by Hercules and buried there. Or certainly he named it after his son Pallas who was killed by Turnus and buried there. When Hercules stayed there for some time and pastured the cattle that he had led away after he killed Geryon, a servant of Evander's, Cacus, stole some cattle for himself. He dragged them by the tail to a cave, so that they might not lead anyone seeking their tracks to the cave, since their foot tracks were turned around. But Hercules found them after seeking them for a long time when the lowing of one ox came forth from the cave. He killed Cacus, who was dragged by the heel from the cave; he was spewing forth a smoky mist. Also, this same Cacus who was spewing fire and smoke from his mouth is said to have been the son of Vulcan. He devastated all the neighboring lands by fire. But the truth is this: Cacus was a most wicked servant of Evander, for we know that "evil" is called cacon by the Greeks. He was said to spew fire because he devastated the fields by fire. Therefore all malice belches smoke because it is contrary to truth, that is, to light. His own sister of the same name [Caca] betrayed him. Hence she merited the little shrine in which the Vestal Virgins offer sacrifice to her. When Hercules proved his strength by killing Cacus, a very great altar to him was established, which Delphic Apollo had predicted there would be to Hercules in Italy. And so, when Hercules dedicated cattle from his own herd for his sacrificial rites, two old men were called upon, Pinarius and Potitius. To them he showed how he wanted to be worshipped, namely, that sacrifice be offered in the morning and the evening. After the morning sacrifice was completed, when the rites were to be repeated around sunset, Potitius arrived first. Later, when the entrails had been offered, Pinarius arrived. Thus an angry Hercules decreed that the family of the Pinarii would serve the Potitii as they feasted and fulfilled the sacred rites.

177. On Admetus.

Admetus, a king of Greece, sought Alcestis in marriage. Her father had proclaimed that if anyone could yoke two dissimilar wild beasts to his chariot, that man could marry her. Admetus asked Apollo and Hercules for help; they yoked a lion and a boar to his chariot for him. Thus he took Alcestis in marriage. When Admetus fell sick and death hung over him, he received a response from an oracle saying that he could live if there were anyone who would be willing to die in his place. When Alcestis learned that by dying she could prolong the life of her husband, she offered herself to death. When Admetus grieved inconsolably over her after she was dead, Hercules, when he descended to the Underworld to fetch the three-headed hound, brought Alcestis back from there and restored her to Admetus. He is named as if people were intending to say *adire metus*, "fears approach." Boldness is called *alce*. Therefore, hoping that boldness is joined to itself, fear yokes two wild beasts to its chariot, that is, it acquires the two strengths of soul and body, the lion as the strength of soul and the boar as the strength of body. It makes Apollo and Hercules, that is, wisdom and strength, favorable to itself. Thus boldness offers itself to death for the soul. Strength recalls this boldness that fails in death from the Underworld, as Hercules did.

178. On the Snake Killed by Hercules.

Near the Sagaris, a river in Lydia, Hercules destroyed a snake that was killing many people and stripping the river banks of their fruits. Given many rewards for this deed by Queen Omphale, who reigned there, he was sent back to Argos. Hercules was so violently inflamed with love for her that he took up the delicate threads of the distaff and turned the wheel of the spindle with his thumb. Hercules is said to be *eron cleos*, "the fame of brave men," and *omphalon* means "the navel." Indeed,

desire rules women in the navel. Hence it is shown that desire can overcome unconquered strength because although the greatness of the world
could not defeat Hercules, burning desire overpowered him.

179. On Eryx.

Eryx was the son of Venus and Butes. According to other sources, he was
the son of Neptune and Venus. Outstanding in strength, he challenged
strangers to boxing matches and killed them when they were defeated.
He was killed by Hercules when he challenged him also. Eryx gave his
name to the mountain where he was buried, on which he had also set up
a temple to his mother, Venus.

180. On Busiris.

Busiris was a king of Egypt who used to sacrifice guests whom he had
welcomed. He was killed by Hercules when he also wanted to slay him.
Socrates[65] sang his praises.

181. On Hercules.

Hercules ravished Megara, the daughter of Creon of Thebes. By Megara
he sired Oxean and Creontiades; he killed them when he was seized by
madness sent upon him by Juno.

182. On Eurytus.

Eurytus, King of Oechalia, refused to let Hercules have his daughter Iole,
who had been promised to him earlier. He dissuaded her thus: he told her
that Hercules had killed his wife Megara and the children born of her, a
deed done under the influence of Juno. Hercules was thus angered that
she was denied to him. After he overthrew the city, he killed Eurytus and
took Iole.

183. On the Two Lions That Hercules Conquered.

Hercules overcame two lions, one Theumesian and the other Clionean.
Theumesus is a mountain in Boeotia, and Nemeus is a mountain, also
called Clioneus, in Arcadia. When Eurystheus sent Hercules to slay the
Nemean lion, he was welcomed hospitably by Molorchos, whose son the
lion had killed. After he overcame the lion, Hercules established games
which were named Nemean, after the place.

184. On Avernus and Lucrinus.

On the bay of Baiae in Campania, opposite the town of Puteoli, there are two lakes, Avernus and Lucrinus. Because of their abundant fish, these lakes once offered great revenues to the Romans. But when the fury of the sea frequently assailed them and drove the fish away from there, the rulers suffered serious losses. They appealed to the senate. C. Julius Caesar went there, constructed moles and shut out the part of the sea which was harmful before. He also left a small space through Avernus by which abundant fish could enter and the waves would not be troublesome. This was called the Julian Works.

185. On Erymanthus and Stymphalus.

In Arcadia there are two mountains: Erymanthus and Stymphalus. On one of these, Erymanthus, Hercules captured the boar, which he brought alive to Eurystheus. On the other, Stymphalus, he killed the birds called Stymphalides. Statius calls this Stymphalus "bronze-sounding"[66] (aerisonus) because Hercules killed these birds not with arrows, but with the sounding of bronze.

186. On the Golden Apples Presented to Jove by Earth.

When Jupiter took Juno as his wife, Earth came bearing golden fruits, along with their branches. Admiring these, Juno asked Earth to plant them in her gardens, which were near Mount Atlas. Since Aegle, Arethusa, and Hesperethusa, daughters of Atlas, often picked the apples from the trees, Juno set a watchful dragon there as a guardian. Sent there by Eurystheus for the fruits of the Hesperides, Hercules killed the dragon and carried off the golden fruits. In truth, however, they were noble girls whose flocks Hercules drove off after he killed their watchman. Thus he is thought to have carried off apples (mala), that is, sheep, for they are called *mala*, and the shepherd is called *melonomos*.

187. On Hercules and Deianira.

When Hercules visited King Hexamirus as his guest, he seduced his daughter, Deianira, and pledged that he would take her as his wife. After his departure, Eurycion sought Deianira. Fearing violence, her father promised her to Eurycion, who came with his brothers on the day set for the wedding. By chance, on this day when the wedding rites were being celebrated, Alcides* arrived. He killed the Centaurs and unexpectedly joined Deianira to himself in marriage.

188. On Lerna, the Marsh.

Lerna was a marsh that had fifty heads [sources], or, as others say, seven. In this marsh lived the Hydra, a beast that is called *excetra*, "serpent," in Latin. Indeed, while Hercules was battling this beast, after he cut off one head, three new heads grew. He finally defeated it with fire. But it is well known that Hydra was a place gushing waters that laid waste the neighboring city. Since this place often dried up and then waters burst forth all the more, with three sources emerging in place of one, Hercules understood that the arteries in the earth could be shut by fire. So, after he drained this place, Hercules applied fire and thus shut off the path of the water. He made this place in Arcadia habitable.

189. On Antaeus and Hercules.

Antaeus, the son of Earth, was King of Libya. He killed many men in single combat and placed their heads on the doorposts of his house as an indicator of his strength. When Hercules visited him, Antaeus began to wrestle with him, and when he was in a position to be conquered by Hercules, he pretended to fall. He always rose up stronger, with his strength restored, as his mother Earth brought him energy. Hercules perceived this, after Minerva warned him. When Antaeus tried to fall again, Hercules lifted him up and strangled him while suspending him above the earth.

190. On Oeneus.

Oeneus, the son of Parthaon and father of Tydeus, was King of Aetolia. He had a daughter named Deianira, whom many men desired in marriage. When both Hercules and Achelous, a river of Aetolia, sought her at the same time, they accepted a condition set forth by Oeneus that the one who prevailed in strength would marry Deianira. And so they came together in combat. When Achelous was being defeated by Hercules, he changed first into a youth, then into a serpent, and third into a bull. As Hercules grappled with this struggling bull, he broke off its horn, which he had grasped with his hands. He consecrated this horn to Fortune; she

*i.e., Hercules.

produced wealth with it. Then nymphs, the Naiads, daughters of the river, caused what had been torn away to be filled with autumnal bounty. Thus it is called "Horn of Plenty,"[67] since, just as the horn grows above the flesh, so riches accompany a man on the outside. The strength of animals is in the horn and the power of Fortune resides in riches, as it is said: "High birth and virtue are more worthless than seaweed, unless they come with property."[68] Moreover, Hercules is said to have taken away the horn from this same river because, although it flowed in two channels, Hercules blocked one and stopped it up.

191. On the Death of Hercules.

After he defeated Achelous, Hercules took Deianira as his wife, and by her he produced a son named Hylus. When Hercules came to the River Eubenus, also called Licormas, he put her down and took across with him his club and the rest of his arms, so that first unburdened, he might then carry her unimpeded. When he was ready to return to carry her across, Hercules saw Nessus having intercourse with her. He shot an arrow and killed Nessus. As he was dying, Nessus gave Deianira a garment stained with his own blood to avenge himself, for he told her that if she wanted Hercules to love her forever, she should give him this garment to wear. Later, after Hercules had overthrown Euchalia, the city of Eurytus on the island of Euboea, and taken his daughter Iole to his own country, Deianira saw that her husband's affection was alienated from her. She feared that his mistress might be preferred to her. When Hercules was about to sacrifice to Jove, she gave the tunic to Lyca, her servant, to bring to him. When Hercules approached the altar wearing it, the garment grew hot and, polluted with poison, it clung to his flesh. In the greatest torment when he could not tear the garment away from his body, Hercules plunged Lyca the servant, who was accused of giving the gift, into the Euboean Sea. Thetis changed Lyca, who was innocent of the crime, into a rocky crag. But when Hercules realized that he could not return to his way of life, and he was afflicted by the burning of the poison, he climbed onto a pyre on Mount Oeta of his own will and thus was carried up among the gods.

192. On the Arrows of Hercules.

When Hercules laid aside his human body on Mount Oeta, he revealed everything concerning his remains to Philoctetes, the son of Poeas, who was from the city of Meliboea. He made him swear an oath not to tell anyone about his body. Also, as a gift, Hercules gave him arrows tinged with the Hydra's gall. Later, during the Trojan War, an oracle said that Hercules' arrows were needed for the attack on Troy. Thus Philoctetes was found. Although he denied at first that he knew where Hercules was buried, finally he acknowledged that he was dead. Then when he was violently forced to reveal his grave, he struck the earth with his foot, since he was unwilling to tell. Afterward, on his way to the war, Philoctetes was using the arrows and was wounded by a falling arrow on the foot with which he had struck the tomb. When the Greeks could not bear the stench of his incurable wound, at last they left him on Lemnos, although he was led about for a long time on account of the oracle. The arrows were taken from him. Later, because of the horror of his wound, he refused to return to his homeland, but founded for himself Little Petilia in the region of Calabria. It is called Petilia because, after he left Ilion, where he was taken by the Greeks, he sought (petivit) this town.

193. On the Sanctuary of Hercules' Grandsons.

After Hercules departed from the earth, his sons and grandsons feared the plots that their grandfather had provoked. First, they established for themselves at Athens a sanctuary, that is, a temple of refuge, consecrated under this precept: that a person accused of any crime might flee to it and be free of all harm, and no one would dare to lead him away from there or to injure him. This is also where Orestes at last recovered his senses when his friend Pylades brought him there. Men say that sanctuary (asylum) is called that from the words *antetrahendo spolium*, "bringing plunder before." This right of religious custom is not in all temples, but in those to which it has been granted by this precept of consecration.

194. On Phorcys.

Phorcys, son of Thoose the nymph and Neptune, was King of Corsica and Sardinia. When he and a great part of his army were overwhelmed by King Atlas in a naval battle, his comrades supposed that he had been transformed into a sea god.

195. On Glaucus.

Glaucus, the son of Antedon, was a fisherman who cast the fishes he took from the sea onto the shore. At the touch of the grass, the fishes came back to life. Glaucus thought that the nature of that turf was such that those who tasted it would become immortal, and so he plucked some and tasted it. When he did this, he lost his mind and hurled himself from a height into the sea. After his human body was thus destroyed, he is thought to have been turned into a sea god.

196. On Scylla, Beloved by Glaucus.

Scylla was the daughter of Phorcys and Cretheis the nymph. Glaucus, a sea god, son of Antedon, loved her. He was loved by Circe, and since he was more inclined to favor Scylla, an angry Circe poisoned the spring in which Scylla used to bathe. When Scylla descended into the spring, she was changed into various shapes up as far as her private parts. Thus horrified at her own deformity, she hurled herself into the sea. Later, Glaucus made her a sea goddess. She is reported to have destroyed the fleet of Ulysses and his companions. Homer says that Scylla was a deathless monster. Sallust says that she was a rock resembling a shape known to those who saw it in the distance. Indeed, because of this, dogs and wolves are thought to be born of her, because those places are full of sea monsters, and the roughness of the rocks there sounds like the barking of beasts.

197. On Charybdis.

Charybdis was a very voracious woman. Because she stole the cattle of Hercules, she was struck by Jove's lightning and hurled into the sea. There Charybdis still preserves her former nature, for she swallows everything. According to Sallust, she dwells around the Tauromanian shore.

198. On the Tyrrhenians and Father Liber.

When Father Liber was sleeping on the seashore, Tyrrhenian sailors carried him off. When he awakened on their ship, he asked where he was being taken. They answered: "where you wish." Liber asked that they return him to the island of Naxos, to the nymphs who were his nurses. Induced by the hope of gain, they began to turn their sails elsewhere. Angered by this, the deity made tigers consecrated to himself appear before their eyes. Filled with terror, the sailors threw themselves into the waves and became dolphins.

199. *On Arion of Lesbos.*

Arion of Lesbos was the best cithara player. When he was traveling from Tarentum to Corinth with many riches, he saw that ambushes were laid for him by the sailors at sea. He asked that he be allowed to play for a little while on the cithara. As he was playing, dolphins gathered around at this sound. Arion leaped upon one and was carried to the Tenarian shore. Thus he escaped imminent danger.

200. *On Arethusa.*

According to the stories, Arethusa was a huntress. While she washed herself in the River Alpheus after her toil, he desired her. Fleeing for a long time, Arethusa was changed through the mercy of the gods into a spring that flowed through hidden passages to Sicily. Alpheus pursued her all the way to Sicily, and there he is said to mingle with her waters.

201. *On Polyphemus.*

Polyphemus the Cyclops is said to have loved Galatea the nymph. Since she loved a certain shepherd, Acis, and spurned Polyphemus, in his anger the Cyclops killed Acis, who was later changed through the mercy of Galatea into a spring. Today this spring is called Acilius, after Acis. Many writers say that Polyphemus had one eye, others say two, and others say three, which is totally incredible. In truth, he was a very wise man who, for this reason, is said to have had an eye in his head next to the brain, since wisdom seems to perceive more acutely than bodily sight. Since Polyphemus was surpassed in wisdom by Ulysses, he is thought to have been blinded by him.

202. *On Ceyx.*

Ceyx, son of Lucifer, had a wife, Alcyone. After she prohibited him from consulting Apollo about the state of his kingdom, he perished in a shipwreck. When his body floated back to his wife Alcyone, she threw herself into the sea. Later, through the mercy of Thetis and Lucifer, both were changed into sea birds called halcyons. Of course, it should be known that when we speak about these birds, he and she became halcyons, and the males and the females are halcyons; when we speak only about the woman, she is Alcyone. These birds make their nests on the sea in midwinter. During this time there is so great a calm that nothing at all moves.

203. On Mergus.

Mergus was the son of Priam. He threw himself down from a wall and did not perish. When he did this often, he was changed through the mercy of the gods into a bird that still does the same thing in imitation of its former ways.

204. On Cyparissus.

While Cyparissus, a handsome boy, was hunting in the forest, he inspired Apollo to love him. From Apollo he received a very beautiful, tame stag as a gift. He loved this stag. When he was weary, Cyparissus fell asleep under a tree. Roused by a sudden noise, he saw the stag at a distance, and, thinking it was a wild stag, he killed it with an arrow. After he recognized it, Cyparissus pined away to such an extent that he abstained from all food and drink. As Cyparissus was pining away, Apollo pitied him and turned him into a tree with his own name: Cypress.

205. A Second Telling of the Same Story.

Silvanus, a forest god, loved a boy named Cyparissus, who had a very tame deer. When Silvanus unknowingly killed this deer, the boy died of sorrow. The god, his lover, turned him into a cypress, a tree with his own name, which Silvanus is said to carry about as a consolation for the dead boy.

206. On Priapus.

When Priapus pursued Lotus, a nymph he loved, she was turned into a tree through the mercy of the gods. The tree is commonly called the Syrian bean.

207. On Lyriope.

Lyriope the nymph gave birth to Narcissus; his father was the River Cephisus. Tiresias promised Narcissus that he would prosper in everything if he did not trust too much in his own beauty. When Echo, daughter of Juno, loved him and found no way to possess him, she pined away for love of the youth. She pursued him with her last cries as he fled. Now only her voice is heard, since she was turned into stone and hidden in the mountains. This happened to her at the instigation of Juno because she often delayed the goddess by her chattering. Thus Juno could not catch

Jove as he pursued nymphs in the mountains. Because of this offense and because of her deformity, she was hidden in the mountains, so that nothing of her except her voice could be perceived. Also, because of the excessive disdain and cruelty that he showed toward Echo, Nemesis, that is, Fortuna, avenger of those who are haughty, came to the above-named Narcissus and forced him to love himself, so that he burned with no less a flame than Echo did. According to others, this happened when in jest he and Apollo had entered a discus-throwing contest and he could not avoid the weight cast on high by Apollo before he felt it strike his head. When Narcissus reclined next to a spring from the weariness caused by constant hunting, and he was drinking the water, he caught sight of his own likeness. Thinking it was another's likeness, he fell in love with it and pined away with desire to such an extent that he died. From his remains a flower grew; the water nymphs, weeping over their brother's death, called this by his name, Narcissus.

208. On the Boy, Hyacinth.

A boy, Hyacinth, was loved by Boreas and by Apollo, but he rejoiced more in Apollo's love. While he exercised with a discus, he was killed with the same discus by an angry Boreas and changed into a flower of his own name. This flower, which traces out on itself the first letter of "Iacinth," is red, like the lily.

209. On the Boy, Amaracus.

A boy, Amaracus, was a royal perfumer. By accident he fell while he was carrying perfumes and created a better fragrance from their mingling together. Therefore the best perfumes are now called *amaraca*. Later he was turned into the marjoram plant, which we now call *amaracum*.

210. On Pilumnus and Pitumnus.

The gods Pilumnus and Pitumnus were brothers. One of these two, Pitumnus, discovered the practice of manuring (stercorandum) the fields, and thus he was called Sterculinus. Pilumnus discovered the practice of crushing grain, and he is worshipped by bakers. The pestle (pilum) is named after him.

211. On Two Brothers Who Were Called Divine.

In the city of Praeneste, located not far from Rome, there were two brothers who were called Divine. While their sister was sitting before the hearth, a leaping spark struck her belly. From this, she conceived. Later, she brought forth a boy next to the temple of Jove, and she abandoned him. Maidens on their way to fetch water found him next to the fire and took him. Thus they said that he was Vulcan's son. They called him Caeculus, "Little Blind Boy," because he had narrow eyes, which the pungency of smoke generally causes. Later, after he had gathered a multitude around him, he was a robber for a long time. Then he founded the city of Praeneste in the mountains. When he invited the neighboring peoples on the day of the games, he began to encourage them to dwell with him, and, for glory, he boasted that he was the son of Vulcan. When they did not believe this, the entire multitude gathered there was surrounded by flames. When this happened, the frightened people dwelt together with him and believed that he was Vulcan's son.

212. On the Telchines, Three Brothers.

The Telchines are said to have been three brothers who were insane with envy. When they saw their neighbors' fields fruitful with produce and blessed by nature, they sprinkled them with Stygian water to render them infertile. Fearing punishment for this crime, they left their country and went to live with the Cyclopes.

213. On Tenes.

A certain Tenes was disgraced because he had slept with his stepmother. He made the island called Tenedos open to inhabitants. Thus it is called Tenedos.

214. On Ebalus.

Ebalus was the son of Telon and the nymph Sebetris. For a long time this Telon reigned on Capri, the island situated opposite Naples. His son was not content with his father's kingdom and crossed over to Campania. After many peoples were subjugated, he extended his own sway.

215. On Maleus.

Maleus was King of the Tusculans. He first discovered the trumpet. When he was practicing piracy and the sea was troubled by storms, he settled on the mountain now called Malea after him. He called Apollo "Maleoti-cum" and named the mountain "Malea" after his own name.

216. On Codrus.

Codrus was a leader of the Athenians. After a war started between the Spartans and Athenians, an oracle predicted that those whose leader perished would be victorious. Codrus proceeded in humble garb to the nearby tents of the enemy. There, by railing at them, he incited them to his own destruction. He was recognized by no one and proved the oracle correct.

217. On Croesus.

Croesus, King of the Lydians, was captured once by Cyrus, King of the Persians, who ordered him to be placed upon a pyre. Suddenly, so great a rain shower arose that the fire was extinguished, and he found an opportunity to escape. Croesus later bragged that this matter had turned out favorably for him, and he boasted about the vastness of his wealth. Solon, one of the Seven Sages, told him that no one ought to brag about riches and prosperity, since we do not know what the coming day might bring. That same night Croesus saw in his dreams that Jove drenched him with water, and the Sun dried him. When he told this to his daughter Phamae,[69] she wisely explained how the matter stood, saying that he would be fastened to a cross, drenched by rain and dried by the sun. Later this happened so, for he was again captured by Cyrus and hanged.

218. On Alcon.

Alcon of Crete was an archer. When a dragon attacked his son, he shot an arrow with such great skill that it flew and fixed itself in this serpent, and yet it did not injure the son.

219. On Jove and Electra.

Jupiter slept with Electra, the daughter of Atlas and wife of Corythus, a king in Italy. Dardanus was born from the seed of Jove, and Iasius was born from the seed of Corythus. Iasius ruled Thrace, where Samos is. He named it Samothrace, for there is another Samos belonging to Juno. Thus, when the Trojans received an oracle that said "seek out your ancient mother," Aeneas proceeded to Thrace and carried off the Samothracian gods from there because of his mother's origin. In fact, because of an oracle, Dardanus changed location and came to Phrygia. Setting up small buildings in the valleys, he founded Troy and named it Dardania after his own name. After his death, Teucer came from Crete and united the companions of Dardanus to himself. Teucer established defenses and walls. After him Ericthonius, the son of Dardanus, ruled. His son Tros succeeded him, calling the place Troy, after himself. He sired two sons, Ilus and Assaracus. The elder one, Ilus, obtained the kingdom, calling Troy "Ilium" after his own name. Ilus sired Laomedon, Priam's father.

220. On Laomedon.

When Laomedon, the Trojan king, was about to build Troy, he promised a certain amount of money for building temples to Neptune and Apollo, who had been hired for the construction of the city. While these sanctuaries were rising, he transferred this money to the building of the walls. When he denied to Neptune and Apollo the promised reward for the walls, an angry Neptune sent sea monsters against Troy. When Apollo was consulted, he gave hostile responses, since he himself was angry; he said that noble girls had to be offered to the beasts. The Trojan leaders demanded that Laomedon end this plague by handing over his own daughter to a beast. Theseus, bolder than all the others, accused the king because he was unwilling to offer his daughter to the beast. The angry king ordered Theseus killed, and later, in his anger, he said that the daughters of all should be handed over to the beast. And so, many men, terrified by the king's threats, entrusted their daughters to merchants to be transported elsewhere. They were ready to endure their absence more easily than their death. While this was happening, a certain nobleman, Hippotes, feared that his daughter Egesta would be tied up for the sea monsters. He sent her on a ship to wherever chance should take her. Carried to Sicily, she was seized by the River Crimisus after he was changed into a bear or a dog. She gave birth to Acestes, who founded a city that today is called Segesta, from his mother's name.

221. On Tithonus and Aurora.

Tithonus was the brother of Laomedon. Aurora loved him and raised him up to heaven. Afterward, when he lamented his length of life, he was changed into a cricket. Also, he sent his son Memnon the Ethiopian, born of Aurora, to the aid of Troy.

222. On Anchises.

Anchises the shepherd was the son of Capys, son of Assaracus. Venus loved him and slept with him; from this union she gave birth to Aeneas near the River Simois in Troy. Indeed, goddesses or nymphs bear children near streams or groves. When Anchises was feasting with men of his own age, he boasted about sleeping with Venus. When Venus complained to Jove about this, she obtained this judgment: thunderbolts would be hurled against Anchises. But when Venus saw that he could be killed by a thunderbolt, she pitied the youth and deflected the thunderbolt elsewhere. Yet, touched by the celestial fire, Anchises lived forever infirm.

223. On Cassandra.

Cassandra was the daughter of Priam, the Trojan king. Apollo granted her the faculty of prophecy. Deceived by her in his hope of intercourse, Apollo took away credence from her even though she spoke the truth. Thus, when Cassandra predicted that Troy would be destroyed because of the arrival of Helen, the Trojans did not believe her on account of Apollo's command.

224. The Story of Helenus.

Helenus was captured by the Greeks at Arisba and ordered to reveal to them the fate of Troy, including that concerning the Palladium. He is said to have obtained realms from Pyrrhus, for he had shown Pyrrhus that he should return home by land, warning him that all the Greeks would perish by shipwreck. Indeed, this happened. Afterward, Diomedes and Ulysses entered the citadel by underground passages, as some say, or by sewers, as others say. They killed the guards and carried off the statue. Later, when Diomedes had this statue, he believed that it was not meant for him because of its dangers. He tried to give it to Aeneas as he was passing through his land. But when Aeneas turned away while offering sacrifice with his head covered, a certain Nautes took the statue. For this reason, the Julian clan does not keep the sacred rites of Minerva, but the Nautae do. Thus Vergil says in Book Five: "one whom Tritonian Pallas taught."[70] Although some say that this statue was hidden by the Trojans in a wall, they later knew that Troy would fall. Afterward, in the war with Mithridates, a certain Roman, Fimbria, is said to have revealed the discovered statue, which, it is well known, was brought to Rome. It had been prophesied that supreme power would reside where the Palladium was. After Mamurius the sculptor was summoned, he made many similar statues. But they recognized the true one by the movement of its spear and eyes.

225. On Hecuba.

By Arisbe, Priam had a son who was a seer. This son declared that a boy would be born who would overthrow Troy. The wife of Thymoetes and Hecuba, who was Priam's lawful wife, both gave birth at the same time. But Priam ordered the son of Thymoetes, and his wife herself, to be killed. When Hecuba, the daughter of Ciseus and wife of King Priam, was pregnant with Paris, she saw herself bring forth a torch by which the city was burned. When she reported this to Priam, he understood that the boy who was born would be the cause of burning the city. When the father ordered that his son die, the mother handed him over secretly to a shepherd to be raised. Nourished by him, Paris became so strong that in the festival contests at Troy he overcame all, even Hector himself. When Hector drew his sword in anger against Paris, the latter declared that he was his brother. Since this seemed astonishing, his rattles from childhood were brought forth, and he was proved to be Hector's brother. Paris was admitted by his father into the fellowship of his brothers.

226. On Ganymede.

Ganymede was the son of Troilus, King of the Trojans, and Callirrhoe. So that he might not suffer the shame of male intercourse because of the beauty of his body, an eagle snatched him up to the sky while he was hunting in the forest on Mount Ida. He was made cupbearer to the gods after Hebe, Juno's daughter, was removed [from that office]. Thus Juno was angry at the Trojans. Poets love to adorn their babble with false illusions, so Anacreon, a most-ancient author, wrote that while Jupiter waged war against the Titans, the sons of Titanus, who was Saturn's brother, he offered a sacrifice to Coelus. An eagle in flight appeared to him, and he saw this as a favorable sign of victory. In return for this happy omen, especially since victory followed, he placed an eagle on his ensigns and consecrated it as a guardian. Thus the Romans use ensigns of this kind. Indeed, while he waged war with these ensigns preceding him, Jupiter snatched Ganymede, just as he snatched Europa on a bull, that is, on a ship having the picture of a bull.

227. On Hercules and Hylas.

When Hercules became the comrade of the Argonauts, he took with him a young man of wondrous beauty, Hylas, the son of Theodamas. Because of his strength in rowing, Hylas broke his oar in the sea. Proceeding to Mysia to repair it, he entered a forest there. When Hylas went to fetch water with a jar, he fell into a river from which nymphs snatched him. While Hercules searched for him, he was restrained by the Argonauts, and Hylas was left behind on Mysia. Afterward, when it was learned that Hylas had perished in a stream, sacred rites were established for him. In these it was the custom to cry out his name in the mountains. In imitation of this Vergil says: "The whole shore resounds with Hylas, Hylas."[71] After Hylas was lost and Mysia had been searched, Hercules proceeded to Colchis. He came with his ships to Troy. When Laomedon, King of the Trojans, kept him away from Troy's harbor, Hercules pretended to depart. From the promontory of Troy, called Sigeum because of his silence (for *sige* means silence), he arrived at Troy unforeseen. Hercules conquered the city and killed King Laomedon. He handed over his daughter Hesione, taken by right of war, to his companion Telamon, who had been first to ascend the wall. This same Hesione gave birth to Teucer, for it is known that Ajax was born of another woman [of that name]. Then Hercules also rescued Priam from his neighboring foes and established him in his father's kingdom. Later, when Priam grew up, he wished to take back his sister. He went with emissaries to Salamina, where it was known that she ruled, but he was not able to take her back, for the Greeks said that they had her by rights of war. Then an angry Priam sent Paris with an army to take something, such as either the king's wife or daughter. Paris went to Greece and began to seduce Helen, the wife of Menelaus. When she refused to conspire with him, he went out and besieged the city. When it was overthrown, he seized Helen. Later, she deserved to be recovered by her husband. Moved by their grief, the Greeks besieged Troy after certain brave warriors of Greece were gathered together. Finally, in the tenth year, they conquered Troy.

228. On Aminoe (Amymone).

While Aminoe, the daughter of Danaus, was zealously practicing [with a javelin] on an island, she struck a satyr without knowing it, and when the satyr wanted to violate her, she implored Neptune for help. After Neptune chased the satyr away, he had intercourse with her. From this union Nauplius was born, whose son Palamedes was born in the seventh generation after Belus. When he was recruiting men throughout Greece, Palamedes led away an unwilling Ulysses, who was feigning madness. Ulysses had yoked animals of a different nature together and was sowing salt. Palamedes placed his son in his way. When he saw his son, Ulysses stopped. Led off to war, he had a just cause for animosity. Later, when Ulysses was sent to fetch grain and brought nothing back to Troy,[72] he was rebuked vehemently by Palamedes. Ulysses said that by no means should he be blamed for negligence; indeed, if Palamedes himself were to go, he could not bring back anything. Palamedes went and brought back endless amounts of grain. With his enmity increased through envy of this, Ulysses sent to Palamedes a false letter in Priam's name. In it Priam gave thanks for Palamdes' betrayal of the Greeks and reminded him that a secret mass of gold had been sent to him. Ulysses gave the letter to a Trojan captive, and he had him killed on his journey. This letter was found, and, in the military custom, brought to the king and read to the assembled captains. Then Ulysses pretended that he was supporting Palamedes. He said: "If you believe this, search for the gold in his tent." When this was done and the gold was found, which Ulysses had bribed servants to hide there in the night, Palamedes was stoned to death. Yet it is well known that he was a wise man, for he invented a board game to repress the insurrections of an idle army, as Varro testifies. Certain writers say that he discovered letters, which is perhaps a doubtful thing, yet it is certain that he invented X (chi) with an aspiration (h).

229. On Nauplius.

Palamedes' father, Nauplius, the son of Aminoe and Neptune, grieved over the death of his son. When the Greeks were returning after Troy had fallen, they were struggling in a storm. Nauplius climbed Mount Caphareus, and with a torch he gave the signal that a harbor was nearby. Deceived by this, the Greeks suffered shipwreck on the craggy rocks.

230. On Dodona.

Dodona is a city in Epirus. Near it is a grove consecrated to Jove that abounds in acorns. In fact, Sestos and Abydos are cities on the Hellespont separated by a narrow, dangerous sea.

231. On Leucas.

Leucas is a high mountain on a promontory of Epirus near the city of Ambrachia. Augustus called this city Nicopolis after Antony and Cleopatra were defeated there. In that place he set up a temple to Apollo of Actium, and he named the games there "Actian."

232. On Pelorus.

Pelorus is a promontory on Sicily. According to Sallust, it was named after Hannibal's pilot, who was buried there. Pelorus was killed through the king's lack of information when he believed that he had been deceived by Pelorus' guile.

233. On Euboea.

Euboea is an island. From a city on this island the Chalchidians set out to seek new dwelling places. Not far from Baiae, they found an empty shore. This place took its name from Baius, Ulysses' companion who was buried there. They founded a city there after they observed a pregnant woman. This showed that their republic would be fertile. They called it Cumae, either from *egkumos,* "pregnant," or they named it from *apo ton kumaton,* "from the waves." Moreover, the Romans turn *y* into *u,* as when *byrria* becomes *burria.*

234. On Pachynus.

Pachynus is a promontory on Sicily, looking south. It is named from the density of the air, for dense is called *pachys.* Drepanum is a city not far from Mount Eryx, across from Lilybaeum. The city is called this either because of the curvature of the shore on which it is situated, or because Saturn threw down his sickle there after his father Coelus' genitals had been cut off. A sickle is called *drapanon* in Greek.

235. On the Syracusans.

At a certain time, the victorious Syracusans captured a vast multitude of Athenians. They made this throng cut away mountains and add fortifications to the city. Also, when the walls were built, they constructed a trench on the outside. They let a stream flow into it, filled it, and rendered the city more fortified. Thus, because of the suffering of their enemies and the harm done to them, they called this trench Hibris.[73] Later on,

Sicilians proceeded to Italy and held the part where Rome is now, as far as to the Rutuli and Ardea. Thus it is written: "A boundary extending to the Sicani."[74] And for its likeness to the trench at Syracuse, they called the Albula River "Tiber," as if to say "Hibris." Also, Theocritus says that the trench around Syracuse was named Hybris.

236. On Tullus Hostilius.

When Tarquin captured the city of Utriculana, a certain captive woman in his house gave birth to Servius Tullus Hostilius. When the child was sleeping, suddenly a flame took hold of his head. When Tarquin wanted to put it out, Tanaquil, the king's wife, prevented him, for she had knowledge of omens. The flame left the boy when he awakened. From this she knew that he would be illustrious right to the end of his life.

237. On Brutus.

When Brutus and the sons of Tarquin consulted the oracle of Apollo at Delphi, the response was that supreme power would belong to the man who first kissed his mother on his return home. Only Brutus understood this. Disembarking from his ship, he pretended to fall, and he kissed the earth. Thus he possessed the supreme power. The seven kings of Rome were: Romulus, Numa Pompilius, Tullus Hostilius, Ancus Martius, Tarquinius Priscus, Servius Tullius, and Tarquinius Superbus. When Romulus died, the senate ruled in the first year through *decuriae*, "groups of ten," but this seemed irksome, and a king was sought. When no one suitable was found in the city, the good reputation of Pompilius came up. He lived at Cures, a city of the Sabines. So, entreated by legates, he accepted the supreme power and brought the ferocity of a warlike people to the sacred rites. For this reason he was called Numa, from *apo ton nomon*. Also, he was gray haired from childhood.

238. On Tarquinius Superbus (Tarquin the Proud).

Tarquin was called Proud for many reasons, but especially for the following one. He once ordered a certain follower of his to kill all the leading men of a certain town. When that man went there, he found a great multitude. When he reported back to Tarquin, who was walking with a stick in his gardens, the king in response struck off the heads of poppies so that his follower might understand what he wanted done. In like manner, his son violated Lucretia, a most noble matron. Grieving over this, she killed herself. Then Brutus, her uncle, snatched the sword from her body; he went before the people and addressed them on this matter. After he did this, it pleased all that the king, who was then attacking Ardea, should not be accepted back. Because of this, Tarquin, along with his children, joined Porsena, King of Tuscany, and he waged a very harsh war against the Roman people. Then two men became consuls, Brutus and Tricipitinus, the father of Lucretia, who was also called Tarquin. Because of this alone, he was expelled from the city, and Valerius Publicola was chosen in his place. After his death, likewise another was made consul, and, similarly, another. But the sons of Brutus were friends with the sons of Tarquin, with whom they devised a plan to let them in at night. They were betrayed by Venditius, a servant, and killed by their father.

239. On Brenus (Brennus).

After the Roman legions had been annihilated near the River Allia, Brennus led the Gauls and they destroyed the city of Rome, except for the Capitol. For this favor they accepted a vast amount of money. Then Camillus was made dictator. He had been absent a long time, since he was in exile near Ardea because he had not shared the booty from Veia equally. He pursued the departing Gauls, and after they were killed, he took all their gold and their standards. Since he weighed this gold there, he gave a name to the city. It is called Pisaurum because gold (aurum) was weighed (pensatum) there. After this, Brennus returned to exile.

240. On the Civil War.

Civil wars were waged seven times. There were three by Caesar: against Pompey in Thessaly; against his son Magnus in Spain; and against Juba and Cato in Africa. There were four waged by Augustus: against Cassius and Brutus in Thessaly; against Lucius Antonius in Perusia, a city in Tuscany; against Pompey in Sicily; and against Antony and Cleopatra in Epirus.

241. On Fabius.

There were three hundred Fabii from one family who swore oaths with their slaves and retainers, and waged war against the Veientians. They were slain in an ambush near the River Cremera. Only one, Fabius Maximus, survived. Because of his still-tender youth, he had remained in the city. Later, when he could not resist the attack of Hannibal, Fabius avoided him by delay. He drew Hannibal to Campania, where his strength was weakened by pleasures. About this man Ennius says: "One who restored our state to us by delaying."[75]

242. On Marcellus.

Marcellus conquered the Gauls and the Carthaginians in a cavalry battle. With his own hand he even killed Viridomarus, the leader of the Gauls, and brought back the spoils of honor (spolia opima) that he took from that general. Another Marcellus, whom Augustus adopted, was the son of Octavia, his sister. In his sixteenth year, while he held the office of Aedile, this boy fell sick, and he died in his seventeenth year at Baiae. The City grieved exceedingly over his death, for he was affable, as well as Augustus' son. To glorify his funeral procession, Augustus ordered six hundred biers to enter the City. In fact, among our ancestors this was glorious and was granted in accordance with one's prosperity, for Sulla had six thousand. Thus Marcellus was carried in a mighty procession and buried in the Campus Martius.

243. On the Shield (Ancile).

A shield fell from the sky at Rome in the time of Numa Pompilius. An oracular response declared that dominion over the world would be there, where the shield was.[76] So that no enemy might recognize this shield, Mamurius the craftsman made many similar ones. A day was consecrated to the shield, and on this day they strike its hide in the manner of an art. We call this a shield, although in his lyrics Horace says: "of shields."[77] We know that at first there were three divisions of the Roman people: one of Tatienses, named after Tatius, a leader of the Sabines who was a friend at that time after treaties were concluded with him; another of Ramnenses; a third of Luceres, whose name and origin are unknown, according to Livy. But Varro says that while Romulus was fighting against Titus Tatius, he asked for help from the Lucumones. Thus a certain one came with an army. Then when Tatius was captured, part of the city was given to him. The Tuscan quarter in the city is named after him. Horace says: "The impious mob of the Tuscan quarter."[78] Therefore the

Luceres are named after the Lucumones. Also, it is known that the people are divided into three parts, so that those who preside over individual parts are called tribunes. Thus they call payments that they used to give to the people "tribute." After the rape of the Sabine women, a treaty was made between Romulus and Titus Tatius. Then the Sabines were accepted into the city, but under this law: they would be Roman citizens in all things except the right to vote, for magisterial offices were not created from among them.

244. On the Rostra.

Augustus was the conqueror of all Egypt, which Caesar had conquered in part. Augustus carried off many rostra from a naval battle. With these he made four columns, which were later placed in the Capitol by the Emperor Domitian.

245. On Agamemnon.

When the Greeks came to Aulis, King Agamemnon unwittingly killed a doe that belonged to Diana. Thus the angry goddess took away the blowing winds. When the Greeks could not sail away because of this, and they endured a pestilence as well, the oracles said that Diana must be placated by the blood of Agamemnon. When Ulysses, who was very shrewd, abducted Agamemnon's daughter Iphigeneia under the pretext of marriage, and she was ready to be sacrificed, she was rescued through the mercy of the goddess. A doe was put in her place, and Iphigeneia was transported to the Taurian territory and handed over to King Thoas. She was made a priestess of Diana Dictynna. Moreover, when Agamemnon returned from Troy, his wife Clytemnestra brought him a garment without an opening for the head. When he tried to put it on and could not find an opening for his head, he was murdered by Aegisthus the adulterer, son of Thyestes and his own daughter Pelopia. Later, when Orestes grew up, he killed Aegisthus, together with his mother Clytemnestra, to avenge his father. He became insane because of this crime. While he was raving mad, he entered the temple of Apollo, at the urging of his friend Pylades, to escape the Furies. When he wanted to leave the temple, the Furies assailed him. Thus it was written: "The avenging Dirae sit on the threshold."[79] When Orestes could not free himself of his insanity, he went to the oracle. It responded that he could be cured in this way: if he would

carry off the statue of Scythian Diana from Taurica. Then, when he went
to Colchis with his friend Pylades to free himself of madness, his sister
recognized him as she was appeasing the goddess with human blood, according to custom. After King Thoas was killed with her consent, she
carried off the statue hidden in a bundle of sticks. Thus it is called Fascelis,
not only from the torch (face) with which it is depicted, but also from
the bundle of sticks. It is also called Lucifera, "Light-Bearer." Iphigeneia
brought this to Italy and placed it in a grove of Aricia. Later, when the
cruelty of the sacred rites were displeasing to the Romans, even though
slaves were being sacrificed, Diana was transferred to the Laconians.
There, the custom of the sacrifice was preserved in the scourging of
young men who were called Bomonicae. They were whipped for a long
time, until blood flowed from the human body, for they were placed upon
altars and strove to see who could endure more strokes. In fact, Orestes'
bones were transferred from Aricia to Rome and placed before the temple
of Saturn, which is in front of the Capitol, next to the temple of Concord.

246. On Jove and Aegina.

Jupiter changed into an eagle and snatched Aegina, daughter of the River
Asopus. He violated her and got by her a son named Aeacus. Her father
could not patiently bear the fact that his daughter had been raped, and he
was also incited by a whole army of rivers. He assailed heaven, waging
war against Jove. When he did this, he was struck down by Jove's thunderbolt. So that the memory of this infamy might last forever, today we
say that Asopus flowed with burning coals at that time when he was
struck.

247. On Aeacus.

When Aeacus, the son of Jove and Aegina, was living on the island of
Asopis, he endured a grievous pestilence because of Juno's anger.
Through prayers he secured the mercy of Jove. Indeed, when he observed
ants, that is, *myrmicae*, on a fig tree, he wished that so many companions
might come to him. Immediately the ants were turned into men. Thus
they were called Myrmidons. But these are fables. The truth is that the
Myrmidons were named after King Myrmidonus.

248. On Peleus and Thetis.

Although Jupiter wanted to marry Thetis, the mother of the nymphs, the
Fates prevented him because the offspring that might be born would drive

Jove from his realm. Jupiter joined her to Peleus. And so, when Peleus married Thetis, he held a magnificent banquet for all the gods and goddesses. Discord alone was not allowed to attend. Angered by this, she threw a golden apple into the banquet hall where Venus, Minerva, and Juno were. On it was written: "A most beautiful gift for the most beautiful goddess." Paris, the son of Priam, was chosen as a judge while the goddesses were boasting among themselves about which was the most beautiful and to whom he owed the apple. He preferred the beauty of Venus to that of Juno and Minerva and awarded the golden apple to her. Later, when he was attacking Sparta, he stole Helen with the help of Venus, but because of the judgment of Paris, Juno forever after was hostile to the Trojans. By Peleus, Thetis gave birth to Achilles. When she was afraid for his death because he was mortal on his father's side, she lamented over this in the presence of Neptune. Neptune said that she should not be afraid concerning him, because he would be such a man that people would think he was sired by a god. Yet, fearing the fate of Achilles, Thetis dipped him in the Stygian swamp. Thus he was invulnerable in his entire body, except in his heel, by which he had been held. While waging war around the walls of Troy, Achilles refused to go forth against the Trojans because he was in a rage against Agamemnon because of Briseis. But he was asked at least to offer his arms, fashioned by the hand of Vulcan, to his comrade Patroclus. Earlier in the Trojan War, Patroclus had killed Sarpedon, the son of Jove and Laodamia.[80] At last, Ulysses persuaded him and Achilles gave in. Thus Patroclus went forth wearing the arms of Achilles. He was killed by Hector, stripped of the arms, and laid to rest. Then Thetis again obtained arms from Vulcan for Achilles, who could not bear the death of his companion. Achilles wore these arms when he challenged Hector, killed him, and avenged Patroclus. He bound Hector's corpse to his chariot and dragged him around the walls. Priam asked Achilles to allow him to take the ransomed body of his lifeless son. When he did this, Polixena, Hector's sister, stood on a tower and cast down her bracelets and earrings to the man from whom her brother's body was being ransomed. Achilles promised that if the girl he had seen were given to him, he would return Hector's body and make peace between the Trojans and the Greeks, but with Helen returned. But after the Trojans promised Polixena to Achilles and gathered in the temple of Apollo Thymbraeus to ratify the agreement, Paris hid in ambush behind a statue. He shot an arrow and Achilles died from his wounds. Before his death, he asked that Polixena be sacrificed at his tomb after Troy was conquered. Later, his son Pyrrhus fulfilled this request.

249. The Explanation of This Story.

Men say that water is called Thetis, for which reason she is also called a nymph. When Jupiter wanted to take her as his wife, he was prevented by the Fates, lest he should be driven from his realm by the offspring that might be born. This is because fire, that is, Jupiter, is extinguished by the power of water, if it is mingled with water. Moreover, Jupiter joined her to Peleus, for *pelops* in Greek means "mud." Thus men say that earth mixed with water produced man. Furthermore, all the gods are thought to have been present at the wedding because, according to the pagans, they have power over the individual parts in man, such as Jove the head, Minerva the eyes, Juno the arms, Neptune the breast, Mars the heart, Venus the kidney and groin, and Mercury the feet. Also, Discord alone was not admitted to the marriage of water and earth, that is, of Thetis and Peleus, because both elements are in harmony so that man might be brought forth. The coming together in this marriage indicates this, for Peleus as earth, that is, flesh, is united to Thetis as water, that is, fluid, and Jupiter as fire, that is, soul, is said to join both. Discord threw in the golden apple, that is, desire, for you might see a golden apple, but you cannot eat it. Also, considering the tripartite manner of mankind, that is, speculation, practice and love of ease, the poets have set forth the contest of three goddesses contending over the nature of beauty. Minerva signifies speculation, that is, contemplative life; Juno signifies practice, that is, active life; and Venus signifies love of ease, that is, life devoted to pleasure. Moreover, the contemplative life is that which pertains to the search for wisdom and truth; the active life, striving after adornment, gapes at life's useful goods; the life devoted to pleasure, seeking only life's corruption, addicted only to lust, considers no honorable thing to be good. Thus the poets said that Jove could not pass judgment on these, either because they did not know about the judgment after the end of the world, or since they believed that man was established in freedom of the will. If Jupiter had judged as a god, by condemning two of them, he would send down only one way of life to the earth. But the poets handed over the judgment to a man, who is owed the free will to choose. Truly, the shepherd was not sure with an arrow, not good with a javelin, not handsome of face, not quick of wit. As is the way of the herd, he turned his gaze toward lust, which he put before virtues and riches. Finally, his mother dipped her son Achilles in the Stygian waters, for there are veins in the heel that are said to affect the system of the kidneys and masculine parts. Wounded in the heel, Achilles perished for love of Polixena, for in Greek *polixenae* means "stranger of many men," since love makes minds wander as strangers. Indeed, human virtue is fortified for all events, yet lies exposed to the blows of lust.

250. On Diomedes.

Diomedes discovered that his wife was living shamefully at Argos because of the wrath of Venus, who had been wounded by him. He refused to return there, but took possession of parts of Apulia. After he conquered all the people on Mount Garganus, he founded many cities in that same region: Beneventum, Equus Tuticus, and Arpos, which is also called Argiripa.

251. On the Priest of Neptune.

After the Greeks came to Troy, the priest of Neptune was stoned to death because he had not prevented their coming by his sacrifices. Later, as the Greeks were departing, when the Trojans wanted to sacrifice to Neptune, Laocoon, priest of Apollo Thymbraeus, was chosen by lot, as used to happen when a certain priest was lacking. Laocoon had committed a sin by copulating with his wife in front of a statue of the deity. Because of this he was destroyed, along with his sons, when serpents were dispatched against them.

252. On Pyrrhus.

After Troy was conquered, Pyrrhus received by lot Andromache, the wife of Hector, along with Helenus, the son of Priam. It was then a custom of kings that, not having a lawful wife, they might nevertheless have someone, even a captive, in place of a lawful wife, so that children born of her could succeed them. Pyrrhus took Andromache as if she were his lawful wife, and by her he had a son, Molossus, who succeeded his father. Molossia, a region of Epirus, was named after him. Later, Helenus named this place after his brother Chaon, whom he is said to have killed unknowingly while hunting. He called it Chaonia, as a consolation for his dead brother. Afterward, Pyrrhus wanted to take Hermione, the daughter of Menelaus and Helen, as his wife. She had been betrothed before then to Orestes, who killed Pyrrhus in the temple of Apollo at Delphi. As he was dying, Pyrrhus ordered that Andromache, who held the place of a wife in his house, be given to Helenus because of a good deed. Helenus had prevented him from sailing home by prophesying to him that all the Greeks would perish in a shipwreck, and this came about. Thus it happened that after Pyrrhus died, Helenus ruled.

253. On Hecuba and Polymestor.

When the booty of captured Troy was divided, Hecuba, the wife of Priam, fell by lot to Ulysses. She was bitterly grieving last of all over two calamities, the untimely deaths of Astyanax and Polyxena, who was slain at the grave of Achilles. Hecuba was brought by ship to Thrace. Deprived of the rest of her children, she hoped that her son Polydorus would remain unharmed. She had entrusted him secretly to Polymestor, King of Thrace. But she observed him on the shore, lifeless, cast up by the waves onto the land. Induced by greed for gold that little Polydorus had handed over to him, Polymestor killed him. To conceal the crime, he hurled him into the deep. After she discovered this, Hecuba pretended that she wanted to visit the king, promising that she would add gold beyond that which she had handed over to him before with her son. Thinking that this was true, the tyrant consented to her request for a private conversation. Hecuba blinded him. As the Thracians pursued her, she was turned into a dog.

254. On Idomeneus.

Idomeneus, King of the Cretans, was returning home after the fall of Troy. In order to calm a storm, he vowed that he would sacrifice from his property that which first presented itself to him on his return. And so it happened that his son ran to meet him. When he had immolated him, or, as others say, he wanted to immolate him, the citizens drove Idomeneus from his realm. He took possession of the Salentine promontory in Calabria. Near there he founded a city.

255. On Circe.

Circe was the daughter of the Sun. She changed men who visited her into wild beasts. Ulysses came to her by chance after Troy had been conquered. He sent Eurylochus to visit her, with twenty-two companions. Circe soon changed these from their human shape. Eurylochus fled from there and told Ulysses. As Ulysses proceeded alone to meet Circe, Mercury gave him an antidote and showed him how he might trick her. After Ulysses came to her, he mixed Mercury's antidote in the drink that he accepted from her. With his sword drawn, he threatened death to her unless she restored his companions to him. Then, perceiving that this was done with the consent of the gods, Circe gave him assurances. She restored his companions to Ulysses and married him. She gave birth to Telegonus.

256. The Interpretation of This Story.

Circe is said to mean "work of the hand," as if from *cironore*, for a lustful woman does not value labor of the hands. Blameless Ulysses ignored her because wisdom despises lust. Thus he is also said to have had a chaste wife, Penelope, because all chastity is joined to wisdom. Circe is imagined to be the daughter of the Sun because nothing is brighter than the sun. By her lust and flattery, Circe leads men away from human life toward the beastly life, so that they serve lust and pleasures. This is the point of the story.

257. On Picus.

Picus loved Pomona, the goddess of fruits, and married her. Since Circe loved him and was spurned, she was angry. She changed him into a bird, the martial woodpecker (picus), for the magpie (pica) is another bird. The story is fashioned this way because Picus was an augur and had in his house a woodpecker, through which he learned the future.

258. On Phyllis.

Phyllis was the Queen of the Thracians. As Demophoon, son of Theseus and King of the Athenians, was returning from the Trojan War, she fell in love with him and proposed marriage to him. He replied that first he would set his affairs in order and then return for his wedding. He departed, and when he tarried, Phyllis hanged herself. She did this because of the impatience of love and the influence of sorrow, since she believed that she had been spurned. She was transformed into an almond tree without leaves. When Demophoon returned later and learned the truth, he embraced the tree trunk. As if the tree sensed the bridegroom's arrival, it put forth leaves.

259. On Laodamia.

Laodamia was the wife of Protesilaus. When she learned that her husband had been the first to perish in the Trojan War, she wished that she might visit his spirit. When this was granted, she was unwilling to forsake the spirit, and she died in its embrace.

260. On Procris.

Procris, the daughter of Iphilis, was the wife of Cephalus. When he was taken with a zeal for hunting and exhausted by the effort, he used to go to a certain place and there to summon the wind to refresh him. Since he did this often, he stirred the love of Aurora toward himself. She gave him a very swift hound named Lelapa and two unavoidable spears, since he was a hunter. She asked him to embrace her, but he said that he had sworn an oath of mutual chastity with his spouse. When she heard this, Aurora responded: "To test your spouse's chastity, transform yourself into a merchant." When this was done, he went to his wife. When he came to Procris, he offered gifts and procured intercourse; then he revealed himself as her husband. Grieving over this, Procris went to the forest and hid among the bushes to catch her husband, since she had heard from a rustic that Cephalus loved Aurora and used to summon her. When he called Aurora in his usual way, Procris tried to come forth and rustled the bushes. Expecting it to be a wild animal, Cephalus hurled his unavoidable spear and unknowingly killed his wife. Yet, as she was dying, Procris begged that he not marry Aurora.

261. On Tereus.

Tereus was King of the Thracians. He married the daughter of Pandion, King of Athens, whose name was Procne. After a short time she asked him to fetch Philomela, her sister, for a visit. He proceeded to Athens. While he was bringing the girl back with him, he violated her on the way and cut out her tongue so that she would not tell of his wicked deed. But the girl sent the true story to her sister depicted in her own blood on a tapestry. When this accusation became clear, Procne killed her own son, Itys, and set him before his father to be eaten. Afterward, all were changed into birds: Tereus into a hoopoe, Itys into a pheasant, Procne into a swallow, and Philomela into a nightingale.

262. On Leander and Hero.

Leander of Abydos and Hero of Sestos were lovers. Leander used to visit Hero by swimming through the Strait of the Hellespont, which flowed between the cities of Sestos and Abydos. But after the torch that Hero used to hold up at the appointed time was by chance extinguished in a storm, the young man perished. When his body was carried to the girl, she hurled herself into the sea.

263. On Hymenaeus.

Hymenaeus, as some say, is the god of marriage. Others say that he was a certain youth overwhelmed by catastrophe on the day of his marriage. Thus he is called upon at weddings for the sake of expiation. But this is false, for his name ought to be avoided more than retained. Yet the story that follows is the truth. Hymenaeus was a boy of the Athenian nation. When he surpassed the years of boyhood and still could not achieve manhood, he is said to have been endowed with beauty so that he might imitate being a woman. When one of his fellow citizens, a noble maiden, loved him, he despaired of marriage, since he was born of common parents. Yet he did what he could: loving her at a distance with his heart alone, he made himself a girl in appearance. When the noble women and maidens were celebrating the sacred rites of Eleusinian Ceres, pirates arrived suddenly and captured them. Among the women was also Hymenaeus, who had followed that beloved maiden, and the girl was entrusted to him. When the pirates had carried their booty over the distant seas, finally, swept along, they reached a certain region and there, overcome by sleep, they were slain by those pursuing them. Hymenaeus left the maidens there and returned to Athens. He was promised marriage to his beloved by the citizens if he would restore their own daughters to them. When Hymenaeus restored them in accordance with his vow, he received his desired wife. Because their union was happy, it pleased the Athenians to join the name of Hymenaeus to marriage. For this reason, those who are marrying still invoke the name of the liberator of virginity, as it were. Thus also among the Romans Talassio is invoked. During the rape of the Sabine women, a certain plebeian took a very beautiful woman who had been seized. Lest she be taken away from him by others, the noble woman pretended to belong to the leader, Talassio. Because of his name, the girl's virginity remained intact.

264. On Licambes.

A certain Licambes had a daughter, Neobole. When Archilochus asked for her in marriage, the father promised her, but then denied that she had been promised. The angry Archilochus composed a poem, a curse against him. So, driven by grief, Licambes hanged himself, along with his only daughter.

265. On Bubalus.

They say that Bubalus was a certain painter at Laudomena, a city of Asia. As a joke, he painted Hiponactes, a certain poet, as deformed. Moved by rage, the poet attacked Bubalus with such a poem that he hated his own life and hanged himself with a noose.

266. On Dirceus.

The poet Dirceus, an Athenian, was misshapen in all his limbs. He first invented the war trumpet. The Lacedaemonians used this to lead them and conquered the Messanians. The war between the Lacedaemonians and the Messanians was drawn out for a long time. When the Lacedaemonians consulted him, Apollo responded that they could not otherwise conquer the Messanians, unless they should fight with an Athenian as their leader. When they requested one, the Athenians sent Dirceus. So the Lacedaemonians conquered their enemies when the new sound of the war trumpet terrified them.

267. On Iarbita.

Iarbita was a Moor by birth. He tried without success to imitate Timagines the philosopher, who was declaiming in a learned way. Iarbita is said to have burst, so to speak, with envy.

268. On Mopsus.

Mopsus was the son of Apollo and Imas. He and Calchas held a contest over their skill in prophesy in a grove consecrated to Apollo in Gryneum. When they contended over the number of fruits on a certain tree, the glory went to Mopsus. Because of his grief over this matter, Calchas died.

269. On Apicius.

Apicius was a certain very voracious man who wrote many works about spices. After he squandered his entire inheritance and finally began to be in need, he could not endure the shame. He died by poison.

270. The Story of Opimius.

A certain man, Opimius,[81] was so greedy that although he abounded in great wealth, he would drink the worst wine of Veii on holidays, and on private occasions he drank vapid wine that was worse than that of Veii. By chance this man fell into a coma on account of his excessive anxiety. Then his cheerful heir began to run around among the coffers and keys, hoping that Opimius would die quickly. A faithful doctor came and recognized the cause of the malady. He counted out all the money before him and he spoke to the sick man thus: "Unless you guard your possessions, there is no difference whether you perish from hunger or from sickness." Waking up, Opimius said: "Who will take my possessions from me?" So he became well.

271. On Alcinous.

Alcinous, King of Phaecia, was plagued by the Harpies. When Hercules came to visit him and recognized this, he waited for their approach as they came in their accustomed way to the table. After Hercules wounded the Harpies, he drove them from the kingdom. The Harpies are said to be hounds of Jove, named after plundering (rapiendo). Ovid calls them "Stymphalian."

272. The Story of Ixion.

When Ixion took the daughter of Eponeus as his wife and gave a dowry unwillingly, he made a ditch that he filled with fire, and he covered the top with ash. Pretending that he had invited Eponeus to a meal, he thrust him into this ditch, along with his companions, and thus he let him be consumed by fire. Because of this he is called perfidious.

273. A Narrative.

When Romulus waged war against the Sabines, he handed over the citadel to a certain Tarpeius to be defended. This man's daughter fell among the enemy when she went to fetch water. When they incited her to betrayal, she demanded the adornments on their left hands, that is, their bracelets, as a reward. After she carried out the betrayal of the citadel, the enemy kept their promise and paid her with an ingenious death. They killed her by laying their shields, the adornments of their left hands, upon her. Buried there, she gave her name to the Tarpeian Rock.

274. On Responsive Song.

It is a responsive song (amoebeum carmen) as often as some sing and employ an equal number of verses, and the response is such that it says either something greater or something contrary.

275. The Accursed Hunger for Gold.

"The accursed hunger for gold."[82] That saying arose from a custom of the Gauls. For as often as pestilence afflicted the Massilians, one of the poor was brought forth to be fed for a whole year by the foremost men of the city. Afterward, adorned with sacred boughs and dressed in sacred garments, this man was conducted through the whole city and led about with curses. This is so that the evils of the whole city might fall upon him, and thus he was cast down.

THIRD MYTHOGRAPHER

On the Gods of the Pagan Nations and Their Allegories

There was in Egypt a very rich man named Syrophanes. He had an only-begotten son whom he loved beyond measure. It happened that the son died. Out of excessive feelings of love, the father set up in his house a statue of his son, and while he sought a cure for sorrow, he found rather a seed bed of grief. That statue was called *eidolon*, which in Latin we call an "image of sorrow" (speciem doloris). As an act of homage toward the master, his whole household used to weave garlands for the statue; they brought flowers and lighted incense. Even the accused took refuge at the statue, obtained pardon from the master, and venerated that statue more from a feeling of fear than of love. Thus it is said: "Fear first made gods in the world."[1] After this the long-standing human error in the worship of pagan idols began to be diffused everywhere. But this same ignorance did not envelop all men, nor did all think these same rites should be accepted. For the philosophers, whose authority passed on to many peoples either the way of truth or the assertion of reason, declare that there is one god, without doubt the creator of heaven and earth and all things. Yet these same philosophers likewise call this god by various names because of the manifold dispositions by which the world is governed in diverse ways. For he is called Vitumnus because he bestows life (vitam), and Sentinus because he bestows sensation (sensum). The god is called Jove or Jupiter in the sky, Juno in the air, Diana on earth, and there are many other names of this same god, just as there are names of most things. And generally, one and the same god is called not only by diverse names, but also by different sexes, according to those verses of Valerius Serranus:

"Almighty Jupiter, inventor of things and of kings,
  Father and mother of gods, one and the same god."[2]

So also there is that speech of Jove: "Heaven-dwellers, my limbs, gods, whom our power, diverse in offices, makes." So, as Remigius says, a god, in his mighty dispositions, is addressed as if he were of masculine gender, but in lesser dispositions, a god receives somehow a feminine name. Or, according to Servius, passing on the teaching of the Stoics, a god is called a male from "acting" (agendo), but a female when the poets give to the god the nature of being passive (patiendi). Thus it is written: "He sank deep into the lap of the joyful spouse."[3] Moreover, according to the same writer, a god is named from his acts, as Jupiter is called *juvans pater*, "Helping Father." Mercury is so called because he presides over merchandise (mercibus); Liber is given his name from liberty (libertas). Varro says that although a man is one and the same person, he is called a man (homo) because of his body, but a wise man (sapiens) because of his soul. Therefore, because of the diversity in his ordering of affairs, a god, though one and the same, is thought of by many names.

But now, let us refute in turn some unexplained errors of antiquity, and if we cannot pour light into them, at least let us drive away in some measure the mists of ignorance with the scourge of mightier authorities.

1. Saturn

1. Men consider Saturn the first of the gods. They imagine him to be sad, an old man, gray haired, having his head covered with a grayish mantle. He is the devourer of his own children, bearing a scythe and even holding in his right hand a fire-breathing dragon that devours the end of its own tail. Different writers perceive some of these attributes in the same way, but others differently.

2. The story says that Saturn the father and Jove the son possessed realms in Crete. After a war started between them, Jupiter prevailed. Saturn was driven away and fled to Italy. Janus, who was reigning there then, welcomed him. When Saturn taught him the use of vines and the pruning hook, he was admitted into a share of the realm, and he made a town for himself. Saturn devoted great skill to agriculture. Drawing people to himself through the distribution of grain, he deserved to be called Saturn, from *saturando*, that is, "saturating."

3. Thus poets everywhere describe this god as sad because he was conquered in war and violently thrust out of his realm. But astrologers consider the matter more subtly. They say that he is so sad because the star

allotted to Saturn always announces sadness at its rising. Positioned in Capricorn, it produces the heaviest rains, but especially in Italy. Thus it is written: "Or Capricorn, monarch of the Western waves."[4] In fact, it brings hail in Scorpio, and likewise lightning in another sign, winds in another, and other hurtful things in others. Astrologers even add that Saturn is so sad because his constellation is the slowest, for it spends thirty years traveling through its cycle. Another of the wandering stars might pass through its cycle in a month, as the moon does, or others in a year, as Mercury, Venus and the Sun do, another in two years, as Mars does, or another in the space of twelve years, as Jupiter does.

4. Poets depict him as an old man because, just like an old man, he has been robbed of the warmth of youth. He struggles with the cold, for the blood is thinner in those old men, and thus they tremble. So also his star is thought to be the coldest. No wonder, since it is farthest from the sun, from which all warmth proceeds, and since it is near the waters above the heavens. Also it has its dwelling place among the most remote signs, namely Aquarius and Capricorn, which are thought to be cold from the influence of their season. In these, even if Saturn is placed with the sun, he brings upon us the most oppressive blast of cold. But there are those who assert that he is not called cold from his own shade, but from the effect of the cold, because, of course, he kills men with his destructive constellation. Indeed, dead men are cold. If this is true, he is not inappropriately imagined to be an old man, since it is in the nature of old men to be always near death. Yet he is called cold by some only because he is hurtful. Servius intimates that "cold" is put in place of "hurtful." You have an example in Vergil, where he says: "O Boys, flee from here! A cold snake lurks in the grass."[5] Finally, Saturn also seems not unsuitably called cold on this account: just as old men by nature have an abundance of cold and phlegmatic humor, so also from the signs Capricorn and Aquarius, over which he presides, we know that in individual years cold and rains come to us, namely in the months of January and February. Because of this also they depict him as gray haired, since there is no doubt that at that same time he produces frosts and snow. He has his head covered, so that, just as a frigid old man fortifies himself against the cold, Saturn is also thought to remind us of the same thing. Thus he is covered with a grayish mantle because his star is of a watery, cold nature.

5. But let us pass on to the explanation of other points. The philosophers also accept Saturn as a figure of time. Thus they call him Cronus in Greek, that is, "Time." So also, some assert that his head is covered on this account: because the beginning of time is unknown. Thus he was driven away by his son because the following time, which in a certain manner is born from the preceding time, drives away the past by succeeding it. But also he is called Tex by the Greeks because among them *T* signifies three hundred, *e* five, and *x* sixty, and this, as those who compute it say, is the number of days in the whole year. Tex is also interpreted as "eating" or "consuming." Thus he is also said to have devoured his own children. This is thought to be so because time consumes whatever it has brought forth, for all things that have arisen perish, and what has advanced grows old.

6. Saturn carries a scythe, either because the fruits that time produces are harvested with a scythe, or because, as we said above, he first taught the use of the scythe to the Romans, or because all the seasons turn back upon themselves in imitation of curved scythes. For this same reason he holds a fire-breathing dragon in his right hand. The dragon denotes the year. It rightly devours the end of its own tail because the year also returns to itself by its own tracks, and it devours the yearly fecundity and the yield of all fruits. So also that dragon is called fire breathing, that is, devouring all, just as fire consumes all things. There are those who say that Saturn is of no harm as he goes forward. In fact, since he goes backward, he is harmful, and thus he has a scythe, since a scythe in going forward has no force, but pulled back it cuts down whatever stands before it. Fulgentius says that Saturn has his head covered because fruits, which the seasons bring forth, are covered by the shade of leaves.

7. Also, the fables say that this god cut off the manly parts of his own father, Sky, and cast them into the sea. From their blood and the foam of the sea Venus was born. Or, they say he himself was castrated by his son, and in the same way Venus came forth from his manly parts thrown into the sea. But from this difference we perceive the same thing. According to Fulgentius, the cut-off testicles of either one represent the fruits of nature that the seasons produce. These, of course, are brought forth from earlier seed plots, and they are born fit for creating new ones from themselves. If they are propagated in their own way, they spring forth. It is necessary that Venus, that is, desire, produce these fruits that have been

gathered and planted in the pit of the stomach as if in the sea. Thus the comic poet says: "Without Ceres and Bacchus, Venus is cold."[6] The natural philosophers assert that we imagine this so, because nothing at all is created unless moisture descends from the sky to earth. As you will hear in the following passages, the natural philosophers say that Venus is "the beauty of the earth." In fact, others offer a reason that Venus was born from the blood of manly parts and the foam of the sea. All strength, they declare, is weakened by sexual intercourse. Thus it is thought that Venus was born through loss. Moreover, concerning the sea, they affirm what natural science teaches: that sweat, which sexual union always brings out, is salty. So also the myrtle is sacred to Venus because it delights in the seashore. They also add that she arose chiefly from the foam because the pleasure of passion, like foam, quickly disappears, and passing away very swiftly, leaves nothing except a goad to repentance in the conscience.

8. Now let us return to the beginning. Although Saturn, according to the story, is an old man, he is able to become a boy. This fiction arose from this fact: in each year time seems to grow old in the winter and to come to life again in the spring. He is also thought to have the face of a dragon because of the excess of cold. At one time he has a lion's mouth due to the excessive heat of summer, and at another time a helmet with boar's teeth because of the frequent intemperateness of the elements. Clearly, these conditions come about through the changes of the seasons. Also, add the fact that since the star of Saturn is destructive, according to the astronomers, and is an unpropitious constellation, as we have said, he is called a malicious god because of these. Finally, lest you imagine from what was said before that my foot is in a tight spot, Servius says that this god devoured his sons for this reason only: he is the god of the seasons, which revolve forever. So also Cicero says that he was named Saturn because "he is saturated with years,"[7] that he was overcome by Jove so that he would not have unrestrained movement, and so that he might be bound by chains of stars through which time is set in order.

9. Fulgentius says that Saturn is the son of Pollux, either from *pollendo*, "being mighty," or from *pollucibilitate*, "magnificence," which we more commonly call "humane character." Indeed, they say that the age was golden while he was still reigning. Although we seem to ramble a little, men say that after a plot was formed, Saturn was driven from his realm by his own son, as we said, and Jove threw into disorder the peace

that had thrived in the time of Saturn. Thus the golden age, named after the golden morals that thrived up to that time, he changed to the age of silver. Truly, it is known that in the time of Jove there were many wise men among his earthly subjects. So also, after Saturn was conquered and put to flight, other tyrants set about to deprive Jove of his paternal inheritance. Since he overcame them with engines of war, he is thought to have blasted the Giants with thunderbolts.

10. Now concerning these matters that Varro writes about, I considered them either of little importance to the present subject, or scarcely worthy to be committed to memory. For he says that in the time of the flood certain men fled to the mountains. Later, they were attacked in a war by those who came from other mountains; they easily defeated these from their higher places. Thus it happened that the higher ones were called gods, but the lower ones were called earth-born. Also, either because of the serpentine shrewdness that they had, or because they crept from the lower places to the higher, they were said to have had serpents in place of feet. Indeed, men at that time were said to be born from rocks and tree trunks. This was because of the ancient habitations of men, for they dwelt in hollow trees or in caves before houses were made. When they emerged from them or led out their offspring, they were said to be engendered from there. Beyond this, as Lactantius says, while the use of houses was lacking to them, they used to roam about in the manner of herds. They sheltered their children either in the hollows of trees or mountain caves. Those passing by thought these children were the young of trees or rocks.

11. Thus it is that the Arcadians are said to have existed before the stars and moon, for they were born and raised in dense forests. When they finally went out into the plains, they had not seen the moon or stars before, nor had they thought that these existed. When the Arcadians contested the Phrygians over their antiquity, they shut up individual little ones with individual nurses from whom they learned speech, to prove whether language was inborn or learned, and if it was inborn, which it would be: of the Phrygians or the Arcadians. In fact, the children who were brought forward uttered "bekos," which means "bread" in the tongue of the Phrygians.Therefore they learned that the Arcadians were not the original race. Moreover, the fact that the Arcadians are called noble has been treated elsewhere. In his first book, Thucydides reports

that the Greeks had a custom. When they were compelled to go into foreign lands that they knew to be fertile, they emptied them of their old inhabitants. The Arcadians alone were not moved because of the sterility of their fields, and so, he says, they were thought to be nobles.

2. Cybele

1. Saturn's wife is thought to be the mother of the gods. The Greeks call this goddess Rhea or Berecynthia or Cybele, but the Romans call her Ops. Thus Ops, as Servius seems to intimate, signifies the same in Latin as Rhea in Greek. As Fulgentius says, this name was selected from the fact that she brought aid to the hungry by bestowing fruits. In fact, according to the same author, men called her Berecynthia as if to say "mistress of the mountains." She is mother of the gods because they are called gods through pride, and they dwell on Olympus, as if to say they are lofty and proud. They are called *daemones*, "supernatural spirits," because they strove to subjugate many men and to be above people, for *demos* means "people" and *eis* means "one." So also among the Romans, he says, they are called *indigetes*, "local deities," as if to say *nullis indigentes*, "in need of nothing." Remigius, however, posits other interpretations of supernatural spirits. They are called *daemones*, he says, from *demouchos*, that is, "preeminence among the people" (principatu populi). Or they are called *daemones* as if to say *diamones*, "knowing all," seeing that they are messengers of god, whom the Romans called *medioximos*, "placed in the middle." Indeed, *medioxemus* [sic] means "nearest the middle," for they run about between god and man. In fact, some deities are only celestial, some only terrestrial, and some in the middle, whom Apuleius calls *medioximos*. Moreover, as Servius says, these are ones who were changed from men into gods. Regarding a deity of this kind, they assert that Vergil said: "Summon the common god," namely Hercules, a man who was made immortal. But about these matters I shall write elsewhere.

2. Also, as we considered a while ago in the teaching of Fulgentius, the Greeks called her Berecynthia, as if to say *verni cynthos*, "flower of springtime," for a flower is called *cynthos* in the Attic tongue. Thus she is also called *huas cynthos*, "sole flower," namely, more perfect than all others. Moreover, Berecynthia is understood as power. Therefore she is also called Cybele, "the steadfastness of glory." Thus also Homer says:

"On whom Jupiter bestowed glory." So also she is depicted with a tur-reted crown because every uplifting of power is in the head. She glitters in manifold garments, and she employs lions to draw her chariot, since all power is adorned, and all power is also granted to virtue. She bears a scepter because all power is near royal authority. She is called the mother of the gods because among the ancients, gods or daemones or indigetes were named from *divitiis*, "riches." Moreover, power is the mother of riches. This goddess is said to have loved Attis, a most handsome boy, whom she castrated after she became inflamed by excessive jealousy. Therefore glorious power is always consumed with love of its own vast family fortune, and it is tormented by envy. It quickly cuts off what it loves while it also cuts away that which it hates, for even to this day all power does not know how to preserve a lasting affection with respect to its own family. So also, men say that Attis is so called, as if to say *ethon*, for "custom" is called *ethos* in Greek. Thus however much love there is among the powerful, it does not know how to be stable.

3. Regarding this same Ops, Remigius puts forth more evident conclu-sions. He says that Saturn's wife Ops is a mother of great age, and corpu-lent, because the earth is the *procreatrix* of all things. She is corpulent because the element of earth is thicker and more corpulent than the rest. She has a garment of different colors, adorned with gems and metals, for these are collected together in the bowels of the earth or in the sands. She is also called Cybele, as if to say *cubele*, for no element is more solid than earth. In fact, they say that *cubus* means solid, and hence we call solid numbers cubes. Or, as the same author has it, she is called Cybele by a Greek because in Latin this signifies "rotation of the head" (rotatio capitis), since men recall that in her sacred rites her priests employ those called "Galli."[8] Servius observes nearly the same thing about this god-dess, but a little more, for he says that she is the nourishing mother of the gods. Earth is called "nourishing" (alma) because she feeds (alat) us. But he says we improperly bestow this epithet on other deities also. Moreover, we know that the earth is the mother of the gods. Thus her statue is depicted with a key, for the earth is open in the spring season and closed in the winter. She is carried about by lions to show clearly that maternal love conquers all. Indeed, all fierceness is subject to mater-nal affection and subjugated to it. She rides in a chariot because the earth is suspended. Thus wheels support her because the world rotates and

revolves. So the Corybantes, who are depicted with drawn swords, were her attendants to signify that all men ought to fight for their own land. The fact that she wears a turreted crown shows that cities are placed upon the earth, and we know that these are distinguished by towers.

4. Remigius relates a little bit about the fact that she loved Attis. Attis, he says, means "flower." In this figure of speech the sun is meant, for it is the flower and prince of stars, and the cause of all flowers. Berecynthia, that is, earth, loved him, for the earth, bound by the cold of winter, desires to be loosened and revived by the warmth of the sun. John Scotus says that the boy Attis means "impulse" (impetum) or "the nearest one" (proximum). Timbrels are given to Ops because the earth is surrounded by two celestial hemispheres. Also, cymbals are in her care because these are similar to the celestial half circles that encompass the earth. Martianus imagines that Vesta, the goddess of fire, clings to her, since fire is found in the bowels of the earth. Indeed, we see that fire is stricken from flint stones.

5. Since the case of Vesta has arisen, let our discourse about her proceed somewhat. We read in this same Martianus that this goddess was the nurse of Jove and that she nourished him at her own bosom. Remigius says that this was imagined for this reason: because philosophers say that heavenly fire, understood as Jove, is nourished by earthly fire, understood as Vesta. The fact that fire is kept unextinguished in her temple can serve as proof that she is believed to be the goddess of fire. In fact, in his book of Fasti, Ovid intimates that this goddess was called "hearth" by our ancestors.[9] But also, at the entrance of her temple there used to be fire at one time, and at this place all devoted their attention to her sacred rites. In fact, they were forbidden to enter the inner sanctuary. Thus he thinks this place was called the vestibule, from Vesta, that is, from the hearth. He adds also that the ancients attributed no effigy to Vesta, just as no effigy was attributed fire, which is always in motion. But also, because fire deserved to be a deity, and because Jupiter had fire in his temple, we say that Vesta must be considered the most powerful goddess of religious worship. Indeed, without fire there was no sacrifice, as we read, nor was any religious worship practiced without it. Thus this goddess, like Janus, was invoked at all sacrifices. So also, I think, men of old added a water pitcher (futis) to her ministry. The futis, as Servius says, was a certain vessel with a wide mouth and a narrow base that

priests used in the sacred rites of Vesta. Indeed, water drawn for her rites was not placed on the ground because it was a sacrilege if this happened. Thus a vessel was devised that could not stand by itself but, put down, immediately poured out whatever it contained. This, I think, signifies as follows: just as water was not poured out from the hand, so at no time must we cease from religious worship.

6. Ovid leaves this same Vesta to be understood as fire, and also as earth. Thus he says that a temple is assigned to her, and also a dome of the temple, both round things, in the likeness of the earth.[10] Also he tries to prove this clearly through the etymology of her name, asserting that the earth is called Vesta because it stands alone, as if to say *vi sua*, "by its own power," although it is clear that all the other elements are in motion without interruption. For this reason not a few writers contend that Vesta and Cybele were the same goddess. Yet the name Vesta is from the Greeks, according to Cicero.[11] Indeed, she is the one, he says, whom they called Hestia. Her power extends to altars and hearths. Finally, the true name of the deity is Vesta because, according to the law of her sacred rites, it was forbidden to know where at Rome she presided. A certain tribune of the people, as we read, dared to divulge this and was crucified. So we say that Vergil used this periphrasis: "Mother Vesta, you who guard the Tuscan Tiber and the palaces of Rome."[12] Also, Pales, whom we call the goddess of fodder in the writings of Vergil, and for whom the sacred rites called Palilia were fulfilled on April 21, is meant to be mother of the earth by some, Vesta by others. Vergil addresses this goddess in the feminine gender, but others, including Varro, in the masculine gender.

Some writers interpret Saturn to mean *sacrum sensum*, "sacred sense," that is, divine providence creating all things, or the sower of all things. They assign his four children as follows: first Jove, second Juno, third Neptune, fourth Pluto, or Dis. They also say that he is the son of Pollux, as if to say *poly filium*, "having many children," namely, begetting the four elements. Natural philosophers understand Jove to be *aether*, "upper air," that is, fire; Juno as air; Neptune as water; Pluto as earth. But let us begin our treatise about Jove.

3. Jupiter

1. They say that Jove and Juno, that is, fire and air, are brother and sister because these elements seem to be equal in thinness. Because Juno,

air, is subject to fire, her husband's name was rightly placed higher. But they say that both of these come from *juvando*, "supporting." Indeed, nothing fosters all things so much as warmth, nor can any animal live without air. Jupiter is called Zeus in Greek, which means warmth (calor) or life (vita) in Latin, because, of course, this element is warm, and because, as Heraclitus asserts, all things are animated by vital fire. Thus he is called Jupiter, as if to say *juvans pater*, "supporting father," and he is the same as the one named Lucceius in the language of the Oscans, from light, which he is thought to give to men. By the Romans he is named Diespiter, that is, *dieipater*, "father of the day."

2. Vergil calls this god the eternal ruler of men and gods. Probus assigns one title according to the natural philosophers, another according to the astrologers. Indeed, he says Jupiter is the ruler of the gods because he is the upper air, which has preeminence among the elements. He is the ruler of men because the favorable brilliance of Jove's star bestows honors upon men. His rule is eternal because of his separation from the other deities, for we read that even Apollo set aside his divine power, and that Hercules and Father Liber were not always gods. Also, we read what the poets invented: that Juno placates Jove when mortal men anger him. She restrains him from his purpose, for Jove, or Jupiter, is the *aether*, "upper air," but Juno is *aer*, "air." Thus when the seeds shrivel in winter, and earth begs for its accustomed nourishment from Jove, that is, from the ethereal fire, this can only happen by Juno, that is, air, interceding and mediating, as it were. The air receives the warmth of ethereal fire and brings its accustomed fertility to the earth.

3. Also, Martianus calls Jove the will (fatum) of the gods, for he is said to govern divine affairs, that is, those above, by himself, but human affairs, namely those below, by the fates. We offer the reason for this fact: the nature of *aether* is such that it does not need the lower elements, but the lower elements need it. Thus things below subsist by various supports of the elements, which are understood as the fates, but things above are content to preserve themselves by the stability of their own nature alone. The fact that poets call Jove "beneficent" (benignum) alludes to his star, which is beneficial and most temperate. Indeed, positioned as it is between Mars and Saturn, that star is thought to borrow its temperateness from both, drawing warmth from Mars but moisture from Saturn. Thus Vergil writes: "Look upon us—only this."[13] In fact,

those who are favored by the rays of Jove's star doubtlessly live well. Elsewhere the same author wrote: "He turns his eyes away from the fields of the Rutuli,"[14] that is, by looking back he made that place more fruitful. So also, on the other hand, we read about a hostile deity: "Turned away, the goddess held her gaze fixed on the ground."[15] Thus we call angry gods "averse," as also, concerning that same place, according to Servius, we read: "For her statue could not turn itself." And elsewhere Vergil wrote: "Turned away long before, she regarded him as he was saying such things."[16] Indeed, how do you understand "turned away," except as "angry?" Neither does it seem to be contrary that in the Fourth Book of the *Aeneid*, when Jove is turning his gaze toward the walls of Carthage to drive Aeneas away from there, that all things are thrown into disorder, for he frees Aeneas and Dido from a foul reputation. So it follows: "And the lovers, forgetful of their better reputation."[17]

One imagines that Jove sends lightning and thunderbolts, since it is clear from natural science that these things come from above. Furthermore, coming from the left side, they herald prosperity, because things that seem on the left to us as we look at the sky are on the right there. That is not to say that things on the left are good, but that things on the right in the sky appear on the left to us. Indeed, we read that the left signifies adversity in earthly affairs and prosperity in heavenly affairs.

4. Men place the eagle under Jove's protection. This results from the story that says that the eagle furnished thunderbolts to Jove when he fought against the giants. The natural philosophers give this reason: the eagle by nature is of very great warmth, so that it can cook even the eggs upon which it broods unless it applies *gagates*, a very cold stone. Hence Lucan says: "stones made warm under the eagle."[18] Also they add that the eagle's vision is so keen that it never turns away its eye from the brightest rays of the sun. Also, as they say, the mothers turn their own chicks toward the rising sun so that if they keep their eyes fixed on the sun's rays, they are kept alive, but if not, they are cast out of the nest. Thus in his Ninth Book Lucan says: "as when the bird of Jove brings forth from the warm egg," etc.[19] Therefore in the warmest and clearest element, the upper air, this bird strives after that which abounds in both warmth and sharp sightedness. Men give this as the reason that the Roman ensigns were eagles: just as the eagle is believed to rule over all birds, so the Romans desired and were thought to obtain dominion over

all peoples. Yet about this matter others think differently. Anacreon, an ancient author, wrote that Jupiter was a king of Crete. He waged war against the Titans, sons of Titanus, who was Saturn's brother. When he offered sacrifice to the Sky, he observed favorable auspices of victory. An eagle in flight appeared to him. When he was victorious because of this augury, Jupiter made a golden eagle for his battle standards, and since victory followed those auspices, it was imagined that the eagle had furnished thunderbolts to him as he fought. So also, from a happy augury it came about that eagles follow the soldiers' banner.

5. Next, so that you will not be unaware of what the poets have written about the Titans, their fables say that Earth begot them for her vengeance when she was angry against the gods. Thus they deserve to be called Titans, as if to say *apo tes tiseos* (from vengeance). Of these, only the Sun held back from injury to the deities. Thus he merited the sky and still keeps the former name, for he is called Titan. Also, while the ensigns were passing before them, Jupiter snatched Ganymede, son of Troilus, King of the Trojans, amidst other plunder of war. He is said to have transformed himself into an eagle to seize him. Ganymede was carried into the sky, according to the story, and he is employed in serving drinking cups. In fact, there is a constellation Ganymede, which we call Aquarius, which is known to be rainy. Also, in a similar way Europa was carried off by Jupiter in the form of a bull, that is, having the picture of a bull on his ship. In the form of a cow, he carried off Isis, that is, having a picture of this kind on his ship. Finally, so that you might believe this more surely, an Egyptian worships the ship of Isis. Also, Danae, daughter of Acrisius, was shut up in a golden tower to safeguard her chastity, as they say, but she was seduced by this same Jove with gold, not by a golden shower. Thus Horace wrote elegantly: "For a god changed into money."[20]

6. The fable says that Jove changed into a swan and had intercourse with Leda. She conceived and brought forth an egg from which three children were born: Castor, Pollux, and Helen. Fulgentius explains this fiction. Jupiter, he says, is regarded as "power," but Leda is so called as if from *loide*, which is interpreted as "envy" (invidia) or "injury" (injuria). And so, all power, while stooping to bring injury to someone, is mingled with the injury and changes the appearance of its own nobility. Thus Jupiter transformed himself when he came to Leda. In fact, he became a

swan because the natural scientists say that this bird is full of uproar, so that when it cries out the rest of the birds that are present keep silent. So also, as often as a noble and powerful man hastens to abuse others, he descends from his state of modesty and does not blush to produce contentions. But what is conceived from this circumstance is an egg, that is, a shell full of liquid that is thick, cloudy and sticky, for in the carrying out of injury there is only foulness and filth. From this egg are born three offspring: Helen, Castor, and Pollux. Helen is the seedbed of scandal and discord, as it were, for she incited the Greeks and Trojans to war. Indeed, who does not see that discord and strife proceed from inflicted injury? But also Pollux, interpreted as "perdition" (perditio), and Castor, interpreted as "utmost evil" (malum extremum), were born from the same egg. For very often the fear of vengeance, represented by Pollux, and everlasting punishment, represented by Castor, follow the injury which anyone inflicts upon another.

7. And so, to sum up the foregoing discussion briefly: any powerful person, like Jupiter, degenerates from the dignity of his own character into bestial habits when he plots injury to someone. Indeed, from the infliction of injury there immediately comes an egg, that is, the foulness of infamy and filth arises in the polluted conscience. From the kindling of these things certain evil children come forth, namely, hatred of others and detraction, like Helen; fear of vengeance, like Pollux; and perennial punishment, like Castor. Another fable says that Helen and Pollux were immortal, the children of Jove, and Castor was mortal, the son of Tyndareus. Fraternal love redeemed him from death by its own destruction, and with the permission of Jove it divided its own divinity in half for him. In fact, it is said that Pollux allowed himself to be killed in his mortal part so that Castor might gain immortality, and thus he shared his own divinity with him. The story is fashioned this way because their stars act in such a way that while one rises, the other is still hidden, and likewise after the setting of the first one, the later one still is visible for a while. In fact, that one rises while the other is setting and one sets while the other is rising, as is said by many, cannot be true in any way, since their stars are contiguous and form the same sign, which we call The Twins (Gemini).

8. Now let us certainly not abandon the counsel to search for the truth. Time indicates that Helen was immortal, for it is well known that

her brothers were with the Argonauts. The sons of the Argonauts fought with the Thebans. Likewise, their sons waged war against the Trojans. And so, if Helen were not immortal, no doubt she could not have endured for so many generations. Moreover, we read that she was first seized by Theseus and entrusted to Proteus in Egypt. Persuaded by this fact, some authors say that the war was fought at Troy not because of her seizure, but for certain other reasons. Servius, however, does not agree with them. According to him, Ilion was conquered and Laomedon killed because he prevented Hercules from entering his harbor after Hylas was lost and Hercules had scoured Mysia. Hercules gave Laomedon's daughter Hesione to Telamon because he was the first to climb the walls of Troy. Servius also says that the fiction about Hesione being set free is celebrated in fable. He writes that Priam had been captured by Hercules but redeemed by his neighbors and restored to his kingdom. Legates accompanied Priam, but he could not get Hesione back, since the Greeks said that they held her by rights of war. Provoked by this, Priam sent Paris into Greece with an army. He abducted from there something, namely, the wife or the daughter of the king. Thus Paris, welcomed with hospitality, first committed adultery. Then when he solicited Helen but she was unwilling to follow him, he went forth and besieged the city of Sparta. When this place was destroyed, he seized Helen. Thus she deserved to be taken back by her husband. Therefore the treaty that we know had been established before between the Greeks and Trojans, and which had been kept for a long time, at last was broken and they went to war. Finally, according to a higher science or opinion, Helen's star was thought to be harmful and the bringer of storms, but the stars of her brothers are propitious. Thus, suitably, Helen seems to have been a cause of evil. So it is written: "When now the Spartans' sails were damaged by their sister's fire, the brothers fled."[21]

9. But let us return to Jove. Certain philosophers accept him as a figure of this world. They say that he is called Jove, "universal force" (universalis vis). Thus they attribute eternity to the world, not because it always remains the same, which is truly eternity, but because by enduring and renewing its cycles, it seems to bind itself to a certain form of eternity. But more often we accept Jove as the sky. So also, those who celebrate triumphs hold the insignia of Jove: the scepter and palmed tunic. Thus Juvenal writes: "on the tunic of Jove."[22] They also smear the face with

red in imitation of the ethereal color. In Libya this god is also called Ammon, "of sand," from the Libyan sands, for sand is called *ammos* in Greek. Where his statue is fashioned with a ram's head, it is because in the same place very obscure oracular responses are given. But also he is said to have taught the future through doves in the grove of Epirus because in the Thessalian language both doves and prophetesses are called *pleiades*. He was nurtured in Crete, since it is well known that the Cretans discovered religion first, as Sallust says.

4. Juno

1. As we have said, men consider Juno, air, to be the wife of Jove, sky. The natural scientists call both of these elements male, but water and earth female. Indeed, these hang above and those lie below; these are active and those are passive. They also confirm the fact that masculine names are given to these and feminine names to those. Ignoring this consideration, the poets call one male and the other female. According to Cicero, air is effeminate because nothing is more gentle, and as a wife is subject to her husband, so is air subject to the sky. The poets see that it draws heat from the sky by which it warms the regions below just like semen received into the female womb. Thus they imagine them to be married since more than the others these two elements are thin and have less of dregs, as we have said. The poets call this one brother, but that one sister (not brother), as if they were born of the same parents, so that they might keep the sex associated with marriage. They imagine Juno to be the foster child of Neptune because, according to natural science, air is made dense by seawater. They suppose that as often as Juno is about to do something, she employs the help of another, such as of Aeolus or Iris or the nymphs, because it is the nature of air to do nothing by itself. To produce something, air always employs another connection, as of the winds, which create clouds and rain.

2. To this goddess the poets also assign Iris, the rainbow, as an attendant. Iris is a watery cloud penetrated by a ray of the sun, about which Vergil wrote: "trailing a thousand varied hues across the opposing sun."[23] Thus she always appears from the region of the sun. According to the story, this goddess was the daughter of Thaumas, and so she is called Thaumantias. In fact, the truth is that she received this name from the wonder and astonishment caused by her colors, for in Greek *thaumatos*

means "wondrous." According to the natural scientists, this is the reason for this variety of hues: because it is necessary that clear water and bright air and a dark cloud, when illuminated, create varied hues. Since this goddess appears in the air, and is in the air, she is thought to serve Juno. The fable also says that although Juno persecuted all her rivals, she loved Maia. The story is fashioned this way because when the Sun is positioned in Taurus in the month of May, he makes his way through the Pleiades, one of which is Maia. They are in the knee of Taurus. Then the warmth of the air is tempered by spring showers, and from its temperateness seems to be joyful, as it were.

3. This goddess, Juno, is also said to preside over marriages and births. Thus men assign many names to her. She is called Lucina because she leads those being born into the light (lucem), and for this reason she is called the goddess of gates because she offers those being born a gateway to the light. She is called Fluonia, from the flowing (fluoribus) of seeds, because she frees women in childbirth. She is called Februalis or Februa because she purges them after childbirth when the afterbirth comes forth, for *februo* in Greek is *purgo* in Latin. Thus Pluto is also called Februus because he presides over the purgation of souls. Because of this also the month when the ancients celebrated the expiation of souls is called February. Juno is also called "introducer" (introduca) because she "leads in" girls who are being married. She is called "house-leader" (domoduca) since she leads them to the houses (domos) of their husbands. She is also called Unxia, "anointing goddess," from *unguendo*, "anointing," because brides used to be anointed with various ointments, or because they used to anoint the doorposts of their houses as they entered. Therefore men call their wives *uxores*, as if they were being called *unxores*. She is also called, through antiphrasis, Cinxia, "Goddess of the girdle," from *cingendo*, "girding," because she loosens the girdle of chastity. Also she is called Socicena, "She who unites," because she unites male and female, or she is called Saticena, "Goddess of sowing," from *satione*. Indeed, Juno is said to free women in the toil of copulating, which is also called their war. Thus Vergil writes: "but not slack toward Venus and the nightly wars."[24] The same author also writes elsewhere about an old steed: "If ever he comes to battle, his mad passion is in vain."[25] Men also call her Populonia because she multiplies peoples (populos). Also they call her Curitis, "royal," or "brave," or "powerful," or, according to Servius,

"from a chariot" (curru), since those who wage war use chariots, over which she presides.

4. Since we are discussing brides, Varro says that according to custom they do not touch the threshold. This is so that they will not begin marriage with a sacrilege if, as they are about to give up their virginity, they tread upon a thing consecrated to Vesta, the most chaste deity. So it is written: "She forbids her to touch the threshhold with her foot," for individual parts of the house are sacred to the gods, as the threshold to Vesta, the kitchen to the Penates, and the wall that encircles the house to Jove Herceus. They say that torches were carried before them because in earlier times brides were not led away by their spouses except at night. They provide this reason for the nuts that are scattered at weddings: so that marriage might be celebrated with the favorable omen of Jove, and so that the bride might become a matron, like Juno, for nuts are in the keeping of Jove. Thus they are called walnuts (juglandes), as if to say *Jovis glandes*. Also it is commonly said that nuts are scattered so that there might be rattling sounds while the boys are picking them up, so that the voice of the girl being deflowered might not be heard. But also as the brides reached the husband's threshold, but before they entered, they used to adorn the doorposts with woolen ribbons. Thus Vergil wrote: "with snow-white fleeces."[26] Also, Juno is thought to precede Venus at weddings since the office of Juno comes first in marriage, and the enjoyment of Venus in intercourse comes after.

5. Fulgentius says that in the *Aeneid* Juno petitioned Aeolus, King of the Winds, to cause shipwreck for the Trojans, and she promised him marriage to Deiopea because shipwreck represents a perilous birth in which there is both the loss of the mother in giving birth and peril for the infants in being born. So that you might understand this more clearly: offspring come from Juno, but they are brought forth for shipwreck, for she incites Aeolus. Aeolus is interpreted to mean "destruction of an age," as if to say *aionelos*, for the human race is universally involved in this destiny. She promised Deiopea to Aeolus, for *demos* in Greek means "public" and *ope* means "eye" or "vision." Thus for those being born into the world there is a secular danger in being born, yet, for the completing of the birth, a public vision is promised by the goddess of birth. No less do men assert that Juno is the mistress of riches. Thus they also depict her with a scepter because riches are nearest to kingdoms.

Indeed, one who abounds in riches more easily aspires to a kingdom. They present her with her head veiled because all riches are commonly concealed. They also say that Juno is the goddess of birth, since riches are pregnant, as it were, for by riches are new riches always engendered. But also these are generally miscarried, and both fortune and wealth are lost together. Juno has the peacock under her protection, since a life of riches is always seeking adornment. Just as the peacock adorns its front parts, rounding out the many-eyed curve of its tail, but shamefully bares its backside, so do riches and worldly glory adorn for the moment, but later leave bare those whom they have adorned. Thus a certain writer said: "Consider what remains." And Solomon said: "In the death of a man is the uncovering of his works."[27]

6. They attach Iris to this goddess because, just as she flees in a moment while painting various adornments, so also fortune is fleeting, although adorned for the present. Some writers want her called Iris as if to say *eris*, "strife," and they make her Juno's attendant because very often strife and quarrels arise from the poison of riches. So it is that Iris is sent to stir up discord, but Mercury is frequently sent for the sake of concord. Also many say that Juno is the goddess of kingdoms. Thus they fabricate this story: Ixion sought marriage with Juno. She made a cloud in her own likeness and Ixion had intercourse with it. He sired the Centaurs. So Juno is the goddess of kingdoms, as we have said. Ixion is interpreted to mean "dignity." Indeed, any dignity in this life, that is, a person of dignity as great as you please who strives after a kingdom, merits only a cloud, that is, the temporary likeness of a kingdom. For that is truly a kingdom that will endure forever, not one that is transitory. Moreover, we read also in history that Ixion was the first man in Greece to strive after the glory of a kingdom. He was the first of all to gather a hundred horsemen to himself. Hence they were called Centaurs, as if to say *centum armati*, "a hundred armed men." Thus in a brief time he swiftly obtained a kingdom, and then he was driven out of his kingdom. He is also said to have been punished on a wheel because the whirling of a wheel immediately casts down those things that are on top. In this example we see that those who strive after a kingdom through arms and violence are raised up suddenly and suddenly thrown down, just like a wheel, which does not have a stable top point.

7. Now about the poets' invention of the Centaurs, Servius tells the following story. When a certain Thessalian king ordered his attendants to go and recover cattle that had been chased by a gadfly, and they were not up to such running, the men mounted horses and pursued the cattle by means of their swiftness. They drove them back to their stables with whips. But either because they went swiftly or because their horses were drinking at the River Peneus with heads bent forward, they created an occasion for the story, so that they were thought to be Centaurs: half men, half horses. They are called Centaurs from the Greek *centaurois*. Others assert that the story of the Centaurs was invented to express the swiftness of human life, since it is well known that a horse is very swift. Of course, about these and other things that are said to happen contrary to nature, we must understand, as the Stoics and Academics say, not that they happen, but usually that they seem to happen. On this matter Jerome reports a suitable example in his book *On the Lives of the Fathers* where he treats of the miracles of Macarius. He says that the maiden daughter of a certain head-of-household seemed to men to have been turned through magic phantasms into a horse, so that indeed she was thought to be a mare and not a girl. When her parents brought this girl to Saint Macarius and he asked what they wanted, they said: "This mare that your eyes behold was a maiden and our daughter, but wicked men have changed her through magical arts into this animal that you see. We beseech you, therefore, to pray to the Lord to change her back to that which she was." But he said: "I see no trace of the herd in this girl whom you point out. On the contrary, this which you speak of is not in her body, but in the eyes of the beholders, for those phantasms are not true things as they are, but they are caused by demons." When he led this girl and her parents into his little cell and prayed to the Lord and anointed her with oil in the Lord's name, every deception of sight was dispelled. He caused the maiden to be seen by all as she was seen by him. Thus all magic art was expelled by the Romans, as Pliny the Elder teaches in his *Natural History*.

8. But let us return from our digression to that with which we began. From what we said about Juno being air, we fashion this tale about her quarrel with Jove over pleasure. The fable says that Tiresias observed two serpents copulating. When he struck them with a stick, he was changed into a woman. Then, after a period of time, namely in the seventh year,

he saw the same serpents copulating and likewise, after he struck them, he was restored to his former shape. On account of this, when Juno and Jupiter had a quarrel about the quality of love, they chose him as judge. He declared that a man has a single part of love's pleasure, but a woman has nine. For this reason Juno, in her anger, took away his sight, but Jupiter, to make restitution in some measure for what he had lost, gave Tiresias knowledge of the future. Tiresias is interpreted to mean "perpetuity of summer." He is also established as a figure of time. Thus in the winter months, when Time produces no sprouts because the lands are held fast by cold, he has, in a manner of speaking, a masculine form. When spring arrives, Tiresias sees the animals now exercising their lasciviousness and copulating. He strikes them with his stick, that is, with the heat of passion, and then he changes into the female sex, that is, into summer's fruitfulness. In fact, men consider summer to be like a woman because in this season all the sprouts coming forth emerge from their pods as if from the womb of a mother. Also, there are two seasons of conception in nature, spring and autumn. In autumn, when animals copulate again and seeds are sown, Tiresias, that is, Time tending toward winter, strikes them again with his stick, that is, with his blast of cold, and so at last returns to his former appearance. Autumn so contracts everything that even the grass withers, the sap of trees dries up, leaves fall, and thus Time, declining toward winter's cold, returns to its masculine sterility. Neither is it said inappropriately that Tiresias changed his sex in the seventh year, for it is clear that in the seventh month the sun changes the position of the seasons. Finally, Tiresias is sought as judge for the two gods, fire and air, quarreling over pleasure, that is, over the nature of procreation, and, seeing that he has experienced this himself, he renders a just judgment. Indeed, in fructifying sprouts, a triple matter proceeds from air rather than fire, for the moisture of air fosters sprouts in the soil and produces them in leaves and multiplies them in pods; in fact, the warmth of fire only knows how to ripen them in seeds. Then Juno blinds Tiresias clearly for this reason, that the season of winter grows dark because of the dark cloudiness of the air. Yet, relieving winter's harshness even a little on individual days, Jupiter at least promises and, as it were, now forecasts a crop from the seeds sown. So is he thought to have granted knowledge of the future.

9. Also, Janus is depicted as having two faces for this reason: he looks back at past events and looks forward to future events. But some want him to be lord of the entire year, which, it is well known, is divided into four seasons, and so they depict this same god as having four faces. This fact proves that he is lord of the year: the first part of the year is named after him, January. By some he is called god of the day, and because of his rising and setting he is depicted with two faces. Thus Horace writes: "Father of the Morning, or do you more willingly hear the name Janus."[28] Also, every beginning is consecrated to this same god, and he is called Janus because he opens the door (janua) of the year. So the beginning of the year is not named after him inappropriately. In fact, according to Servius, the reason for opening and closing his temple is varied. Some say that while Romulus was fighting against the Sabines, when he was at the point of being defeated, hot water burst forth from that place and put the Sabines' army to flight. For this reason the custom was handed on that those about to fight would open the temple that had been set up in that place as an image of the former aid. Others say that Tatius and Romulus built the temple in this place after a treaty was made. Thus they also say that Janus has two faces so that he might clearly show his recognition of the two kings. There is also another reason that seems better: that those going to war ought to think about peace and to wish for a turning back.

10. Since we mentioned Aeolus above, Varro reports that he was the king of nine islands. From their foggy mists and the smoke of Vulcan's island, he predicted future events in the blasts of winds. Hence he is believed by ignorant folk to have had the winds in his power. These islands are below the Strait of Sicily; they are called Aeoliae after this same Aeolus, the son of Hippotae, although they also have their own names. About one of them Vergil says: "Aeolian Lipara."[29] We find the names of others in Martianus. But he discusses only seven islands, and he asserts that we call these Vulcanian. Also, he recalls that Aeolus ruled in one of these called Strongyle. From flame bursting forth nearby or from smoke on this island, which the wind would blow, he perceived the future. Today, he says, it is known that inhabitants of this place have foreknowledge. According to natural reasoning, Aeolus is thought to reside in a cave because it is natural that hollow places are full of wind. Juno is thought to have given him a kingdom since the motion of air, that is, of

Juno, creates winds, over which Aeolus presides. According to certain authors, winds are created by the motion of water. Thus, in the *Aeneid*, according to Servius, Juno betrothed a nymph to Aeolus since the origin of winds is rightly united to him because he is king of the winds. Moreover, Juno is said to have nymphs under her sway for a reason, since she is air, from which clouds are formed. Thus it is written: "And the air is forced into a cloud."[30] From the clouds, rains are sent down, which, there is no doubt, are nymphs. In fact, the critics censure Vergil because he promises a wife to Aeolus, a husband already, but his regal license properly excuses this. Thus Sallust writes: "Some men have ten wives, others more, but kings have more than that."[31] Moreover, since Vergil does not say that Aeolus restrains the winds, but that he soothes their spirits and tempers their wrath, he shows by transition that vices of nature are changed in no way, but they can be mitigated somewhat. Besides, who is able to hold the winds, that is, something void, by force? Thus also, expressing the ungovernableness of his kingdom, Aeolus says: "Whatever kind of a kingdom this is."[32] Misenus, the son of Aeolus, was called a trumpeter because it is well known that every sound is formed from wind.

5. Neptune

1. They say that Saturn's third offspring is Neptune, the element of water. According to Cicero, they call him Neptune from *natando*, "swimming," with the letters altered a little, just as Portumnus comes from *portu*, "harbor." The Greeks call this god Poseidon, which in Latin is translated *faciens imaginem*, "making an image," clearly for the reason that water forms images of those who look into it. This happens in no other of the four elements. He is also called Earth-Shaker, that is, *terram movens*, "moving earth." Of course, as certain opinions assert, earthquakes happen because of the violent jarring of water. Neptune bears a trident because waters have a triple quality, for they are fluid, fertile, and potable. We assign Amphitrite to this god in marriage, for, as we read in Fulgentius' On the Aeneid, *amphe* means "around" (circum) and *triton* means "worn down" (contritum). This is as if to say tetrimmenon, clearly because water is enclosed in three elements and, as it were, "worn down" by them: in the sky, as in waters above the heavens; in air, as in

the clouds; in earth, as in springs and wells, or because water, as Macrobius demonstrates, surrounds and wears down the earth. Thus sea gods (Tritones) are said to serve Neptune, since waters wear down (terunt) the lands. The fact that Doris is called the wife of Triton is based on the following story. Dorus was a king of Greece who perished with his army in the sea. Thus he was called a sea goddess and his army was called his daughters, sea nymphs, by the poets, who everywhere serve flattery and fiction. Also, as Varro reports, Phorcus was a King of Corsica and Sardinia. Since King Atlas overwhelmed him and a great part of his army in a naval battle, his comrades imagined that he had likewise been turned into a sea god.

2. Indeed, in his book entitled *Philosopher*,[33] Plato testifies that poets have invented many superstitions. He reports that the race of ancient men, woodcutters and shepherds, used to worship, in place of gods, the causes and powers given by divine grace to men for their use in living, such as agriculture, grape cultivation and more examples of that kind. Then, for the sake of gain and favor, poets portrayed these sciences individually and designated them by their own names, calling the science of tilling the fields "Ceres" and caring for vineyards "Bacchus." They revered even the shameful acts of men, such as lust and passion, among the gods. And thus was born the superstition of religion. Moreover, this term, according to Servius, was taken from the word for little old women who survived (superstites) beyond the customary length of human life. Indeed, we believe that the first inventions about deities of this kind were those of these women who are now decrepit and doting through excessive age. According to Lucretius, superstition is so called from things standing above us (superstantibus), that is, heavenly and divine things of which our fear is empty and unnecessary.

3. Also, Cicero tells us that people's way of life and common custom raise up to heaven men who excel in good deeds because of their fame and good will. Thus he says Hercules, Castor and Pollux, and Aesculapius all merited deification. Later, however, care was taken among the Athenians and Romans so that no one would introduce new religions. So Socrates was condemned, and also Jews or Chaldeans were expelled from the city. Thus Vergil wrote elegantly in Book Eight: "No empty superstition or one ignorant of ancient gods imposed on us these solemn rites."[34] He is saying two things: either we do not so worship Hercules because we

think all religon is true, or because we do not know the ancient gods. The etymology of the name is the reason that men dedicate the nymphs to Neptune, for they are called nymphs as if from *lymphae*, "waters." In fact, Servius offers this difference among the nymphs: the goddesses of springs are called naiads, he says, for water is called *nais*. Oreads are goddesses of mountains, for *oros* is translated as *mons*, "mountain"; the goddesses of forests are dryads, for *drus* means "oak" (quercus). Thus also, as Aristotle says, those who are born and die with trees are called amadryades, that is, "loving oak." Goddesses of the sea are called nereids, from the sea god, Nereus. Neptune is also said to preside over the winds because, according to the natural scientists, wind is created by the motion of water.

4. The fable says that when Neptune and Minerva were quarreling about the name of Athens, it pleased the gods that the city be called after the one who bestowed the better gift on mortal men. Then, when he struck the shore, Neptune brought forth the horse, an animal suited to war. When she hurled her spear, Minerva created the olive tree, which, as a sign of peace, was judged the better thing. Thus the goddess gave her own name to the city, for Athena and Minerva are the same goddess, and each name means "immortality." Some authors want to call the horse that Neptune produced Scinthius, others Chiron, and others Arion. Athens is situated, as I have learned, near the seashore. The adjoining region is Acte, from *acte*, which is translated "shore," or Attica, and the Athenians themselves are called Attici. Furthermore, I think that land is very fertile for olive trees. After Athens was established, I believe that its founder, Cecrops, contemplated these two advantages of the city: it had proximity to the sea and an abundance of olive groves. He stood in doubt for a long time, then gave a name to the city from each thing. Thus we imagine that the deities contended with each other. At last, preferring the fruit of olive trees to the uses of the sea, he named the city after the goddess of these. Moreover, you will hear subsequently why olives are assigned to Pallas. Also, Neptune is said to have created the horse because the sea is mobile and swift. So also he is called Ocean, from *okus* in Greek, which is translated "swift." For that reason too, as Servius says, Castor and Pollux are said to hold horses under their protection, since their stars are very swift.

5. They say that Neptune sired the Harpies, for he is thought to be the father of almost all monsters. No wonder, since all things are procreated from moisture, according to Thales of Miletus. Thus it is written: "and Ocean, the father of things."[35] So also, we call foreigners whose country and kin we do not know "sons of Neptune." The Harpies are called "hounds of Jove," since they are also said to be Furies. Greedy men are thought to endure the Furies, since they hold back from their own portion. Fulgentius sets forth the story of the Harpies as follows. The first of the Harpies, he says, is Aello, the second Ocypete, and the third is called Celaeno, for there are only three. Harpy (harpuia) is translated as "plundering." Aello is translated as "taking away another's property," Ocypete as "carrying off quickly," and Celaeno as "dark." Indeed, in plundering, the first thing is to desire another's property, the second is to seize what is desired, the third is to conceal what you have seized. And so, these Harpies were sent to punish Phineus. This is the story: Phineus the king blinded his own sons who had been accused of incest by their stepmother. On account of this, Jupiter blinded him also, and sent the Harpies to torment him besides. Partly they plundered his food and partly they polluted it with their excrements. Later, however, they were driven away by Zetes and Calais, the sons of Boreas.

6. Phineus, named from *fenerando*, "lending at interest," is put forth as an example of avarice. His sons seem to be rightly called "riches." They are procured with much toil, both preserved and increased with sagacious solicitude, just as with fatherly nurturing. While these riches are suitably spent for good purposes, there is no doubt that they shine with their own brightness and make their owners illustrious too. But when riches are stored up out of perverse parsimony, the stepmother of proper economic management, for the wrong purpose of preserving them more than of spending them, in fact when they are kept concealed in a treasury, they cannot be seen nor shine brightly, neither do they render their masters illustrious for the glory of their generosity. So it seems to be that because of the stepmother's accusation, blindness was inflicted upon both the sons and the father. Also, as Fulgentius says, Phineus is thought to be blind because every greedy man fails to see his own property. He does not ever consider the possessions he has, while he forever wants things to possess. Thus the Harpies seize his food because grasping parsimony does not permit him to taste anything of his own. But truly,

the fact that they pollute his meals with their excrement signifies the life of money lenders, which is filthy in every way, as Horace shows. Zetes and Calais drove them from his sight, since we call "seeking good" *zeton kalon* in Greek. These two are said to be winged because no search for good is ever mingled with earthly things. Thus they are sons of Aquilo because every search for good is spiritual, not carnal. And so, when goodness arrives, all plundering is put to flight.

7. Also, the fable says that Neptune built the walls of Troy with Apollo, but we know that Laomedon had promised a certain amount of money to the above-named gods for making holy shrines. When enemies were menacing him, he transferred this money to the building of walls. Therefore the gods are said to have made the walls and to have been offended. Also, Neptune's son was called Messapus, since he came over the sea to Italy. He was even said to be invulnerable, since nowhere did he perish in war. Indeed, no one marvels that Neptune is called the king of rivers, since the waters are his, and they rush down into his realm, the sea. So rivers are depicted with horns, either because they imitate the bellowing of oxen by the murmuring of their waters, or because generally we see their banks curved in the likeness of horns, or because of the impetus of waters.

6. Pluto

1. Men say that Saturn's fourth child is Pluto, and they assert that he is King of the Lower Regions, he who presides over the earth. In the *Thebaid*, Statius calls him the begetter and terminator of things because all bodies are created from the earth, which Pluto presides over, and all are dissolved into the same earth. *Plutos* is translated as "riches." Thus he is otherwise called Dis, "rich" (dives), because, clearly, either riches are believed to be in the earth alone, or because nothing in the universe is richer than the world below. Although this god receives all things, he is never sated. So it is that this same god is called Vedius, "evil god," and Vejovis, "evil Jove." He is also named Orcus, for *orco* in Greek means "I swear," as if he swears and affirms that he will dismiss none of the souls without examination and punishment. According to Cicero, Pluto is called rich because all things return to earth and arise from earth. He is thought to be in eternal shadows because earth's matter alone is darker than all the elements. Therefore I say . . .[36] if you give heed to the views

of the philosophers, Lucretius, especially, and others, teach correctly that the realms of the underworld indeed cannot exist. In fact, what the truth is about the underworld—namely, whether it exists, and if it exists, what, or what kind of place, or finally, where it is—let true theologians seek this. For us it suffices if we render the fictions of the poets less obscure in some measure.

2. Let us discuss the poetical fictions and pass on the philosophic material. The greatest of the ancients say that this earth on which we live is the lower regions. It is the lowest of all the circles, namely the seven planets—Saturn, Jove, Mars, Sun, Venus, Mercury, Moon—and of the two great circles. Thus it is said: "and the Styx holding them in with nine circles,"[37] for the earth is surrounded by nine circles. Therefore all things that are invented about the lower regions, we shall also show to be on earth. First, those who have described the things belonging to the lower regions have said that there are four rivers in the Underworld—Lethe, Cocytus, Phlegethon, and Acheron—and the fifth, Styx, is a swamp. Lethe is translated as "forgetfulness," Cocytus means "sorrow," Phlegethon means "burning," Acheron means "without joy" or "without health," for a means "without" and chaire means "joy" or "Hail." Thus also in hymns we sing out with joy "Kuria Chaire," that is, "Hail Mistress." Styx is translated as "sadness." They say that Acheron arises from the depths of Tartarus; the channels of this river create the Styx, and from the Styx arises the Cocytus. The reason for this etymology is that one who lacks joy easily falls into sadness. Moreover, sadness is neighbor to sorrow. Who does not know that this [sorrow] disturbs human spirits on earth? Of course, it is well known that Acheron is a place in Italy, not far from Baiae, enclosed on all sides by mountains so that it cannot ever see the sun, except at midday. Also, places in the vicinity gush with warm, sulphurated waters. That place is said to be without joy because necromancy and soothsaying were customarily practiced there. These did not happen without the killing of a human being. Indeed, both Aeneas and Ulysses carried out those accursed rites there after Misenus and Elpenor were killed. Cocytus also is a place near Acheron; it too is said to be sorrowful for the same reason.

3. In that book where he treats of the sacred rites of the Egyptians, Seneca reports that the Styx is a muddy swamp near the farthest part of Egypt; that it is thick with papyrus and difficult to cross. Next to this

swamp were finally buried the limbs of Osiris, husband of Isis, who was killed by his brother Typhon and found after a long search by the Egyptians. This swamp, which brings sadness to those crossing it, deserved to be called Styx. We read that the neighboring people carry the corpses of their dead in boats through this swamp to another region. In fact, if anyone happens to perish in its stream, his final rites are fulfilled after a hundred years. Thus Vergil says: "A hundred years they wander and flit about these shores."[38] We read this about the Styx: "By this the gods fear to swear and to deceive the deity."[39] So, according to the fables, Victory, the daughter of Styx, favored Jove in the war of the Giants. As a reward for this Jupiter granted that the gods who swore by her mother would not dare to deceive, under this confirmed penalty: if anyone swore falsely by her name, he would be forbidden to taste the nectar of ambrosia [sic] for one year and nine days. And this dew is such a little thing! Styx signifies sorrow, for it is named after *stygeo*, "sadness." Indeed, the gods are always happy. Thus they are also truly immortal; they do not feel sorrow. They swear by a thing contrary to their nature, and thus they consider the oath an execration, for to swear an oath properly, with the gods from somewhere invoked as witnesses, is to wish for prosperity, but an execration is to ask for adversity. The fact that Victory's mother is called Styx, "sadness," seems to be on account of this fiction: that in struggles, when more diligent and, so to say, more anxious solicitude is applied, a reason to conquer is more at hand, since this is not irrelevant to the situation. "When she [Victoria] was not propitious, Ilios was defended by arms; when she was propitious, Ilios took in the horse filled with soldiers." This same Styx is called both the nurse and friend of the gods, since the gods of earth gained their heavenly fellowship through purgation, which Styx signifies for certain theologians.

4. Phlegethon is named after *phlox*, "flame." Indeed, the entire river surrounding the lower world is fiery, signifying figuratively the fires of wrath and greed that inflame human souls. Yet those who seem to have understood this more profoundly assert that this river represents the turbid and corpulent nature of this lower air which, clearly, is made thick by fire drawn from the regions above, and by water drawn from the regions below, where sinful souls are cleansed. Some, who believe that the underworld begins in the sky, call this same Phlegethon the circle of Mars, just as also they maintain that the Elysian Fields, which fable has placed in

the lower regions, are the circle of Jove. Yet others, as Servius says, believe the Elysian Fields are on the Blessed Isles. Moreover, *lusis* means "release," because, of course, souls there are released from the faults of the flesh and thought to enjoy beatitude.

5. Lucretius offers appropriate theories about the infernal punishments, and he affirms that all the things that are imagined about the lower regions exist in our life. He says that Tityos exposing his liver to be gnawed by vultures is love, that is, lust, which according to the natural scientists is in the liver, just as laughter is in the spleen and irascibility in bile. So also the liver devoured by the vulture is renewed as a punishment. In fact, after the deed has been done, it is not enough for lust, which always breaks out again. Thus Horace says: "The liver of intemperate Tityos."[40] He is also said to be damned in the Underworld for his impurity, since, clearly, he tried to seduce Latona because of his lewdness. Lucretius also says that the superstitious are meant by those over whom there hangs a stone about to fall, as we read concerning Phlegyas. These people always fear in vain. They think badly of the gods and those above, for truly religious men fear out of reverence. Phlegyas deserved that punishment for destroying Apollo's temple. Those who roll a rock, as Sisyphus does, signify striving and refusing, he says, since those repeaters who are always refused do not cease to strive. Sisyphus also seems not unsuitably to have incurred that punishment for robbery. Although robbers might often be exposed to danger, they do not desist from their iniquity. By those rotated on a wheel, as Ixion is, Lucretius indicates tradesmen who are always rolled about by tempests and whirlwinds. Ixion, who deserved punishment of this kind, was first enriched by a kingdom, as we have said. Then he was expelled from his kingdom and suffered shame in place of his former glory.

6. Macrobius differs somewhat on these subjects. He says that according to certain philosophers, the vulture feeding off the immortal liver signifies the torments of a perverse conscience. It continually condemns itself according to the law by which no one doing harm is absolved when he judges himself, neither can he avoid his own judgment about himself. Macrobius says that those stretched out to hang from the spokes of wheels signify men who entrust themselves and all their acts to fortune. They foresee nothing by deliberation, moderate nothing by reason, regulate nothing by virtues. They are always whirled about by fortuitous

events. He says that those who waste their life on ineffectual and toil-some endeavors roll a mighty rock. He also says that a black rock aways about to fall, and like one falling, threatens the heads of those always striving after high offices and lofty powers, but who will never be suc-cessful without fear; those who force themselves to hate the subject popu-lace while they fear them; those who always seem to bring upon themselves the destruction that they deserve. Now concerning Acheron, Cocytus, and Styx, Macrobius agrees sufficiently with Lucretius.

7. He indicates that the river Lethe, which means "forgetfulness," as we have said, signifies nothing other than the straying of the soul that forgets the majesty of its former life. According to the philosophers, it possessed this before it was sent into the body, and yet thinks that life is in the body. But there are other men of great authority and reputation who discuss the river Lethe and whether it is one of those nine circles surrounding the lower regions, and they separate this one from those. They think that Lethe is the image of old age. They say that our souls thrive and are active and full of memory from childhood right up to vig-orous old age, but later, in extreme old age, all memory fades away. After memory has faded away, death occurs. Thus the river Lethe is senile for-getfulness, always near to death. Furthermore, the fact that souls are thought to want to return to their bodies after they have tasted Lethe belongs to the loftier teachings of philosophers. Since I know that this is difficult for the inexperienced, I have judged it unsuitable for this treatise.

8. Nevertheless, let us draw out just a few, very easy theories from these indefinite and inexplicable materials so that we might not be ex-pressly accused of inappropriate silence in these matters on which much effort has been expended. According to the opinions of philosophers, or of triflers, as certain ones say, souls were created from the beginning of the world and placed among corresponding stars so that they might contemplate there the rational motion of the firmament. They were en-dowed with the hope and desire for the highest beatitude, so that they might rule their bodies rationally according to the motion of the firma-ment. Also, dwelling there free from every bodily contagion, as they say, the souls possessed the heavens. They had perfect understanding of all things past, present, and future. But looking down from that highest emi-nence and everlasting light, the soul pondered with latent desire that longing for a body and for this that on earth we call "life." Because of

this weight of earthly meditation, the soul slipped downward little by little. It did not suddenly put on a body of clay from its perfect incorporeality, but gradually through silent losses, through a lengthy receding of simple and most absolute purity, the soul swelled up into certain increases of the body. In fact, in the individual spheres that are subject to the sky, the soul is clothed in a certain aetherial enveloping, so that through these it is brought by degrees into union with this earthly covering.[41] And as much as the soul is everywhere enveloped in this corporeal circuit, so much the more does it allow there the perfection of its pristine knowledge, which it possessed, and the subtlety of its virtues, which to this point it had followed alone, to be overwhelmed. For, as the philosophers affirm, it draws to itself sluggishness from Saturn, irascibility from Mars, lust from Venus, greed for gain from Mercury, and desire for a kingdom from Jove. These things, as they say, cause disorder for the soul so that it cannot use its own vigor and its proper strengths. Also, by this reasoning the astrologers assert that we are linked to the powers of individual deities.

9. The rest of the theories that antiquity sanctioned on these matters seem to pertain less to this subject, yet something about them will be touched upon in its own place below. Indeed, as it descends from the planets through the lower regions, the soul is driven by various tempests of hail and snow, rains and winds. Finally, covered by the shadows of the body, the soul is so weighted down by the body's hard mass that it forgets everything that it had known before and recalls nothing of its prior state. This is even apparent in the foolishness of children who are injured when they have been deceived by glowing charcoal. Furthermore, different writers feel differently about whether or not souls receive bodies in those envelopings.[42] Those who deny that the soul receives a body in them assert that through this its clarity is only obscured, just as an image is obscured by smoke. But those who assert that the soul is united to them and then receives a body draw their argument from this: the fact that, as Macrobius testifies, souls finally returning from the body lead these same covers back there whence they took them. After those have been left behind, they recover again entirely the former strengths that they lost there. But if they did not receive bodies in those covers, they say, they would neither convey them to bodies nor would they carry them back there on their return. If it occurs to them that the soul thus incorporated

is made a living being even before it receives a true body, they answer that this is not a necessary thing, since a soul joined to a finger does not immediately make a living being. This is because many things also affect the nature of a living being besides a body and soul, such as sensibility and other things that natural scientists teach. In fact, they say three things by nature are adapted to the soul enclosed in the body, by which it deserves to be restored to its former stage. These are wrath, which repels evil; concupiscence, which seeks good; and reason, which distinguishes between both. Besides, two things are judged to be purposefully added. The first is teaching, by which the soul leads back into its memory what it had surrendered to oblivion. Thus what among us is called *lectio*, "lesson," and is called *repetita cognitio*, "recollected knowledge" among the Greeks. The second is virtue, by which the soul leads what it has rightly wished for to its effect.

10. Since we have begun to discuss the soul, let us extend our discourse on this a little. Some teach that the soul is a certain part or portion of the divine essence. In fact, they say, all things are created from the four elements and the divine spirit. Spread throughout the four elements, this produces everything. Therefore, if all things proceed from the elements and God, they have a single origin, and the nature of all things is, in a certain manner, equal. But, they say, let us see what is thought to be in us from God, and what from the elements. As much as it is given us to understand, they say, we possess the body from the elements, the soul from God. They prove this as follows. Earth, water, breath, and heat are in the body. All of these, just as also the elements, are observed in the bodily senses, but the spirit, just as also God, is subject to no senses. Furthermore, those elements, just as also the body, are devoid of reason. On the other hand, the spirit, just as also God, has understanding. Then the elements are thought to perish, which is peculiar to them, just as also to the body. On the other hand, it is clear that God does not perish. Thus we infer that neither does the spirit perish, which takes its origin from Him. But this occurs to us: if spirits are immortal and have one beginning, for what reason do they thrive more in these people than in those? They say that this difference proceeds not from spirits, but from bodies. To the extent that they were lively or listless, so also they make their spirits, which can be shown in one and the same living body. Indeed, in a healthy body there is unencumbered liveliness of mind, but in a sick

body the mind is more sluggish. Also, in a weak enough body, there is a lack of reason, as we observe in delirious people. Thus when the soul comes to the body, it does not use its own nature, but is altered by the nature of the body. Therefore we see that Africans are cunning, Greeks are capricious, Gauls are of sluggish disposition, which in a certain way the nature of their climates causes. Ptolemy perceived this when he said that a man transported to another climate changes his nature in part, for he cannot change it entirely, since he receives the allotted condition of his own body in the beginning. Thus the soul exists according to the nature of the body.

11. But it occurs to us: why is the better thing in the power of the worse? The divine spirit ought to rule over the mortal body absolutely; the mortal body should not corrupt the nature of the spirit. This happens so, they say, because that which contains is more than that which is contained. Indeed, as a lion, if it is confined in a pit, though impeded, does not lose its strength, but cannot exercise it. So the spirit does not go over to the vices of the body, but it is impeded by its union with the body and does not exercise its own strength. Now this occurs to us: anything that is corrupted is not eternal, but the spirit is corrupted, for it becomes angry and insane, it desires and fears. Therefore it lacks eternity, to which those things are contrary, for passion destroys eternity. Reason opposes this conclusion, they say, since the spirit suffers nothing by itself, but it is troubled through its union with the body. Indeed, it is one thing to be corrupted through its own nature and, conversely, another to be corrupted through the nature of another thing. In fact, we see something of this kind in a lamp that is bright by itself, and without doubt it illuminates the place where it stands. If ever this lamp is withdrawn and shut away, it ceases to illuminate the place, but it does not lose its own brilliance. And so when the impediment has been removed, it appears. Neither is its brightness, although impeded, thus also corrupted. So therefore the spirit, they say, as long as it is in the body, likewise suffers its contamination, but when it has put aside the body, the spirit recovers its ancient vigor and employs its own nature.

12. This occurs to us: if the spirit recovers its own nature, why does it suffer punishments in the Underworld? It is so, they say, because even though the body has been put aside, the soul does not return to its own splendor, nor can it. Just as if you might soil a shining pearl that has been

put in the mud and you immediately remove it from there, it is not therefore free from filth, but requires cleansing. So too, a soul still defiled by contamination of the body, even if it puts aside the body, needs to be purged. After this has been done, it begins to be brighter. Thus Vergil says: "until a distant day, after the cycle of time has been completed, takes away the stain that has grown."[43] So it is that some souls are said to have a lunar orbit and others a solar orbit for their way of perfection. So also, both Palinurus and Dido, who had not yet reached places of perfection, are discovered in the Underworld surrounded by dark shadows. About Palinurus we read: "He scarcely recognized the unhappy man in the dark shadows."[44] Concerning Dido we read: "And he recognized her dark form in the shadows."[45] But it occurs to us: if souls are purged and recover their own nature, why do they want to return to bodies? Many philosophers have taught about palingenesis, that is, multiple generation, and metempsychosis, that is, the transmigration of souls. The souls drink forgetfulness, they say. But there is an uncertainty whether they do this to forget their past punishments, or so that they might be ignorant of the future. However, they desire to return to bodies. We explain that forgetfulness of the former perfect knowledge of those souls as "annulment." All souls suffer this in their descent and incorporation. Yet, according to these same philosophers, we must know that not all souls return to bodies. Indeed, some return because of a wicked life, others because of the necessity of fate, but others attain the eternal fellowship of the gods through apotheosis because of the merits of their life.

13. Of course, since we said above that the soul is immortal, our ancestors inquired whether it is begotten or unbegotten, for the authority of Plato seems to intimate both. It seems to be begotten in the first book of the Timaeus, where he says: "The most excellent was made from the most excellent," and likewise in the second book: "A sowing of the whole race." But in the Phaedo, it seems to be unbegotten, where he says: "And the soul is not born, and it is eternal." The philosophers solve this controversy as follows. He calls the soul unbegotten, they say, for this reason: because it does not yield to the law of things that have been begotten, namely, that it might be dissolved either naturally or actively. For all begotten things, except the world and divine matter, are dissolved actively, but the world and divine matter are dissolved naturally. In fact, although they are never dissolved by nature, yet if the creator willed it,

they would undergo dissolution. For whatever is put together, it is natural for that to be dissolved. So, then, the soul is said to be unbegotten. But he intimates that it is begotten as follows: because according to many the soul also has *hyle,* "preexistent matter." Although Plato nowhere asserts this, he nowhere contradicts it.

14. Some philosophers said that there is only one soul, the world soul, which alone animates all things and confers strength on each one according to its own ability. It confers strength on the stars, which we find to have a divine form, that is, round; on men, who alone among transitory things imitate the divine form with a spherical head, it confers reason and sensibility. Although the divine soul does not much exercise its sensibility because of its excessive contemplation, it confers sense and power of growth on other living things, and only power of growth on trees and plants. Just as one face appears in many mirrors, or many faces in one mirror, so the soul is the same in different things and everywhere has strengths, although it might have a different function in different things according to the ability of their bodies. According to this way of thinking, no one dies, that is, so that he suffers separation from the soul, since they say that this is never separated from the four elements into which all bodies are dissolved. But someone is said to die when the soul in that person abandons the exercise of its former strengths. Although the soul might have equal power in all bodies with respect to itself, as we have said, in some, where the mass of the body stands in the way, it cannot exercise this power. Other philosophers said that this same world soul is in a man equally with a human soul, and from this worms are brought to life in the man. And so they asserted that the same man has two souls.

15. Also, some say that human souls were created from the beginning of the world and placed in matching stars, just as in vehicles, while they descend daily in their zeal to receive a body. Indeed, they think they have evidence by virtue of Abel because it is written: "See, the voice of your brother's blood cries out to me from the earth,"[46] that is, as they say, souls that had to be incorporated into bodies born from the blood of Abel. Thus they cried out, they say, because they wished to merit perfect beatitude in their bodies. In fact, they said that the soul that is graced by laudable merits in life is of greater significance than one that is not incorporated. But God makes nothing superfluous. Therefore this way of thinking must also be judged worthless. But these who, as we said above,

used to say that the soul is part of the divine essence drew upon that place where it is written: "He breathed upon his face the breath of life."[47] Moreover, they say, this particle does not return any more to be united with God. So also, it can sin. Thus these philosophers treat of God as if He belongs to a place and is divisible. Some assert that souls are born of angelic substances, others that they are born of hereditary seed, so that just as the body of a son is separated from the substance of his father, so is the soul also thought to come forth, and they draw their evidence from the similarity of their ways. Yet it is a matter of undoubted faith that souls are born or created neither from here nor from there, nor are they brought from another place, but they are born together with the body itself. There is a certain time determined after the conception of seed, which is taken into the human body, in which the soul is born with the body.

16. There are two strengths of the soul, one superior and the other inferior. The superior strength of the soul adheres to heavenly and incorruptible things, and desires those; it is called rationality, spirit, mistress, mind, soul. The inferior strength accords with the pleasure of the body and is called sensuality, animal nature, handmaid, heart. It is in the nature of the superior to rule the inferior, but sometimes because of the negligence of the superior, the inferior prevails and leads the superior astray. Also under this figure are Adam and Eve, for if the superior Adam had ruled himself with reason, the inferior Eve would not have led him astray. Thus it is that philosophers, following reason and opinion more than truth, inquire into the detriments of the soul in this manner and in the manner of poets, and they think that they understand them. If the soul is eternal, they say, and part of the highest spirit, for in the soul all men are made similar to God, why does it not see everything while in the body? Why is it not of such great vivacity that it can know all things? Because, they say, when it begins to descend into the body, the soul drinks in foolishness and forgetfulness. Thus, after forgetting its own nature, it cannot fulfill the strength of its own divinity. We have described above what that forgetfulness is. And so that we might be versed in the poetic and philosophic doctrines: the soul descending from Heaven forgets past things, according to the poets, and future things, according to the philosophers. Thus Vergil holds the middle ground by saying: "They drink forgetfulness."[48]

17. Truly, among the philosophers there is a remarkable explanation of the return of souls. [They explain] how or why the souls of the guilty, according to some of them, just as of the innocent, return to the stars after they have been freed from the body. The souls do this so that they might either be presented with the greatest reward of eternal light as the wages of life, or they might be banished from these stars for deeds committed wickedly, or taken up, not to perish, but that they might be cast down. So also that same Vergil, not a stupid man, says: "Certainly, all things, now released, are returned and then brought back hither; there is no place for death, but alive, they fly up to join the number of stars and climb to the high heaven."[49] And Lucan says: "He made the innocent in life endure the lowest ether and gathered the souls to their eternal orbits."[50] No wonder, since it is clear that all things return to their own origin, for there is nothing that can perish utterly, since there is, according to the philosophers, *to pan*, "the whole," to which all things return. The thing called death, as Servius says, is not death, but release, which in fact causes nothing to perish. Thus it was wonderfully called *interitus*, "going between," by many, as if there is a thing coming between and loosening the connection of mingled things. Because of this it does not befall these bodies that they die, since they do not perish, but they are released into the elements.

18. In truth, they hold wondrous opinions about the cleansing of souls, as Vergil bears witness, saying: "Some are spread out, suspended before the empty winds; for others, the sin by which they have been stained is washed away under a vast whirlpool or burned away by fire."[51] There he preserves the poetic and does not depart from philosophy, for according to the philosophers there is a triple cleansing of souls. They are cleansed on earth, clearly because they are devoted to bodily delights and weighed down by different kinds of filth. These cross over into earthly bodies and are said to be cleansed by fire, for fire, which burns up all things, is from the earth; certainly, celestial fire burns up nothing. Or, souls are cleansed in water, that is, they cross over into marine bodies, if they have lived a little better. Or, surely, they are cleansed by crossing over into air, that is, by receiving aerial bodies, if they have lived well enough. Thus we also read this in Statius, where he treats of auguries. So in all sacred rites there are those three complete purifications, for either they are cleansed by pitch or sulphur, or washed in water, or swung

in the air. This customarily happens in the sacred rites of Father Liber. Thus it is written, "and for you, delicate little images hang from the lofty pine,"[52] for this was a kind of cleansing. Also, in these cleansings Vergil followed a proper order of merits, so that he spoke first of aerial cleansing, then of water, and later of fire. Also, they say that these souls that have lived wickedly return immediately to being embodied; those that lived better, more slowly; those that lived best are with the deities for the longest time. Vergil adds, "we suffer, each of us, his own shades (manes)."[53] Either he leaves this to be understood as the various punishments among the shades, as if someone might say "we suffer a judgment," that is, these things that are contained in a judgment, or something else, which according to Servius is truer. When we are born, he says, we are allotted two guiding spirits (genii). There is one that urges us toward good and another that seduces us toward evil. They are not called *genii* inappropriately, since when any man is born (genitus), observers are immediately assigned to him. With these assisting us, after death we are either freed for a better life or condemned to a worse one. Through them we merit either wandering, that is, ascension to the world above, or a return to bodies. Therefore he calls the shades that we are allotted with our life "genii."

19. There was a long search by Plotinus the philosopher and many others as to whether our mind's eye is moved toward desires and purposes by itself, or rather by the influence of some deity. The foremost ones said that human minds are moved by their own accord. Yet they understood that we are driven toward all good things by our guiding spirit and by a certain familiar deity given to us when we are born, but we desire and long for wicked things with our own mind. It cannot happen, they say, that we desire wicked things through the will of deities, for we know that nothing evil is pleasing to them. So elsewhere Vergil says: "Do the gods add this ardor to our minds, Euryalus, or does his own dreadful desire become a god for each man?"[54] as if he were saying, "Oh Euryalus, do the gods implant desires in our minds, or does the mind's desire itself become a god?" Remigius says that the guiding spirit is a natural god that presides over the generation of all things. But we say that we yield to the guiding spirit as often as we pay attention to pleasure. On the opposite side, we have in Terence: "or while denying pleasure to the guiding spirit."[55] But the ancients said that there is no

place without a guiding spirit. Thus we read in the Fifth Book of the *Aeneid* about a snake bursting forth from the tomb of Anchises: "uncertain whether it is the guiding spirit of the place."[56] Indeed, what is added, "or the attendant spirit of his father," seems to be drawn from ancient custom. For it was the way of our ancestors that, whenever kings died, their beloved horses or slaves and the dearer one of their wives were burned up with them, and among these wives there was great contention over this. Thus we can accept that an attendant slave was buried with Anchises, or the poet showed that he was made a god through apotheosis. Thus he gives him an attendant as his servant. The superior individual deities, they say, have inferior powers as their servants, as Venus has Adonis, the Mother of the gods has Attis, Minerva has Erichthonius, Diana has Virbius, Bacchus has Marsyas. Certainly it was thought to be so from the assertion of Pythagoras, who first understood that a snake is formed from the marrow in a man's spine. Ovid recalls this among the teachings of Pythagoras in Book Fifteen of *Metamorphoses*. Furthermore, we know that a snaky appearance is generally given to the guiding spirit, as Persius says: "Paint two snakes."[57] The ignorant used to think that snakes discovered in the inner rooms of houses are the spirits of Roman citizens, as Servius intimates. The Romans, he says, call these *genii*.

20. Vergil divides the Underworld into nine circles. He says that the first holds the souls of infants, the second of those who were unable to look after themselves because of their simplicity, the third of those who killed themselves to avoid hardships, the fourth of lovers, the fifth of brave men, the sixth of those wicked ones who are punished by judges, the seventh where souls are cleansed, the eighth of those souls already cleansed so that they might return, and the ninth is the Elysian Fields, from which souls do not return. Either the whole account is an incredible fable, or, as Servius says, it was very cleverly devised. He says that those who have thought deeply about the plan of the world declare that within these nine circles of the world are included virtues, that is, powers endowed with a lesser perfection. Clearly, these are spirits (daemones), among which are both wrath and cupidity, from which sadness is born, that is, Styx. Therefore by these and within these bounds it is clear that all souls that undergo punishment are punished. Thus they say that there are nine circles of the Styx that surround the lower regions, that is, the

earth. Clearly, these are the spirits and their dwelling places. They say that there are other cleansings beyond these nine circles, powers that serve only good and do no violence to anyone. Now those are the clever inventions of Fulgentius on these circles, but I have judged them unworthy to be handed on; in fact, they bring about a perverse morality, but they do not comprehend the views of natural science. In fact, we read that entrance to the lower regions is open to anyone night and day, but exit is difficult. This was said either poetically, or it proceeded from the opinion of those who contend that all souls indeed descend and can receive bodies, but the souls of those who live rightly return easily to the upper circles, that is, to their own origin. Lucan ascribes this condition to Pompey. Moreover, they contend that the souls of those who live wickedly remain longer in these bodies according to a different mutation, and thus they are always in the lower regions. Vergil agrees that only those whom Jupiter loves are able to return often, that is, those whom the favorable appearance of the stars shines upon at their birth. Thus Juvenal wrote: "Indeed it makes a difference which stars receive you when now you begin to put forth your first squalling."[58] Also, those whom prudence raises up, that is, "whom ardent virtue carries up to the stars."[59] And religious men, who are born of the gods, he says, for it follows that the offspring of the gods are open to religions.

21. On Tantalus, who is punished in the Underworld, the story says that he was a king of the Corinthians and a friend to the deities. He entertained them frequently. When he held a banquet for them at a certain time, he killed his own son Pelops and served him to the gods to eat. Then, although all the gods abstained from eating, Ceres gulped down his shoulder. When the gods wanted Mercury to summon Pelops to the heavens, an ivory shoulder was fashioned for him. Ceres is said to have eaten for this reason: she is the earth, which dissolves bodies. It is thought that Mercury summoned Pelops for this reason: he is the god of intelligence, according to certain sources, by which the philosophers comprehend palingenesis, "repeated generation," or metempsychosis, "transmigration of the soul." *Palin* means "again" and *genesis* means "generation." Likewise *meta* means "beyond" and *psyche* means "soul." Tantalus was condemned to punishment in the lower regions according to this stipulation: standing in the Eridanus, a river of the Underworld, he could not partake of the waters that were there nor the fruit orchards

that were nearby. Thus he represents avarice. For this reason also he is called Tantalus, which means "wishing for a vision." And so, the avaricious man, deprived of the faculty of deriving enjoyment, is fed by the vision of his own possessions. In fact, Aratus says that the Eridanus, in which Tantalus is thought to stand, is in the sky not far from the constellation called "The Whale," but also it is on the earth, namely in the country of the Veneti, which is part of Italy, and it is called Po. Some writers want to keep this river in the Underworld, others want it to originate in the Underworld and to come forth from the earth. These stories are conceived in this way because the river arises in a part of the Apennines that looks toward the lower sea, that is the Tyrrhenian Sea. This encircles Italy from the west and extends all the way to the upper sea, the Adriatic, which is from the east.

22. The philosophers understand three-headed Cerberus to be "hatred." They place him at the feet of Pluto. Cerberus is interpreted to mean "devouring flesh." Now hatred is practiced on earth in three ways: one is natural hatred, as of men and snakes; another is causal hatred, as that which is aroused by an injury that has been inflicted; another is casual hatred, as when hatred is often incurred for a single word, unless it is appeased. Some philosophers think of Cerberus as the tripartite earth: Asia, Africa, and Europe. This earth, swallowing up bodies, sends souls to Tartarus. What others might think about this, we shall say below. It should be noted that the individuals among the three brothers have similar insignia in part, for Jupiter holds a three-forked thunderbolt, Neptune a trident, and Pluto has a dog with three heads. And not undeservedly, for these three deities, although they have different dominions, are thought to have a common power in the entire realm, as if those very physical elements which they possess are joined among themselves in a certain way. Thus it is unnecessary to note that, in the first book of the *Aeneid*, Neptune complains about the other elements, saying: "Now, Winds, do you stir up the sky and earth without my authority."[60]

23. Likewise, three Furies serve Pluto, that is, they are at work on earth. According to Fulgentius, the first of these, Alecto, is interpreted to mean "not pausing"; the second, Tisiphone, is as if to say *touton phone*, "their voice"; the third, Megaera, is as if to say *megage eris*, "great contention." In fact, the first thing, he says, is to become furious by not pausing, the second is to burst into speech, and the third is to bring forth

strife. But others say that Megaera is second, Tisiphone third, whom also, or similarly, they interpret to be "their voice" or "the vengeance of death." In the same way they assert that the first thing is to incur a burning wrath after a disturbance of the peace; second is to produce much contention after the stirring up of wrath; third is to exercise only malevolence and detraction after strife and wrath, or consequently to inflict vengeance and punishment. Also, we assign to this same Pluto the three Fates, whom we call Parcae through antiphrasis, since they spare (parcant) no one. According to Servius, one of these speaks, another writes, and the third draws out the thread of life. According to Homer, one carries a strainer, the other draws water and the third breaks the container. Although they are secretaries and scribes of Jove, surely because they put into effect the dispositions of the highest god, we give them as servants to Pluto for this reason: their services are seen especially on earth. Clotho is interpreted to mean "summoning," Lachesis means "lot," and Atropos means "without order." Through these names the entire disposition of human life is signified. Indeed, men are first summoned from non-being to being, or from their mother's womb into the light; then comes their lot, how each one must live; finally, death brings an end to life. Atropos is called "without order" because, observing no rank and sparing no age, she draws all things to herself indiscriminately.

24. On the twin gates of dreams, one of true dreams and the other of false, which we have placed in the lower regions, Philosophy holds these views: by the gate of horn, She says, are signified the eyes, which are the color of horn and harder than the other members of the body. They do not feel the cold, as Cicero attests in his book *On the Nature of the Gods*. By the gate of ivory is signified the mouth, along with its teeth. In fact, we know that what we say can be false, but those things that we see are especially true. For that reason Aeneas, who was both let into the Underworld and sent forth from there, according to the poets, went out through the gate of ivory. Another thing is understood from this. We know that Sleep is depicted with a horn. Those who have written about dreams say that the ones that seem to be in accord with our fortune and that may be possible, very often come to pass. And these, they say, are seen through horn; thus the gate of true dreams is imagined to be made of horn. But those dreams that are beyond our fortune, the ones that have excessive ornament and diverse ostentation, they affirm to be false.

Thus the gate of ivory, as the more ornate, is given to false dreams. Yet, as Macrobius says, Porphyry extensively and in a contrary way followed the description of these gates handed down from Homer. All truth lies hidden, he says, but the soul, when it is freed a little from the functions of the body in sleep, sometimes sees [the truth], sometimes directs its sight, yet does not perceive. And when it sees, it still does not see with free, direct light, but with a covering interposed, which the nexus of a dark nature draws over it. Vergil asserts that this is in nature when he says: "See, for the entire cloud that is now drawn over you and dulls your mortal vision, and with its mist covers all around with darkness, I shall snatch away."[61] When he grants this covering in sleep to the true eye of the soul looking inward, it is believed to be horn, whose very nature is such that, in its thinness, it becomes pervious to sight. But when the covering dulls the sight and repels our sight from the truth, it is thought to be ivory, whose body is so thick in its nature that, scraped to any extremity of thinness you like, it will be penetrated by no sight tending toward the inner parts. Moreover, Servius left it to be understood that that cloud was a mist arisen from the earth that hinders our seeing. Thus he says an eagle sees more, since it is above the mist. Vergil declares that empty dreams cling to the bottoms of leaves, since those who treat of dreams have said that dreams are empty at the time when leaves fall from the trees.

25. Dreams and Sleep, War and Fear, Grief and Want, and other similar things, they say, occupy the approach to the Underworld, either because they seem allied to death, or they are created after death, or they are in death. And rightly are they thought to be in the Underworld, since it is necessary that the one whom these things befall is mortal. Thus we call the gods immortal, since they do not experience these. But Centaurs and Scyllas, Gorgons and Harpies, and other monstrous creatures are said thus to have their abode at the entrance, according to Servius, since those things that are created contrary to nature perish immediately. In fact, some say that the lower regions are under the earth, thinking that they have proof from the cosmographers and geographers who represent the earth as a globe and say that it is supported by water and air. But if this is so, it is possible for ships to reach the antipodes, which, as far as it appears to us, are below, as we are to them. For this reason also they think it was said to Aeneas in the Underworld: "Do you come now,

driven in your wanderings on the sea?"[62] Also, Tiberianus introduces a letter brought by the wind that has the words: "Those above bring greetings to those below." Here he is treating this as a reciprocal fact. But wiser men have taught that souls, as if through metempsychosis, have crossed over to bodies of another climate, and that they do not remain in the world in which they were before. Thus Lucan wrote: "The same spirit rules the limbs in another world."[63] In fact, according to Plato and Aristotle, metempsychosis now preserves the sex, now changes it. So Caeneus is said to have returned to her own sex after death. Caeneus was a maiden who obtained a change of sex from Neptune as payment for her shame. As a man Caeneus was invulnerable; while fighting for the Lapiths against the Centaurs, he was driven little by little into the ground and fixed there by the repeated blows of clubs. Therefore it seems true to me that Caeneus was a great-souled youth who, although he did nothing manfully among his compatriots in his youthful age, was carried abroad over the sea, and through much toil and virtue made a very great name for himself. Moreover, any virtue you please yields to a greater number.

26. Black cattle are sacrificed to Pluto because sacrificial animals are chosen for the deities either through resemblance or through contrast. Through resemblance, as black cattle to Pluto; through contrariety, as a sow, which harms the fruits of the fields, to Ceres; as a she-goat to Aesculapius, since he is the god of health, since a she-goat is never without a fever; as an ass to Priapus because by its braying it indicated his baseness in having intercourse with a certain nymph. Also, as Servius reports, Priapus was from Lampsacus, a city of the Hellespont. Because of the great size of his manly member, he was driven away by the citizens. But he later deserved to be accepted into the number of the gods as the deity of gardens. About him Horace wrote: "For my right hand restrains thieves, and also the red stake stretched out from my obscene groin, but the reed-crown fixed on my head frightens the troublesome birds."[64] Priapus is rightfully said to preside over gardens because of their fertility, for although other ground might produce something once in the year, some gardens are never without fruit. But he is also the god of married women; he is, as they say, conveyed among the gods by a company of them. Also, it should be known that there are different sacrifices to other deities according to the nature of their regions, as the sacrifice of incense to Venus at Paphos. Thus it is written: "By no means am I worthy of

such honor."[65] To the Mother Goddess, the Roman one, there is an immolation of sacrificial animals. A goat is sacrificed to Liber everywhere. The reason that men entice souls to a tomb with milk and blood is this: the body is nourished by milk; after the body's union with the soul, the soul also is never without blood. When this has been poured out, the soul departs. Also, we read that the souls of the unburied roam about, but after a lawful burial has been rendered, they return to the repose of the grave. The Stoics follow a middle course; that is, they are divided. They say that souls endure as long as the body endures. Thus the Egyptians, who are experienced in established wisdom, preserve bodies longer so that the soul might endure for a long time and be subject to the body, and that it might not pass over quickly to others. But the Romans used to do the opposite, burning corpses so that the soul might return immediately to a state of generality, that is, to its own nature.

27. We said that the Stoics follow a middle course because Plato says that the soul is eternal and makes the transition to different bodies immediately, according to the merits of its former life. Yet Pythagoras says that there is not a transfer, but a palingenesis. This is, indeed, to return, but after a time. Besides, others disagree with the Stoics when they say that the soul endures equally with the body; these others assert that souls do not perish with bodies, but in fact they delight in them and remain with them as long as anything is left of them. And thus, they say, corpses are interred with spices, so that, lasting for a long time, they might not withdraw their delight from the soul. It is not true that the soul abandons the body, although, rather, the body abandons the soul. Thus both Simonides the poet and also Statius in the Eighth Book of the *Thebaid*, affirm this: "I hate these limbs, and this frail use of the body, the forsaker of the spirit."[66] Moreover, in his *Natural History*, Pliny gives the reason that the dead were washed with warm water and were lamented at intervals of time. He says that the vital spirit frequently is thought to have left a corpse, and this deceives people. Then, he says, a certain person placed upon the pyre would be aroused when the fire was applied, and he could not be rescued. So corpses were kept for seven days and washed with warm water, and after a final lamentation, they were burned. Thus Terence exclaimed: "Stop! Now the lamentation is done!"[67] Indeed, it was the custom that if anyone were killed far from his home, he would be brought back to his own home. Thus Vergil wrote: "Bring him back

to his own dwelling place."[68] In like manner he would be kept there for seven days, set afire on the eighth day, and finally be buried on the ninth. Thus Horace wrote: "to scatter the ashes on the ninth day."[69] For this reason also the games celebrated in honor of a dead man are called *novemdiales*, "ninth day." Also, it should be known that they were buried in their own home. So this custom first arose, that the household gods are worshipped in homes.

28. Cypress was used at funerals, according to Lactantius, because with this tree the Romans marked households that had been defiled; or because a sterile tree was judged suitable for the dead; or because the cypress was under the protection of the inhabitants of the Underworld; or more likely, according to Servius, because, cut down, it does not sprout forth again, just as a dead man does not come back to life; or because a house is shown to be in mourning by means of this tree. So also the cypress is called "gloomy" because it signifies the hearth gods (Lares) in mourning, just as leafy boughs of festive laurel, olive, and the like indicate joyous hearth gods. In fact, it was a Roman custom that a branch of cypress was placed before a house in mourning lest any high priest be defiled by entering through ignorance, for if they were defiled by a dead body, priests were forbidden to offer sacrifice. But if it happened that someone was defiled and at the same time compelled to attend to sacrifices, he would take pains to complete the sacred rites before he acknowledged the corpse. Thus, as we read in Livy, when a certain high priest was about to dedicate the Capitol and it was reported to him that his son had been killed by enemies, he responded "let the corpse be," so that he would not dedicate it while defiled. And he was unwilling to acknowledge the corpse until he had dedicated the temples. Thus rivers were shown to Aeneas in the Sixth Book of the *Aeneid*. He had been defiled by the death of Palinurus, not because he had seen him dead, but since he had acknowledged his corpse, and then had grieved. So it was said: "shaken in spirit by the fall of a friend,"[70] for these pollute us that we acknowledge and over which we grieve. Aeneas needed to approach these rivers to be purified before he came to the sacred rites. Also, according to the same source, in the Eleventh Book, the custom was introduced to attend to the sacred rites before, and then to return to the burial of comrades. But Varro says that pyres were surrounded by cypress because of the strong stench of burned corpses, so that the circle of people standing around them might not be

offended. Indeed, this circle of people used to stand, responding to the weeping of the woman hired to lead the mourning, that is, the leader of the lamentations, until after the corpse was consumed and the bones collected. Then the very last word was said: *ilicet*, "you may go," which stands for *ire licet*, "it is permitted to leave." For *vale*, "farewell," used to be said after the solemn ceremonies at the tomb were completed. The women hired to lead the mourning were called leaders of the lamentation, not of the grief itself. They used to call the women to whom the dead person (funus) was related—as a mother, sister, paternal aunt, maternal aunt—*funerae*, as if to say "belonging to the corpse." Thus the mother of Euryalus said: "And I, your mother, did not lead you to your funeral."[71]

29. In fact, they maintain that *vale*, "farewell," is said to the dead not because they can fare well or be safe, but because we are departing from them, never to see them again. Thus it came about that *vale* has the signification of a curse, as Terence says: "Let those who want discord between us be gone!" [valeant][72] That is, let them depart from us and perish, so that they might never return to our sight. Thus Vergil wrote: "Farewell, Forests!"[73] For what he says elsewhere—"Live fruitfully" [vale]—is of one wishing well, not of one cursing. These curses have been invented as opposites, so that reverence might be preserved, as it were. Therefore, when *vale* is said to a dead person, custom must be considered, not etymology, since we say *vale* to no one, except one from whom we are being separated. Also, among different peoples there were diverse kinds of funeral rites. In one place the dead were buried, in another they were burned, in another they were sent back to their first homelands, in another, rites were conducted during the day, in another at night. Heraclitus, who affirms that all things are composed of fire, says that bodies ought to be dissolved into fire. Thales of Miletus, who affirms that all things are created from moisture, contends that bodies should be buried, so that they are dissolved into moisture. Among the ancients it was a custom to kill the captives of brave men in their tombs. We also read in Homer that this was carried out at the funeral obsequies of Patroclus, and Vergil makes mention of this at the funeral of Pallas. Also, where this practice seemed excessively cruel, it was acceptable for gladiators to fight before the tombs; they were called *bustuarii*, from *bustis*, "tombs." It is no wonder that cruel rites are tendered to the dead, that is, to the

sacred offices of the dead, especially those who are guilty of crimes. Indeed, it is the opinion of Varro that women mutilate their faces at a funeral so that, when blood has been shown, it satisfies the dead. So also we read that these dead were called *manes*, "shades," by the poets through antiphrasis, for *manum* means "good." This is according to Servius, who says: "Mane, for what is better?"[74] But also the word *immanis*, "savage," comes from this.

30. Certainly, various opinions are held about the shades (manes), as to what or how or whence or where or even if they exist, and the most contradictory traditions are found concerning them. Since I feel that all of these are full of uncertainty and think that none can be affirmed for certain, I return to more common matters. Now since we have been discussing the dead, I mention the following so that you will not be unacquainted with the proper signification of names whose misuse confounds us: *funus*, strictly speaking, is a cadaver in the process of actually burning, according to Servius. While this corpse is being carried, we call it *exequias*, "funeral"; when it has been cremated, we call it *reliquias*, "remains." When it has now been interred, we call it *sepultum*, "buried."

Sacrifice to Pluto, as to other deities, used to be carried out with the head covered. This was observed in all sacred rites, lest anything might present itself to wandering eyes during the ceremony. The Saturnalia, however, was excepted, so that there would not seem to be imitation of the deity. So in the Third Book of the *Aeneid*, Helenus says: "lest any hostile face might appear before the sacred fires in honor of the gods and disturb everything."[75] For the sacred rites to be interrupted was a sin. Thus in the Eighth Book Vergil writes: "Bold Pallas forbids them to interrupt the sacred rites."[76] Accordingly, when games were being celebrated in the Circus in honor of Apollo, and it was reported that Hannibal was attacking the city around the Colline Gate, all took up arms and rushed to oppose him. When they returned later and feared for their sin, they found a certain old man still dancing in the Circus. When he was asked why and responded that he had not interrupted his dance, this proverb was born: "The State is safe while an old man dances."[77] But it was not lawful for the annual sacred rites to be deferred because, according to the law, they could not be repeated. Thus, likewise, in the same place we read: "the annual rites, which it is a crime to defer."[78] If ever the sacred rites of the Calends were deferred for any reason, they were lawfully repeated, nor was a sin committed by their interruption. Moreover, in reference to sacred rites, the position of both soul and body is equal. Indeed, generally, what cannot happen with respect to the soul is allowed with respect to the body, as to loose or to bind; by this the soul is able to sense through this relationship what it cannot sense by itself. Thus it was written: "having removed the cords from one foot, and in a loosened garment."[79] For at a sacrifice it was a crime for anything to be bound. Thus in Vergil, as Helenus was about to prophecy, he loosened all the cords on his body so that he might not approach the deity with any part of his spirit bound. In these sacred rites alone was this observed.

Juvenal shows that victims were allowed to be bound before sacrifices when he says: "The frisky victim shakes the far-stretched rope."[80] Also, it should be known that in sacred rites, pretended things are taken for real ones. Thus when the sacrifice should be of animals that are difficult to find, they are carried out with bread or wax, and these are accepted in place of real animals. So it is written: "She had sprinkled waters pretended to be from the spring of Avernus."[81] Also, in the temple of Isis, sprinkled water was said to be from the Nile.

31. Yet there was much diversity and exceedingly-superstitious curiosity in the rituals of sacred ceremonies. Those sacrificing to the gods below were sprinkled with water, as in: "sprinkling with a little dew from the branch of a fertile olive tree."[82] Those sacrificing to the gods above were washed, as in: "until I shall have washed myself in a running stream."[83] Only to the gods above did they pour libations, as in: "In the midst of the hall they poured out cups of wine."[84] But while pouring libations to the gods below, they used to throw the vessels into the fire, as in: "Cups after the olive oil was poured."[85] Statius also mentions this at the burial of Archemorus. In the veneration of the gods below, they used to observe an equal number, which, according to arithmeticians, is of a lesser dignity, as in: "See, two for you, Daphnis."[86] In veneration of the gods above, they observed an unequal number, as in: "The god rejoices in an unequal number."[87] But also, they sacrificed to some gods after a little trench had been made, to others above the ground, but to the gods of the heavens, after a fireplace was constructed. Thus also, these were properly called high altars (altaria). But for the gods above, there are altars (arae) and high altars (altaria), but only altars (arae) for the gods below. Moreover, altar (ara) is named from the prayers, which the

Greeks call *aras*. Also, in the sacred rites for the gods above, they used to pour wine (*fundere*), as in: "He poured between the horns."[88] In the rites for the gods below, they poured wine upon them (*invergere*), as in: "The priest pours wine upon its brow."[89] Furthermore, *fundere* means to pour a libation with the hand bent backward, but *invergere* means to pour with the hand inclined toward the left side so that the libation bowl is turned. These were not really the sacrifices themselves, but they pertained to the testing of the sacrificial victims, for it they were not stunned, they were considered suitable.

32. Also, the victims were wreathed with fillets, and the forehead, the fireplace, and the knives were sprinkled with salted barley meal, that is, with salt and grain mixed. This was called *mola salsa*. It came from this year's barley and this year's salt, as Horace said: "this year's grain."[90] Also, they used to draw a slanting knife from the victim's forehead all the way to the tail before its immolation. So we read: "They mark the tops of the beasts' heads with steel."[91] There were also inspections to determine whether the animal consecrated to a god was suitable for sacrifice, that is, if it would endure everything patiently, as in: "And I shall place a young bullock with its forehead gilded before the altars."[92] This means adorned with gold, as sometimes happened. Elsewhere we read: "And a sacred he-goat led by the horns will stand before the altar."[93] As often as a victim resisted, it showed itself to be unsuitable, as Lucan says: "The bull fled from the overturned altar."[94] Also, they used to place bristles plucked from the head of the sacrificial animal as the first offerings on the altars before the immolation, and so the victim was marked for immolation beforehand. Thus it was written: "designated heads." When they were offering sacrificial animals, they sacrificed whole victims, as in: "And he placed whole carcasses of bulls on the flames,"[95] that is, a whole burnt offering (*holocaustum*). After the entrails were withdrawn, this was placed upon the altars. At times these entrails were also offered, after they had been washed and boiled. Thus in the same place this is also said: "pouring [oil] on the burning entrails." Or they sacrificed a part of the body, as in: "I shall cast the entrails into the salty streams."[96] Or they sacrificed the blood alone, which was poured onto the altars, as in: "bowls of sacred blood." Also, it was a priestly custom that some held the knives below while others struck the victims above, so that they would die thus. So it was written: "Others apply knives from below"; that is, they cut

the sacrificial animals' throats. The word used in sacred rites, where they avoided words of evil omen, was *macte*. This word stands for *magis aucte*, "be more honored!" As often as either incense was added or wine was poured over the animal, this was said: "The victim is honored with wine and incense!" that is, it was set apart and more honored. From this, the poet took his verse: "Be honored, Boy, for your new strength; thus does one advance toward the stars!"[97] That is, "Be the more honored for the glory to which you have aspired." And elsewhere we read: "Be honored in spirit, you who are deemed worthy of such great arms." Also, we read that *reddere*, "to offer," was a priestly word, as in: "We offer living entrails on curved platters,"[98] for entrails were said to be offered. These were placed upon the altar after they had been approved and boiled. Moreover, they took care lest the sheep to be immolated might have a spotted tail or a black tongue or a cleft ear. Thus we read that those animals chosen for sacred ceremonies were everywhere called *bidentes*, animals whose two rows of teeth are complete, for they were not admitted to the sacred rites unless nothing was lacking to them. So also concerning the oxen it was said: "now from the herd unbroken."[99] According to Servius, they are called *bidentes* as if to say *biennes*, "of two years," since it was not permitted to immolate those younger or older. Also, in certain sheep there are two prominent teeth among eight; these do not appear except around the age of two, and these sheep alone are thought suitable for sacrifice. Moreover, they used to give their own epithet to sheep: "chosen," to pigs; "excellent," to oxen; "unbroken," that is, untamed, not having borne the yoke.

33. According to the ceremony of sacred rites, when the first sacrifices were not pleasing, which generally was determined from portents immediately following, they were repeated more carefully. Thus, after the nuisance of the Harpies, we read in Vergil: "And we placed the fire again on the altars."[100] But in the renewal of sacred rites, statues were accustomed to be moved. So Horace says: "Neither shall I shake you, Bright Bassareus, when you are unwilling."[101] Vergil writes: "Thyias, aroused when the sacred images have been moved."[102] And it should be known that a place was consecrated to the deity whose sacred image was placed in its midst, for if others were positioned there, they pertained only to decoration. Thus this same Vergil says the same thing elsewhere: "Caesar will

be in the midst for me and will have his temple";[103] that is, "I shall consecrate a temple to him." The fact that he says "in the midst" indicates that
it will be his temple. The fact that he adds "and will have his temple"
means that he is using the language of a high priest, for the one dedicat-
ing a temple used to say, while holding the doorpost, that he gave himself
to the deity; that it would be necessary now to be possessed by the god
and to forsake human justice. But also, we read that it was a Roman
custom that as they were about to wage war, they promised something
from the share of the plunder to the deities. So at Rome there was one
temple of Jove the Plunderer, not because he presided over plunder, but
because something from the plunder was given to him. Thus Vergil composed this verse: "We rush in with the sword, and we summon the gods
and Jove himself to a share of the plunder."[104] Also, as they were coming
from a battle, the victors sometimes went with a multitude of people to
meet the lesser deities. There, since they had put their enemies to flight,
they used to immolate sheep with the giving of thanks and a display of
rejoicing. Also, they exclaimed *ovans*, "exulting," for an *ovatio*, "ova-
tion," was properly a lesser triumph. In fact, one who merited an *ovatio*
used a single horse and was led to the temple by the plebs or the Roman
knights. He made a sacrifice of sheep. One who celebrated a triumph
used four white horses and, as the senate preceded him to the Capitol, he
slaughtered bulls.

34. Those who were praying sometimes looked down, sometimes up,
according to the nature of the deities, for, as we said, some are heavenly
powers, some are earthly, some are mixed together. Thus it is that those
praying to Apollo used to prostrate themselves on the ground, as in: "We
fell prostrate upon the ground."[105] As we said, he is also a god of the
lower regions, so inner chambers are given to him. Those venerating Jove
used to stand, and they raised their hands and eyes on high. Thus it was
written: "But Father Anchises raised his eyes with joy toward the stars
and stretched his palms to the sky with these words."[106] *Ore favete*, "be
silent,"[107] used to be uttered amidst the supplications because this saying
seemed suited both to sacrifices and to games. Indeed, silence is necessary
at sacrifices and favor at games. Moreover, anyone "favors his tongue"
through silence. Thus Horace wrote: "Favor your tongues"(favete lin-
guis).[108] Of course, we read that the fillet that adorned priests in the sacred
rites was a band resembling a diadem from which ribbons hung down on

each side; this was commonly twined from white and scarlet wool. But the rod on top of the priest's cap, which likewise they remember using, is properly called a "woolly wand" (virga lanata), that is, there was a little wool at its extremity. We know that Ascanius first established this custom at Alba. This was done to show the eminence of the priesthood, just as pillars are placed over dead noblemen to signify their lofty stature. Or it was done because they wanted to frighten away birds with the top of these wands when they were offering sacrifice at Laurolavinium and birds from the nearby groves frequently snatched the entrails from them. From this also the custom remained that those who offered sacrifice at Laurolavinium used to have huge wands, not short ones, as in the City. Yet sometimes when the felt caps of this kind were a burden to wear because of the heat, they used to bind their heads with only a fillet so that they would not proceed with their heads entirely uncovered, which was a sin. So also from the fillet (filo) that they used they were called *flamines*, as if to say *filamines*, "those who wear a fillet." But on festal days, after the fillet was put aside, it was necessary to wear the felt caps. So much for these matters.

35. Whoever seeks to know fully what sacrificial victims were decreed for the individual deities, and why, as we touched upon in part, briefly, a little before, let him peruse the pontifical books at his leisure. Neither are all the gods worshipped in a single way nor are the same gifts offered to all, for there are certain gifts that are offered to individual deities. Thus it was written: "And I shall heap up the altars with their own gifts,"[109] that is, with suitable ones. According to Roman rites, it was not lawful to sacrifice a bull to Jove, so that when Aeneas slaughtered one to Jove in Thrace, we read that a monster came forth immediately from the bloody baskets. Thus a bullock was immolated to Jove, but a bull never, except sometimes in a triumph. Yet this was allowed because at that time sacrifice was being offered not only to Jove, but also to other gods who bring aid in war. With respect to the sacrificial victims, it was required that animals of a certain age be offered to certain deities. Moreover, this is the reason that there is dancing among the religious ceremonies: the ancients wanted there to be no part of us that did not feel the ceremony, for singing pertains to the spirit and dancing to the mobility of the body. So we read of Dido: "She promenaded before the faces of the gods to their altars rich in fat,"[110] for matrons and those women about to sacrifice were

lead around the altars holding little torches. This was done with a certain gesticulation. Thus Sallust wrote: "To dance more elegantly than was necessary for a virtuous woman."[111]

7. Proserpina

1. Men say that Proserpina, the daughter of Ceres, was married to Pluto. Ceres is interpreted to mean joy (gaudium). Thus they imagine her to be the goddess of grain because where there is abundance of grain, there joys must abound. They said that Proserpina means "growing corn," that is, proserpentem, "creeping forth" by roots through the ground. But she is also called Hecate by the Greeks, for hekaton means "one hundred" (centum). She was assigned this name because the growing corn brings forth produce a hundredfold. Ceres is said to search with torches for this daughter seized by Pluto, that is, sown in the ground. So are the "days of torches" consecrated to Ceres, clearly for this reason: at the time of harvest, produce is joyfully sought for reaping with torches, that is, the heat of the sun. Remigius says that Proserpina was named from proserpendo, "creeping forth," and also that she is a girl because seeds spring forth and are renewed in individual years. The same writer accepts Proserpina as the power of herbs and all seeds that arise from the ground. Finally, he says that Ceres was so called as if to say Creerem, from creando, "creating," and crescendo, "growing." He affirms, as also does Servius, that she is the earth, which creates all things. Cicero asserts that Ceres was named Geres, as it were, from gerendo, "bringing forth," with the first letter changed by chance, because she brings forth (gerat) produce. She is said to be golden-yellow because of the ripeness of ears of corn. While this goddess seeks her daughter, she forgets her childlessness, and Jove urges her on with the poppy as her food. In truth, the poppy produces a stupor. When we use this, even if we have been cast down sometimes by the summertime scarcity of the grain supply, we bear less severely the wait for its ripening. Ceres is very deservedly called Alma, "bountiful," from alendo. She has her own rituals, just as Liber has his orgies. She is said to have invented laws, since before Ceres discovered grain, as Servius says, men used to wander about here and there without law. This savagery was stopped when the use of grains was discovered, since legal rights arose from the partition of fields. Ceres is said

to have loved Triptolemus because he first invented the plow and a great part of agriculture in Greece, just as Osiris did in Egypt.

2. It is said that Ceres' daughter had been seized near Aetna because Sicily is very fertile in fruits, as Lucan testifies. So Ceres secured [this concession] from Jove: Proserpina would spend six months in the sky with her mother and six months in the Underworld with her husband. We say that the story was fashioned this way because after sowing, the seeds of plants lie hidden, as it were, for that much time before they bring forth their fruits; or, as Servius says, because this goddess is the same as the Moon. Throughout the year the moon waxes for six months and wanes for six, so that through the individual months she seems to be among the gods while waxing for fifteen days, and among the dead while waning. Or, as Fulgentius says, men place Proserpina, the Moon, among the dead and among the gods for equal lengths of time because she is hidden by day and shines at night, and so she is thought to divide the year, as it were, with the Sun. Or she is thought to be among the dead because, according to the astronomers, she traverses the sky in a lower orbit than all the stars. She rules over the earth and supplies moisture to things, so that not only do stones in the ground sense her losses and gains, but also the brains of living things. And this is more wondrous: even dung senses them. Expelled during the increases of the moon, it produces little worms for the gardens. Also, the marrow of animals and the pith of trees and sea snails and many other things are thought to experience losses and gains through the accession and recession of her light. Men call this same goddess Diana in the woodlands because in a similar way she adds to the sap of trees and plants by the moisture that, according to the natural scientists, she sends down from herself. She is also said to preside over woodlands because all hunted game feeds especially at night, but sleeps in the daytime. Cicero says that the Moon is called Diana because at night she creates the day (diem), as it were. This goddess is thus summoned to births because these are sometimes ready after seven courses of the moon, or nine courses generally; these courses of the moon are called months (menses) because they complete measured (mensa) lengths of time, Cicero says.

3. The Moon is thought to have loved Endymion the shepherd because he was the first to understand the course of the moon. Thus he is said to have slept with her for thirty years, which is the time he spent looking

into this subject. Or the Moon is said to have burned so with love for the shepherd Endymion because the moisture of nocturnal dew, which they say is produced by the moon, is infused into the living juices of plants. This is very beneficial to the successes of shepherds. A story has it that Actaeon saw Diana while she was bathing, and he was changed by her into a stag and torn to pieces by his own hounds, which did not recognize him. In the book in which he discusses ancient paintings, Anaximenes reports that Actaeon loved hunting very much. When he reached a mature age and considered the perils of hunting, seeing the bare rationale for this skill, as it were, he became fearful and had, as it were, the heart of a stag. So Homer wrote: "Drunkard, having the eyes of a dog and the heart of a stag." But while Actaeon fled from the peril of hunting, he did not abandon his fondness for the hounds; by feeding them to no purpose, he wasted his whole fortune. For this reason he is said to have been devoured by his hounds. Also, they say that Perdix pined away with love, first for Diana and then with incestuous love for his own mother. They say that this same Perdix discovered the use of the saw. This man was also a hunter who renounced his former way of life when he likewise learned the great hardship of hunting and its very small profit, and he saw that Actaeon, Adonis and Hippolytus had come to a sad end. He gave his attention to agriculture and was brought by constant toil in this to the point of wasting away. Thus Perdix is also said to have loved his mother, that is, the Earth, she that produces all things. She is also called Polycarpe, which means "many fruits," for the Earth brings forth all fruits. Since Perdix disparaged all hunters because of the disgrace of their ancient skill, he is thought to have invented the saw, that is, evil speaking (maliloquium).

4. We also call Diana by the name Dictynna, from *diktus*, which means "net," and we give her a bow and arrows since hunters, whom she rules, use these. We also said that the moisture in things proceeds from the moon. This seems to be confirmed by the authority of Remigius. He says that the sphere of the moon, its mirror, as it were, is composed of dew. Thus also Diana presides over moisture, and she casts back the splendor of the sun that she has received, that is, she can reflect it. The Moon is also said to hold a rattle because of the first sound of earthly harmony, which extends from earth up to the moon. The rattle is a kind of trumpet [sic] or musical instrument that only the Egyptians use; it is

depicted in the representation of Isis. As Servius says, Isis is a guardian deity of Egypt who signifies the approaches and retreats of the Nile through the motion of the rattle that she bears in her right hand, but through the bucket that she holds in her left hand, she shows the flowing of all streams of water. In fact, in the language of the Egyptians, *isis* means "earth," which they also say Isis is. But others hold that she was brought by ship from Greece and reigned in Egypt, and that this same Isis was the first to invent the Egyptian alphabet. But let us return to what was discussed above. Some understand the marriage of Pluto and Proserpina as the union of earth and the moisture inherent in it. The earth, over which he presides, is signified by Pluto, and by Proserpina the moisture that makes the earth fertile. As they say, she is rightly called Proserpina, as if to say *proserpendo nata*, "born by creeping forth," because moisture rises insensibly through plants or thriving trees and promotes growth in them. The fact that Ceres, the goddess of produce, is said to search for Proserpina signifies, as they say, that fruits desire moisture in the season of excessive drought. The fact that poets sometimes venerate Proserpina under the name Juno has come down, we say, from the teaching of the Stoics. As we recalled above, they said that there is one god for whom names are changed according to his actions and offices. Thus we call gods above and gods below by the same names, as in: "called sacred to Juno of the lower world,"[112] that is, to Proserpina. And elsewhere: "sacred to Stygian Jove,"[113] that is, to Pluto.

8. Apollo

1. They say that Apollo is the first son of Jove. Men call him by different names and very often put him under various significations. He is called Apollo, that is, "destroying" or "exterminating," because he seems to drive out all the moisture of plants and trees with his summer heat. He is called Pythius, either from the Python, the serpent that he killed as soon as he was born, according to the story, or from the Greek word *putho*, which means "I ask," for men ask him and consult him, or from *phutios*, "bringing faith." He is also thought to have killed the Python because all false credulity that has arisen through darkness is scattered by the splendor of his rays, for *peitho* means "credulity." According to Cicero, he is called Sol, either because alone (solus) he is so great, apart from all the constellations, or because when he has arisen, he appears

alone, with all the other stars obscured. He is called Lycius from his greatest Lycian shrine at Delos.[114] Thus Vergil wrote: "now . . . the Lycian oracles."[115] Or he is called Lycius from *luko*, that is, from *lupo*, "wolf," for just as the wolf tears the herds to pieces, so the sun dries up all moisture by its raging heat. So also Pan, who is said to be the god of sheep, is called Lycaus because he keeps wolves away from the sheepfold. Since we happened to make mention of Pan, let us add a brief, useful digression about him.

2. Varro, who treats of the powers and natures of the gods, says that Pan is a god of nature and his name means "all." He has horns to resemble the rays of the sun and moon. His face is ruddy in imitation of the upper air. On his breast he has a starred fawnskin in the likeness of the heavens. His lower part is shaggy because of the trees, bushes, and wild beasts. He has goats' feet because of the firmness of the earth. He carries a pipe of seven reeds because of the harmony of the heavens and a *kalauropa*, a shepherd's crook, because of the year, which revolves upon itself. We know that Silvanus is different from this god; the common opinion in religious rites has it that Silvanus is the god of herds and fields. Wiser men say that he is Hylen, which means "woods" (silvam), that is, the sediment of the elements from which all things are created, as Servius says. The Romans called this *hylen* "matter." So much for these things.

3. Apollo is called Delius, "making clear," because the sun illuminates all things, or from Delos, the island where he is thought to have been born. I have decided that the story of his birth must be set forth, since it is obscure in other writers, and that it must be begun from far back so that the entire matter might be clearer. And so, Ceus the Giant had two very beautiful daughters, Asterie and Latona. After Latona had been violated, when Jupiter also wanted to violate her sister Asterie, she begged the gods to be changed into a bird, and she was turned into a quail. When Asterie wished to cross over the sea called Coturnicus, she was blown upon by Jove and changed into a stone; then she was hidden beneath the waves for a long time. But when Latona implored Jove, she was raised up and began to float on the water. Later, when Juno persecuted the pregnant Latona and sent the Python against her, she was driven out of all lands. Finally, she was received by her sister Asterie who brought Latona to her shores, and there she brought forth Diana first, then Apollo. He immediately avenged the injury to his mother when he killed the Python. After

Diana was born, she is said to have performed the duty of midwife to her mother as she gave birth to Apollo. Thus, although Diana is a virgin, she is invoked by women giving birth. According to many writers, she is Diana, Juno,[116] and Proserpina. And so, after the two deities were born, they did not suffer the land of their birth to wander, but they bound it to two islands. Certainly the truth is far otherwise, for since this island is troubled by earthquake, which happens because of winds concealed beneath the land, it lacked an oracle of Apollo because of the earthquakes. In fact, he commanded that a dead man should not be buried there, and he ordered certain sacrifices to be performed. Later, people came from Mykonos and Gyaros, nearby islands, to take possession of it. This is the reason that Diana was born first: it is well known that night was first, whose ornament is the Moon, that is, Diana; then the Sun, who is Apollo, produces the day. The fact that Delos was first named Ortygia is said to have come about from the quail, which is called *ortugometra* in Greek. Also, it is called Delos because it lay hidden for a long time and appeared later, for the Greeks call "clear" *delon*. Or what is thought to be truer: it is called Delos since clear oracles are given there, although everywhere else the responses of Apollo are obscure.

4. Sometimes poets also call Apollo "father," that is, the creator of all things, because, clearly, whatever is born on land or in the sea is created while the splendor of the sun is at work. Yet, although he is a father, they depict him as beardless because in being reborn each day he seems to be younger, as it were. But he is also called Phoebus, "new," either because the sun really appears new every day at its rising, or because it is made of atoms, according to the Epicureans, and it is said to be born with the day and to die with the day. Apollo is depicted as unshorn because he produces rays equal to all the years. He is also said to be golden haired from his golden splendor, and likewise he is an archer because of the shafts of his rays, with which he penetrates the whole world. Philosophers and poets are accustomed to represent Apollo now as the sun itself, now as the god of prophecy or wisdom or healing, now as some soothsayer, now as the world itself, now as any wise man, now as the modulation of the human voice. They assign the laurel to his care. Thus he is said to have loved Daphne, which means "laurel." She was the daughter of the River Peneus. And where is the laurel believed to spring forth except from river water? But especially the banks of that river are said to

abound in laurel. Indeed, laurel is called the friend of Apollo, who, of course, presides over prophecies, for this reason: because as those who have written about the interpretation of dreams promise in their books, if you place laurel near the head of those who are sleeping, they will dream true dreams.

5. Also, Remigius says that a tripod is a kind of laurel having three roots; it abounds especially next to Apollo's temple on the island of Claros. It is pleasing to Apollo because in it there is no small power of prophesying. Moreover, this laurel stands for the triple kind of prophecy: of things present, past, and future. The tripod is also called Apollo's table, and it is covered with the skin of the Pythian serpent. The place around the tripod, from which the oracle was given, is called cortina after this skin (corio). Some say that this was called cortina as if to say *certina*, either because certain (certa) responses were uttered there, or they have handed down the word from Greek etymology. The reason that is certainly truer is that the heart (cor) of the seer was there, according to Servius. For, he said, there was a cavern in the temple of Apollo where his priestess, carried away in ecstasy, used to prophesy, as Lucan also shows us. He writes: "She had recourse to the tripods, and the seer, plunged into the caverns, remained fixed there, and in her breast, unaccustomed to it, she received the deity."[117] Besides the fact that the tripod was covered or wrapped with the skin of the Python, we offer this line of the same Lucan: "Or when the Python was burned by a foreign torch."[118] Indeed, as Fulgentius says, Phoebus is thought to be the god of prophecy either because the sun shows all obscure things in its light, or because in its forward course and at its setting the sun exhibits a sign of many things.

6. They give Phoebus a four-horse team, either because he completes the space of a year with the four-part changes of the seasons, namely spring, summer, autumn, and winter, or because he traverses the space of a day in four different parts. So also they give fitting names to his horses, for Erythraeus means "reddish," Aethon, "shining," Lampos, "bright" or "burning" and Philogeus, "earth-loving." Indeed, each day the sun is red in the morning, which Erythraeus signifies. In the summer or each day at the third hour the sun shines very brightly, which Aethon signifies. In autumn or at midday the sun, positioned at its midpoint, gleams with immense light, which Lampos shows. Setting late in the day

or passing through the lower constellations in the winter season, the sun seeks the lower slopes of the land, which Philogeus signifies. Thus there is that verse of Martianus: "They say that you direct the four swift steeds with your reins, since you alone tame the four-horse team that the elements bestow," that is, the year consisting of four seasons, as Remigius says. According to the natural scientists, there is no doubt that these seasons have the properties of the elements, for summer is compared to fire, autumn to earth, winter to water, spring to air.

7. They also give to Phoebus a crown of twelve precious stones; it is flashing with flames and likewise represents the differences of the year. Three gems are said to be in the front: lychnis, astrites, and ceraunius. Through the impenetrable brightness of their rays, this crown hides his face from recognition by those who desire to see him. They say that one of these precious stones was taken from the brow of Gemini, one from the head of Cancer, and the third from the eyes of Leo. Another six— smaragdus, scythis, jasper, heliotropius, dentritis, and hyacinthius—are said to cause a reddish glow on each side of the crown. They say that Spring and Autumn gave these to Phoebus. The next part of the crown has these precious stones fixed in it: crystal, diamond, and hydatis. Winter is said to have produced them. According to Remigius, the natures and types of these precious stones are as follows. By Apollo's crown, the year is understood. The twelve months and four seasons of the year are signified by the twelve precious stones, counted by threes. By the three gems placed in front are signified three constellations that the sun courses through on summer days, for summer is the foremost part of the year, the brighter and more prominent part. Moreover, lychnis, which India produces, is a fiery red stone shining with the brightness of lamps. From this it takes its name, for *lucerna*, "lamp," is called *lukos* in Greek. Touched with the fingers under the sun, lichnis draws off chaff. It is said to extinguish a fire suddenly, and so it is consecrated to Vulcan. In fact, it is joined to Gemini because of its fiery red color, since while the sun is in the sign of Gemini in the month of June, fiery red flowers burst forth here and there. Astrites is a shining white gem that has within itself a walking star, as it were; thus it receives it name from *astrum*, "star." This stone is joined to Cancer because of the height and clarity of the stars in that sign.

8. The ceraunius is a reddish-yellow stone. It is found where frequent thunderbolts fall from the sky, and it is said to be useful against thunderbolts. It has its name from these, for a thunderbolt (fulmen) is called *keraunos* in Greek. Thus also the mountains of Epirus are called Ceraunia because of the frequency of thunderbolts falling from the sky there. Also, because of their altitude and the hurtling down of thunderbolts, we find that these mountains are more expressly called Acroceraunia, for *acron* means "sharp" and promontories are called acra. Thus men also say that Arcadia is called Nonacria from its nine promontories, just as Sicily is called Trinacria because, as Martianus says, it is considered triangular because of its three promontories. Indeed, as he himself teaches, Pachynus looks to the south, Pelorus to the west, and Lilybaeus to the borders of Africa. But we have read that this same Sicily is called Triquetra, as if from *tribus*, "three," and *quaestu*, "profits," because frequent shipwrecks used to occur around these three promontories, and there were three harbors there. So also frequent profits used to come to the Sicilians, and three tributes were sent to the Romans in a year. Therefore the ceraunius is placed in the constellation of Leo because of the nature of thunderbolts, since, in the manner of a thunderbolt, the heat of the sun penetrates all things. It destroys and burns up all green plants, especially when it is in Leo in the month of August. These three precious stones hide the face of the sun because while the sun lingers in the aforementioned constellations, it is not easy to fix our gaze on it because of its excessive brightness. It is said that the gem called lychnis was taken from the brow of Gemini because of the beauty and pleasantness of that month, June, since, of course, a man's entire beauty is thought to be in his foremost part, and not a small part of his beauty is observed in his face. The astrites was taken from the head of Cancer because of the height and clarity of its stars. The ceraunius came from the eyes of Leo because of the wildness of its passion, for the ferocity of lions is seen especially in their eyes.

9. The smaragdus, scythis, and jasper are green stones. They represent the signs of the spring season, Pisces, Ares, and Taurus, because while the sun traverses those signs, the earth begins to be green and then to put forth flowers. Smaragdus is named from *amaritudo*, "bitterness," because of its excessive greenness, for all growing plants are bitter while they are green. In fact, it is the greenest gem, more than all plants and

leaves. The scythis is named after Scythia, where they say it is found. The jasper is named from *aspide*, "viper," in whose head it is said to be found. There are many kinds of jasper, among which there is even a yellow one; demons and all phantasms are said to be put to flight by this. The heliotropius, dentritis, and hyacinthus represent the changes of the autumn signs. The heliotropius is also a green stone that has blood-colored streaks. Placed in a silver basin full of water, it turns the sun's rays into a blood-red, dark color. If anyone mixes this stone together with the plant of the same name, the heliotrope, and he utters the proper incantations, he removes himself from the sight of others. Old proverbs call the heliotrope "the bride of the sun," a name taken from that story about Gyges the Lydian. The best heliotropius is found in India and Libya. It is a brilliant stone that changes its color with the rising and setting of the sun. It takes its name from this, for *helios* means "sun" and *tropos* means "changing," because it undergoes variations in its color according to the changes in the sun. But also, the plant is said to follow the sun since it is closed in the evening and opened in the morning, as they say, and during the whole day it turns the unfurled breadth of its flower toward the sun's rays. This gem is placed as an ornament in Virgo because of the brightness of the sun still coursing through this sign in the month of September.

10. The dendritis is a stone like a tree, that is, amber, for a tree is called *dendron* in Greek and a twig is called *rabdos*. This gem is given to Libra because around October, when the sun occupies parts of Libra, trees especially exude sap, as we read. The hyacinthus is a dark blue stone of wondrous and varied nature, sometimes cloudy, sometimes clear, like the waves. It is of purple light, although it seems to change with the air, and it is cold when carried in the mouth. The hyacinthus is assigned to Scorpio because of the cloudy color of that time, November. The crystal is a stone hardened by water, and so it has received its name from ice, for ice is called *krystallos* in Greek. It is likened to Sagittarius since in the month when the sun is in Sagittarius, December, water begins to be hardened into ice. The diamond is a stone that cannot be cut. It is like the kernel of a filbert in size and of such great solidity that no force except goat's blood can break it. The diamond is assigned to Capricorn because of the harshness and severity of the month of January, when the sun occupies

Capricorn. The hydatis is a yellow stone, round, having within itself another stone whose rattling is noisy, although some say that the ringing is not from the little stone inside, but from the movement of a certain interior spirit. It exudes water, so that you might think that a flowing spring is shut up in it. So also the hydatis is said to have merited its name from *hudor*, water. It is likened to Aquarius because of the excessive rains that are accustomed to abound in the month of February when the sun occupies Aquarius. Through the twelve gems of the crown men also perceive the twelve hours of the day, which are distinguished through the course of the sun. Thus it was written: "And they say that your hallowed head with twelve rays bears golden lights because you complete just so many months, so many hours." But what other mystical interpretation the theologians perceive about those precious stones, or what natural interpretation the physical scientists perceive, may be sought out in their writings. On this crown Statius wrote in the beginning of his *Thebaid*: "He pressed upon your locks a halo beaming on high."[119]

11. Well, since we have named the signs, it does not seem useless to say a few words about their names and natures according to the perceptions of the ancients, who bestowed numbers and names on the stars. In the first place it should be known that the signs are nothing other than certain spaces in the sky determined through certain limits, as it were, by the wondrous sagacity of astronomers based on the position and order of stars. Through frequent, long night watches they discerned a definite region of the sky that the sun traverses in its yearly travel, so that it never ascends to the North Pole, never descends to the South Pole. It seems bound in that latitude on both sides by two lines. Then they divided the longitude also, that is, that circumference in the sky, into twelve parts. As we have read, posterity followed these astronomers and first called those parts, in general, "signs." And this was not unsuitably done, since through the recognized intervals of these stars, which preserve an unmovable position, the progression of the sun and the various motions of all the planets may be shown. So also this orbit (circulus) is called "sign-bearing" (signifer) in Latin, but "zodiac" in Greek, from *zodio*, "sign." Certainly this seems to have been devised by poetic imagination from the Greek *zoe*, "life" or "soul," and it was called *zodiac*, "living," because of the shapes of living things represented in it. Then, to create a more convenient method for their discourses and doctrines, they assigned certain

names to the individual shapes, and from the diversity of the names they directed their attention to discovering the nature of the seasons for their works. Thus they call that one in which the sun is soon brought forth and positioned the first of the signs. Each year it begins on the fifteenth day before the Calends of April, which they assert to have been the first day from the beginning of the world. They call this sign Aries, "Ram," taking their rationale from the nature of this animal. Or, as we find to have been handed down, they do so since this animal is especially powerful in its horns, just as the sun from this time on begins to apply the force of its rays toward thawing the earth, which is bound by winter's stiffness. Or they do so because from the autumnal[120] equinox, which occurs on the fourth day after the beginning of Aries, through the whole summer all the way to the other equinox, which occurs on the third day before the Calends of October, the sun traverses the right, the higher hemisphere. This is divided from the lower one by the equinoctial colure that touches it, just as that sign for this entire time is said to rest on the right side. For during the remaining half of the year the sun likewise travels through the lower hemisphere, namely, the southern circle, and Aries rests on the left side. But younger scholars thought that they understood things more acutely. Thus, they say, we place the sun in Aries in the month of March because just as rams are weak in their posterior parts and have all their strength in the foremost parts of the body, so when the time of winter is now past, a dead time because of its inclemency, temperateness returns through the approach of the sun. Then the season begins to be altered and, as it were, aroused for the future.

12. They have put Taurus, "The Bull," in the second place because when the sun approaches those regions, the first definite season after the stiffness of winter, oxen begin to toil; or because then their efforts, that is, the crops, tend toward ripeness among many peoples, and among some in the warmer lands, they even are harvested then. According to others, they do so because the bull is much stronger in its foremost parts than the ram. Indeed, they say, the ram has been allotted strength in its forehead only, but the bull in its head and breast and that entire foremost part. So, when the sun is nearer to us, a greater heat begins to prevail. On the rationale for Gemini, "The Twins," that antiquity has put forward, it seems to me more fabulous than true. Thus I have thought that one must

not disagree with the younger scholars. The Twins are depicted as embracing themselves with outstretched arms and reaching puberty, as if in their first time of life, just as in that time also, they say, young trees embrace the earth with their roots stretched below and entwined, but above they grow into plants.

13. The meaning of Cancer, "The Crab," where the sun will be after Gemini, is quite clear because just as this kind of animal walks backward, so the sun, when it reaches this sign, does not want to climb beyond. It seeks the lower parts again, after the solstice has been observed in its fourth stage, that is, on the twelfth day before the Calends of July. They call the next sign Leo, "The Lion," because of the very hot season of that month, August, since the lion is said to surpass all other animals in warmth. So also it is an animal of unbearable wrath. Then also begin the days that they call dog days, from the ferocity of the dog star (Canis Minor), which is especially vigorous then, they think. During these dog days it is not permitted to let blood or to use potions because of the warmth of the season and the motion of the blood. Thus it is said: "Under the Dog and before the Dog, purges are dangerous." Next the sun enters the sign called Virgo, "The Virgin." She is depicted as holding an ear of corn in her hand, for just as a virgin brings forth no fruit, so the earth now ceases to germinate. And among many peoples, the corn, which before was rising up into a plant, now matures into an ear. Libra, "The Balance," which is formed in the likeness of a pair of scales, represents the equinoctial equality of that month, September, which occurs on the third day before the Calends of October. After this follows Scorpio, "The Scorpion," which they say stings with the very fine point of its tail, because we feel the discomforts of cold after the autumnal equinox. Thus Horace wrote: "The morning cold now nips those who are too little cautious."[121] Then Sagittarius, "The Archer," receives the sun, since winter sends hail and storms just like arrows. Moreover, Sagittarius is erect in human form above and sinks down into animal form below, signifying that the sun in that season has been thrust down from the higher to the lower regions. What mystical meaning is sought in Capricorn, "The Goat," is very easy to apprehend even with the eyes, for who does not know that in grazing, a she-goat always seeks the higher places, up from the lowest? So also this sign sends back the sun to us from the lower parts to the higher, after the winter solstice has been completed in the

fourth or third stage, that is, the twelfth day before the Calends of January, just as the summer solstice was completed in Cancer. Thus both this sign and that one are called tropical, that is, "turning," from the Greek *tropos*, "turning around," because in Cancer the sun turns from the higher regions to the lower; in Capricorn, it turns from the lower to the higher. Thus also the philosophers called these two signs the gates of the sun, since in both the approach of the sun is prohibited from advancing by the solstice preventing it. The last signs of the zodiac, Aquarius, "The Water-Bearer," and Pisces, "The Fish," are so called because they are rainy months.

14. They consider the raven to be under the protection of Phoebus, either because, contrary to the nature of things, it alone produces its oviparous offspring in the middle of the hot summer, according to Fulgentius, or because, according to other sources, this bird is most suited to augury. Thus Statius, intimating the ill luck of an augury, complains that the raven, "dark companion of oracles," is absent.[122] According to Ovid in the Second Book of *Fasti*, Phoebus inflicted a disgrace on the raven: as long as figs are ripening and coming to maturity, it cannot drink. Because of this fiction we read that in those days the raven has a perforated throat. According to the fable, the Sun copulated with Clymene the nymph and sired Phaethon. Aspiring to drive his father's chariot, Phaethon caused a ruinous conflagration for himself and the world. Thus it is necessary that the sun, mingling with water, always brings forth some fruits. Since these appear to be leaping from the earth, they are called phaethontes, as if to say *phainontes*, for *phainon* means "appearing." Indeed, these fruits seek the warmth of the sun until maturity, but when they have obtained it, they are scorched by frequent, excessive heat. Phaethon's sisters weep with bright, glistening tears over their brother's conflagration, as Ovid relates in the Second Book of *Metamorphoses*, and they emit golden amber from their ruptured bark.[123] They are called Heliades, daughters of the Sun. Thus without a doubt trees are the sisters of plants and flowers; they are produced by one and the same union of heat and moisture. Furthermore, when the sun is hotter in the months of June and July, it burns the ripe fruits, and it reaches into Cancer and Leo. Then, after their bark has split in the strong heat, those trees that drip amber emit their liquid juice in the river Eridanus to be hardened by its waters into amber. But it should be known that there are three kinds of amber according to Pliny

in his *Natural History*: one from trees, which is called amber; another which is found naturally; a third, which is made from three parts of gold and one of silver. If you dissolve the lump, you will find these parts. Also, the nature of amber is shown by poison. When this has been mingled with it, the amber emits a shrill sound and causes various colors to appear, in the likeness of someone who has been poisoned.

15. Phoebus is deservedly called the god of doctors, either because the herbs that physicians use are generated by the sun's warmth, or because the particular changes of the seasons, which the course of the sun causes, bring balances or imbalances to the humors. These produce health and illnesses. Thus, in his First Book of *Metamorphoses*, Ovid calls autumn imbalanced, that is, sickly; certainly in autumn each year we experience severe pestilences. For autumn to abound in diseases, it produces a borderline of cold and warmth. Although the spring season also has this, it does not cause diseases, since bodies then have been made hardy by the preceding cold. Autumn harms these bodies, finding them weaker from the heat of summer. So also, as Servius says, all who are born with the mother's womb cut open are consecrated to Apollo, as to the god of medicine, through whom they have gained the light. So too, Aesculapius is thought to be his son, since he was cut out of the womb of Coronis. Aesculapius is interpreted to mean "acting harshly." Also, the family of Caesars keeps the sacred rites of Apollo because the first one of their family was born when his mother's womb had been cut open. Thus he was called Caesar, from *caedendo*, "cutting," although various etymologies are given for this name.

16. The Sun is said to sink into the ocean and, worn out, to restore its light there, and to emerge from there, bathed, in the morning. In truth, the sun's flames are nourished by water. Even poetic fiction declares this because Jupiter is said to have been invited by the Ethiopians to banquets, along with other gods. The Ethiopians live next to the ocean, whose water feeds the fires of the seven planets. The story says that when they could not harm each other in their discord, the brothers Atreus and Thyestes returned to a pretended friendship, at which time Thyestes slept with his brother's wife. Then Atreus set Thyestes' own son before him to be eaten. When he saw this, the Sun fled so as not to be defiled. According to Servius, there is little truth in this. Atreus was first among the Mycenaeans to discover the eclipse of the sun. Envying him, his brother departed from their city at that time when his teachings were proved right.

In fact, the deities receive various shapes and diverse names according to places, for Apollo is imagined in human form at Delphi, like a wolf in Lycia, but at Delos he has the shape of a serpent. Also, according to the book of Porphyry, which he called Sun, it is known that Apollo has a triple power, and that the same god is the Sun among the gods, Father Liber on earth, and Apollo in the lower regions. Thus also, sanctuaries are consecrated to him. The interior or secret part of a temple is called the sanctuary through antiphrasis because it is approached by a few, that is, by the priests of the sun. So also, we see three insignia around his statue: the lyre, which shows us the image of celestial harmony; the griffin, which shows him to be an earthly deity; and arrows, by which he is shown to belong to the lower regions and to be a harmful god. Thus Apollo is named from the Greek word *apollein*, "exterminating" or "destroying," as we said. Thus it is that Homer calls him the author of pestilence, just as of health. So also we assign a bow and arrows to an angry Apollo, but to a placid Apollo we assign a cithara. Thus Horace says: "Apollo, mild and placid when your weapon is set aside, hear your suppliant children."[124] Moreover, he has a lyre because all things are tempered through the harmony of warmth and moisture. Also, the astrologers assert that pestilence will follow as often as the sun appears with his bow.

17. Apollo was robbed of his divinity and pastured the herds of Admetus because he killed the Cyclopes. This story seems to depend on natural philosophy, for the Sun brings forth grasses and all the nutriments of the herds. Thus also, according to Servius, he is called Nomius, from the Greek *nomoi*, "pastures." According to the same author, he could have acquired this name from *tonomoi*, "the usage of stringed instruments." The fact that the goddess Celerity, "swiftness," is called the daughter of the sun was imagined so either because no bodily thing is swifter than the sun, or because the astrologers say that in the constellation of the sun, breezes will be fair and swift. Apollo carries a light, that is, a torch, with which the Sun is depicted and by which he is thought to illuminate the world. He is said to wash his locks in the Castalian spring because of this resemblance: locks of hair hide the neck. But in truth, wise men who examine the secrets of philosophy and hidden wisdom also inhabit this place. Apollo is sometimes taken for the human voice too, as we have said. Thus also the nine Muses are attached to him because, according to the philosophers, there are nine things that regulate the

human voice: two lips, four teeth, the tip of the tongue, the hollow of the throat, and the breathing of the lungs. Indeed, if any of these is lacking, the voice will not be complete.

18. Fulgentius calls the nine Muses "modes of learning" and "modes of knowledge." He assigns to them a suitable-enough order according to the meanings of their names. Clio is put first; her name means "fame," for no one, he says, seeks knowledge except one who advances the dignity of his own fame. So the first Muse is called Clio, "the idea of seeking knowledge." We call the second Euterpe, which means "well-pleasing," so that to wish is the first thing and second is to be pleased in that which you wish. The third Muse is called Melpomene, "meditating," so that to wish is the first thing, second is to desire what you wish, third is to pursue by meditating that which you wish. Fourth is Thalia, "capacity" or "planting seeds." Fifth is Polyhymnia, "making much memory," for after capacity, memory is necessary. The sixth Muse is Erato, "finding likeness," for after capacity and memory, the most useful thing for one who is learning is to find something similar on his own. Seventh is Terpsichore, "delighting in instruction," because after finding something it is necessary to distinguish and to judge what you have found. Eighth is Urania, "heavenly," for after judging you choose what you affirm or what you reject. Moreover, it is a heavenly quality to choose what is useful and to reject what is fleeting. Ninth is Calliope, "of best voice." So this will be the order: first is to wish for learning; second, to delight in what you wish; third, to pursue with perseverance that which you desire and in which you have been delighted; fourth, to grasp what you are pursuing; fifth, to remember what you grasp; sixth, to find on your own something similar to that which you remember; seventh, to judge what you have found; eighth, to make a choice about that which you judge; ninth, to advance well what you have chosen. Remigius, in fact, has another order of the Muses, and he wrote another explanation, but it seems to me less clear and pertains only to the reading of Martianus [Capella]. Thus I have not judged it necessary to the present work. Therefore, as we said before, Apollo, the god of wisdom, is deservedly thought to preside over these Muses, the certain steps to wisdom, as it were.

19. According to the natural scientists, Apollo presides over the Muses for a far different reason: because the sun, positioned in the midst of the planets, is thought to rule the whole vastness of the world's harmony.

About the sun Cicero says: "leader and author and ruler of the rest of the stars, mind and moderator of the world."[125] The theories of theologians hold that this planet and the seven spheres subject to it are joined. While their motion continually preserves musical proportions among them, the individual ones make individual sounds, and all together they make the greatest harmony. The natural philosophers add that the nine Muses should be understood as nothing other than the melodies of the seven spheres and that one harmony that is created from all in harmony together. So also, they call the eighth Muse Urania, "heavenly," but the ninth Muse, namely, that wholeness of the eight sounds, they call Calliope, "of the best voice." Yet, according to Remigius, the theory of this harmony is reckoned a little differently, for he seems to intimate that the ninth sound proceeds from the earth, which others say is immobile and without sound. But the sun is the author of this harmony. Established in the midst of the seven spheres, as we have said, the sun is shown by the astrologers to vary their positions, their orbits and reversions, but also to vary their risings and settings by its own force. Among the Greeks Apollo is also called Mousagetes, "leader of the Muses." Also, according to Remigius, the swan is consecrated to him, since it is a songful bird. Some scholars say that although there are nine circles of the world, the highest, which they call Anastron, and the lowest, which is the circle of earth, lack sound. There are seven remaining, making seven different tones, whose harmony, as they assert, Orpheus was the first to grasp. Thus also, he deserved to be called the son of Apollo and Calliope.

20. Moreover, to digress a little, Orpheus was a very great man who was illustrious because of the splendor of his genius as well as the sweetness of his eloquence. He is called a priest because he was a theologian and the first to establish orgies. Also, by the charm of his oratory he turned men who were living irrationally away from their wild and savage ways into mild and gentle people, and he settled them after they were turned from their wandering, harsh ways. Thus he is said to have moved all beasts, birds and streams, rocks and trees. So also is Amphion, founder of Thebes, a man outstanding for his faculty of oratory, thought to have enticed stones by his singing so that, coming together on their own, they built the walls. The fact is that by his mellifluous speaking he persuaded men who were stupid before, ignorant of law, and dwelling here and there, to come together, to live together civilly, and to construct walls for

public defense. In fact, Orpheus means "best voice." About him men tell the following fable. Orpheus loved the nymph Eurydice. Delighting her with the sound of his cithara, he took her as his wife. When Aristaeus the shepherd loved her and pursued her, she stepped on a snake as she was fleeing, and she died. Her husband descended into the Underworld for her and accepted the stipulation that he not turn around and look back at her. He did turn around and, seeing her, he lost her again. According to Fulgentius, this fable is a description of the art of music, for Orpheus, as we have said, means "best voice" and Eurydice means "profound discerning." Orpheus, that is, anyone who devotes attention to music, seeks to be joined to her and takes her as his wife after she has been enticed by the cithara because one who studies music cannot be a musician unless he understands the secret depth of this art and so at last attains this by the repeated, artistic modulation of the voice. In fact, the best men love this depth of knowledge because it denies the commonality of men. So Aristaeus loved it, for "best" is called *ariston* in Greek. Thus it dies from the serpent's bite and migrates to the lower regions, as it were, since it is cut off by the secrets of its own excessive subtlety. But after attaining this art, which must be sought and raised up, the melodious voice descends and is prohibited from looking back, and when it sees, it loses. Even the most accomplished Pythagoras, while he toiled in the study of music and suited its harmonies to the proportions of weight and numbers, still could not give a reason for its effect.

21. But this fiction appears otherwise to Remigius, for he says that Eurydice was called the wife of Orpheus because discernment ought to be the companion of eloquence. Indeed, she descended to the Underworld after the serpent wounded her because, by gaping at earthly profits, she is turned toward a perverse place by the venom of iniquity. She is recalled to the upper regions by the songs of Orpheus because the stimulus for gain is transformed to equanimity by excellent oratory. But if it looks back, it is drawn again to earthly goods and is not restored to the pleading Orpheus. For when the earthly spirit desires worldly things too much, scarcely any oratory raises it up to a state of rectitude, since it is held back by Proserpina, that is, the very great enticement of vices. Furthermore, Servius says that Orpheus really wanted to lead back his wife's soul by certain songs. Since he could not do this, he says, Orpheus is thought by the poets to have lost his wife, when she had already been

won back, because of Pluto's deadly decree. Vergil also wished to show this by saying: "if Orpheus could summon the shade of his wife."[126] For "to summon," he says, properly belongs to one calling forth.

22. But let us return to the Muses. Among the ancients, even rustics recognized that the Muses are the harmony of the world; they called them Camenae, as if to say *canenae*, from *canendo*, "singing." Also, since theologians established that heaven makes music, they added the musical sounds of the heavenly bodies to their sacrifices, which were performed among some with the lyre or cithara, among others with pipes or other musical instruments. In fact, water is called *moys* in Greek; thus Muse means "watery." Indeed, while air is going through the windpipe of one who is singing, it is sprinkled with moisture, and one does not ever sing through the pipe in the throat except with the help of moisture. So also, according to Varro, these Muses are nymphs, and not without cause, as Servius says, for the sound of water produces music, as we see in water organs, that is, aquatic instruments. This same Varro recounts that there are only three Muses: one who is born from the motion of water; another whom the sound of air creates when it is struck; a third who consists only of pure voice. When I consider the obscure differences in these matters, which burden my natural ability, I propose that they be dispersed by others and elucidated by sound interpretation, lest my insignificance should be opposed by the authority of great men, or, while putting forth spurious teachings in understanding thus, I cause myself to understand nothing.

9. Mercury

1. They say that Jove's second son is Mercury, the god of speech and eloquence. They interpret this name to mean *medius currens*, "running in the middle," since speech takes place between two persons, or *mercatorum kyrios*, "lord of merchants." According to Fulgentius his name means *merces curans*, "caring for merchandise," for Mercury presides over merchants, among whom excellence of speech and caution in speech are especially vigorous. He is said to have been born in Arcadia because this region in particular strove after eloquence, as Remigius says. He is present at the weddings of the gods since at weddings speech is very effective, for there many mediations and messages and that kind of thing go back and forth. Mercury is said to have been born after Apollo, for

among wise men counsel comes first in whatever matter is being thought out. This is represented by Apollo, the god of wisdom. Then what has been foreseen is enunciated in speech, which is understood as Mercury. Martianus imagines that Mercury took Philology as his wife, and that she gave him the seven liberal arts for a dowry. Thus Philology is interpreted to mean "study" or "love of reason." Also, she is represented in the person of reason, but Mercury is represented in the likeness of fluency and speech. So when these two come together in a wise man, I mean both acuteness of reason and fluency of speech, then in a certain manner Mercury and Philology are united; then also one comes very easily to a knowledge of the seven liberal arts. In fact, Philology's mother, Phronesis, which means "prudence," is thought to have been mortal. And so, it was necessary that this same Philology, born of a mortal mother, was a mortal and unworthy of marriage to so great a god, unless she received an apotheosis, that is, deification. This was thought to be so, according to Remigius, since secular wisdom of itself is mortal and transitory, unless it acquires immortality through the study of true wisdom. Phronesis is rightly called the mother of Philology, since prudence adorns reason and, in a certain manner, nourishes it, just as a mother does.

2. Also, this same Mercury, whose father was Jove and whose mother was Maia, was half mortal. But then Juno put him to her own breasts and thus filled him with divine milk so that he might become immortal. Therefore speech is suited to setting forth divine subjects, that is, lofty and subtle ones, and also human subjects, that is, lowly ones and those that have less subtlety. Thus he is said to have been begotten by those parents, one immortal and one mortal. So when speech is occupied with only earthly things and inferior ones, it is deservedly thought to be mortal, but while it is lifted up to the breasts of Juno, who is the air, that is, while speech ascends to heavenly things and to discerning the secrets of higher philosophy, it seems in a certain manner to have merited divinity. As far as physical science is concerned, Mercury is thought to have been nourished by the breasts of Juno because speech is effected and sustained in a certain way when a word has been formed from air that has been struck. According to the nonsense of fables, Mercury had intercourse with Venus while he was still a youth, and he sired Hermaphroditus, whose name comes from his own and that of Venus. For in Greek, Mercury is called Hermes, but Venus is named Aphrodite, "foaming," for

foam is called *aphros*. Also, why Venus is called "foaming," we explained clearly when we discussed Saturn. Thus Hermaphroditus is said to be the son of Mercury and Aphrodite. We call people of one sex as well as the other hermaphrodites, and we also call them androgynous, for in Greek a man is called *aner* and a woman is called *gyne*. Hermaphroditus signifies a certain wantonness of speech because superfluous embellishment of speech is generally required when regard for truth is neglected. So we read that Wisdom was unwilling to marry Mercury, for although speech is the great ornament of a rational creature, wisdom spurns the superfluous embellishment of words, not because it runs away from being joined to fluency, but because it does not consent to be mingled with immoderate wordiness.

3. Fulgentius says that Mercury presides over business. So he is called Mercury, as if to say *merces curans*, "caring for merchandise," because tradesmen, whom he rules, are always watching over merchandise; or he is named from the Greek Hermes, which means "to discuss," because knowledge of languages is especially necessary for a tradesman. Therefore Mercury is called the messenger of those above and those below because traders traverse lands; they go upon the sea and cross it. Mercury is the god of theft and himself a thief because merchants, while cheating others by their lies and deceptions, are not far removed from thieves. So also he is said to have killed Argus, after his eyes had been gouged out with a sickle, because sly thieves and tradesmen instructed in the tricks of crooked cunning are also often very wise men, but they cheat and defraud those who are devoid of worldly shrewdness. Indeed, Argus means "void." The cock is considered to be Mercury's sentinel because this bird especially seems to indicate the hour of rising for merchants, over whom he presides. Thus he carries a staff, according to Remigius, because a speech of eloquence is delivered by the right and ready way of reason. Thus the staff is encircled by snakes and called a herald's staff (caduceus) because the speech of an orator "running between" the venomous disputes of adversaries compels every quarrel to end, and he reconciles the adversaries to one another, for those waging war are pacified by the oratory of eloquent men. Legates are called *caduceatores*, according to Livy, for just as wars are declared by the *fetiales*, "college of priests," so peace is arranged by the *caduceatores*, "heralds." I certainly do not approve of the theory that Mercury carries a staff because the

constellation Mercury does not advance through the revolutions of orbits when it is with the sun, just like certain planets, but it moves on a straight path while touching eight parts of the breadth of the zodiac. Based on this view, any planet that traverses more than one of the twelve lines in the breadth of the zodiac must not be thought to proceed on a straight path. Martianus calls that staff of Mercury's "memory," since speech leads anything at all to the memory. Also, this staff brings sleep and takes it away, because clever speech calms some quarrels, as we have said, and also sometimes stirs up others. It also imparts life and snatches it away, since at trials the same speech of orators frees this man and condemns that one.

4. Mercury is also said to wear a cap because of the intricate obscurity of words. Indeed, the authority of Remigius does not disagree with these points, for he connects the faculties of Mercury to these words: Themis, he says, means "obscurity" or "darkness" and Erigone means "contention" or "quarrelsome." These two are very often the companions of Mercury because they suit an orator, since the speech of orators is sometimes obscure, sometimes clear, and sometimes it provokes quarrels and strife. The venomous and sharp eloquence of orators is represented by the two snakes that encircle Mercury's staff. Also, there are two because the speech of orators both condemns and liberates. We interpret Mercury's staff to mean the speech of an orator because, just like a staff, the tenor of justice and truth ought to be both straight and flexible in orators. The top of his staff is golden, the middle is grayish, and the bottom is pitch black because at first the orator's speech seems beautiful, then it is rough, but at last it condemns the accused. Remigius makes these points. But by that staff with snakes wound around it we are able, not foolishly, to perceive the continuous, insatiable purpose of tradesmen, over whom Mercury presides. They are always hurrying with the same desire toward profits, full of serpentine shrewdness, and constantly tormenting themselves with the noxious poison of cares.

5. Now we imagine that Mercury has winged sandals, that is, a winged shoe, and a traveler's cap (petasum), from the Greek word peto, "flying," either because nothing is swifter than speech, or because of the very great swiftness of his constellation. In fact, as Remigius declares, these winged sandals are more properly said to be golden than silver, according to allegory, for in sacred rites gold refers to the purity of understanding, but

silver refers to the clarity of speech. Also, as a sign of his swiftness, Mercury is depicted with his head covered, and deservedly so, for although other stars return slowly to their risings, Mercury is found at his rising point on the eighteenth day, as Servius says. So also he is called Stilbon, which means "quick." Sometimes also, as Remigius says, Mercury climbs above the sun, and often he even approaches the orbit of Mars, but sometimes when he is going backward he descends to the lower orbits and again is brought down almost as far as the border of the lunar orbit. Therefore it is thought that he frequently returns to the sky and to Tartarus. Judging that to be obscure, as far as I am concerned, I leave it to be studied by astronomers. The fact that Mercury is called the attendant of the gods arose because his planet rushes about ascending and descending through the orbits of the other planets like their servant, or because speech renders equal service to greater and to lesser men, or, as Servius teaches, for a certain mathematical reason. For, he said, we should know that two of the five planets, Mars and Saturn, are injurious; two, Jove and Venus, are good; but Mercury is like the one to which it is joined. Thus he is thought to be the attendant of the gods because he submits to their power. So it is that Vergil says: "Into what circles in the sky the Cyllenian fire wanders,"[127] that is, to which of the planets Mercury clings, so that from it the quality of Mercury himself can be recognized.

6. In fact, Pliny describes more extensively the natures of the planets that we have called good or injurious. He also mentions that comets are natural stars, and they appear in all seasons, and these same comets come from the five planets. Thus sometimes they signify good, he says, and sometimes the worst of things, for if they come from Venus or Jove, they announce the best of things, but if they come from Mars or Saturn, they announce worse things. Mercury is always like that planet to which he clings. Thus Pliny also says that Mercury is imagined to be the attendant of the gods. Also, the Stoics say that these planets are beyond the thirty-two whose names and effects Avienus[128] mentions. Sirius is another of these, that is, a star positioned in the mouth of the Dog. This star is pestiferous to the extent that it is in this position, but according to the quality of those nearby it is either overcome or it exercises greater powers. But no doubt it causes pestilence, if the courses of other stars suit this outcome. So it is that, although it always rises at a certain time, it is

not always injurious. Also, its destructive force often lasts for a whole year, often for a few days. Thus it was written: "And Sirius rules for the whole year." Moreover, Canis appears after Orion and is imagined to have been his hound while he was a hunter. In fact, he is called Sirius from "trailing," that is, the length of the constellation, for *suro* means "I trail along." This is the greatest constellation, so that by its greatness it seems to occupy the space of three others. Its rising is said to bring heat because in the month of June, when Canis rises with it and the sun is positioned in Cancer, men are accustomed to suffer from the excessive burning of the sun. Also, Orion rises for many days because of his greatness. Thus his weather is uncertain, even among experienced men. Moreover, he rises when the sun stands in Taurus. It is thought that Orion was killed by the arrows of Diana, or by the sting of a scorpion, as Servius says. But the more likely reality is that a scorpion killed him because he falls when that sign is rising.

7. Neither should you shudder at the fact that prosperity or adversity is said to be determined for us according to the position of stars. Even the Catholic faith truly perceives this and embraces it steadfastly. Yet the opinion of the pagans holds that the vicissitudes of our deeds and successes happen either by the force and power of the stars, or without doubt they are presignified either by those who know or do not know them. Thus even birds, which do not understand them, betoken future events with their feathers or calls, either while flying or standing. No wonder the management of our affairs is ascribed to stars, since all of us, while we live, owe all things to them, according to natural philosophy. Now I am not setting forth Catholic truth in these matters, but the opinions and fictions of the pagans. For truly they say that when we are being born, we receive a soul from the Sun, a body from the Moon, blood from Mars, mental ability from Mercury, a longing for honors from Jove, passionate desires from Venus, a bodily humor from Saturn. They assert that the dead return all of these to the individual planets. Some people teach these views otherwise and more extensively. Here let that teaching of Servius suffice.

8. Remigius says that Mercury is thought to be the inventor of wrestling since his star wrestles with the sun, so to speak, and struggles with it, as it were, wishing to overcome it. Indeed, Mercury always goes with the sun, never standing more than thirty-two paces apart from it. Thus

Mercury is rarely seen. Also, he is depicted as dark because of the heat of the sun. You should know that, in accordance with the variety of his locales, Mercury also receives different names and different shapes. He is called Cyllenius from Mount Cyllene in Arcadia, where it is thought he was born; Mercury from conducting business; Arcas from Arcadia. Really, his proper name is Kyrios, "Lord." Some say that this same Mercury is the god of intelligence. The god who is depicted with a dog's head among the Egyptians is also called Mercury. Clearly this is so because nothing has keener sense than a dog. The fact that it is thought Hecuba had been changed into a dog refers to another story. She was transformed into a barking animal because she reviled the Greeks in vain because of her excessive grief when she was taken captive and recognized the corpse of Polydorus, her son. He had been killed, as we read, by Polymestor. To be sure, Cicero says in his books *On the Nature of the Gods* that there are many Mercurys, but with regard to the gods, we must follow fables, since the truth is unknown.

9. Also in the same book [Cicero] teaches that there is a triple belief about gods. The first is that gods do not exist. The author of this view was burned by the Athenians. The second is that the gods exist and have no concern for things, as the Epicureans affirm, who think that the whole world is turned by fortuitous events. In accord with them, Vergil says in his Fourth Book: "Certainly this is work for the gods above; this care disturbs them as they rest."[129] The third theory is that gods exist and care for all things, as the Stoics say, who teach the necessity of fate. In accord with them, Vergil a little later adds: "if the benevolent deities can do anything."[130] Poets use the sects of philosophers according to the nature of their material, and they do not ever bind themselves to one sect, unless that is especially their purpose, as with Lucretius, who followed only the Epicureans. Moreover, we know that sects are opposed to one another. Thus it happens that in a certain poet we might find contrary views, not because of his ignorance, but because of the variety of sects. In fact, even that which Vergil says in the Fourth Book, "but wretched before her day,"[131] is from the Epicureans, who consign all things to chance, but what he says in the Tenth Book, "each one has his own day,"[132] is from the Stoics, who say that the decrees of fate are preserved. Therefore, although the Stoics always grant birth and death to the fates alone, they assign everything in between to fortune, for all the events of

human life, they say, are uncertain. Hence Lachesis, the middle one of the sisters [Fates], who represents one's lot in life, is imagined to be the dispenser of our life. Thus, either to show the full teaching of the Stoics, or perhaps following different philosophers, that same Vergil says: "almighty Fortune and inevitable Fate."[133] Indeed, nothing seems so contrary to fate as chance.

10. But according to wiser men, our life depends upon three things: nature, to which is not granted more than one hundred and twenty solar years; fate, for which ninety years, that is, three circuits of Saturn, make an end, unless perhaps the benevolence of other stars surpasses the third circuit; fortune, that is, chance, which pertains to all things that are from without, such as a downfall, fires, slaughters, shipwrecks, and the like. Thus in the same source [Vergil], Dido, about to die, says: "I have completed the course that Fortune gave,"[134] for as she is about to kill herself she rightly ascribes this act to fortune, not to nature or fate. So Cicero writes in Philippics: "For many things seemed to threaten me beyond nature and fate," that is, by the chance of Antony's sword. But there was much dispute among the ancients about the fact that Dido says that her shade (imago) will go beneath the earth. Here let us insert a useful excursus concerning certain profitable subjects in this choice part of the Aeneid. Among some philosophers there was a long search for what it is in us that seeks the Underworld. They taught that a man consists of three parts: soul, which is from above and returns to its source; body, which disappears in the earth; shade, which Lucretius defines as "air deprived of light." Therefore they say a shade is created by the body, as it were, and without doubt perishes with it, nor is anything left of a man which seeks the lower regions. Yet finally they said that they had discovered that there is a certain semblance which, fashioned in the likeness of our body, departs into the lower regions; also there is a bodily appearance that cannot be touched, just as the wind cannot. Thus it was written: "It is unlawful to transport living bodies in my Stygian skiff."[135] Homer inquired into this matter when the semblance of Hercules was seen among the dead. These semblances are also said to belong to those who were made gods through apotheosis. So all are said to have been seen in the lower regions or to have descended there. On Liber, Horace wrote: "Harmless Cerberus saw you adorned with a golden horn."[136] And in Vergil, Charon says: "In truth, I was not happy to take Alcides on this

lake, nor Theseus and Perithous, even though they were sired by gods,"
etc.[137] But poets misuse this information, and they indiscriminately put
down either "semblance" or "shade."

11. Vergil introduces these words into the magical rites that Dido per-
forms to ensnare Aeneas by her love: "And the love charm snatched away
before the mother."[138] He took this from Pliny, who says in his *Natural
History* that the foals of horses have a certain piece of flesh on their brow
that the mother snatches away from them as soon as they are born. If by
chance anyone snatches this away before her, she hates the foal and re-
fuses her milk to it. Thus Juvenal writes: "Into which Caesonia poured
the whole brow of a trembling foal."[139] Moreover, they rightly suspect
that a love charm is created from flesh, without which the mother does
not nourish the foal that she has created. Vergil relates that Dido suffered
a difficult death because of this: because life seemed to remain in her,
who was dying by chance, not by either fate or nature. And he added
this: "For since she perished not by fate nor by a deserved death,"[140] that
is, natural. Thus he also made Iris cut off a lock of Dido's hair so that she
could die, imitating Euripides, who likewise brought in Mercury to cut
off the hair of Alcestis, since she was dying because of her husband's fate.
For it used to be said that no one could die unless either the Parcae [Fates]
have broken the thread on which a man's life depends, or Proserpina has
marked his name on the doorpost in the Underworld, or she has cut off a
lock of hair from his head, or the Eumenides [Furies] have carried their
torches around him. Also, they assert that everyone has a stone in an urn
in the Underworld, and whose stone comes out first descends first to the
lower regions; whose stone comes out later descends later to the lower
regions.

12. Lying Greece, with its poetic babbling ever adorned by falsehood,
always bestowed its care on cunningly inventing such ridiculous fictions.
And so they say that these fabricated deferrals of death arose from this
fact: that through certain dedications the ancients used to see to it that
they were fortified against all assaults of fortune, and they could not die,
as Servius says, unless that dedication was carried out. Thus those stories
were preserved about Dido. Furthermore, they accept, not foolishly, that
the urn is the world itself, always tottering and turning everything and
sending those whom it holds to the Underworld. Thus Horace writes:
"The urn of all is turned, and the lot comes out later or sooner."[141] But

also this seems to have been taken from history, for the Greeks, as we read, when they were about to send legates to any place, used to put lots into an urn, and they sent those whom the lot destined. About the dying Dido, Vergil wrote: "The warmth flowed away."[142] He imitated those who say that the soul is warmth and when this recedes, the body is cold, "and life departs into the winds," that is, the soul [departs]. Or he followed those who say that the soul is air; that is, it returns to its own substance, as elsewhere he wrote "they draw the fine substance of life."[143] Or surely he followed the Epicureans, who say that the soul perishes with the body. So that we might understand the point: it vanished. For this reason, according to these same ones, it was said: "The loss of a grave is easily borne."[144]

13. Also, Vergil introduces Aeneas' bride offering sacrifice at the founding of Carthage: "to fruit-bearing Ceres and Phoebus and Father Lyaeus."[145] But above all she sacrifices to Juno. [She sacrifices] to Ceres, of course, so that she might grant fruitfulness to the crops; to Phoebus because he presides over the divine omens by which cities are ruled, as we said above; to Lyaeus, that is, Bacchus, who is rightly the god of freedom for cities, as we shall teach in the following passages. Thus also his attendant, Marsyas, is a sign of freedom in city-states. If other gods are invoked during the first offerings of cities, it pertains to a private cause, as in that same place we read: "Before all to Juno, whose care is for the bonds of matrimony."[146] Although this was represented as a benefit to the commonwealth, it was also the special cause of Dido. The common opinion is this: she offered sacrifice first to the deities who preside over the city, as if she were about to marry for the benefit of the commonwealth; then to Juno, to whom belongs the concern for marriage. But some have deeper understanding, for, they say, as we are about to do something, we first appease the hostile gods, and thus we invoke the propitious ones, as in "a black sheep to Winter, a white one to the favorable Zephyrs."[147] So, now about to marry, Dido first appeases Ceres, who curses marriage because of the ravishing of her daughter; Apollo, who is without a wife; Liber who could not marry the girl he had seduced, as we read. Thus she procures the favor of Juno. Such also is that saying of Apollo when he addresses Iulus in the Ninth Book when Iulus killed Numanus with his arrow after Jove was invoked: "Mighty Apollo grants this first glory to you."[148] He says that he has granted this because he is

the god of arrows, and although Jupiter aided Iulus, Apollo claims his own part, saying that he had granted this, since he did not prevent it. These favors that we ask of other deities are then fulfilled, if other gods are not opposed, and especially those gods to whom these things belong. So also in the Fourth Book, Juno, discussing Dido and Aeneas, says to Venus: "I shall be there, and, if your good will toward me is assured, I shall unite them in firm wedlock."[149] This means, "I shall unite them, which is in my power; it remains for you to be willing to fulfill your duty."

10. Pallas

1. They say that Pallas is the eldest daughter of Jove. Men call her the goddess of war, wisdom, and all arts, as Ovid says in his book, *Fasti*. They also assign different names to her, for the same goddess is called Pallas, Minerva, Tritonia, and she is Athena among the Greeks. Either she is called Pallas from the Greek *pallein*, that is, from "shaking a spear," which clearly this goddess does, or since, according to the story, she killed the giant Pallas near the River Triton. According to Remigius, this is thought to be so because wisdom killed foolishness as it lay in the mud of wretched ignorance. Pallas also means "new," for wisdom knows no decay and no old age. For this reason she also deserved to be called Minerva, "not mortal," for *min* means "not" and *erva* means "mortal." Athena means the same thing, for Athena is as if to say *athanatos*, "immortal." According to Remigius, she was named Tritonia as if to say *tritonoia*, "three ideas," for philosophers toiled with their minds to understand only so much, namely, the creator, the creature and the soul, which they judged to be in the middle. We have touched upon this [the soul] elsewhere. But Fulgentius understands this name another way; according to him, Triton, as we said above, is as if to say *tetrimenon*. In Latin we say *contritum*. Thus, he says, Tritonia is called the goddess of wisdom because all *contritio*, "contrition," produces wisdom. According to Servius, *trein* means "to fear." She was called Tritonia as if to say *terribilis*, "frightful," according to him. Now the fact that she gained this name from a marsh in Libya because there she celebrated her descent from heaven and her ascent to heaven, is known to be a poetic invention, for we read: "And she called herself Tritonia, after her beloved waters."[150]

2. It is thought that Pallas was born without a mother because wisdom is without a beginning or an end. Thus she is a virgin because wisdom admits no corruption of vice, but rejoices in the perpetual blamelessness of good morals. Martianus imagines that Pallas descended from a loftier and brighter place because Wisdom clearly dwells on high and surmounts all the vileness of earthly dregs. You have her saying: "I have dwelt in the highest places, and my throne is on a pillar of cloud."[151] Men imagine too that this goddess clung to the head of Jove because, according to the story, she was born from the head of Jove. One can agree with this fiction because wisdom was produced by the mind of the supreme God. She says: "I proceeded from the mouth of the Most High."[152] So too, the fact that Pallas is represented without a mother shows that everlasting wisdom had its beginning not from other existing things, but from the essence of God. Thus also, since she is a virgin and without a mother, the number seven is consecrated to her, since that number alone within the limit of ten, as is taught in arithmetic, neither produces another from itself nor is it produced by any other number, except from oneness alone, which is the mother of all numbers. Pallas bears the Gorgon's head on her breast as an image of terror, for there, as Servius says, is all prudence, which confounds others and proves them to be ignorant and hard as stone. She has a triple vesture, either because all wisdom is multiple, or because it is concealed. Men place the owl under her protection because wisdom possesses its own brightness even in darkness. Many say that Pallas was born from Jove's head because the seat of genius and wisdom is said to be in the brain. Thus we say that citadels and the loftier and more remote ramparts of cities are consecrated to her, for we read: "Let Pallas herself dwell in the citadels she has built."[153] So also in the overthrow of Troy, Vergil properly says that she occupied the citadels, for he very deliberately gives to the deities their own parts to be thrown down: gates to Juno, whose goddess she is, as we have said; citadels to Pallas, walls to Neptune, to whom foundations are consecrated and by whose will they are also said to be shaken. Indeed, he is also called *enosigthon*, "earth shaker," as we have said.

3. The story says this about Pallas and Vulcan: when Vulcan fashioned thunderbolts for Jove, he received permission from him to undertake whatever he wished. Vulcan asked for Minerva as his wife. But Jupiter ordered Minerva to defend her virginity with arms. When they entered

the bedchamber and Pallas resisted him, Vulcan cast his seed upon the floor. From this a boy with dragons' feet was born; he was called Erichthonius, as if he were begotten from earth and strife, for *chthon* means "earth" and *eris* means "strife," according to Servius. He was the first man to use a chariot, to conceal the hideousness of his feet. Concerning his name, Fulgentius thinks otherwise. He says that a struggle is called *eris* in Greek, earth is *chthon*, or envy is *phthonos*. Minerva concealed that fetus in a basket, with a serpent placed over it as a guard. She entrusted it to two sisters, Pandora and Aglaurus. They say that Vulcan is understood to mean "the fire of fury." Thus, according to Fulgentius, he was called Vulcan, "the ardor of the will." Finally, he also makes thunderbolts for Jove, that is, he incites fury in citizens. Thus he seeks marriage to Minerva, since fury sometimes creeps stealthily even into wise men. In fact, Pallas defends her virginity with arms because every wise man struggles with strength of spirit to defend the integrity of his good morals against fury. So Erichthonius is born, that is, the struggle of envy or of earth. Of earth, I say, because just as earth consumes bodies, so also envy consumes earthly glory. And what else can fury creeping stealthily into wisdom create, other than the struggle of envy? Minerva hides this envy in a basket, that is, the wise man conceals it in his heart, for a wise man is calmer and does not expose his grief. She places a serpent as a guard over it, that is, she devotes care to it. Also, she entrusts Erichthonius to two virgins, Pandora and Aglaurus. In fact, Pandora means "universal gift," but Aglaurus means "oblivion of sorrow." Indeed, if a wise man bears any wrath or rancor against anyone, he either entrusts it to kindness, which is naturally the gift of all; that is, out of kindness he pardons it, or while he defers taking vengeance, he consigns it to oblivion.

4. Since we made mention of Vulcan above, Remigius and Servius call him Volicanum, as if to say *volantem candorem*, "flying brightness." As Remigius says in a certain place, Vulcan is represented in the shape of earthly fire, just as heavenly fire is represented by Jove. He is thought to be lame, since fire never appears straight, but crooked. Vulcan is also represented as the fire of obscene desire. Thus he is thought to be the husband of Venus. Also, he is rightly called Lemnius, "muddy," because obscene pleasure abides in none but "muddy" minds. In fact, *limne* means "lake." He is also called Mulciber, "airy fire," as if to say *mulcens*

imber, "softening rainstorm," for when clouds seek the higher places they are dissolved into rain showers by the heat. In fact, we say that among Jove and Vulcan and Vesta, this is the difference: Jove is celestial fire, simple and harmless, burning nothing; Vesta is public fire, suited to mortal uses; Vulcan, however, is understood to be harmful fire and burning, such as lightning is. So it is thought he is called Vulcan, as if to say "flying brightness," because, clearly, [lightning] flies through the air, for it proceeds from the clouds, according to the natural scientists. Also, Vulcan is thought to have been born from Juno's thigh. He was cast down from the sky because of his deformity, so that he became lame. He fell onto the island of Lemnos and first received the name Lemnius from Lemnos. Accordingly, Juno is air. Vulcan was born of her because all lightning falls from the air. He was thus born from her thigh because lightning bolts proceed from air alone. Thus Lucan says: "The air nearer to earth is inflamed by lightning-bolts . . . the highest places have peace."[154] Moreover, since frequent lightning is hurled down upon the island of Lemnos, so Vulcan is said to have fallen onto this island.

5. There is a natural reason why Vulcan is thought to have his workshop between Aetna and Lipare. Clearly it is because of the fire and winds, which are suited to craftsmen. In fact, Aetna is a volcanic mountain, but Lipare is one of the islands that Aeolus rules. Vulcan's servants fashion thunderbolts; they are Brontes, Steropes, and Pyracmon. Brontes takes his name from "thunder," Steropes from "lightning," and Pyracmon from "glowing anvil," for *pyr* means "fire" and *acmon* means "anvil." For the origins of the prior names, inquire of the Greeks. Vergil says that those thunderbolts are sent forth from the whole sky, as Servius attests. The philosophers say that thunderbolts are hurled toward the earth from sixteen parts of the sky. What Vergil adds in the same place ("They had added three rays of crooked rain, three of watery cloud, three of red fire and of winged wind")[155] insinuates that thunderbolts fall to earth all year. Through these periphrases he shows the seasons of the whole year, which clearly are four, and they have three months each. By "three rays of crooked rain," that is, constricted and condensed into hail, Vergil designates winter, when we know that hail abounds. By "three of watery cloud" he designates spring, in which season there are excessive rains, as he himself says elsewhere: "And rainy spring rushes on."[156] By "three of red fire" he means summer. By "three of winged wind" he

means autumn, when there are frequent blasts of wind. In all of these he wisely expresses the nature of the thunderbolt, since only clouds and winds produce it. But what we have read, namely that the thunderbolt is three-forked or three-pointed, looks to another reason, for there is a kind of thunderbolt that blows and there is one that splits. Now there do not seem to be others besides the four kinds of thunderbolts that he talks about. There is a thunderbolt that frightens us, he says, as in: "You rule with everlasting authority and frighten us with your thunderbolt."[157] There is a kind that breathes, as in: "He blew with the winds of his thunderbolt."[158] There is a kind that punishes, as in: "Or the almighty father might drive me to the shadows with his thunderbolt."[159] And there is a kind that presages, as in: "I recall that the oaks struck from the sky foretold."[160] According to Servius, Vulcan is thought to be the husband of Venus because the service of Venus does not exist without heat. So Vergil wrote: "The older one is cool to Love."[161] He is called Mulciber because fire weakens and softens (demulcet) the hardness of iron.

6. Now let us return to Pallas. The story says that Minerva was angry at the Greeks because of Cassandra's defilement, or because the victors, in their pride, were unwilling to sacrifice to her. So as they were returning home, she harassed them with severe storms and scattered them over diverse seas. Thus Horace wrote: "when Pallas turned her wrath from burned Ilion."[162] But in truth, we know that the Greeks were afflicted by storms during the vernal equinox, when the sun is positioned in Aries and when Minerva's lightning, that is, the casting down of thunderbolts, stirs up the most severe storms. These deities that we do not observe among the constellations, although they do not have their own signs, are mingled together with others in their power, as Ophiuchus is Aesculapius, and also Gemini is said to be the sign of Apollo and Hercules. So also Aries is known to be the sign of Minerva. So Minerva is said to have punished the Greeks because they were in peril under that sign. In fact, we read in the books of the Etruscans that there are certain deities who are masters at hurling thunderbolts: Jove, Vulcan, and Minerva. Thus among poets we find everywhere the warning that they not presume to give their thunderbolts to others. The olive, a sign of peace, is rightly consecrated to Pallas, the goddess of wisdom, because it is in the nature of wise men both to love peace and to restore it as quickly as possible among those in conflict. Thus also the olive seems to have gotten its

name, for *eleos* in Greek means "mercy." It is partly consideration of the story, partly consideration of nature that causes the olive branch with fillets to be offered in petitioning for peace, for when Neptune and Minerva were contending over the name of Athens, as we described above, Minerva brought forth the olive and immediately won the contest. Thus when the olive branch is offered to someone it indicates that he is the better man. Thus also that proverb was spoken, "I give grass"; that is, "I concede the victory." Finally, as Varro says, in games someone used to give grass in the manner of a palm to him with whom he did not attempt to contend, and so he admitted that the recipient was the better man. The olive branch has fillets, that is, woolen ribbons, to show the inertia and weakness of the one offering it, for we know that sheep always need the help of another. In fact, *vittae*, "ribbons," are named after *vinciendo*, "binding."

7. Minerva is also said to have devised the pipes. When she made music with them at a banquet of the gods and all the gods laughed at her puffed up cheeks, she went to Lake Triton and, after she saw her distorted face in the water, she threw the pipes away. After Marsyas found them and played them, he challenged Apollo to a contest. They chose King Midas to be the judge. Because he judged unjustly, Apollo shamed him with the ears of an ass. Midas showed this mark of his offense only to his barber, and promised him a part of his kingdom to keep silent. The barber was unable to conceal it, nor did he dare to reveal it openly. He dug in the earth, told the story to the hole he had dug, and covered it over. In that very place a reed sprang forth from which a certain shepherd made a reed pipe for himself. When this was played, it said: "King Midas has the ears of an ass." So Orpheus writes in his *Theogony*. This was found by musicians to be a fable, for the musicians proposed two classes for their art, and then they added a third of lesser power: of singers, of cithara players, and of pipe players. So the first is the living voice, which very swiftly comes to their assistance in all the necessary circumstances of music. The second is the cithara, which, although it seems to equal the living voice in many ways, does not satisfy some needs that the living voice can. But, in fact, the pipe scarcely suffices to fulfill the least part of the art of music, for of the five harmonies that the living voice or the cithara render, the pipe scarcely achieves one and a half. Thus Minerva, that is, any wise person, not yet knowing the defect of pipes, indeed

devises them, yet everyone learned in music rejects them when they are known because of their paucity of sounds. Indeed, the gods are said to have laughed at her inflated cheeks because the pipe makes a windy sound in music, and since the peculiar quality of artistic flexibility of voices has been lost, the pipe whistles its song rather than modulating it musically. Thus everyone who is learned in the art of music rightly laughs at one who makes noise through it by too much blowing. So also Minerva, that is, wisdom, cast aside those accursed pipes that Marsyas picked up, for Marsyas means "fool." He alone in the art of music was willing to prefer the pipes to the cithara, and thus he is rightly depicted with a pig's tail.

8. Midas sat in judgment over the contestants as an ignorant judge, for his name means "knowing nothing." He is also said to have the ears of an ass because everyone who is devoid of discernment does not differ from an ass. For this reason also the servant is said to have disclosed the disgrace of his ears. As is read, we ought to keep our natural inclination in the position of a servant who submits to everything we want and who carefully conceals our secrets. The reed pipe through which that disgrace was made known signifies the windpipe in the throat through which one speaking shows his own ignorance. The shepherd who hears it stands for those people who nourish their spirits with doctrines; they first discovered ignorance. This same Midas, as Ovid reports, sought and obtained this favor from Bacchus: that whatever he touched might become gold. This gift was turned into revenge against him, for whatever he touched was turned into gold. Even his food and drink hardened into gold. And so again Midas begged that Bacchus might take away the evil thing he had desired, and he received the response that he should put his head in the River Pactolus. After this was done, Pactolus flowed with golden sands. They say that this story refers to men's insatiable cupidity. Indeed, those who serve avarice and always desire to increase their gold and to multiply it from any situation, die of hunger; for instance, although gold was freely at hand for him, yet Midas, who was devoted to avarice, could not enjoy his own goods. History records of him that, after the sum of his money had been gathered together, he diverted the River Pactolus through countless courses to irrigate his territory. It used to run through only a single channel to the sea. Thus when his own money was spent, he made the river fertile. Since Midas spent his wealth in this way, he is said to have put his head in the river. Also, the river is said to have flowed

with golden sand because it was made fruitful. Finally, as we said, he was called Midas, "knowing nothing," because an avaricious man is such a fool that he does not know how to benefit himself.

9. Prometheus used Minerva's help. They fashion the following story about him. Prometheus formed a man out of mud and made him inanimate and insensible. Minerva marveled at his work and promised him whatever he wanted from the gifts of heaven to aid his work. He said that he did not know what good things there were among the heavenly gifts, but he asked that, if it could happen, she might raise him up even to the gods above so that he might see and choose what would suit his work. And so Minerva placed him on her shield and carried him to heaven. When Prometheus saw heavenly bodies animated by flaming vapors living there, he secretly applied a fennel branch to Phoebus' chariot wheel and stole fire, which he applied to the man's breast and made his body animate. Then, they say, he was bound and forever offers his liver to a vulture. Nicagoras reports, and Petronius Arbiter testifies, that Prometheus had formed the first idol and offered his liver to a vulture because envious men bit him with the tooth of detraction. In fact, Fulgentius asserts that Prometheus means "the foresight of God," but Minerva is "heavenly wisdom," and the divine fire is understood to be wisdom or the soul. So when Pallas, who is the goddess of wisdom, that is, she makes a man wise, was observing divine providence, she saw that a soul is necessary for him to live. She divinely breathed this, which had been drawn from heaven, as it were, into him. Prometheus rightly kindled his torch from the sun because, according to the natural scientists, although we receive other things from other planets, we receive life from the sun. Indeed, Fulgentius wants the vulture gnawing at his liver to be accepted as a figure of the world because the world both turns with a certain swiftness of flight, and it feeds on the perpetuity of corpses of those being born and those perishing. And finally, after mankind was made, Minerva is said to have formed Pandora, for *pandora* in Greek means "gift of all," since life is the universal gift of all.

10. Servius hands down another tradition about Prometheus. He says that after he created mankind, Prometheus ascended to heaven with Minerva's help. When a torch was held to the chariot wheel of the Sun, he stole fire, which he made known to mankind. For this reason, Servius says, the angry gods sent two evils upon the earth, diseases and poverty,

just as Sappho and Hesiod recount. Also touching on this, Horace says: "After fire was brought down from its heavenly home, poverty and a new cohort of fevers came over the land."[163] Also, with the help of Mercury, the gods bound this same Prometheus to a rock on Mount Caucasus and an eagle was summoned to devour his heart. Servius says that all these things were devised with good reason, for Prometheus was a most intelligent man. Thus he was named after the Greek word *prometheia*, "foresight." He first taught the Assyrians astrology, which he studied with great care and solicitude while living on the heights of Caucasus. This mountain is located near the Assyrians, almost next to the constellations. So also he pointed out the greater stars and diligently noted their risings and settings. An eagle is said to devour his heart because solicitude, by which he understood all the eclipses and motions of the constellations, is unrelenting. And since he did this through prudence, with Mercury, who is the god of prudence and reason, as his guide, it is said he had been bound to a rock. Beyond this, he comprehended the nature of thunderbolts and taught it to mankind; thus he is said to have stolen fire from heaven. Also, through a certain art shown by him, the fire from above was called down. This benefited mortal men while they used it well. Later, through the wicked use of mankind, it was turned to their destruction, just as we read in Livy about Tullus Hostilius, who was consumed by this with all his possessions. In fact, Numa Pompilius used it with impunity only in the sacred rites of the gods. Thus it is that when fire was stolen, diseases are said to have been sent down upon mankind by the angry deities.

11. *Venus*

1. We said enough about the birth of Venus when we discussed Saturn earlier. The Epicureans, who strive after pleasure, call her a good thing, but the Stoics, who renounce pleasure, call her a vain thing. We read in Cicero that she was called Venus because she comes (veniat) to all things. She is depicted nude, either because the crime of lust is not concealed, or because it suits those who are nude, or because lust lays bare anyone's purpose and does not allow it to be concealed. Roses are assigned to her, for roses are red and they prick. Likewise, lust brings a red blush because of the reproach of shame, and it pricks because of the sting of sin. Indeed, just as a rose delights us but is taken away by the swift motion of time,

so also with lust. Doves are consecrated to Venus because those birds, as their frequent breeding indicates, are believed to be especially fervid in sexual union. Men depict her as swimming in the sea because there is no doubt that lust brings ruin [shipwreck] to things. Thus Porphyrio wrote in an epigram: "Naked, needy, shipwrecked on the sea of Venus." Venus is also depicted as carrying a sea conch because this animal is united in sexual intercourse with its whole body exposed at once. The myrtle is allotted to her, either because this tree delights in the seashore, and Venus is said to have been born of the sea, or because it is a neighbor to the salt sea, and sweat, which sexual intercourse always brings out, is salty, as we have said; or because, as the books of physicians say, this tree is suited to many necessities of women. Venus is appeased by sacred boughs of myrtle because this plant does not emit seed. So it was written: "the altar encircled with chaste boughs."[164] She is called Cypris, which means "mixture," from the island of Cyprus, which abounds in fragrances.

2. The three Graces, who are called Charites, are women of singular beauty; they are assigned to Venus as attendants, and are named Pasithea, Aglaia, and Euphrosyne. They are depicted nude, since grace ought to be without rouge, that is, not feigned and contrived, but pure and sincere. The Graces are joined together because it is fitting that friendships be indissoluble. Thus Horace wrote: "and the Graces, slow to loosen the knot."[165] Indeed, this is the reason that one is turned away, but two are depicted as looking back: because grace proceeds from us singly, but is wont to return double. They are called daughters of Venus and Liber because favors (gratiae) are very often gained through the gifts of these deities, namely, of Venus, who is pleasure, and Liber, who is wine. Also, as I seem to have heard, Pasithea means "attracting," Aglaia means "soothing," and Euphrosyne means "retaining," since in acquiring friendships the first thing is to attract the unknown persons, second is to soothe those attracted by flattery, and third is to retain by compliance those whom you have soothed. It is thought that Hymenaeus was born of Venus and Bacchus because, as Remigius says, lust is accustomed to be aroused through the wantonness of wine. Also, the membrane that belongs exclusively to the female sex, the one where childbirths are said to happen, is called *hymen* in Greek. Thus Hymenaeus is called the god of weddings.

3. Lactantius tells a story drawn from history, that Hymenaeus presides over weddings. Servius also attests to this, for he says that Hymenaeus was a young Athenian of such great beauty that he imitated being a woman. When one of his fellow citizens, a noble maiden, loved him, he despaired of marriage because he was born of common parents. But once, when Athenian maidens were celebrating sacred rites near the seashore, they were seized and carried off by pirates who arrived suddenly. Among them was also Hymenaeus, who had followed his beloved maiden in female garb; he was believed to be a girl. But after the pirates reached port in a faraway land, pursuers killed them. And so, with the maidens left behind, Hymenaeus returned to Athens; the citizens promised him marriage to his beloved if he should restore their daughters to them. When he restored them according to his promise, he married the wife he desired. Since a happy marriage fell to his lot, it happened that his name is invoked at weddings. Servius asserts that it is false that the young Hymenaeus, as some say, was overwhelmed by disaster on the day of his wedding, and so his name is invoked at weddings for the sake of expiation.

4. Vergil imagines that Jove met with Venus in the highest heaven when Aeneas was driven to Libya. He seems to fashion this metonymy according to astrology, for when the star of Jove is positioned in its own altitude with the star of Venus, it is said to signify that some happiness will come about through a woman. Thus, since Aeneas had to be granted access to part of his realm on the occasion of his marriage, so the poet put this first. Also, in the same place you will notice this: he very-expertly said that Venus was sadder than Jove at that time. By this he signifies the unhappy death of Aeneas' wife to come, for Dido finally kills herself. The fact that Vergil has Mercury glide down from Jove and descend toward the sunset, that is, to the lowest part of the earth, shows that indeed there will be friendships, but they will not endure for long. Also, the astronomers say that when Venus is positioned in Virgo, a merciful woman is born. Vergil imagines that Venus came to Aeneas in the attire of a virgin huntress. Thus, later, he both discovered a merciful queen and was joined with her in hunting. The fact that Vergil gives him Achates as a companion everywhere is thought to be for this reason: *achos* means "solicitude," which is always the companion of kings, or because he was amiable to all. In fact, about the agate (achates) Pliny

writes that if anyone has this stone in a ring, he is more pleasing. Or, as Fulgentius says, the agate is called "the custom of sadness," for human nature is joined to tribulations from infancy.

5. There is also a theological view, that those who are unacquainted with the practice of sex are said to see deities. Thus in his Second Book, when Venus envelops herself in the thick shadows of night, this same Vergil rightly recounts that Aeneas saw gods. Moreover, he says that after the departure of Venus, dreadful shapes and hostile deities appeared. This seems to have been devised according to astrology. Indeed, when the rays of Venus are present, they temper the anerotic planets opposing them, that is, the harmful planets: Mars and Saturn. If these drive away the origin of generation with their rays, they are thought to destroy the cause of life. Thus it was written: "Jove, your shining guardian, rescued you from wicked Saturn and slowed the wings of Fate."[166] And well did he slow them, since the inevitableness of fate is said to be able to be impeded, not entirely eluded. Thus it is written: "Nor did the fates forbid Priam to endure and to survive for another ten years." But what he added after a few verses, "and with the god leading the way," that is, Venus, was spoken in accord with those who affirm that deities have a share in each sex, as we said above. Thus Gallus wrote: "Venus, a potent god."[167] Also, Vergil said elsewhere: "The god did not assist the erring right hand" when it meant either Juno or Alecto. Also, on Cyprus there is a statue of a bearded maiden, that is, of Venus. It is no wonder, Servius affirms, that deities are thought to be of both sexes. In fact, they are incorporeal, and to be seen they take on the body that they want, for unless they put on bodies, they cannot appear to human sight. Indeed, according to the teaching of the poets, one should know that deities are unwilling to be seen unless it is out of extreme necessity. Thus about the appearance of Venus there, it was called a marvel: "my dear mother, making herself known as a goddess."[168] And because of this Vergil writes elsewhere: "Throw them over your head and do not look back."[169] Moreover, what Venus promised to Aeneas in that same place, that she would not fail to assist him, seems to come from the supposition that, as Varro teaches, from the time when Aeneas left Troy until he came to the Laurentian land, he always saw the star of Venus. So also Vergil wrote: "With his goddess mother showing the way."[170] And elsewhere: "And now the Morningstar was rising on the ridges of lofty Ida."[171] And when

she was going back from there, Venus did not appear to him right away. Thus Aeneas knew that he had come to the destined lands. But also, since he used her favorable constellation, just as everywhere he used his mother's help, we cannot think that he foolishly called it his mother.

6. When Glaucus scorned her sacred rites, an angry Venus is said to have sent a raging fury upon the mares that he used for his chariot; they tore him to pieces with their teeth. The story was fashioned this way because Glaucus was torn to pieces by mares that were wild from excessive desire, since he kept them from sexual intercourse so that they would be faster. Also, Mars is said to have had intercourse secretly with Venus. The Sun observed this and told Vulcan. He bound them together with chains of steel as they were having intercourse and exposed them shamefully lying together to all the gods. Grieving over this, Venus inflamed the five daughters of the Sun—Pasiphae, Medea, Phaedra, Circe, and Dirce—with abominable love. And so Mars was defiled by the embrace of Venus, that is, virtue was corrupted by the enticements of lust; with the sun as witness, he is shown in public, that is, virtue is at last perceived to be guilty through disclosure of the truth. This virtue, enticed by perverse habit, is shown to be fettered by very thick chains. Thus by this corruption Venus darkens the Sun's five daughters, that is, the five human senses dedicated to light and truth, and given, as if they were the Sun's offspring, for the varied perception of things, as the philosophers demonstrate. In fact, there is no sense that pleasure does not infect by its own enticements. You will read more suitably in Martianus about the corruptions with which pleasure vexes individuals. The names are fitting for the Sun's daughters, for the first is called Pasiphae, "appearing to all." She represents sight. Indeed, unless it is placed in our midst, a sight is not seen. Second is Medea, "no vision," designating hearing, for no sound is corporeal. Third is Circe, "judgment of hands," which is understood to be touch. Fourth is Phaedra, "bringing sweetness," which signifies what is smelled. Fifth is Dirce, which means "judging keenly," for taste is the judge of flavor.

7. Pasiphae is said to have loved a bull, and she gave birth to the Minotaur. Servius says that this story is taken from actual events, for he asserts that Taurus was the clerk of Minos. Pasiphae, the wife of Minos, loved him secretly, he says, and had intercourse with him in the house of Daedalus. Since she gave birth to twins, one by Minos and the other by

Taurus, she is said to have brought forth the Minotaur. Thus Vergil wrote: "Mixed race."[172] Since Daedalus gave his consent to this affair, the angry king thrust him into prison, but the queen bribed the guards and freed him. After his son was lost at sea, Daedalus came by ship to Cumae. Vergil also touches on this when he says "by the oarage of wings,"[173] for there are wings of birds and wings of ships. Thus the same writer says elsewhere: "We unfurl the wings of our sails."[174] Indeed, I think that the sons of the Athenians who were sent to the Minotaur to be devoured must be taken to be weights of gold and silver sent as tribute to Minos after Athens was conquered. Also, according to Servius, Circe is thought to be the daughter of the Sun for this reason only: she was a very illustrious harlot, and nothing is more illustrious than the sun. He says that by her lust and blandishments she led men from a human way of life to that of wild animals so that they might give their attention to lust and pleasures.

8. About the fact that Circe transformed Scylla the following fable was invented. Glaucus loved Scylla, a very beautiful maiden. According to most sources he was born in the city of Anthedon, but according to Fulgentius he was the son of Anthedon. Circe, the daughter of the Sun, loved him. In her envy of Scylla she infected the spring where Scylla used to bathe. When Scylla went down into it, wolves and dogs were grafted onto her lower body. But the truth is far otherwise. Anthedon means "seeing the opposite," Glaucus means "one-eyed," Scylla means "confusion." Since the outcome of sloth and carelessness is corruption of morals and utmost ruin, they seem to see the opposites of truth and salvation. Therefore because of sloth and carelessness the blurred vision of the mind loves Scylla, who was born of ignorance; that is, whoever has fallen into senselessness through vices of this kind indulges in lust, which makes men confused. Glaucus is rightly called one eyed, because one who devotes himself to lust is blind and foolish and rotten. Wolves and dogs were joined to Scylla's lower parts because women who serve men's lust cannot satisfy the meretricious desire for devouring them, nor can those given to pleasures themselves drag their own substance away from their corruptors. Thus Juvenal wrote: "A wasteful woman does not realize that her wealth is vanishing."[175] In fact, as Servius says, dogs and wolves are thought to have sprung forth from her for this reason: because those places [where Scylla is] are full of the greatest monsters, and the sound

of waves crashing upon the rocks sounds like barking. I think that Glaucus was transformed into a monster, as the story says, because the impatience of lust is the shame and ruin of the male sex no less than of the female. Circe is said to have hated Scylla and transformed her because Circe, as we said above, means "judgment of the hands" or "working of the hands." Also, a lustful woman scorns labor, namely, the judgment or working of the hands; one who at last renounces lust at some time transfers that lascivious leisure to the performing of works.

9. Ulysses passed by Scylla unharmed because lust does not fetter wise men. So he is said to have had a very chaste wife, Penelope, because every wise man strives to preserve modesty. We must expand on something else about him. Polyphemus was a very prudent man, as Servius recounts, and because of this he had a single eye in his forehead, that is, next to his brain, since his prudence saw more. Thus he seems to have been aptly called Polyphemus, "of much light." Even so, Ulysses overcame him and so is thought to have blinded him. This same Ulysses deserved to be called *olon xenos*, as if to say "stranger to all things," because wisdom makes men strangers to all worldly things. Thus he killed the Sirens by scorning them. According to the story, there were three Sirens, part maidens, part birds, daughters of the River Achelous and Calliope the Muse. One of them used to make music with her voice, another with pipes, the third with a lyre. They lived first near Pelorus, later on Capreae; they led those enticed by their singing to shipwreck. As he was about to sail past them, Ulysses blocked the ears of his comrades with wax. Then he tied himself to the mast and passed by them unharmed. The Sirens bore this with sorrow and died because they could not endure their grief. Therefore the Sirens clearly signify bodily enticements. Thus they also deserved a suitable name, because bodily pleasures draw the minds of men to themselves. Indeed, *siro*, as we have said, means "I draw." So also tracts of sand are called *syrtes*. Furthermore, a wise man blocks the ears of his men so that they do not hear their melodies; that is, he instructs them with salutary precepts, lest they be entangled in secular delights. But he himself passes by tied to the mast, that is, relying on virtue. Although he knows the enticements of worldly vicissitudes, in scorning them he directs his course toward his homeland of everlasting happiness. Also, because of this bypassing, the Sirens perished in sorrow because in the heart of a wise man carnal desire dies

when it is scorned. But some contend that these three sisters were very beautiful harlots. Since they led those approaching them into poverty, they were said to bring shipwreck upon them. They deserved to be depicted with wings, either because lovers' discernment quickly perishes, or because the love of harlots passes away swiftly. They have feet of fowls because the passion of lust uselessly scatters all possessions. Plato said that the individual Sirens occupied individual orbits. This signified that a most-pleasing harmony was presented to the deities by the motion of the spheres. He said this when he was discussing the volubility of the celestial spheres in his Republic. In another sense, the word Siren, Macrobius said, has the force of "singing to god," according to the Greek meaning. In fact, Sallust says that to those seeing it from afar, Scylla is a rock similar to a renowned shape. As Servius says, hounds and wolves are thought to be born of her for this reason: these places are full of huge monstrosities, and the sound of the waves crashing upon the rocks resembles barking.

10. But since we made mention of Mars earlier, this same Mars is called Gradivus according to Remigius, either because he proceeds into battle step by step (gradatim), or from *apo tou gradein*, "brandishing of a spear," or, according to the same author, as if to say *gratus divus*, "pleasing god." This means, he says, "he is a powerful god." Mars was very often called Gradivus when he was raging, and Quirinus when he was calm. Finally, Mars merited two temples from the Romans, one within the city, as if he were a guardian and calm, the other outside the city, as if he were the warrior Gradivus. He seems to be called the deity of those who wage war because the star assigned to him is very hot, as it is located in the next place above the sun. Established in its own planetary domicile, this star is thought to presage war. Thus Vergil also calls Scorpio "burning," clearly because it is the planetary domicile of Mars, for certainly that season is cold; in fact, November is the month of this sign. Grass is dedicated to Mars because, according to Pliny in his *Natural History*, it is produced from human blood. Also, grass is a species of herb, although generally every herb is called grass, just as all wood is called oak, although it is also a species of wood. Thus also it was a Roman custom to set up altars of grass when there was talk of war and sacrifice was offered to Mars. I suspect that he is said to have been born of Juno without the union of a father because if his star appears alone in the air, that is, Juno, in any of the planetary domiciles at all, it is thought to

signify that the ardent desire for war will grow. But if Jupiter or Venus arises, it is believed to mitigate the violence of Mars and to nullify his effect.

11. It is well known that Romulus and Remus were thought to be sons of Mars because they were warlike men. That they are said to have been nourished by a she-wolf is a fabulous invention to conceal the baseness of the ancestors of the Roman race, and it was not invented unsuitably, for we also call harlots "she-wolves" (lupae) from the similitude of their obscenity and stench and rapacity. So also we speak of *lupanaria*, "brothels." It is also well known that this animal is under the protection of Mars. The woodpecker (picus), which is said to have brought food to those exposed twins, is consecrated to Mars because this bird pierces the hardest wood with the sharpness of its beak just as with the point of a spear. That fable about Picus the king has nothing to do with this matter, for Pomona, the goddess of fruits (pomorum), loved that Picus and married him, as Servius says. Ovid tells this story about a nymph named Canens in the Fourteenth Book of *Metamorphoses*. He reports that there was another Pomona and that she married Vertumnus. Later, when Circe loved this same Picus and was spurned, in her anger she turned him into the bird sacred to Mars, for the magpie (pica) is another bird. This story was fashioned this way because Picus was a soothsayer who had a woodpecker that taught him the future, just as the pontifical books indicate. Thus also Vergil gives an augur's wand to his statue. The augurs' staff is a crooked wand that they used for designating spaces in the sky, since to do so with the hand was not allowed. In fact, they marked out certain limits in the sky within which they contemplated the omens of flying birds. I think that Circe, whom they say was a sorceress, was scorned by Picus because he renounced sorceresses.

12. Since this opportunity reminded us about soothsayers, the subject now seems to demand that we touch on the superstitious absurdities of soothsayers here, not elsewhere, since poets are sometimes concerned with these. Since all men do not know all things, we also wanted to begin this little work above for the ignorant, that is, for those like us. And so, as they say, the generally accepted magic comprises five kinds: deceptions (praestigia), fortunetelling (sortilegia), sorcery (maleficia), divination (manticen), and delusive astrology (matematica). Deceptions occur when

human senses have been tricked by an imaginary illusion and unbelievable mutations of things seem to be seen through demonic art. Thus, since these magicians change things fantastically in such a way, they are called tricksters. Sorcerers practice sorcery; through demonic incantations or bindings or other kinds of sacrilege of this type, they commit impious acts with the cooperation and inspiration of demons. Fortunetellers are intent upon fortunetelling; through lots they are able to foresee the future, or they strive to. Divination is divided into five parts. First is necromancy, which, as we have read, means "divination among the dead," for *nekros* in Greek means "dead" and *mantike* means "divination." Indeed, this kind of divination used to happen through the sacrifice of human blood, for which demons are said to thirst. Second is geomancy, that is "divination in earth," for *ge* means "earth." From this word the Georgicon is named, a book about cultivation of the earth, for *ergon* in Greek means "cultivation." So also, all sacred rites among the Greeks were called *orgia*. The Romans call them *caerimoniae*, "ceremonies." Although public practice preserved orgies, such as those of Bacchus, as we said above, the rest were called "ceremonies." Third is hydromancy, "divination in water," for *hydor* in Greek means "water." From this word comes also hydropicus, one who perishes from an excessive appetite for water. We know that water organs are called *hydraulia* or *hydraula*, and *aulai* are "organ pipes." Fourth is aeromancy, "divination in air." Fifth is pyromancy, "divination in fire," for fire is called *pyr* in Greek. Thus they said *pyre* and Pyriphlegethon, "fiery." Statius in the Tenth Book of his *Thebaid* seems to introduce Tiresias as employing this kind of divination.

13. Therefore, the first kind of magic, necromancy, is seen to pertain to the dead, the second to earth, the third to water, the fourth to air, the fifth to fire. Mathematica means "theoretical" when the second syllable is short and aspirated. Also, as it is believed to be finally understood, this is the first part of speculation, containing in itself the quadrivium: arithmetic, music, geometry and astronomy. But when the second syllable is lengthened and without an "h," matematica means "falsehood." Haruspicina, horoscopica, and the science of divination through birds, that is, augury, are species assigned to this matematica. Also, haruspicina is so-called as if to say *ararum inspectio*, "inspection of altars," because

soothsayers (haruspices) inspect altars and contemplate the future in organs and entrails of sacrificial victims. These same ones sometimes deserved to be called *harioli*, that is, those who pray around altars or those who divine the future on altars, or *salisatores*, "palpitators," because they divined the future from palpitating limbs or from the pulse. So it was written: "Or the deity that leaps in slaughtered entrails."[176] Horoscopica, which we have read is also called "constellation," is that by which the fates of men are sought in the stars. Calculators of nativities (genethliaci), who study men's births, employ this. They are commonly called astrologers (mathematici), although we read that formerly they were specifically called *magi*, "magicians." Those who cast horoscopes are named after horoscopica, that is, inspecting the fates of the hours. Concerning divination of this kind, Juvenal wrote: "No uncondemned astrologer will have his genius."[177] According to the teachings of this art, birds are either "singing birds," that is, those that sing about the future, or "flying birds," those that show the future by their flight. Therefore knowledge of divination through birds is sometimes exercised by the eye and properly called auspices, as if to say *avispicium*, "looking at birds," because the flight and motion of birds are observed. Sometimes divination through birds is exercised by the ears and properly called augury, as if to say *garritus avium*, "chattering of birds." Common usage calls both augury indiscriminately, with the origin of the names disregarded.

14. Some auguries are freely given (oblativa), that is, which are not asked for; others are obtained by entreaty (impetrativa), that is, which occur after they have been wished for. With respect to the one obtained by entreaty, Statius wrote: "almighty Jupiter, for you on swift wings,"[178] etc. With respect to the one freely given, Vergil wrote: "when by chance twin doves,"[179] etc., for unless it were freely given, he would not have added "by chance." Sometimes, however, by their magic spells augurs have caused those to be obtained by entreaty that had come about freely of themselves. Thus in the same place was added: "Oh, be my guides, if there is any way."[180] We read that it was a characteristic of augural observation that those taking the auguries designated certain spaces in which they wanted things seen to pertain to themselves, as we have said. Thus it was very skillfully interjected, "flying from the sky, they came past the man's face and settled upon the green sward,"[181] clearly because, if they flew farther off, they would not seem to pertain to him. Thus, about

the appearance of an eagle in Book Twelve, it was written: "And by this portent he deceived," for Vergil indicates that that augury lacked trust, with its place denied. Indeed, wherever Maro introduces a firm augury, he gives it a very firm place. Thus in the *Bucolics* he wrote: "Often from a hollow oak on the left, a crow warned me."[182] Also in this augury he says that a released swan had fallen into the water, since it is clear that it was an unreliable augury. No wonder, since in fact it was not freely given nor obtained by entreaty, but sent because of the actions of Juturna. At any rate, we know that Vergil preserved this method everywhere, so that in situations for which a way out was denied, he also supplied weak beginnings. Thus he says that when Aeneas was settled in Thrace, which he was soon to leave, he made sacrifice of a bull to Jove, contrary to custom. So also in the Third Book after the appearance of the deities, which seemed to announce good fortune, it was written: "I rose up from my couch,"[183] for right away a storm followed. Likewise in the Second Book it was written: "I am roused from sleep,"[184] and soon destruction was brought upon the city. In fact, as often as sleep abruptly flees, as Servius says, it signifies an unfortunate omen. And not undeservedly, for, he says, if sleep is a gift of the gods, as in "and by the gift of the gods, most pleasing rest overspreads them,"[185] then not without misfortune does the gift of the gods abruptly depart.

15. Also, in auguries freely given, the one seeing them was the judge of whether he wanted what was seen to pertain to himself, or whether he would refute it and seek to avert it. Thus also in the same augury, the augur added: "I accept and acknowledge the gods";[186] that is, "I willingly embrace this augury, and I acknowledge the favor of the gods toward us." And then, deceived, he acted as if the augury were freely given. Likewise, in Book Five we read: "Neither did mighty Aeneas deny the omen."[187] Also, it was a Roman custom that if they were not content with a single augury, they would not begin something unless the first one was confirmed by a similar one. Thus was written: "And these firm omens," for if the later auguries seemed dissimilar, the earlier ones were dismissed. Thus it was written: "just as Chaonian doves when an eagle comes,"[188] for without doubt an eagle is more powerful than doves. Also in Vergil, an augury is rightly given to Aeneas in the Sixth Book, inasmuch as he is the son of Venus and a king, for doves were consecrated to Venus because of their frequent copulation and their fertility, as we have said.

Their augury pertains to kings because doves are never alone, just as kings are not unattended. And it is not without purpose that in the same place there is added after the speech of Aeneas: "Having spoken thus, he checked his steps,"[189] for the utterances of augurs are, strictly speaking, prayers. So also, the mounds of earth behind open boundaries, where they used to take auguries, were called "utterances," and after prayers they were accustomed either to sit or stand without moving to take the auguries. Moreover, some of the prophetic birds hold to the upper air, as Servius says, and they are properly called swift of flight (praepetes); others keep to the lower air and are called inferior (inferae). But both these and those are called by the common word *praepetes*, because all flying birds seek the first places (priora petunt).

16. Men rightly subject haruspicina, horoscopica, and augury to matematica, that is, to falsehood, because in these they determine the fates of men and examine them; according to true theologians, this is an abominable superstition and a fruitless labor, although we do not hesitate to say the same of other kinds of divination. In fact, what happens by nature to a genus often assumes the use of a species. Certainly, all practical knowledge of divination is divided into two parts, as Cicero says: either it is inspired frenzy, as in prophesying, or an art, as among soothsayers, augurs, calculators of nativities and the like. These all depend on themselves, although they are held in check by their own limits. Vergil gives all of these to the one whom he wants to be perceived as perfect, as in: "You who know about tripods and the laurel of Apollo (Clarius), the stars and tongues of birds and omens of swift-winged birds."[190] And elsewhere he writes: "to whom lie open the entrails of cattle, stars in the sky, tongues of birds and fires of the prophetic thunderbolt."[191] These were interpretations of lightning strikes; that is, there were lightning interpreters who either produced the lightning through incantations or who foretold it.

17. But lest we be accused of wandering too much, let us turn back from this subject to Venus. In the winter season, the beauty of all things perishes through a certain passing away. From this fact was invented that fable about Adonis and Venus, and it was elucidated by Remigius as follows. Venus, he says, bewailed Adonis with copious tears when he was killed by a boar because the beauty of earth, which is signified by Venus, bewails the sun, which is represented by Adonis, as it descends toward

its southern orbits, killed by filth and winter's stiffness as if by the tusks of a boar. Then the earth brings forth the tears of rain and streams. Fulgentius has a different understanding of the beloved Adonis. So this might be made clearer, let us begin with another story. Myrrha is said to have loved her father and to have had intercourse with him when he was drunk. When he learned the truth, he pursued her with his sword drawn. She was turned into a myrrh tree. When her father struck this tree with his sword, Adonis was born from it. Thus the myrrh is a kind of tree in India that is scorched by the heat of the Sun, whom, as we said above, men call the father of all things because with his help every variety of sprout grows. Thus she is said to have loved her father. When Myrrha became a larger tree she split open because of the heat of the sun, and through this crack she exuded a sap that is likewise called myrrh. For this reason she is said to have given birth to Adonis, which means "sweetness," for this kind of sap is sweet in its scent. Furthermore, Venus is said to have loved him because this kind of juice is very hot. Thus also Petronius Arbiter reports that he drank a draught of myrrh as an incentive to lust.

18. Everyone knows why Love (Amor) is called the son of Venus: because it is certain that love is born of the desire for pleasure. Love is depicted as a boy because shameful passion is foolish and because speech among lovers is imperfect, just as among children. Thus Vergil says of Dido in love: "She begins to speak and halts in mid word."[192] Love is depicted as winged because nothing is more fickle or changeable than lovers. He carries arrows, which are both unsure and swift, or, as Remigius says, since knowledge of a crime perpetrated vexes the mind. A golden arrow brings love, a leaden one takes it away, since love seems beautiful to a lover, like gold, but it is a heavy burden to one not in love, like lead. So also Love is naked, since this shamefulness is carried out by naked people, or since in this shamefulness nothing is concealed. According to this same Remigius, there are two Venuses. One is chaste and modest; she presides over virtuous love, and he says that she is Vulcan's wife. The other is said to be devoted to pleasure, the goddess of passions; her son, he says, was Hermaphroditus. Likewise, there are two Loves. One is good and modest; because of this one, wisdom and virtues are loved. The other love is immodest and evil; because of this one, we are inclined to vices.

Thus, also, with regard to the distinction of good love, we generally call both "Love."

19. The fable invented about Hero and Leander relates to the reality of this love, for Hero means "love" [Eros] and Leander means "dissolution of men." Thus, a youth, Leander, loved Hero, a girl from beyond the sea. When he would swim to her at night, she stood on the land opposite and lighted a torch for him so that he would not stray far from her shore. On a certain night when a storm had arisen and the torch was extinguished, the young man was drowned. When the maiden saw his body cast ashore, she hurled herself headlong into the sea. Therefore Leander, that is, "the dissolution of men," loves Hero because of the abandonment of virtue and the indulgence of idleness; that is, he rushed into love and lust. But anyone who is inflamed by lust, while he proceeds toward that which he ardently loves, never really sees what is expedient, for he also swims at night; that is, he essays dangers in the dark. Hero lights a torch for him so that he might not go astray. And what else does love bring on other than a burning flame? Also, she shows a perilous way to the one who desires her. Moreover, her torch is immediately extinguished because the flame of young love does not last long. And finally, he swims naked, for this reason, of course, that the allure of love is accustomed to strip those who strive after it of property and purpose, and to throw them into peril, just as into the sea. Also, the fact that the extinguished torch is the cause of death for each of them clearly signifies, according to Fulgentius, that lust abides in each sex. Finally, both perish in the sea, that is, in old age they forget the agitations of lust, for since old age is cold and wet, it seems comparable to the sea. The storm in which Leander perished signifies the disposal of property. Consideration of this very often kills the fire of lust.

20. Finally, the philosophers have represented Venus as an example of a life of ease, and they have correctly judged her contest with Pallas and Juno. To explain this fiction, let us proceed a little more deeply. Although Jupiter loved Thetis, he was prevented by Proteus from lying with her so that he would not sire the one who would expel him from his realm. He was persuaded and gave her to Peleus as his wife. Jupiter was present at their wedding, with all the gods and goddesses except Discord. That angry goddess cast a golden apple in the midst of three goddesses: Juno, Pallas,

and Venus; it was inscribed "a gift for the most beautiful." And so, contending over the excellence of their beauty, they chose Jove as their judge. Unwilling to offend two of them if he preferred the third, Jove sent them to Paris to be judged. Although Juno promised him a kingdom and Pallas promised virtue, Paris judged Venus most beautiful because of her promise of Helen.

21. Then Achilles was born of Peleus and Thetis; his life is known to all. And so, men said that water is called Thetis; thus they also called her a nymph. Jupiter, as a god, joined her to Peleus, for *pelos* means "mud" in Greek. Therefore they say that earth mixed with water produced a man. They say that Jove himself wished for intercourse with Thetis, but it was forbidden lest he might sire one greater than himself, since fire, that is, Jupiter, if it mixes with water, is extinguished by the water's power. At the joining of water and earth, that is, of Thetis and Peleus, discord alone was not invited because it is rather the concord of both elements that is necessary for a man to be born. Thus, in the generation of a man, Peleus is present as earth, that is, flesh; Thetis is present as water, that is, moisture; and Jupiter, who joined both elements together, is there as fire, that is, soul. Furthermore, in the same place the three goddesses contend with one another, for the man who is born still does not know what way of life he might choose.

22. The philosophers say that mankind's way of life is tripartite. They name the first speculative (theoretica), the second practical (practica), the third fond of ease (philargica). In Latin we call these contemplative, active, and pleasure-loving. Thus that is speculative or contemplative which they lead who are open to contemplation alone, raising the mind up from all earthly things and continually searching out wisdom's secrets. Among us, monks practice this way of life, and among the ancients, philosophers practiced it. No desire for worldly goods affects followers of this way of life, no frenzy of anger, no poison of envy, no ardor of lust. Their only concern is to track truth and contemplate justice; fame distinguishes them and hope nourishes them. The practical or active life is that which consists of actions and affairs, that which is anxious only about the goods of life; it is greedy for adornments, insatiable in possessing, desirous of plundering and anxious in preserving. This way of life does not consider what is expedient, where it is going, what it might seize. Among the ancients, some tyrants exhibited this way of life; among us, the whole world does.

The life fond of ease, or pleasure-loving, is that which is addicted to pleasure only; striving after the corruption of life alone, it thinks that no
honest thing is good. Among the ancients, only the Epicureans exhibited
this way of life. Among us, a life of this sort is in the nature of things; it
is no crime.

23. And so, considering this, the poets described the contest of the
three goddesses, Minerva, Juno, and Venus, who were contending over
their beauty. They represented the speculative life through Minerva,
goddess of wisdom; the practical life through Juno, the goddess of kingdoms and riches; and the life fond of ease through Venus, who presides
over pleasures. Jupiter is imagined as unwilling to judge them, lest by
preferring one, he might seem to disapprove of two. Indeed, the freedom
of our will would seem to be destroyed if the god should put forth one of
these three ways of life for us to lead, with the other two condemned.
Thus he transferred the judgment to a man, to whom the free will of
choosing is both owed and given. That man did something stupid, as is
the habit of wild beasts and herds. He had no regard for the virtue of
Minerva or the riches of Juno, but he turned his gaze toward lust and
chose the life fond of ease, just as the outcome of the story later indicated.
But the fact that all the gods are said to have been called to the marriage
signifies that mankind is created through the cooperation of all the elements and the consent of the stars; or because the pagans used to think
that individual gods governed individual parts of the human body: Juno
the arms, Neptune the breast, Mars the middle, Venus the kidneys and
groin, Mercury the feet, and Minerva the fingers. They consecrated the
ears to Memory and thus was written, "Cynthius [Apollo] plucked my
ear";[193] the forehead to Genius, so while venerating that god, they used
to touch the forehead; the right hand to Faith; the knees to Mercy, so
those who beg for mercy touch them.

24. Finally, Achilles was born a perfect human being, as it were. His
mother dipped him in the waters of the Styx, that is, she fortified him
against all hardships. His heel alone she did not dip. The meaning of the
story is as follows. Veins in the heel pertain to the function of the kidneys
and thighs and manly parts. From here other veins also extend as far as
the big toe, and Orpheus indicates that the principal place of lust is in the
heel. Therefore it is clearly shown that human virtue, though fortified
against all eventualities, lies open to attacks of lust. Thus also, Achilles is

brought to the palace of Lycomedes, that is, to the kingdom of lust. Lycomedes means "sweet nothing," for indeed all lust is sweet and it is nothing. Finally, Achilles perished at Troy for love of Polyxena, and he was struck in the heel because of his lust. Polyxena in Greek means "stranger to many men," either because love makes our minds wander away from their diligence as strangers, or, as Fulgentius says, because lust roams among many men as it travels about. On the death of Achilles, Servius writes as follows. Achilles, he says, was submerged in the Stygian swamp. He was invulnerable in his entire body, except the part by which he was held. When he had decided to take his beloved Polyxena in a temple, he was killed, ambushed by Paris hiding behind the statue of Apollo. Thus in Vergil it is rightly said to Apollo: "you who directed the Dardanian arrows of Paris,"[194] and so on; "you directed," to the vulnerable spot, of course, but "Dardanian" so that the god might seem to have done that not for the adulterer, but for his people, for it is thought that Paris directed the arrows against Achilles, while Apollo held them. In fact, here we might seem to stray a little. The same Paris was a very brave man, according to the *Troica* of Nero, so that in the games of the Agonalia at Troy he surpassed even Hector himself, along with all the others. When the angry Hector drew his sword against him, Paris said that he was his brother, which he proved when his childhood rattles were brought forth.

25. But since we made mention of Proteus above, let us say something about him. It is said that he did not give oracular responses unless he was bound. They say that this fiction has a natural explanation, as Servius declares, for a man has in himself, he asserts, lust, foolishness, ferocity, and guile. While these thrive in him, that part through which he is close to divinity, that is, prudence, is not apparent; when those are bound, that is, when anyone lacks all vices, then prudence can keep its strength. Thus we read that Proteus then could prophecy and receive the power of divining, when in him were bound his cupidity, wild fierceness, and lapse of mind, which is similar to the changeableness of water. According to the story about him, we read this in the Fourth Book of the *Georgics*: "The seer knows all things, those which are, which were, which soon will be done."[195] In fact, only so much was understood, for he is said to have received a temporary power of divining. Otherwise, he could have learned that they were going to put chains on him. Also, in the same place was

added, not inappropriately: "Indeed, so it seemed good to Neptune." For as often as a reason is not apparent, "so it seemed good" is interposed. Thus when Horace showed that love does not belong to beauty, he said: "So it seemed good to Venus." And rightly does the accusation against the gods maintain a certain respect; otherwise, it is a sacrilege. Thus at the beginning of the Third Book of the *Aeneid* we read: "After it seemed good to the gods above to overthrow the might of Asia and the guiltless race of Priam."[196] But some also say that this is praise for Troy, which none but the gods could have overthrown. They imagine Proteus to be an old man, just as almost all the sea gods were, because their heads are said to be white from the foam of the waves.

12. Bacchus

1. Bacchus, the deity that presides over vines, is also said to be the son of Jove. To him, just as to others, men assign different names. He is called Liber, since even drunken slaves seem free (liberi) to themselves. Thus also we read: "Then the poor man assumes horns,"[197] that is, elation and confidence; or, as they say, because this god frees males when their seeds are sown, for females are said to be freed and cleansed through Juno and males through Liber. He also deserves to be called Liber because he frees men from cares; or Liber, since his sacred rites pertain to cleansing of the soul. Thus according to wiser men, as we remarked above, it was said: "And for You they hang gentle little masks from the lofty pine."[198] So too the winnowing fan, that is, a sieve for wheat, is dedicated to him, because just as grains are cleansed by winnowing fans, so men are cleansed by his sacred mysteries. For this reason Vergil also calls the winnowing fan "mystical." Very many writers also confirm that he is the god of liberty. Therefore, among the sacred rites of cities being founded, sacrifice was made to him also, along with other protector deities, so that he might preserve liberty for the citizens, for cities were either tributary or confederate or free. In free cities there was a statue of Marsyas as a sign of liberty, for he was under the protection of Father Liber. Also, it was a Roman custom, as Ovid reminds us in his book of *Fasti*, that the toga of liberty was given to youths during the festival of Liber as a sign of the freer way of life to come that had been granted to them. Thus he was named Liber from the fact that he liberates.

2. Also, he is called Lenaeus, either from the Greek word *lenos*, "lake," or, according to Donatus, from the fact that he soothes (deleniat) the mind. Servius declares that he did not promote the first view, since, clearly, the Greek name would not admit a Latin etymology. On this point Cicero, as we indicated above, and many others, seem to disagree. Finally, Varro says:

> Etymology does not have a certain right of possession, but it comes about according to the capacity of the intellect. Indeed, "vestibule" is so called, according to some, because it surrounds (vestiat) the door; according to others, it comes from Vesta, for a doorway is consecrated to Vesta. But, as others say, it is because no one stands (stet) there, for even as people say *vesanus*, "insane," instead of *non sanus*, so we use "vestibule" as if to say *non stabulum*, "not a standing-place," for in a doorway there is only a passage. [De Lingua Latina]

But we must be well disposed to each side; as far as this dispute about opposing rules goes, I leave it to be sifted. Also, although "Father" is a general name for all gods, it is always properly attached to "Liber," for he is called Father Liber. Yet it should be known that, according to the nature of things or persons, the highest god is assuredly called "Father," for anyone calls the god whom he especially venerates "highest." Thus we read: "Apollo, highest of gods, guardian of sacred Sorace.'"[199] Yet this epithet was given particularly to Jove, as in: "Son, you who scorn the Typhoean darts of the highest father."[200] There are other names of this god and other gods about whom we have spoken and about whom I have not read authentic writings. In fact, the name Iacchus is applied to Liber, or he is named Evius, which they say means "good boy." Likewise he is also called Briseus, "pressing out," since Liber first pressed out wine from grapes, milk from the breast, honey from the honeycomb; or Briseus means "hairy," for he is said to have had two statues in Greece, one hairy, called Briseus, and the other smooth, called Lenaeus. He is also called Bassareus from his garment that hung down as far as his feet. This word was taken from the place in Lydia where he was, as Horace writes: "shining Bassareus."[201] His attendants were called Bassarides after this place. Nero wrote: "a Bacchante [Bassaris] and a Maenad about to guide a lynx with an ivy-cluster."[202] Since I have not found these names in any authentic accounts, I consider them commonplaces or hastily invented or false or apocryphal.

3. According to Fulgentius, Bacchus is said to have conquered the Indians for this reason: because the sun makes them drinkers, or because the Falernian or Mareotic wine was here. The potency of this wine is so great, he says, that scarcely any wine lover drinks a whole sextarius[203] in a month. Thus Lucan wrote: "Meroe forcing the untamed Falernian to foam."[204] It is said that this wine cannot be made milder by adding water. We also read in history that Liber discovered the use of wine among the Indians when he had triumphed over them, just as Osiris, the husband of Isis, did among the Egyptians. Liber is said to have been nourished by Maro, as if to say Mero, for Mero means "nourisher of wine drinking." He sits upon tigers, either because wine drinking begets fierceness or because savage minds are soothed by wine. So also, according to Fulgentius, he is called Lenaeus, as if to say *lenitatem praestans*, "offering gentleness." For these same reasons also we consecrate to him the Bacchae, named from *bacchando*, "raving in honor of Bacchus," or after Bacchus himself. Sometimes we call these Mimallones, either from the language of the Macedonians, as Lactantius says, or, as we read elsewhere, from Greek, because this term means "madness." We say that Maenads are given to him as attendants. They are named from the Greek word *maenein*, which likewise means "to be mad," as we have read. In fact, it seems more contrived than true that they were named Maenads from *mene*, "moon," [luna in Latin] "lunatics," as it were, that is, raving in the manner of lunatics. I think that lynxes were assigned to him because of the very keen sharp-sightedness for which we hear that they are noted, for as the natural scientists say, wine taken in moderation sharpens the intellect.

4. Bacchus is depicted as a young man because drunkenness is never mature. Also, he is naked, either because drunken men generally become naked by whirling themselves about through the night, according to Fulgentius; or because men drunk on wine denude themselves of their property while they indulge in their cups; or because a drunken man cannot keep secrets, nor does he know how. Bacchus is thought to have been sewn into the thigh of Jove and been born from there since, as Martianus says in his *Cosmographia*, in a certain region there is the city of Nysa,

sacred to Father Liber, and Mount Merus, sacred to Jove. Thus, he says, the story is that he was born from Jove's thigh (merou). But in Remigius we read that Nysa is a mountain in India where even today the childhood rattles of Liber are said to be. In fact, we find that he is called Nysaeus, from Nysa, or Dionysus, "god of Nysa" (deus Nysae). Garlands of ivy deserved to be part of his sacred rites either because of their similarity to bunches of grapes and clusters of fruit, or because evergreen plants are suited to an ever-young god. Thus poets are crowned with ivy, either because they are consecrated to Liber or because ivy is always thriving, just as poems merit eternity. Like the Bacchae, poets are insane, and thus Horace wrote: "Liber included insane poets among the Satyrs and Fauns."[205] A story says that King Lycurgus of Thrace cut off his own legs while cutting down vines in his scorn for Bacchus. In truth, however, he was a man who refrained from wine, as Servius says. It is well known that such men are of a more-zealous nature, which also was said about Demosthenes.

5. I recall reading nothing that I have judged worthy to be handed on as to why it is said Bacchus was born of Semele, one of the daughters of Cadmus, when Jove's lightning shone before her. But I have decided not to pass over the fact that there were four sisters: Ino, Autonoe, Semele, and Agave. And, as Fulgentius says, there are four kinds of drunkenness: from wine, forgetfulness of things, lust, and insanity. The first is Ino, which means "wine"; second is Autonoe, "not knowing herself"; third is Semele, which means "unfettered body"; fourth is Agave, whom I pass over, because the meaning of this name happens to seem unsuitable, or it was unknown to the Romans. But we shall compare her to insanity because, as we read in the story, the drunken* Agave cut off the head of her own son, Pentheus. Furthermore, so that we might seem to go more deeply, the story says that the Giants found Bacchus inebriated. After they tore him to pieces limb by limb, they buried the bits, and a little while later he arose alive and whole. We read that the disciples of Orpheus interpreted this fiction. They asserted that Bacchus should be understood as nothing other than the world-soul. The philosophers say that although this soul might be divided among the bodies of the world limb by limb, as it were, it always seems to make itself whole again, emerging

*Accepting *vinolenta* for *violenter*.

from the bodies and forming itself. Always continuing one and the same, it allows no division of its singleness. Also, we read that they represent this story in his sacred rites.

13. Hercules

1. They say that Hercules was also the son of Jove. He was unconquered by others, but for love he subjected himself to Omphale, who forced him to weave and to perform women's duties. Therefore "Hercules" is as if to say *heron cleos,* which means "the glory of strong men." He is said to be the grandson of Alcaeus, and thus he is also named Alcides, for *alce* in Greek means "boldness." He also has Alcmena for his mother; her name means "salted." No wonder, for the glory of strong men is born from the fire of intellect, as from Jove; from boldness, that is, courage, as from his grandfather Alcaeus; from the salt of wisdom, as from his mother Alcmena. Yet this glory is overcome by lust, for the navel is called *omphale* in Greek. Moreover, lust in their navel rules women. Thus it is shown that lust even overcomes unconquered strength. Cacus is said to have stolen oxen from this same Hercules and to have hidden them in a cave after they were dragged there by their tails. While Cacus belched forth smoke and vapor, Hercules strangled him. *Cacos* means "bad." He coveted the goods of Hercules because all malice is contrary to virtue. He was hidden in a cave because malice is never free of earthly things. But Hercules, that is, virtue, kills bad men and claims its own goods. Cacus emits smoke and vapor, which harm the sight, because malice always undertakes hidden deceptions. So also malice is said to be double, since it is multiformed, not simple. Malice harms in a triple way: either openly, as more powerful; or more subtly, as a false friend; or secretly, as a thief. So also he dragged the oxen with their tracks reversed because thefts are carried off through trackless ways. But Servius feels otherwise about Cacus. He says that Cacus was Vulcan's son, according to the story. Spewing fire and smoke, he devastated everything nearby. Yet, according to the philosophers and historians, the truth is that Cacus was a very wicked slave of Evander, and a thief. We know that evil is called *cacon* by the Greeks, and the Arcadians used to call this man so at that time. He is said to have spewed fire because he destroyed the fields by fire. His sister of the same name betrayed him. So also she merited the little shrine where Vestal virgins used to sacrifice to her.

2. Antaeus the Giant was also the son of Earth. His mother granted this gift to him: as often as he was lying upon the earth, he would have his strength doubled. When Hercules learned this, he lifted him off the ground and strangled him to death. Antaeus is represented as a figure of lust, for "contrary" is called *antion* in Greek. Thus it is thought that he was born of earth because lust is conceived of the flesh. Finally, he rose up more vigorous and more powerful when he touched the earth because the more flesh consents to lust, the more harmful lust grows. But Antaeus is overcome by glorious virtue, that is, by Hercules, and he dies at the same time as contact with the earth is denied to him. Raised on high, he cannot get his mother's help because while someone denies himself carnal desires and raises his mind on high lest it seek carnal pleasures, he immediately rises up as a conqueror. Hercules is also said to have completed a divine struggle because it is a precious and heavenly fight that is joined with concupiscence and vices. Concerning this subject, in his moral works Plato says: "Wise men wage a greater fight with vices than with enemies."[206] Indeed, the fact that Hercules set Alcestis free seems to look to virtue. Thus there is the following story.

3. They say that Admetus, a king of Greece, sought Alcestis in marriage. Her father had put forth an edict declaring that if anyone should yoke two different wild beasts to his chariot, he could marry her. Admetus asked Apollo and Hercules for help, and they harnessed a lion and a boar to his chariot. And so he received Alcestis as his wife. When Admetus fell ill and realized that he was dying, he begged for Apollo's mercy. The god responded that he could offer nothing to him unless one of his relatives would die voluntarily in his place. His wife did this most willingly. When Hercules descended to the Underworld to drag Cerberus out of there, he also led her back from the lower regions. Thus Admetus signifies the mind, and he is called Admetus as if to say *adire metus*, "to approach fear," for the mind, not the body, submits to fear. He desired Alcestis in marriage because "boldness" is called *alce* in the Attic language, as we have said before. And so a timid mind, observing that boldness, that is, courage, is necessary for itself, desires union with it. To obtain this, it needs to yoke two different wild beasts to its chariot, that is, it takes to itself two strengths of life, namely, of soul and of body. It subjugates the lion, that is, strength of soul, and the boar, that is,

strength of body. Finally, it appeases Apollo and Hercules, that is, wisdom and strength. Thus boldness offers itself to death for the soul, as Alcestis did, that is, courage willingly incurs dangers to defend the vitality of the soul. But even though the soul is expiring and in danger of death, the strength of virtue recalls it from the lower regions, as Hercules did for Alcestis.

4. Finally, as Servius says, wiser men consider Hercules to be strong more in mind than in body, so that his twelve labors can be traced back to something. Although Hercules accomplished more, only twelve labors are attributed to him because of the twelve signs of the year. In fact, Atlas taught him astronomy. Thus Hercules is also thought to have held up the sky, which he received from Atlas because of the knowledge of the sky that was taught to him, of course. Indeed, we know that Hercules was a philosopher, and this is the reason why he is said to have overcome all those monsters. Certainly this is the reason that he dragged Cerberus up from the Underworld: because he despised and subdued all passionate desires and all earthly vices, for Cerberus is earth, the devourer of all bodies. Thus he is called Cerberus, as if to say *creoboros*, "devouring flesh." This same Hercules also killed the Hydra by burning. According to the story, the Hydra was a serpent in Lerna, a swamp of the Argives; three heads used to grow on this Hydra when one was cut off. Thus it was also called *excetra*, "snake," by the Romans. But we know that Hydra was a place spewing forth water that devastated the nearby country through which many channels burst forth when one was blocked. Observing this, Hercules burned many places in its circuit and so blocked the channels of water. Surely it was called Hydra from *hudor*, "water." Vergil indicates that this could happen when he says: "The blemish is burned away and the useless moisture sweats out."[207] Hercules broke off one horn of Achelous and gave the broken piece to Copia because, as they say, he dried up one channel whose unrestrained eruptions used to flood the fields, and he made it fertile again.

5. But Hercules is also said to have robbed the Hesperides, about whom the following story is told. The Hesperides, daughters of Atlas, King of Africa, had a garden in which there were golden apples consecrated to Venus. Hercules was sent there by Eurystheus and carried off the apples after he killed the dragon that watched over them. But in fact,

according to Servius, the Hesperides were noble girls whose flocks Hercules drove off after their guard was killed. Thus he is thought to have carried off *mala*, "sheep,"[208] for sheep are called *mala* [n Greek]. He is also called Malonomos, "shepherd of sheep." But Fulgentius has a more subtle understanding of this fiction. He says that the four Hesperides are called Aegle, Hesperis, Medusa, and Phaethusa, which in Latin we call "study," "understanding," "memory," and "eloquence." Hercules took the golden apples from their garden since one comes to philosophy through these, since to study is first, to understand is second, to remember what you have understood is third, and to adorn what you remember in speech is fourth. Certainly from the names set forth we have caused a difficulty for the reader! We have discovered that Eurystheus was a king of Greece, a descendant of Perseus. At the instigation of Juno he commanded Hercules to overcome various monsters so that they would kill him. Thus Vergil rightly calls him "unfeeling," one who surely could be capable of putting into action a stepmother's hatred. But we read that there were three Atlases: one was a Mauretanian; he was the mightiest. Another was Italian, the father of Electra; Dardanus was begotten by him. The third was Arcadian, the father of Maia; Mercury was begotten by him. But because of the similarity of the names, Vergil makes an error in his Seventh Book,[209] calling Electra and Maia, the mothers of Dardanus and Mercury, daughters of the mightiest Atlas. He says with good reason: "And the mightiest Atlas sired her," for he had daughters with these names, that is, Electra and Maia. The fact that Vergil calls Maia "shining" refers to the star, for Maia is one of the Pleiades; she is the most brilliant among them.

6. Also, Geryon was a king of Spain who is thought to have had three sets of limbs because he ruled three islands that lie near Spain: Balearica Majorca, Balearica Minorca, and Pityusa [Ebusa]. He is thought to have had a two-headed dog because he was very powerful in both land and naval combat. Hercules conquered him and is thought to have been transported to Geryon in a bronze jar because he had a powerful ship fortified with bronze. Also, according to the story, Charybdis was a very voracious woman. Since she stole Hercules' cattle, she was struck by Jove's lightning and cast into the sea, but she kept her former nature, for she swallows up everything. According to Sallust, she dwells near the Tauromenian shore.

7. We also read that Hercules came to Italy with the herds of the conquered Geryon and was at last welcomed by Evander, who was reigning at that time. When Hercules said that he was Jove's son and proved his strength by killing Cacus, he was regarded as a deity and merited an altar, which was called "the greatest altar"; Delphian Apollo predicted that this would be his in Italy. But Hercules was not accepted at first, for strangers were rarely accepted among our ancestors unless they had a law of hospitality because it was uncertain with what intention they were coming. When Hercules dedicated animals from his own herd for his sacrificial rites, he showed two old men, Pinarius and Potitius, how he wanted to be worshipped, and he ordered that sacrifice be offered to him both morning and evening. And so, after the morning sacrifice was completed, when the sacred rites were to be repeated around sunset, Potitius arrived first, Pinarius afterward, when the entrails were already offered. Thus an angry Hercules decreed that the family of Pinarii would only serve the Potitii as they were feasting and carrying out the sacred rites. For this reason also the Pinarii are named from the Greek *pina*, "hunger," for it is known that Pinarius, that old man, was called by another name. So it is that Vergil, in describing the sacred rites of Hercules, only makes mention of Potitius, saying: "And Potitius went first."[210] What he said before, "and the household of Pinarius, guardian of the sacred rites of Hercules,"[211] is not contrary to this, for we know that "guardian" (custos) is used in place of "servant," as the same author wrote in Book Eleven: "But Diana's guardian, Opis, sits high on the mountain tops,"[212] that is, her "servant." We also read in ancient books that Hercules brought with him to Italy a huge wooden cup that he used in sacred rites. So that the cup would not be consumed by decay, it was kept smeared with pitch. Vergil intimates its great size when he says: "the sacred cup filled his right hand."[213] This same Vergil mentions chosen youths in the midst of the sacred ceremonies since neither slaves nor freedmen were present at the rites of Hercules. Thus we read that Appius, who transferred these sacred rites to freedmen, both lost his sight and ruined the whole family of the Pinarii within a year. Critics fault Vergil because he led in Hercules to be praised over the fall of Troy with Trojans present; they do not consider that his respect for the hymns, from which it is a sacrilege to remove anything, caused this.

8. Vergil calls Hercules a "shared" (communis) god either because he attained apotheosis after being a man and deserved to be numbered among the "middle gods," as we have said, or because, according to the pontifical custom, he is the same Hercules who is also Mars, for they are said to have a single star. But Cicero also calls Mars a shared god. Vergil even allots Salian priests to Hercules, who, there is no doubt, belong to Mars. In fact, according to men of higher knowledge, when he says in Book Twelve, "and altars for the shared gods,"[214] he left us to understand gods of no definite places (azonos), that is, gods who do not inhabit definite regions, but who are worshipped commonly by all because they are thought to be everywhere. Thus Cybele is believed to be in every zone; so also she is called Mother of the gods because, they say, her power is common to all. But the fact that Vergil is thought to have called the Sun and Moon, Pluto and Mars, "shared gods" because the veneration of people everywhere is shown to these deities, or he calls Mars, Bellona, and Victory "shared gods" because they can favor each side in a war, is a very common saying and believed to flow from a poor source. In fact, just as Varro says, all who acted bravely were called "Hercules," although he enumerated forty-three of these in his First Book. Thus it is that we read of Tyrinthian, Argive, Theban, and Libyan Hercules. And do not let it disturb you if in diverse places some things are affirmed about the gods that do not seem to be consistent, for their stories are confused and, as we said above, they should be followed only with regard to the gods, since the truth is unknown.

14. Perseus

1. They say that Perseus also was among the sons of Jove. The truth is that he was a very rich king of Asia. It is said that he was winged because he traversed many regions in his ship, and he conquered Africa in war. Let us treat this subject more extensively. King Phorcys had three daughters: Stheno, Euyryale, and Medusa. They used a single eye, and they changed men who looked upon them into stone. Perseus was sent against them with a shield of crystal and a sickle-shaped sword, which is a kind of falchion. With Minerva's help he killed them. But, as Servius reports, they were in fact three sisters of singular beauty. Thus it was imagined that they used a single eye. Furthermore, they were very wealthy. So they were called Gorgons, as if to say *georgoi*, "cultivators

of the earth," for *ge* means "earth" and *ergia* [*sic*] means "cultivation." After their father died, the eldest of the sisters, Medusa, succeeded to his realm. Since she was subtler than the others, she is depicted with a serpent's head. To slay her, Perseus used a shield reflecting images, that is, one made of crystal, because when his spies foresaw her purposes, he thwarted her often with an unexpected attack and she fled. Finally, after Medusa was killed and her head was cut off, that is, her fortune was taken away, Perseus was made richer and obtained realms neither small nor few. At last, invading also the realm of Atlas with the help of Medusa's wealth, he forced him to flee to a mountain. Thus Perseus is thought to have changed Atlas into a mountain by [displaying] Medusa's head.

2. Fulgentius seems to offer more subtle interpretations of the slaying of the Gorgons, for, he says, *gorgo* means "fear." Men called them the three Gorgons because there are three kinds of fear and three effects of fear. This is even indicated by the names of these three, for Stheno means "weakness," the beginning of fear, which only weakens the mind; Euryale means "vast depth," that is, stupor or madness, which scatters the mind through a certain profound fear; Medusa means "forgetfulness," which not only throws the mind's considerations into confusion, but even brings on an actual dullness of sight. Indeed, this fear operates in all people. Perseus is seen as a figure of virtue. With Minerva helping him, he killed the Gorgon, since virtue conquers all fears with the help of wisdom. Thus he flies backward because one who is turned away has no regard for fear anywhere. Perseus carries a reflecting shield because all fear passes away not only in the heart, but also in outward appearance.

3. It is said Pegasus was born from the Gorgon's blood. He is established as a figure of fame. His name means "fame," according to Remigius, for while virtue overcomes all things and cuts off fear, it consequently produces fame. Thus also Pegasus is said to fly because fame is swift. He produced a spring for the Muses with his hoof, and poets drink from it because poets have the fame of heroes as their subject for writing. According to some authors, Pegasus means "eternal fountain," and he is set forth as a figure of wisdom. He is winged because wisdom traverses the whole nature of the world with its swift thought. He is thought to have brought forth the spring of the Muses with his hoof because wisdom serves poets, whatever they say. He was born from the blood of the Gorgon; this means "fear" because fear is the beginning

of wisdom. This is the reason given by philosophers that fear is the beginning of wisdom, as we have said: wisdom increases in disciples because of fear of the master, and one who has feared fame will be a wise man. And they say that Pegasus rightly arose from the slain Gorgon because when fear of folly has ended and been annihilated, then wisdom enters a person, for foolishness is always fearful. Thus also the Gorgon, "the image of fear," is fashioned on the breast of Pallas, so that she might seem always to strike fear in the foolish.

4. With the help of Pegasus, Bellerophon killed the Chimaera. The story is as follows. Proteus had a wife, Antia, who loved Bellerophon. Because he would not assent to her wickedness, she accused him to her husband, and Proteus sent him to kill the Chimaera. Riding upon Pegasus, Bellerophon killed the Chimaera. Accordingly, Proteus means "filthy" in the language of Pamphylia, and Antia means "contrary," which is taken to imply lust, since nothing is so contrary to virtue as lust. Proteus had her as his wife, for to whom can lust be ascribed unless to one who is filthy? But Bellerophon means "consultant of wisdom." He did not consent to Antia because one who toils in the search for wisdom strives to keep all lust far away from himself. Thus he is sent to slay the Chimaera, for Chimaera means "the agitation of love." And so, one who renounces lust must take up the fight against love, which a man endowed with virtue easily overcomes on Pegasus the horse, that means, aided by wisdom. But it should be noted that this same Pegasus is also called the horse of Neptune in Greek, since *pege* means "fountain." Moreover, this is the common name of all streams, since streams have the nature of a packhorse because of the swiftness of their course. Also, they say that "the country" (pagum) comes from this same *pege*, since villages are accustomed to be established near water. Thus also country people are called *pagani*, as if to say "drinking from one fountain."

5. But since we made mention of the Chimaera, let us say something about this. It is depicted as tri-formed, namely, having a lion's head, a goat's belly and a serpent's tail, because in love there are likewise three steps. According to Fulgentius, these are to begin, to proceed and to finish. Indeed, in youth love first attacks us fiercely, like a lion. Then the satisfying of lust follows, which is signified by the she-goat, since this animal is very ready for lust. So also Satyrs are depicted with goats' horns since they are never satisfied in their lusts. The Chimaera is

dragon-like in its lowest parts because, after acts of lust, the sting of penitence pricks the mind. Therefore the first thing in love is to commence, second is to complete, and third is to repent for the sin committed. Anyone can distinguish this through the ages of life, or to note it in any copulation at all. Horace indicates that the Chimaera signifies love when he says to the lover: "Pegasus will scarcely free you, bound as you are by the three-formed Chimaera."[215] Servius turns this story into history. In truth, he says, Chimaera is a mountain in Cilicia whose peak burns even today, but lions live near the peak. Moreover, there are meadows in the middle of the mountain, but the lowest parts are full of snakes. Bellerophon made this mountain habitable. Thus he is said to have killed the Chimaera. Ovid describes this mountain clearly enough, but fabulously, when he says: "And on this ridge the Chimaera had fire in its middle parts, and on its breast the face of a lioness, and the tail of a serpent."[216]

15. The Twelve Signs in the Sky

1. There are twelve signs in the sky: Aries, Taurus, Gemini, Cancer, Leo, Virgo, Libra, Scorpio, Sagittarius, Capricorn, Aquarius, and Pisces.

By a certain nymph, Jupiter sired Nephele, whom Athamas, a Theban king, took as his wife. Athamas sired Phrixus and Helle by her. After his wife died, Athamas placed Ino, the daughter of Cadmus, over his children. In the manner of a stepmother, Ino hated them so much that she caused them to be driven out of the house. When they had come to the sea, their grandfather Jupiter or, as others say, their aunt Isis gave them a ram with golden fleece on which they might cross over the sea, under this condition: that they not look back. But Helle, being intemperate and frightened, looked back, and thus she was plunged into the sea. From then on the sea was called Hellespont. Phrixus crossed over, skinned the ram, filled its hide with gold and dedicated it to Mars on the island of Colchis. But the flesh was carried up into the sky and from it was made the sign in the heavens called Aries. And since the ram looked back when it was on the shore, as if it wished to see Helle, it appears so in the sky. According to natural science, the sun is said to be in Aries because from the vernal equinox to the autumnal it courses through the right side of the hemisphere, just as at that time Aries always inclines toward the right side. And just as the sun proceeds through the left side from the autumnal equinox to the vernal, so at that time Aries always inclines toward the left side.

2. Agenor, a king of Lydia, who also reigned in Tyre and Sidon, had a daughter of wondrous beauty named Europa. Assuming the appearance of a shining-white bull, Jupiter ravished her. Thus, later, as a token of honor, the bull was carried up into the sky, and from this was made the sign called Taurus. Others say that it was a cow, in whose shape it was Io, daughter of the River Inachus, who was carried up into the sky as a sign of her love of Jove. Thus Ovid wrote in the *Metamorphoses*: "Now the goddess is worshipped with festive rites by a throng in linen robes."[217] And in the book of *Fasti* he says: "Whether a cow or bull, it is not easy to know,"[218] since the forepart is seen, but the hind part is not seen. According to natural science, the sun is said to be in Taurus, since the labors of bulls begin then, or since, just as a bull is stronger because of its horns, so the sun then begins to be hotter.

3. Jupiter had intercourse with Leda in the form of a swan. By her he produced two eggs. From one, Helen and Clytemnestra were born; from the other, Pollux and Castor, who were the most skilled and most honorable rulers in Greece. They used force to seize the two daughters of Zetypus the peasant. Phoebe and Mollisena were taken at the time of their wedding to the brothers Idas and Sicidas, who had themselves seized them from this same Zetypus. Thus discord arose among them. Idas was killed and Castor was wounded. Since Castor was mortal, he died. Meanwhile, since his brother Pollux was immortal, and therefore was not killed in that quarrel, he asked his father Jove out of fraternal loyalty to share his life with his brother. For this reason, one always appears in an alternate position in the sky in one place, the other in another place, or, as others say, one stands in the sky, the other sinks into the ocean. The sun is said to be in Gemini because in any of the signs the sun remains for only thirty days, but in Gemini for thirty-two.

4. When Chiron's son, the grandson of Saturn and Philyres, was walking near the sea, he stepped on a certain crab of immense size that injured him pitiably. In return, Chiron shot the crab with his arrows and freed his son, in whose memory that crab was carried up into the sky and became a celestial sign. The sun is said to be in Cancer because just as the crab moves to each side, forward and backward, so the sun, when it

approaches Cancer, always goes forward, but when it is in Cancer, it recedes and cannot go forward any farther.

5. The country folk in the Nemean forest spurned Jove and were unwilling to sacrifice to him. Thus an angry Jupiter sent against them a lion of immense size that devastated all their property. And when they were crushed by want, at last Hercules arrived, the tamer of monsters. He killed the lion, and it was carried up into the sky. From it was made the celestial sign. The sun is said to be in Leo because just as a lion rages, so when the sun passes through that sign, it sends violent heat upon the world.

6. When Icarius,[219] a priest of Bacchus and King of Athens, and the best of hunters too, gave wine to the peasants to drink, they became inebriated. Thinking that they had taken poison, they killed him and, to conceal the crime, they threw him into a well. But a little dog that was with him returned home to Erigone, the daughter of this same Icarius, and by its sorrow and whatever signs it could, the little dog led her to the well. When Erigone wept at the well for a long time, at last she was carried up into the sky with the little dog and became the sign called Virgo. The little dog became the principal constellation that is next to Virgo. When the sun is in this, the days called "dog days" are hot and hurtful, like a little dog. The sun is said to be in Virgo because, just as a virgin is barren, so when the sun courses through that sign, the earth is barren and dry, for it produces nothing because of the burning sun.

7. In the Theban War, Pallas, along with certain other gods, favored the Greeks. Since Bacchus was Theban, he, along with certain other gods, favored the Thebans. Thus among the gods there arose a quarrel as to who should gain the victory. Observing this, Jupiter sat on Mount Parnassus, which is near Thebes, holding in his hand a golden balance (libra) to weigh each side. But he saw that at the end of the war the judgment was equal. But soon, at the destruction of Thebes, Jupiter perceived that the Greeks had the victory; he decided against the Thebans and exalted the Greeks. Thus, in memory of this event, the balance was raised up to the sky and became the celestial sign. According to a different account, Libra was made from the scorpion's arms. These are called *chelae*, as will be described below. The sun is said to be in Libra because when it passes through that sign it is the equinox, and nighttime and daytime are equal.

8. When Chiron was passing through a forest with his son, a scorpion of immense size almost swallowed the son. Chiron, the best of archers, shot the scorpion and freed his son, and thus the scorpion was carried up into the sky. According to a different account, Jupiter, Neptune, and Mercury, along with certain other gods, were traveling around various regions. On a certain day, as the sun was setting, they came to the house of Oenopion, a peasant. He welcomed them with respect and set before them as food the only ox that he had. Now when the gods were refreshed, they wanted to repay him. They told Oenopion to ask for whatever he wished and it would be given to him. Since he had no children, he asked that they give him a son. The gods pissed in the oxhide and, when it was full, they buried it. From this, after nine months, was born Orion, or Ourion, "begotten of urine," who became a hunter. He wanted to have intercourse with Diana. The angry goddess sent a scorpion of immense size against him, and while they were battling each other, they were carried up into the sky, for the gods were unwilling that their offspring should die, nor did Diana want her scorpion to perish. Orion is called the "Sword-bearer" because he was girt with a sword. According to another fable, two signs were made from the scorpion. From the arms, which are called *chelae*, was made the sign called Libra, and from the body was made the sign called Scorpio. The sun is said to be in Scorpio because just as a scorpion stings with its tail, so also when the sun is in part of that sign, the cold stings us, for the first cold is more hurtful.

9. Chiron—the best of archers, teacher of Achilles, the one who raised Aesculapius—was carried up into the sky because of his shooting of the scorpion, about which we spoke above. He became the sign called Sagittarius. The sun is said to be in Sagittarius because just as arrows are sent forth from a bow, so also when the sun courses through this sign, snow is sent forth from the sky.

10. Saturn, son of the Sky, learned through oracular responses from Themis that he would have a son who would expel him from his realm. Thus he told Rhea, or Ops, his sister and wife, that she should give to him whatever she might bring forth. First, therefore, she handed over Neptune to him; Saturn submerged him in the sea and he became a sea god. Second, she gave him Pluto, whom he suffocated in a ditch, and he became god of the lower regions. Finally, when Jove was born, a child of wondrous beauty, she had pity on him. She sent to Saturn a stone called

abidir, which he crushed to dust and devoured. Then it was vomited out and formed into human shape and brought to life. In fact, his mother handed Jove over to a certain she-wolf. Since this she-wolf did not have abundant milk, Amalthea the she-goat nourished him. When he was grown up, Jove expelled Saturn from his realm, as is made known in another story. He also carried Amalthea, the she-goat that had nourished him, up into the sky, and she became the sign called Capricorn. The sun is said to be in Capricorn because just as a she-goat seeks high places, so when the sun is in the middle of this sign, since it cannot descend more, then it begins to ascend.

11. Ganymede was the son of Troilus, King of Troy. He was very handsome and the best of hunters. Jove loved him. He changed into an eagle, the messenger of Jove, and snatched Ganymede in the woods on Mount Ida. Then Hebe, the daughter of Juno and goddess of youth, was driven away; she was the first cup-bearer of the gods. Ganymede became Jove's cup-bearer. Because of the charm of his drinking toasts, Ganymede deserved to become the celestial sign called Aquarius, and thus he is said to carry an urn in his hand because of the peculiar nature of the season.

12. When the war of the Giants was imminent, Venus was sitting with her son Cupid above the seashore in the region of Palestine. Thus when she heard the tumult of war, she believed that Typhoeus was pursuing her to seize her, and because of her excessive fear she hurled herself, with her son, into the sea. But two fish of immense size placed themselves under their shoulders and transported them over the sea. Indeed, the gods observed their flight. To mark this deed, they carried these fish up into the sky, and they became the sign called Pisces. The sun is said to be in Aquarius and Pisces because of their peculiar nature, for at that time much rain and snow fall. In fact, a water-bearer carries an urn, and fish are always in water.

FINIS

NOTES

INTRODUCTION

1. Edwin A. Quain, S. J., "The Medieval Accessus ad Auctores," *Traditio* 3 (reprint edition, 1986): 9–10. See also Z. P. Thundy, "Sources of Spoliatio Aegyptiorum," *Annuale Mediaevale* 21 (1981): 77–90.

2. Jean Seznec, *The Survival of the Pagan Gods* (New York: Harper & Row, 1953): 13–20.

3. Seznec, 90.

4. Alan Cameron, *Greek Mythography in the Roman World* (Oxford: Oxford UP, 2004): 221.

5. Jane Chance, *Medieval Mythography: From Roman North Africa to the School of Chartres, A.D. 433–1177* (Gainsville, FL: UP of Florida, 1994): 4.

6. Chance, 5.

7. *Patrologia Latina* 171, 1007.

8. E. Langlois, *Origines et Sources du Roman de la Rose* (Paris: 1891): 134–135.

9. Seznec, 171–178.

10. Seznec, 179.

11. Richard Schulz, *De Mythographi Vaticani Primi fontibus* (Halle, 1905): 74.

12. Chance, 162.

13. Nevio Zorzetti and Jacques Berlioz, ed. and trans. *Le Premier Mythographe du Vatican* (Paris: Les Belles Lettres, 1995): IX.

14. Cameron, 308.

15. Cameron, 4.

16. Zorzetti and Berlioz, XII.

17. K. O. Elliott and J. P. Elder, "A Critical Edition of the Vatican Mythographers," *Transactions of the American Philological Association* 78 (1947): 200.

18. Gregory Hays, "The Date and Identity of the Mythographer Fulgentius," *The Journal of Medieval Latin* 13 (2003): 173.

19. Chance, 300.

20. Philippe Dain, *Mythographe du Vatican T.2.* (Paris, 2001): 8–9.

21. R. M. Krill, "The 'Vatican Mythographers': Their Place in Ancient Mythography," *Manuscripta* 23 (1979): 176.

22. Eleanor Rathbone, "Master Alberic of London, 'Mythographus Tertius Vaticanus,'" *Medieval and Renaissance Studies* 1 (1941–1943): 37.

23. R. W. Hunt, *The Schools and the Cloister: The Life and Writings of Alexander Neckam (1157–1217)* (Oxford: Clarendon Press, 1984): 19.
24. Seznec, 170–179.
25. Seznec, 172.
26. Seznec, 171.
27. Elliott and Elder, 192–193.
28. Zorzetti and Berlioz, XLIX.

FIRST MYTHOGRAPHER

1. The text has "Icarus."
2. The text has "Ephigenia."
3. The text calls him "Oeta."
4. The text has *pellem,* which actually means "hide."
5. *Urina* in Latin can also mean "semen."
6. Cf. Carm, 3.4.71.
7. 9.836.
8. My conjecture; the text has "Thrace."
9. *Mater Domini* in the text should probably be *Mater deorum,* "Mother of the gods," as in Augustine's De Civ. Dei.
10. Cf. ch. 40 above.
11. Vergil, Aen. 1.305.
12. Aen. 3.520.
13. Aen. 2.82.
14. Aen. 5.759.
15. Fast. 2.273.
16. Carm. 1.17.14
17. Hercules.
18. Theb. 12.497.
19. Aen. 8.342.
20. 8.272.
21. Vergil, Georg. 1.88.
22. In fact, the stories of Hercules' labors are well known.
23. *Durum,* Vergil, Georg. 3.4.
24. Aeacus is surely intended, though the text has Cacus.
25. The text has "Sinicros."
26. "Little Blind One."
27. Arion is described as *inter delfinas,* "among the dolphins"; cf. Verg. Ecl. 8.56.
28. The text has "Cethus."
29. Ecl. 2.24.
30. I.e. chelyone.
31. Cf. ch. 39 above.
32. Aen. 4.511.
33. Juvenal 9.2.

34. This quotation is actually from Horace, Sat. 1.8.4–7.
35. Aen. 6.646.
36. Ecl. 10.69.
37. The text erroneously has "Aegisthus."
38. So I have translated *hostibus* here, literally "the enemies."
39. Aen. 11.757.
40. The text has "Latinas."
41. Aen. 4.473.
42. The text has "Hermione" in this and the next chapter.
43. Kulcsar's text omits "Dea," which is in Juvenal 6.172–4.
44. Eun. 588.
45. Aen.7.304.
46. Aen. 6.324.
47. Or, following the text in Bode: "as this bird is hostile to snakes."
48. Epod. 10.13.
49. Aen. 1.132.
50. Aen. 4.705.
51. I.e., *circa enses*.
52. Cf. Myth. II.235.
53. Ecl. 10.50.
54. Aen. 3.400.
55. In most versions of the story, Meleager was killed by Althea, his own mother.
56. Aen. 7.485.
57. Tethys (?).
58. The name Jupiter is omitted at lines 33 and 41 in the Latin text.
59. Ovid. Her. 17.231.
60. Theb. 1.713
61. Aen. 6.620.
62. Laconians: Spartans.
63. Aen. 2.275.
64. Cilla.
65. 9.979.
66. Aen. 12.360.
67. Cf. Fulgentius, Myth. 2.99–100.

SECOND MYTHOGRAPHER

1. The definitions that follow are taken from Isidore, Orig. 1.40.
2. Cf. Lucretius, 5.905.
3. Lucan 6.676.
4. *Thaumas* in Greek means "admiration."
5. Vergil, Aen. 9.803.
6. Lucretius, De rer. natura 6.1090ff.

7. Aen. 6.606.

8. Aen. 3.252.

9. Lucan 6.733.

10. Aen. 6.257.

11. Parcae, from *parcere*, "to spare."

12. *Proserpere* means "to creep forth."

13. Hist. frag. 1.83.

14. Aen. 6.887.

15. Lucan 9.6–11.

16. Lucan 3.460.

17. Aen. 4.511.

18. Prudentius, Symm. 1.365.

19. "Satiety" from Saturn, "venereal" from Venus.

20. Vergil, Georg. 3.97.

21. Georg. 2.112.

22. This last sentence is repeated from the previous chapter.

23. Myrtea is surely intended here, though the text has Myrina.

24. Ecl. 4.62.

25. I.e., sought her protection.

26. 3.113.

27. Terence, Eun. 4.5.6.

28. "Epopeus" is meant here.

29. Aen. 6.646.

30. Vergil, Ecl. 10.69.

31. Orig. frag. 1.11.

32. 1.3.3.

33. Hist. frag. 2.15.

34. Aen. 9.716.

35. Georg. 1.392.

36. Nat. Hist. 18.357.

37. This curious passage seems out of place in the text and is absent from some mss.

38. Icarius? Cf. Myth. I.19.

39. I.e. chelyone.

40. *Semper* is indeed repeated in this line.

41. The text has "Hermione."

42. Theb. 4.570.

43. Patronus.

44. Erythrea.

45. The Mythographer here confuses Ceres' story with that of Latona.

46. The text has "Lycus."

47. I.e., the lynx is spotted to show its "true colors."

48. Celeus.

49. Sat. 1.1.69. Several mss. omit the final sentence of this passage.

50. The text has "Aegestus."

51. The text has "Tityon."

52. Cf. De rer. nat. 3.978ff. The citation of Lucretius is noteworthy, since he was a rare author in the Middle Ages.

53. Carm. 1.2.19.

54. The text has "Stennio."

55. Carm. 4.7.25.

56. The text has "Oenorion."

57. Cf. Myth. 1.32 above.

58. The text has "Bellorophon."

59. The text mistakenly has "Tyndaridis."

60. Aen. 6.617.

61. 2.717.

62. The text has "Melope."

63. Aen. 8.297.

64. The text has "Pityusa."

65. Isocrates.

66. Theb. 4.298.

67. Horace, Carm. saec. 59.

68. Horace, Sat. 2.5.8.

69. Phania.

70. Aen. 5.704.

71. Ecl.6.43.

72. "Thrace" in some mss.

73. From hubris, "harm"?

74. Ann. 11.317.

75. Aen. 12.360.

76. Cf. Myth. 2.224.

77. Cf. Carm. 3.5.10.

78. Sat. 2.3.228.

79. Aen. 4.473

80. The text has "Laudomia."

81. A pun on opimus, "rich." Cf. Horace, Sat. 2.3.142ff.

82. Aen. 3.57.

THIRD MYTHOGRAPHER

1. Statius, Theb. 3.661.

2. Cf. Aug, De civ. Dei 7.9

3. Vergil, Georg. 2.326.

4. Horace, Carm. 2.17.20.

5. Ecl. 3.93.

6. Terence, Eun. 4.5.6.

7. Cicero, De nat. deorum 2.64.

8. Cf. Ovid, Fasti 4.361.

9. 6.267.

10. Fasti 6.282ff.

11. De nat. deorum 2.67

12. Georg. 3.1.

13. Vergil, Aen. 2.690.

14. Aen. 10.473.

15. Aen. 1.482.

16. Aen. 4.362.

17. Aen. 4.221.

18. 6.676.

19. 902.

20. Carm. 3.16.8.

21. Theb. 7.793.

22. 10.38.

23. Aen. 4.701.

24. Aen. 11.736.

25. Georg. 3.100.

26. Aen. 4.459.

27. Cf. Ecclus. 11.29.

28. Sat. 2.6.20.

29. Aen. 8.417.

30. De nat. deorum 2.39.101.

31. Jug. 80.6

32. Aen. 1.78.

33. Plato was himself known as "The Philosopher."

34. Aen. 8.185.

35. Georg. 4.382.

36. There seems to be a lacuna in the text here.

37. Georg. 4.480 and Aen. 6.439.

38. Aen. 6.329.

39. Aen. 6.324.

40. Carm. 3.4.77.

41. This passage closely follows Macrobius, Somn. Scip. 1.11.12.

42. Cf. paragraph above.

43. Aen. 6.746.

44. Aen. 6.340.

45. Aen. 6.452.

46. Genesis 4.10.

47. Genesis 2.7.

48. Aen. 6.715.

49. Georg. 4.227–229.
50. 9.8–9.
51. Aen. 6.740ff.
52. Georg. 2.389.
53. Aen.6.743.
54. Aen. 9.182.
55. Phormio 44.
56. 5.95.
57. 1.113.
58. 7.194–196.
59. Aen. 6.130.
60. 1.134.
61. Aen. 2.604–606.
62. Aen. 6.532.
63. 1.457.
64. Sat. 1.8ff.
65. Aen. 1.335.
66. 8.739.
67. Eun. 2.3.5.
68. Aen. 6.152.
69. Epod. 17.48.
70. Aen. 5.869.
71. Aen. 9.486.
72. Andria, 4.2.13.
73. Vergil, Ecl. 8.58.
74. Servius, Ad Aen. 6.139.
75. 3.406–407.
76. 8.110.
77. Ad Aen. 8.110
78. Aen. 8.173.
79. Aen. 4.518.
80. 12.5.
81. Aen. 4.512.
82. Aen. 6.230.
83. Aen. 2.719.
84. Aen. 3.354.
85. Aen. 6.225.
86. Ecl. 5.66.
87. Ecl. 8.75.
88. Aen. 4.61.
89. Aen. 6.244.
90. Carm. 3.23.3.
91. Aen. 12.174.

92. Aen. 9.627.

93. Georg. 2.395.

94. Lucan, 7.165.

95. Cf. Aen. 6.246–254 for these several quotes.

96. Aen. 5.238.

97. Aen. 9.641.

98. Georg. 2.194.

99. Aen. 6.38.

100. Aen. 3.231.

101. Carm. 1.18.11.

102. Aen.4.302.

103. Georg. 3.16.

104. Aen. 3.222.

105. Aen. 3.93.

106. Aen. 2.687–88.

107. Cf. Aen. 5.71.

108. Carm. 3.1.2.

109. Aen. 5.54.

110. Aen. 4.62.

111. Cat. 25.2.

112. Aen. 6.138.

113. Aen. 4.638.

114. Our author seems confused here. Lycia is a country of Asia Minor, Delos an island in the Aegean Sea.

115. Aen. 4.346.

116. Luna?

117. 5.162–163.

118. 5.134.

119. 1.28.

120. This should be "vernal," though the text has "autumnal."

121. Sat. 2.6.45.

122. Theb. 3.506.

123. They had been turned into trees.

124. Carm. Saec. 33–34.

125. Rep. 6.17.

126. Aen. 6.49.

127. Georg. 1.337.

128. Avienius.

129. Aen. 4.379.

130. 4.382.

131. 4.697.

132. 10.467.

133. 8.334.

134. Aen. 4.653.
135. Aen. 6.391.
136. Carm. 2.19.29.
137. Aen. 6.392.
138. Aen. 4.516.
139. 6.616.
140. Aen. 4.694.
141. Carm. 2.3.26.
142. Aen. 4.705.
143. Georg. 4.224.
144. Aen. 2.646.
145. Aen. 4.58.
146. Aen. 4.59.
147. Aen.3.120.
148. Aen.9.654.
149. 4.125.
150. Lucan, 9.354.
151. Ecclesiasticus, 24.7.
152. Eccl. 24.5.
153. Ecl. 2.61.
154. 2.269–273.
155. Aen. 8.429–430.
156. Georg. 1.313.
157. Aen. 1.230.
158. Aen. 2.649.
159. Aen. 4.25.
160. Ecl. 1.17.
161. Georg. 3.93.
162. Epod. 10.13.
163. Carm. 1.3.29–31.
164. Horace, Carm. 4.11.7.
165. Carm. 3.21.22.
166. Carm. 2.17.23.
167. Calvus, Poet. 7.
168. Aen. 2.591.
169. Ecl. 8.102.
170. Aen. 1.382.
171. Aen.2.801.
172. Aen. 6.25
173. Aen. 1.301.
174. Aen. 3.520.
175. 6.362.
176. Theb. 8.178.

177. 6.562.
178. Theb. 3.471.
179. Aen. 6.194.
180. Aen.6.194.
181. Aen.6.191–92.
182. Ecl.9.15.
183. Aen.3.176.
184. Aen.2.302.
185. Aen. 2.269.
186. Aen. 12.260.
187. 5.531.
188. Ecl.9.13.
189. Aen. 6.197.
190. Aen.3.360–61.
191. Aen. 10.176–77.
192. Aen.4.76.
193. Ecl. 6.4.
194. Aen. 6.57.
195. 4.392–93.
196. 3.1–2.
197. Ovid, AA 1.239.
198. Georg. 2.389.
199. Aen.11.785.
200. Aen.1.665.
201. Carm. 1.18.11.
202. Quoted by Persius, Satire 1:10.
203. A liquid measure; Fulgentius actually has the words "in a whole month."
204. 10.163.
205. Ep. 1.19.4.
206. Quoted from Fulgentius, Myth. 2.4.
207. Georg.1.88.
208. Mala means "apples" in Latin, "sheep" in Greek.
209. Actually, Book 8:138.
210. Aen.8.270.
211. 8.269.
212. Aen.11.836.
213. Aen.8.278.
214. Aen. 12.118.
215. Carm. 1.27.24.
216. Met.9.647–48.
217. 1.747.
218. 4.717.
219. The text has "Icarus."

SELECT BIBLIOGRAPHY

EDITIONS/TRANSLATIONS

Bode, Georg. H. *Scriptores rerum mythicarum Latini tres Romae nuper reperti.* 2 Vols. Celle, 1834; repr. Hildesheim, 1968.

Dain, Philippe. *Mythographe du Vatican I: Traduction et Commentaire.* Paris, 1995.

———. *Mythographe du Vatican T.2.* Paris, 2001.

Kulcsar, Peter. *Mythographi Vaticani I et II.* Turnholt: Brepols, 1987.

Mai, Angelo. *Classicorum auctorum e Vaticanis codicibus editorum Tomus III.* Rome, 1831.

Zorzetti, Nevio and Jacques Berlioz, ed. and trans. *Le Premier Mythographe du Vatican.* Paris: Les Belles Lettres, 1995.

SECONDARY SOURCES

Barbino, G. "Per una nuova edizione del Mitografo Vaticano II." *Mythos: Scripta in honorem Marii Untersteiner.* Genova, (1970): 59–72.

Buehler, Winfried. "Die pariser Horazscholien—eine neue Quelle der Mythographi Vaticani 1 und 2." *Philologus* 105 (1961): 123–135.

Buhler, W. "Theodulus' Ecloga and Mythographus Vaticanus I." *California Studies in Classical Antiquity* 1 (1968): 65-71.

Burnett, Charles S. F. "A Note on the Origins of the Third Vatican Mythographer." *Journal of the Warburg and Courtauld Institute* 44 (1981): 160–166.

Cameron, Alan. *Greek Mythography in the Roman World.* Oxford: Oxford UP, 2004.

Chance, Jane. *Medieval Mythography: From Roman North Africa to the School of Chartres, A.D. 433–1177.* Gainsville, FL: UP of Florida, 1994.

Elliott, K. O. and J. P. Elder. "A Critical Edition of the Vatican Mythographers." *Transactions of the American Philological Association* 78 (1947): 189–207.

Garfagnini, G. C. "Un 'accessus' ad Apuleio e un nuovo codice del Terzo Mitografo Vaticano." *Studi Medievali* 17 (1976): 307–362.

Hays, Gregory. "The Date and Identity of the Mythographer Fulgentius." *The Journal of Medieval Latin* 13 (2003): 163–252.

Hunt, R. W. *The Schools and the Cloister: The Life and Writings of Alexander Neckam (1157–1217).* Oxford: Clarendon Press, 1984.

Keseling, F. *De Mythograhi Vaticani Secundi fontibus*. Halle, 1908.

Krill, R. M. "The 'Vatican Mythographers': Their Place in Ancient Mythography." *Manuscripta* 23 (1979): 173–177.

Langlois, E. *Origines et Sources du Roman de la Rose*. Paris, 1891.

Liebeschutz, Hans. *Fulgentius Metaforalis: ein Beitrag zur Geschichte der antiken Mythologie im Mittelalter*. Leipzig, 1926.

Manitius, Max. *Geschichte der lateinischen Literatur des Mittelalters*. Vol. 1. Munich, 1911.

Pizzorno, Bitto. "Note testuali al Mitografo Vaticano I." *Sandalion* 2 (1979): 231–234.

Quain, Edwin A., S. J. "The Medieval Accessus ad Auctores." *Traditio* 3 (1945), reprint edition (1986): 1–50.

Raschke, Robert. *De Alberico Mythologo*. Breslau, 1913.

Rathbone, Eleanor. "Master Alberic of London, 'Mythographus Tertius Vaticanus.'" *Medieval and Renaissance Studies* 1 (1941–1943): 35–38.

Schulz, Richard. *De Mythographi Vaticani Primi fontibus*. Halle, 1905.

Seznec, Jean. *The Survival of the Pagan Gods*. Trans. fr. French by Barbara Sessions. New York: Harper & Row, 1953.

Sjostrom, H. "Magister Albericus Lundoniensis, Mythographus Tertius Vaticanus." *Classica et Mediaevalia* 29 (1968): 249–264.

Thundy, Z. P. "Sources of Spoliatio Aegyptiorum." *Annuale Mediaevale* 21 (1981): 77–90.

Wetherbee, Winthrop. *Platonism and Poetry*. Princeton, NJ: Princeton UP, 1972.

Zorzetti, Nevio. *La constrizione medievale della mitologia classica: studi sul testo e le fonti dei mitografi Vaticani I e II, I Fabularius A: versione l.O.* Trieste, 1988.